Nigel Nicolson was the younger son of Harold Nicolson and Vita Sackville-West. He grew up in a world which combined Bloomsbury with Knole (his grandfather's great house), Eton with Sissinghurst, and Oxford with some uninhabited islands in the Outer Hebrides, which he bought while still an undergraduate. During World War II he served in the Grenadier Guards (later writing its war history). In the late 1940s he joined George Weidenfeld to found the publishing firm of Weidenfeld & Nicolson. Simultaneously he sought a career in politics (like his father) and was elected Conservative MP for Bournemouth in 1952. He held the seat for seven years, losing it when his constituency association deselected him for supporting the abolition of capital punishment and protesting against the Suez operation of 1956. As a full-time writer thereafter he edited the original edition of his father's diaries (in three volumes), and the six volumes of the letters of Virginia Woolf (whom he befriended at the age of 11 when she was writing her novel *Orlando*). His best-known book is *Portrait of a Marriage*, which describes his mother's love affair with Violet Trefusis and its aftermath. His life of Mary Curzon was awarded the Whitbread Prize for Biography. He also wrote a much-praised life of Field Marshal Alexander of Tunis, books on Jane Austen, domestic architecture, his own county of Kent, and the Himalayas. He published his autobiography, *Long Life*, in 1997. He died in 2004.

HAROLD NICOLSON
DIARIES AND LETTERS
1907–1964

Edited by Nigel Nicolson

PHOENIX

A PHOENIX PAPERBACK

First published in Great Britain in 2004
by Weidenfeld & Nicolson
This paperback edition published in 2005
by Phoenix,
an imprint of Orion Books Ltd,
Orion House, 5 Upper St Martin's Lane,
London WC2H 9EA

1 3 5 7 9 10 8 6 4 2

A CIP catalogue record for this book
is available from the British Library.

ISBN 0 75381 997 X

Typeset by Butler and Tanner Ltd,
Frome and London

Printed and bound in Great Britain by
Clays Ltd, St Ives plc

www.orionbooks.co.uk

CONTENTS

ILLUSTRATIONS

EDITORIAL NOTE

The originals of Harold Nicolson's diaries are at Balliol College, Oxford, and I am grateful to the Master and Fellows, and to the college Librarian, Dr Penelope Bulloch, for their permissions and much other help. The copyright in the 1910–29 diaries remains with Balliol, and that in the 1930–64 diaries has reverted to me from HarperCollins.

The history of their publication is briefly as follows. In 1966, 1967 and 1968 I published with Collins a selection in three volumes, the first two in my father's lifetime, the third shortly after his death. I added some of his letters to my mother, Vita Sackville-West, and hers to him, the originals of which are in the Lilly Library, Indiana University, Bloomington, Indiana, USA, and a few letters to his sons, particularly from the war years when we were both serving overseas.

In 1980 Stanley Olson edited (again for Collins) a one-volume condensed edition, adding previously unpublished passages, but, like myself, he made no use of the pre-1930 diaries now at Balliol, on which I have drawn for the first part of this edition. All that survive from the earliest years are those for 1910, 1912, 1913, 1916 and 1918. They were written in prepared diary-books, allowing my father only a few lines a day, recording where he lunched, dined and spent the night. They are more like annotated engagement books. From 1919 onwards he took more time and pains, writing his daily entries in large notebooks until 1930, when he took to typing them on loose quarto sheets. Missing are the years 1919–20, but before their loss, he copied many entries from them for his book *Peacemaking: 1919* (published in 1933).

In the first of his two-volume Life of Harold Nicolson (1980) James Lees-Milne made some use of the pre-1930 diaries, as did Dr Derek Drinkwater in his doctoral thesis 'Sir Harold Nicolson as International Theorist' (Canberra, 2002) and Professor Norman Rose in his forthcoming biography of my father. They have also quoted from some previously unpublished letters to his parents, of which the originals are retained at Sissinghurst.

This new edition draws together extracts from these different sources – the pre-1930 diaries, the *Peacemaking* diaries, the Olson edition (from which I have omitted much and added much) and the family correspondence, including letters to his sons and parents. The entire diary contains some three million words, of which only about a twentieth part has now been published. The originals can be studied at Balliol, under certain conditions, by previous application to the Librarian.

I am grateful to Susan Fox for her help in editing this volume.

Nigel Nicolson
Sissinghurst
January 2004

INTRODUCTION

Harold Nicolson's diaries were an accompaniment to his life. He once quoted to me a saying of Virginia Woolf, 'Nothing has really happened until it has been described', and he meant described in writing, in a diary or a letter. There was something missing from the day if he had not sat down after breakfast to record the events of the day before, with pen and notebook in the early years, and after 1930 at a typewriter. He did not write his diary for publication, but there are hints in it that he would not consider it an act of treachery to publish extracts from it after his death. As it happened, he allowed me to cull from it three volumes in his lifetime, and when they became best-sellers, he remarked to me, rather ruefully, 'It is sad to think that of my forty books the only ones that will be remembered are the three I didn't realise I'd written.'

There are two reasons why his diaries were so much acclaimed. First, he had led a very active life in diplomacy, politics and literature, and knew, some intimately, the leading figures in all three professions. Therefore his diaries and letters form a record of considerable value to historians and biographers. Secondly, he had unusual powers of observation and recollection, specially of conversations. He recorded not just what people said, but their tone of voice, their gestures, their clothes, possessions and houses, all clues to their characters. The very first entry in this edition, when he is describing in a letter to his parents an old French woman and her clever daughter, written when he was only twenty, illustrates his pictorial style. Thirty-two years later, on June 14, 1939, with the same fecundity of imagery and total recall, he could bring to life Winston Churchill's dramatic intervention at a private dinner party. This was his great gift as a diarist. He was not just a commentator. He was a portraitist.

He was given to self-analysis, never with self-pity, but frequently with self-reproach. His diary received the fantasies of his ambition, and the dregs of his despair. There is no meanness in it, and gossip only in so far as it revealed personality. It is a generous document. To him private pleasures were as important as public success, whether his own or his friends'. His diary reflects his joy in living and his excitement at the turn of events. When he reached the age of fifty, he wrote, 'I have dispersed my energies in life, done too many different things ... But what enjoyment and interest I have derived from my experience! I suppose I am too volatile and fluid. But few people can have extracted such happiness from fluidity.'

A brief summary of that 'fluidity' may be of use to a new generation less familiar with Harold Nicolson's name than his contemporaries. He was born in 1886, in Teheran, Persia, where his father, Sir Arthur Nicolson, later Lord Carnock, was in charge of the British Legation. Harold was educated at Wellington College, which he hated, and at Balliol College, Oxford, which he loved. He entered the diplomatic service in 1909. In 1913 he married Victoria ('Vita') Sackville-West, the poet, novelist and gardener, and they had two sons. His work exempted him from military service in the First World War, and he soon won for himself a leading reputation among the younger Foreign Office officials, playing an important part in the Paris Peace Conference of 1919 and at Lausanne, under Curzon, in 1922–3. He then became successively Counsellor at the Teheran Legation and the Berlin Embassy. In 1929 he resigned from diplomacy in mid-career, mainly because it separated him from Vita, who had better things to do than act the role of a diplomatic wife. After a year in journalism, he joined Oswald Mosley's New Party, leaving it as soon as Mosley turned Fascist. In 1935 he was elected National Labour MP for West Leicester, and became spokesman for his Party on foreign affairs, in close accord with Anthony Eden, the Foreign Secretary. In 1940 Churchill appointed him a junior Minister, and for the remainder of the war he was a Governor of the BBC and the unofficial link between the Government and de Gaulle's Free French. He lost his seat in the 1945 Election, joined the Labour Party, and stood unsuccessfully as its candidate at a by-election in 1948. He devoted the rest of his life to journalism, broadcasting and books, and jointly with his wife created the famous garden at Sissinghurst. He died there in 1968, six years after his wife.

He had a deep interest in the contemporary world, though he was sometimes compared to an eighteenth-century Whig aristocrat. He was at home in half a dozen foreign languages and literatures, including Greek and Latin, loved France but England more, proving himself in the Second World War a patriot of unremitting faith and courage. He was witty and gregarious, the most stimulating of companions. There was a streak of femininity in his personality, and if he had a fault, it was a certain softness ('I have no combative qualities'), but although his gentleness was often mistaken for political impotence, he brought to politics much that was shrewd, effective and deeply felt. He never achieved Cabinet rank, for though Churchill respected his advice, enjoyed his company and admired his oratory ('I envy you your gift'), his abrupt dismissal of Harold after only a year in junior office showed that he regarded him, as Harold once wrote of himself, as expendable because he was not formidable. His early career as a civil servant hampered him. He saw merit in too many sides of every question. He had strong political principles (witness his resolute opposition to the Munich and Suez policies), but lacked the vigour to press home his dissent. In domestic politics his attitude was more ambivalent. He had never known a city like Leicester before he became its Member, and felt ill at ease in its clubs and pubs. He advocated greater equality of opportunity, but could never define exactly what he meant by it. Joining the Labour Party he later regarded as 'the cardinal error of my life'.

His literary achievement gave him more satisfaction. His lightly classical style, his wit, his gift for arranging facts and ideas intelligibly and attractively (a legacy from the writing of innumerable Foreign Office dispatches) soon won him a reputation among the foremost writers of his generation. Even before he left diplomacy, he spent his leisure writing books – biographies of Verlaine, Tennyson, Swinburne and Byron, a novel (*Sweet Waters*), *Some People* and the Life of his father – which broadened his scope and friendships, and provided him with an alternative career. After 1930 he was never without a work in progress. That *Some People* remained his most popular book caused him some annoyance because it had given him least trouble. He thought it too trivial, and on receiving the proofs he was only prevented by Vita from cancelling publication. He considered *Lord Carnock*, in effect a study of the causes of the First World War, his best book, followed by *King George the Fifth: His Life and Reign*, in every sense his *magnum opus*, for which he was knighted in 1953. His journalism included his weekly articles for the *Spectator*, and his book reviews for the *Observer* established him as a leading literary critic. As a lecturer and broadcaster he further widened his public. He was immensely industrious, but never at the expense of enjoying life to the full.

The success of his marriage, after a shaky start, defied every expectation, for he and Vita were not only sexual strangers to each other after the birth of their sons, but different in temperament – he highly sociable, she increasingly a recluse, he classical by upbringing, she a romantic. The garden at Sissinghurst, their joint creation, is one symbol of it. His are the firm lines, the symmetrical placing of urns and statues, the broad steps and paths, the vistas; hers the overflowing vines, figs, roses and clematis. For all his frequent absences, he depended on her absolutely. 'I am a bivalve', he once wrote to her, 'and cannot endure being unicellular.' His diary, read in conjunction with his letters to her, many of which are included in this volume, is as much a tribute to her as a record of his activities. Loving as a husband, stimulating as a father, lovable as a friend, he was a more admirable and attractive man than great diarists of the past like Pepys, Creevey or Greville. He has left behind an incomparable record of what it was like to be alive in those tumultuous years, and of his every mood from exhilaration to despair, in controversy and private happiness.

Nigel Nicolson
Sissinghurst
January 2004

HAROLD NICOLSON
DIARIES AND LETTERS
1907–1964

PART I

FOREIGN OFFICE
AND MARRIAGE
1907–1929

Unexpectedly, Harold was not a successful undergraduate at Balliol College, Oxford. Socially, he did not match the stars of his generation, Julian Grenfell, Patrick Shaw-Stewart and Ronald Knox, and academically he gained only a third-class degree in Honour Mods, a failure, due to lack of application, for which he reproached himself all his life. But he did attract the attention of one senior tutor, 'Sligger' Urquhart, who saw in him unrealised gifts, encouraged him, nurtured him and developed in him a gratitude to Balliol which he described, in a broadcast of 1951, as 'dearer to me than any institution on this earth'.

Harold's father, Sir Arthur Nicolson, was appointed Ambassador to Russia in 1905 and Harold spent several holidays in St Petersburg as an undergraduate and after he left Oxford in 1907. Then he began to study for entry into the Foreign Office, and spent the next two years mainly abroad, in France, Germany and Italy, learning the languages for the highly competitive exam that followed in August 1909. To make up for his indolence at Oxford, he worked extremely hard, and much to his father's surprise, gained one of the only two places available. On hearing the news of his success, he wrote to Sligger, 'My father cast off his ambassadorial dignity and behaved like a schoolboy, and my mother was in tears of joy.' In October 1909 he took up his duties as the most junior Foreign Office official, and in June of the next year his father was appointed Under Secretary of State, the most senior. In the same month Harold first met Vita Sackville-West at a London dinner party.

January 9, 1907

H.N. to his parents   *Paris*

The old Madame[1] is such a very dirty, grimy, smelly old thing, that it requires an amount of courage to grasp her by the hand. She is just

---

[1] She was the mother of Jeanne de Hénaut, who ran an establishment in Paris for British candidates for the Foreign Office. There was room in her squalid house for only three students at a time. Jeanne was a brilliant teacher of French and a hard task-mistress, immortalised under her own name in a chapter of Harold's book *Some People*.

like an old Irish woman, and wears a little fur cape which I would not let Rajah [H.N.'s dog] even sniff at, and spends all day by the fire in the kitchen smoking cigarettes, from where she totters in to meals blear-eyed and sooty. Her daughter, on the other hand, though equally dirty, is like Cleopatra would have been if ugly. She is frankly pagan, and suggestively oriental, and wears a sort of thing between a tea-gown and a dressing-gown, ending in a ruff under her chin. Her hair is a wig which looks like horse-hair and is done down over her ears. She has the blue of a much-shaved moustache on her upper lip, and the laugh of a fat man – while her eyes are like lumps of black coal which suddenly light up when she speaks. Her passion is for cats which she breeds in her bedroom and which cover her hands with long red scratches which catch my eye as she corrects my exercises.

H.N. to his parents

December 6, 1908
London

Remember that before I come to St Petersburg[1] I insist on being guaranteed against:

(1) (a) hash (b) curry (c) Irish stew (d) mince (e) ragout (f) cold mutton (g) pork in any form (h) English potatoes (i) Dutch cheeses (j) cold water to drink (k) celery
(2) The use of the word 'couch' for sofa, or 'serviette' for napkin
(3) The casual reference to younger sons of peers as 'The Honourable'
(4) The expressions 'week-end' or 'out of town'
(5) The wearing of a handkerchief up the sleeve
(6) The leaving of long black hairs in the bath
(7) The pronunciation of the words 'Haldane' as 'Halldane' or 'Derby' as 'Darby'
(8) Any morbid questions as to 'how I liked wrens?'
(9) Any social functions of any sort
(10) Any arguments raised against my having caviare & three baths a day
(11) Any resentment at my interrupting you writing your letters

---

[1] Where he was to spend his Christmas holidays with his parents at the British Embassy.

(12) Any undue affection on arrival
(13) Any exhortations to go down to the Chancery & talk to them
(14) Any discussions as to my health
(15) – or my underclothes
(16) – or my luggage labels
(17) – or to the date of my departure
(18) – or the fact that my fur-coat doesn't button up to the chin
(19) Any suggestion that I buy books which I don't read
(20) – or that I don't grasp the books I do read
(21) Any reflections upon my French –
(22) – or German accent

H.N. to his mother

June 1, 1909
Paris

Please don't fuss me about my health. The last fortnight is the most important,[1] as what one learns then is fresh in one's mind. Ever since I left St Petersburg I have averaged 13 hours a day. I shall continue this until the first of July when I shall stop getting up at 5 a.m., and take a long walk in the morning. I shall then gradually slack off, till by the 26th I shall get down to 8 hours a day. I know you think I have no common sense, but if you knew how the slightest detail is all calculated you would not think so, and after all, I know myself better than anyone else does. Do not be cross, Mother dear, with me, as if I fail I shall not work so hard next year. You always rush to extremes – a little time ago you were distressed because you said I lacked energy, and now you are in a state because I have too much – such is the inconsistency of the eternal feminine. But you are an angel and I love you.

H.N. to his parents

October 19, 1909
London

I was told by the Civil Service Commission to 'Put myself at once into communication with the Foreign Office with a view to entering upon my duties there.' I therefore bought a subdued tie and had my boots

---

[1] In preparation for the Foreign Office exam.

cleaned. I walked down to Whitehall. I was very nervous and envied the gentleman who sells bootlaces in front of the Athenaeum and who is not forced to enter into the full glare of publicity. I went in by the door on Horseguards Parade. I was put in a waiting room and while I was admiring the pictures I was told to go into the Private Secretary's room where I found that little beast Tyrrell.[1] I was then taken into the China department. They were all very shy, and I fear I was too. The head of the department made some fatuous remarks about his being glad to see me. I murmured, 'Not at all,' and pulled out my gloves instead of a handkerchief. After that, I was put down to do indexes, and it was not till then that I realised the full value of a liberal education. I also had to copy a letter, which I did wrong, and write out a telegram in which I had to spell Bangkok but spelt it 'Bancock'.

H.N. to his parents   *November 22, 1909*

I dined with the Alstons[2] last night. They were simply delightful. I do like matrimony. A nice cheap little house in Draycott Avenue with white walls and an old French overmantel with a Romney, some coloured china and large chintz chairs. On the table good silver and a simple but excellent dinner. I am sure it is the sort of life in which one's shaving water would always be hot, and one's breakfast adequate. And then what a joy in the evenings as one leaves the Office to fly back to a big chair, a book and a little cuddly wife who wouldn't talk. And then about 7 p.m. the children would come down and the mother would read them stories and I would go to sleep. In the evening at dinner she would tell me how wonderful I was, and I would accept her admiration, and go to sleep after dinner with no one to laugh at me.

---

[1] Sir William Tyrrell was Private Secretary to the Foreign Secretary, Sir Edward Grey. He disliked Harold and his father intensely, and they therefore much disliked him.

[2] Francis Alston, a career diplomatist, and his wife Hilda. He was then aged forty-one.

H.N. to his parents   *May 21, 1910*

I was woken early by troops marching in the street.[1] My function was to escort the Haiti mission to the funeral at Windsor. They appeared in full and flamboyant uniforms with silver handled umbrellas in their hands which I only managed to persuade them to relinquish by pointing to the sun quivering on the brasswork of the motors in the courtyard. At last we started, and flew along to Paddington between lines of purple draped horses. At Paddington we got into a carriage and the whole way to Windsor was lined with people standing on the house tops. When we were all in order at Windsor the gun carriage arrived drawn by sailors in front and behind. It was very hot underneath the station roof and my niggers perspired. Everyone was chattering in different languages. Suddenly they all stopped and the navy came stiffly to the salute and we all took off our hats. Slowly the big long funeral train slid in. People got out: first two men in frock coats, then the whole platform was flooded with Kings. I caught sight of the King of Bulgaria leaning corpulently on his stick, and of the Kaiser. After him came a double line of Grenadiers carrying the coffin. The guns began to fire in the distance. Between each shot there was a dead silence. The Kings fell into line – Theodore Roosevelt looking quite indescribably beastly – and with an almost theatrical step they started with a roll of muffled drums. When we got to St George's Chapel it was quite cool except for my second nigger who kept on mopping himself with a handkerchief. There was music and prayers and the droning of the Archbishop and then suddenly two old men fainted and were carried out. Afterwards we were given an excellent lunch, but I was ashamed of my niggers who overate enormously.

Diary   *June 29, 1910*

Lunch Apsley House. Lady E. in her dress as Kitty Clive. Dine Mrs Stanley. Sackvilles there. On to *The Speckled Band*.[2]

---

[1] It was the day of King Edward VII's funeral.

[2] This entry was typical of Harold's early diaries, and is only remarkable because he later annotated it, 'This was the first time I met Vita.' She was then eighteen. Lady E. was Eileen Wellesley, to whom Harold was briefly engaged, and Apsley House was

*Harold's friendship with Vita developed slowly. At first her mother, Lady
Sackville, was more attracted by him than her daughter, and invited him to
frequent weekends at Knole in Kent. But when she suspected that Vita was
falling in love with him, she objected that Harold's family was insufficiently
aristocratic and not rich enough to be worthy of the Sackvilles. In 1911 Harold
spent a short time in the Madrid Embassy, and when they became half-engaged
in January 1912, Lady Sackville counselled caution, and almost immediately
Harold was sent to the Constantinople Embassy as a Third Secretary. From
there he succeeded, by correspondence, in maintaining his hold on Vita against
the competition of several rivals, including a girl, Rosamund Grosvenor, with
whom Vita was much in love. In June 1913 he returned to England in time
to hear Vita give her evidence in the famous Scott inheritance case.*

H.N. to his parents	*July 5, 1911* *British Embassy, Madrid*

Everybody has gone away, but it makes no difference to me as I have
not got to know a single solitary soul. I am the most utter failure
socially. I am simply incapable of it – just as Mother would be incapable
of going on a walking tour with Mrs George Keppel [mistress of
Edward VII and mother of Violet Trefusis]. I am excellent at making
friends but hopeless at making acquaintances. You see, not only does
it bore me stiff, but I am so shy that it is as if a shutter was pulled down
in front of my brain and I simply sit there. Of course I know you think
it will be the ruin of my career, but I beg to differ, as I know that later
on, when people expect me to interest and not make love to them, I
shall have a modicum of success. I have always had a success with
people I like, but I hardly like anybody. I think it's a question of
indolence, and still more of modesty. But it's there, and luckily I think
it's the only really Hamilton thing about me.[1]

---

her father's, the Duke of Wellington. Mrs Stanley was the wife of Admiral Victor
Stanley. The play to which they went after dinner was a Sherlock Holmes thriller.

[1] Harold's mother, Katherine, was the daughter of Archibald Rowan-Hamilton, of
Killyleagh, Northern Ireland.

H.N. to his parents

I was amused at your account of Gwen [Harold's younger sister]
meeting Vita. I don't think it will do Gwen any harm at all to find
someone rather above her. And then, when they get to know each
other better, V. will have all the more influence on her, and at the
same time Gwen will feel ashamed of her superficiality. I am only
afraid that she will resent being No. 2. I rather wish she had not raved
so much about V.'s beauty. Of course I think her pretty enough, but I
am so afraid of Father being disappointed if he hears so much about
it. She is tremendously *grande dame* and elegant and this must have
impressed Gwen, who after all does not see many respectable girls. I
get so excited when I think I shall see her soon. I promise not to go
to Knole too often. It is a deep secret, but in her last letter V. says she
simply won't go on in the present terms and that after my leave she is
going to insist on a proper engagement.

February 17, 1913
H.N. to Vita   *Constantinople*

I see that it would be nicer to go to Rome or Tangier or to stay here.
Vienna combines everything which we will both most dislike.[1] But
then I do feel a *duty* to go – I would think less of us if we didn't go –
I would think it a lack of discipline – morally sloppy if we got out of
it. Besides, I really must be the one who 'disposes' in these things. I
tell you this because I want you to understand that this is the basis of
our life that is to be. I will be invariably weak about trifles – but about
big things I am to have the upper hand. I know that in the bottom of
your heart you think, 'Oh yes, it's all very well for him to say that, but
he doesn't know what I give up.' But I *do* know what you give up. I
know that by marrying me you give up vast worldly things – but they
don't matter. And then any girl by marriage gives up her girlhood –
which is so much.

Of course this is common to all, but then the diplomacy thing in

---

[1] Harold had been warned that he might be posted to the Embassy in Vienna soon
after his marriage, but the proposal was cancelled.

your case is worse. Because, Vita, you will be admired (specially in Vienna) in the wrong way. You will be admired in a way that people will be surprised to find you can't dance better. And this (though a tiny thing) is illustrative of the general irritation which their attitude will evoke. Darling Vita.

So you see, I admit the utter weakness of my position. I see how utterly you will hate doing what I am asking you to do, and yet I ask it because deep down I know you will give this up to me, and that you will not let me run away from it when I want to. And, Vita, pull yourself together, you vague person, pull up all the blinds in your mind – and think whether you want it. Darling, be *sure* about it before you decide. And remember that whatever you do – if you never speak to me again – I shall know that you were right.

February 26, 1913
Constantinople

H.N. to Vita

No letter from you for ten days. I know you are not ill, because B.M.[1] in her last letter says, 'V. will have told you all about our last party.' I know no letters can have been lost as I have got regular ones from my family. Oh Vita, this is so dreadful for me – being left without letters. I know, I mean I *hope*, you will be saying, 'Silly boy, why does he get into a state about nothing?'

But *is* it nothing, Vita? You must see how I look on it. I know you have nothing to do – and I am busy all day and yet find time to write to you four times a week. Oh Vita! I know that in a case like this there can be no question of indolence. You can't be too *lazy* to write to me. At least, if you are too lazy it means that you don't care one fig.

Oh Vita! Vita! I am making you angry, and all because I am wretched myself. Yes, wretched – and frightfully disappointed to come back here early and wait for the post because I feel sure there must, *must*, be a letter from you today. And then there is another thing – *not* a little thing – which has hurt me awfully, and in a point where you might have known me frightfully sensitive. You have only been to see my mother once since I left. . . .

---

[1] Lady Sackville, 'Bonne Mama' (which she was not).

Is this a foolish letter to write, Vita? But it is only because my eyes are stinging with disappointment and my heart is sore – sore, Vita – and you are so far away, and I don't know what's happening.

Oh Vita, they are playing in my sitting-room (I am writing this in my bedroom with your photograph there), and, Vita, they are playing *Il pleure dans mon coeur comme il pleut sur la ville* – and I feel it so, and I look over the wet roofs, and Mikky [dog] is by the fire – and No! No! No! I can't bear it. You out there laughing with strange people, people I don't know, people who may have a power over your mind – and sometimes, before dinner, you write me a letter while Rosamund [Grosvenor] is having a bath, and it is written so lightly and it goes so far, and is so important when it gets there.

March 30, 1913
Constantinople

H.N. to his parents

I had a most interesting day yesterday. I went to the front[1] ... I was taken to the field hospital. A red crescent on a pole flapped above it and outside there were several ox-carts with blood stained sacks on the floor. About 30 stretchers were lying in the mud with soldiers on them who had coats thrown over their faces and who had, I conclude, died on the way from the trenches. One of them had a bare foot sticking out from under the cloak, and all the toes were crushed. One of the doctors, an Egyptian, said they were ready to bolt at a moment's notice if the Bulgars came on. A man dashed up and said more wounded were arriving. Some carts were creaking through the mud with men lying on them. They looked dazed and sat in a row holding their hands away from them. The fighting was only three quarters of a mile away from us. When they were lifted off the stretchers they screamed. I could not stand it, and ran upstairs and tried to distance my attention. Then the doctor came in and showed me how to help him make a splint. I could hear the groaning through the floor and then went down again. The house is a filthy place. They were pulling off the men's clothes and one of them was sobbing and chattering and whining like a dog. I was asked to help get them on board the steamer which

---

[1] Bulgaria had declared war on Turkey, and her army had advanced to within thirty miles of Constantinople.

was to take them back to Constantinople. The doctor said, 'Go and look in the cabin of the launch, and you will see humanity at its worst.' So I went down, and saw three young Turkish officers who winced when I came in and whose hands were trembling underneath their coats. They had run away and could hardly speak. The doctor was very curt with them. 'If they were English,' he said, 'I would have them shot straight away.' ... We started off at about 6.45. It was dark and we could see the Bulgar searchlights flashing behind us, and in front the glow of Constantinople. The poor fellows were awfully seasick, and I tried to do what I could. When we got to the city I found a red crescent officer and handed the wounded over to him. Then I jumped into a cab. It was a sight which I shall never forget.

May 19, 1913
H.N. to Vita   *Constantinople*

Vita darling, darling Vita. I got a terrible letter from you today, and it has quite crushed me with apprehension.[1] You put the fierce part in French, half because you were a little ashamed of it and half because you felt it sounded deadly earnest. Vita, I can't answer coherently about it. I have been trying to diminish the effect of it to myself. I have been explaining that you began the letter quite lazily in the garden – and quite thoughtlessly you put that in the end because you were alone, and had come back to England [from Spain] and found your house secure, welcoming and comfortable; and my letters in the bustle of arrival had seemed flat and impersonal, and you had read them in the wrong order, and while people were asking you questions, and they had left no after-glow – and so you ended your letter almost brutally, in an impulse of irritation and in the reaction to the home-coming excitement and the sort of feeling, 'Well there's going to be

---

[1] Vita's letter has not survived. Perhaps Harold destroyed it in his anguish. But clearly she had hinted that their semi-engagement should be ended. At the same time as he wrote this reply, he sent her a telegram, 'Am I to take your letter seriously?', and she replied, again by telegram, 'No, forgive me. Don't believe a word of it.' That was the end of the crisis. On October 1 they were married in the chapel at Knole.

nothing exciting now till Harold comes home, and will that be exciting? I wonder now.'

I feel you may be sounding the ground for worse news in your next
letter.

Vita, surely you could not treat me like that. I feel I should kill you.
And all those bright planned edifices to be pulled down and shoved
away. Vita, is it because I am flippant about us both – and don't talk
heroics – that you think I won't mind? Why, it would alter the whole
substance of things. And, Vita, I was coming back so soon – only six
weeks – and I had planned it all out so. I suppose I felt too sure of you
and this doubt shows me how thin the ice is. And I love you far more
than ever before – the longing after you is like a stretched cord within
me. And, Vita, Vita, why on earth if the [Scott] case is won should we
not get married at once? I always counted on that in my silly ass way.
And now I have nothing to count on. Except that you can't have
meant it, Vita; you can't have meant to write it to me out here; you
would have kept it till I got home.

*Their honeymoon was spent on a long journey to Constantinople where Harold
resumed his diplomatic duties and Vita made her first garden. They returned
to England in June 1914, and Vita's first son, Benedict (Ben) was born at
Knole two days after the outbreak of the First World War. Harold was exempted
from war service because he was considered indispensable to the Foreign Office.
When it was suggested that he should be transferred to the Embassy in Rome,
Sir George Clerk, head of the War Department, exclaimed, 'You don't
seriously suggest that I should let Harold go? The whole department would
collapse if he went', and the Foreign Secretary, Arthur Balfour, agreed.*

*Few written records of Harold's war years survive, since his diary was scrappy
and intermittent and he wrote few personal letters. He returned home each
evening, either to 182 Ebury Street, where his second son was born on January
19, 1917, or to Long Barn, the fifteenth-century farmhouse near Knole,
which he extended with the help of Sir Edwin Lutyens and where Vita made
a garden that became Sissinghurst's prototype. It was also there that they wrote
their first books. Harold was much in demand as an invigorating guest in
London's political and intellectual circles. His only worry was Vita's growing
intimacy with Violet Keppel, later Trefusis, with whom she began a passionate
affair in the last year of the war.*

Harold Nicolson at the time of his marriage in 1913

October 24, 1913
H.N. *to his parents*   *Florence*

We had a great expedition yesterday. We heard of a castle in Volterra
so we drove through the most gorgeous country to a village in the hills
where we spent the night. Next morning Vita and I went to see the
castle. The road is excellent as far as 200 yards from the top and then
there is no road. One has to get out and walk. The sides of the hill are
very rich in olives. The castle is 2,000 years old, having been built by
Sulla in his wars with Marius. It is called Rocca Silliana [Sulla] and the
village is San Dalmazio. V. and I struggled through a mass of fallen
walls to the keep. The view from it is simply marvellous. The priest
had warned us that the interior was in a terrible condition, but when
we opened one door and saw a mass of stones blocking the inside
covered with brambles, our hearts sank. On exploring we found some
good points like an enormous Roman tank fed by a spring, and a huge
vaulted cellar which is in wonderful repair and could make a liveable
room. We felt that we could live in the cellar after very little had been
done to it, and then we could build up the rest. As it is so ruinous we
ought to get it cheap. It will not be comfortable for years but it has so
much character and is so historic and has some wonderful views that
we are both rather in love with it.[1]

December 20, 1913
H.N. *to his mother*   *Constantinople*

Vita says I may tell you of our great secret and you will guess what it
is. She saw the doctor today, who says that he will stake his reputation
on it, but of course Vita is particularly anxious not to tell people so
you will keep it to yourselves. V. had such bright eyes today that I felt
it was true – and we have hoped for some weeks that it might be. It
all sounds so ordinary when written down, but to us it seems the most
extraordinary thing that has ever happened. The doctor said it would

---

[1] This project came to nothing, but the idea was typical of Vita's romanticism. She had
a passion for Italy, castles and ruins. Later she had a yearning to buy Bodiam Castle in
Sussex, now an uninhabitable property of the National Trust, and eventually bought
and restored Sissinghurst Castle in Kent.

be born in July or early August. V. would like to stay here, but of course Lady Sackville may object. V. is so happy, it would make you cry to see her. She is the most beautiful angel in the world.

June 16, 1914
H.N. to his parents   *Paris*

I sent you a telegram from Marseilles. You can imagine how glad we are to have arrived and how relieved I am to have my darling safely back in civilisation. We had a wonderful journey and most comfortable cabins. It was as calm as a river the whole way, and we sat on deck reading the whole time. Vita and I felt so happy lying there, and watching the Greek islands pass. We took a train from Marseilles to Paris. You can imagine the luxury of this brand new hotel [Hotel Edouard VII]. We are here at Lady Sackville's expense, with a large suite of rooms and every possible comfort. She has given us some really beautiful silver from the Rue Lafitte.[1]

May 22, 1916
H.N. to Vita   *Foreign Office*

Dear heart, I do hate to feel that at the end of my beastly bustled days here, I don't get into that soft gentle heaven – when I am alone with you, my gob, and when nothing outside fusses or worries or telephones.

Dearest, how happy we two are, when one gets outside ourselves, and think of our life and two happy homes (Ebury Street rather stern and prim and quiet, and the cottage [Long Barn] all untidy and tinkly), and of our baby [Ben] and the things we do together and like together, and all the many things we will do and like together in the future when this beastly war is over, and all Europe becomes a playground for us to spend money in.

Darling, there are no clouds, are there?, my sweetest, and when and if they rise, I feel we will just go indoors a bit, and sit together in front of the fire and wait till it clears up. Sweetest, it is such a deep strong

---

[1] The house in Paris which Sir John Murray Scott had bequeathed to Lady Sackville, with a large part of the Wallace Collection.

river our love, isn't it?, and there are great meadows on each side of it, and cows, and babies, and guinea pigs and newts.

Dearest, I am so busy – and I write now as there may be a rush at the end.

Ruffle that little head for his daddy.

Goodbye my darling.

August 22, 1917

H.N. to Vita
Foreign Office

A busy day again – but I rather like it. George Clerk is such an angel to work with – so appreciative and encouraging and stimulating. He never snubs one for being uppish, and, oh dear, I was so uppish today. I suggested peace with Austria against everybody's views, and instead of just turning it down, he sends for me to discuss it all and I know how busy he is and how easy it would be for him just to put, 'I think the moment inopportune'. I don't care what Hardinge or Balfour say now.'[1]

H.N. to Vita
October 19, 1917

I was at a loose end last night, so I telephoned to Macned thinking he was a widower too, but oh dear, oh dear, he wasn't, so he had to ask me to Bedford Square, and I am sure it led to a row with Emmie.[2] Anyhow, I went – and a terrible Theosophist friend was there, and poor Macned was such a darling. Emmie is a devil. She nags and jeers and sniffs and sighs at Macned as if he was a naughty schoolgirl, and the poor man is snubbed before that little swine of a Theosophist, who is not worthy to tie his bootlaces. There were only a few rissoles, and the rest, veg. Poor, poor Macned. She *is* a gloom. I do understand why B.M. cheers him up.

---

[1] Lord Hardinge, the ex-Viceroy of India, had succeeded Harold's father in 1916 as Permanent Under Secretary at the Foreign Office. Arthur Balfour had been Foreign Secretary since December 1916.

[2] Macned was Lady Sackville's name for Sir Edwin Lutyens, the architect, whose intimate friend she had become. He had married Lady Emily Lytton, who in 1907 fell under the influence of Mrs Annie Besant, President of the Theosophical Society.

November 11, 1918
H.N. to Vita   *Foreign Office*

They [the Germans] have signed [the Armistice] – at 8.30 this morning.
And I am so busy getting peace terms ready. It is rather fun, though I
feel oddly responsible. I feel that what I do is likely to be accepted –
and that the tracing of my pencil in this familiar room and on my own
familiar maps may mean the fate of millions of unknown people. I feel
almost an impulse – 'God give me the right', and I feel quite solemn
about it.

*In 1919 Harold Nicolson was appointed a member of the British delegation
to the Paris Peace Conference which ended with the signing of the Treaty of
Versailles. The delegation was led by the Prime Minister, Lloyd George, and
Arthur Balfour. Harold's immediate, and much loved, superior was Sir Eyre
Crowe. The other main participants were President Woodrow Wilson, Georges
Clemenceau (Prime Minister of France), and Vittorio Orlando (Prime Minister
of Italy). Together with Lloyd George, these were the Big Four. Harold was
mainly concerned with the Balkans, Czechoslovakia and the relationship
between Greece and Turkey, and was given responsibilities, as he later wrote in
his account of the Conference (Peacemaking, 1933), well above his ranking.
He was still only a Third Secretary. But his performance gained him a
reputation as one of the ablest young Foreign Office officials. It was the most
exciting period of his diplomatic career. He would have loved every moment of
it, had it not been for personal troubles.*

*Unknown to all his colleagues, he was undergoing a severe domestic crisis.
Vita was living with Violet Keppel in Monte Carlo, and in spite of his
desperate pleas, and her protestations of eternal love for him, she refused to join
him in Paris or to return to England. The situation was worsened by Violet's
engagement to Denys Trefusis, for whom she felt no affection whatever.*

*The Treaty was signed at Versailles on June 28, 1919. Harold foresaw the
terrible consequences of a peace dictated not by reason, but by the desire for
revenge on Germany.*

January 21, 1919

Diary   *Paris*

Dine with A.J.B. [Balfour]. He is as charming as usual. He says that
ever since his visit to America he had had a deep regard for President
Wilson as a man and as a scholar, but he had never seen him actually
at work. He is astonished therefore to find him as good round a table
as he was on paper. His attitude at the meetings of the Big Four is
firm, modest, restrained, eloquent, well-informed and convincing.

January 22, 1919

Diary   *Paris*

[Sir Eyre] Crowe is cantankerous about Cyprus and will not allow me
even to mention the subject. I explain (1) that we acquired it by a trick
as disreputable as that by which the Italians collared the Dodecanese.
(2) that it is wholly Greek, and that under any interpretation of self-
determination would opt for union with Greece. (3) that it is of no
use to us strategically or economically. (4) that we are left in a false
moral position if we ask everyone else to surrender possessions in terms
of self-determination and surrender nothing ourselves. How can we
keep Cyprus and express moral indignation at the Italians retaining
Rhodes? He says, 'Nonsense, my dear Nicolson. You are not being
clear-headed. You think that you are being logical and sincere. You
are not. Would you apply self-determination to India, Egypt, Malta
and Gibraltar? If you are not prepared to go as far as this, then you
have no right to claim that you are logical. If you *are* prepared to go as
far as this, then you had better return at once to London.' Dear
Crowe – he has the most truthful brain of any man I know.

January 28, 1919

Diary   *Paris*

Dine with Venizelos.[1] His sitting-room overheated – mimosa and roses

---

[1] Eleutherios Venizelos, formerly the Cretan rebel and now Prime Minister of Greece.
Harold conceived for him an admiration and affection beyond any other foreign
statesman in Paris.

on the table. He is very much the host. He is in great form. He
tells us stories of King Constantine, his lies and equivocations. He
tells us of the old days of the Cretan insurrection, when he escaped
to the mountains and taught himself English by reading *The Times*
with a rifle across his knee. He talks of Greek culture, of modern
Greek and its relation to the classical, and we induce him to recite
Homer. An odd effect, rather moving. He talks of King Ferdinand
and the London Conference after the Balkan wars. The whole gives
us a strange medley of charm, brigandage, *welt-politik*, patriotism,
courage, literature – and above all this large muscular smiling man,
with his eyes glinting through spectacles, and on his head a square
skull–cap of black silk.

February 2, 1919

H.N. to Vita   *Paris*

I am feeling crushed, and sore, and sad today – because it's Sunday –
and I had been packing some things to take round to the flat.[1] I packed
them so tenderly as if they were bits of you, my saint – and I was so
happy, so happy.

And then your letter came – and it was so dark and grim and
horrible. I have never been so disappointed in my life. I didn't know
it could come on one like that.

But it is childish, of course, and disappointment is after all a very
transitory hurt – and nothing compared to poor V's [Violet's] tragic
and hopeless position. Little one, don't think I am angry or sad about
you. I always dissociate these things from you – especially when you
tell me frankly what has happened.

But all the sun has gone from Paris – which has become a cold, grey,
meaningless city where there is a Conference going on somewhere, a
Conference that meant so much to me yesterday, and today is something detached, unreal and inanimate.

But tomorrow it will be all right again – and when you get this *I*
shall be all right again. Only please get a new photograph done of

---

[1] Harold had rented a flat in Paris for himself and Vita, who had promised to come,
but chucked him at the last moment.

yourself and send it to me. I feel you are slipping away, you who are my anchor, my hope, and all my peace.

Dearest, you don't know my devotion to you. What you do can never be wrong.

God bless you, Vita.

February 25, 1919
H.N. to his father   *Paris*

The work is so passionately interesting that one has no time to be exhausted, but I feel that another month or so would wear us all out. Apart from the actual strain of continuous labour, there is the moral exhaustion of realising one's own fallibility and the impossibility of extracting from the lies with which we are surrounded any real impression of what the various countries and nationalities honestly desire. Whatever result is arrived at will be attacked by the champions of all the lost causes; but I must say that this is a matter of complete indifference to me.

I can't tell you the position Venizelos has here! He and Lenin are the only two really great men in Europe.

March 2, 1919
Diary   *Paris*

Dine at the Ritz – a swell affair [Marcel] Proust is there. He is white, unshaven, grubby, slip-faced. He puts his fur-coat on afterwards and sits hunched there in white kid-gloves. Two cups of black coffee he has, with chunks of sugar. Yet in his talk there is no affectation. He asks me questions. Will I please tell him how the Committees work? I say, 'Well, we generally meet at 10. There are secretaries behind ...' *'Mais non, mais non, vous allez trop vite. Recommencez. Vous prenez la voiture de la Délégation. Vous descendez au Quai d'Orsay. Vous montez l'escalier. Vous entrez dans la salle ... Et alors? Précisez, mon cher, précisez.'* So I tell him everything. The sham cordiality of it all; the hand-shakes; the maps; the rustle of papers; the tea in the next room; the macaroons. He listens enthralled, interrupting from time to time – *'Mais précisez, mon cher monsieur, n'allez pas trop vite.'*

March 24, 1919
Paris

H.N. to Vita

I am so depressed about the way the Conference is going. It all seemed
to be humming beautifully when the Committees were doing the
work, but now that the Council of X[1] are supposed to be passing the
work of the Committees it is all hanging fire. You see, the work is all
extremely technical — and our rulers know nothing about it — and
rightly or wrongly hesitate to pass it all. It is so disheartening as there
is no time to waste. Every day makes it less likely that the Germans
will accept our terms. They have always got the trump card, Bolshevism. They will go Bolshevist the moment they feel it is hopeless
to get good terms. The only hope, therefore, is to give them food and
peace *at once*, and if we are going to stop and argue — what will be the
good or the hope? It will be too awful if, after winning the war, we
are to lose the peace, and I must say it all looks as if there was a good
chance of our doing so. In fact, I am very depressed about it. What
we want is a Dictator for Europe and we haven't got one. And never
will have!

April 14, 1919
Paris

Diary

Arnold Toynbee [chief representative of the Treasury] and I plot
together about Constantinople and the Straits. We agree (1) that no
mandatory [power] will be able to run Constantinople without a fairly
large zone behind them. On the other hand, a big zone will include
Greek populations, while cutting the future Turkey off from all communication with the Marmora. (2) That as we have demobilised so
quickly, and as people at home are bored by the future settlement, we
shall be unable to put the Greeks into Smyrna. I mean keep them
there. They can't hold it without allied support and unless the whole
of Turkey behind them is split up among the Allied Powers. Yet, if

---

[1] Originally the deciding body was the Council of Ten (two representatives each for
the USA, Britain, France, Italy and Japan), but this was found unwieldy, and it was
reduced to the Council of Four — Clemenceau (in the Chair), President Wilson,
Lloyd George and Orlando.

they do not get Smyrna, Venizelos will fall from power. (3) We agree, therefore, to propose to cut the Gordian knot. Let the Turks have Anatolia as their own. Give the Greeks European Turkey only. And let the Straits be kept open by a *Commission Fluviale* with powers analogous to those of the Danube Commission. We put this down on paper; we sign it with our names; we send it in. It will not be considered.

Diary

May 8, 1919
Paris

Eric Drummond [Secretary General to the League of Nations] comes in and asks me to 'step aside'. In the passage he says, 'Look here, would you like to join me on the League?' I say I should love to, provided that the F.O. have no objection and I do not lose in salary etc. This means that I do not go to Athens. It also means that I shall work with Drummond in organising the Secretariat of the League – a body which is certain to become one of vital importance. I am delighted beyond words. I could not conceive of a cause, a job, a chief which I would prefer to these.

Diary

May 13, 1919
Paris

I spread out my big map on the dinner table and they all gather round. Ll.G., A.J.B., Milner, Henry Wilson, Mallet and myself. Ll.G. explains that Orlando and Sonnino are due in a few minutes and he wants to know what he can offer Italy. I suggest the Adalia Zone [on the south coast of Turkey], with the rest of Asia Minor to France. Milner, Mallet and Henry Wilson oppose it: A.J.B. neutral.

The flabby Orlando and the sturdy Sonnino are shown into the dining-room. They all sit round the map. The appearance of a pie about to be distributed is thus enhanced. Ll.G. shows them what he suggests. They ask for Scala Nova as well. 'Oh no!' says Ll.G., 'you can't have that – it's full of Greeks.' He goes on to point out that there are further Greeks at Makri, and a whole wedge of them along the coast towards Alexandretta. 'Oh no,' I whisper to him, 'there are not many Greeks there.' 'But yes,' he answers, 'don't you see it's coloured green?' I then realise that he mistakes my map for an ethnological map, and thinks the green means Greeks instead of valleys, and the brown means Turks instead of mountains. Ll.G. takes this correction with great good humour. He is as quick as a kingfisher. Finally they appear ready to accept a mandate over the Adalia region, but it is not quite clear whether in return for this they will abandon Fiume and Rhodes. We get out the League Covenant regarding Mandates. We observe that this article provides for 'the consent and wishes of the people concerned'. They find that phrase very amusing. How they all laugh! Orlando's white cheeks wobble with laughter and his puffy eyes fill with tears of mirth.

May 14, 1919
H.N. to Vita *Paris*

I scribbled you a note yesterday in President Wilson's anteroom when Ll.G. burst in in his impetuous way. 'Come along, Nicolson, and keep your ears wide open.' So I went in. There were Wilson and Ll.G. and Clemenceau with their armchairs drawn close over my map on the hearthrug. I was there about half an hour – talking and objecting. The President was extremely nice and so was Ll.G. Clemenceau was cantankerous, in his '*mais voyons, jeune homme*' style.

It is appalling that these ignorant and irresponsible men should be cutting Asia Minor to bits as if they were dividing a cake. And with no one there except me, who incidentally have nothing to do with Asia Minor. Isn't it terrible the happiness of millions being decided in that way. Their decisions are immoral and impracticable. '*Mais voyez-vous, jeune homme, que voulez-vous qu'on fasse? Il faut aboutir.*'

Lloyd George asked me to draft resolutions at once, and here I did a clever thing. I watered everything down. I tried to introduce at least the elements of sanity into their decisions.

May 17, 1919
H.N. to Vita   *Paris*

There is *such* a thunderstorm brewing here against the Prime Minister.
It is all about this Asia Minor business – and it is difficult for Hadji[1] to
guide his row-boat safely in and out of these fierce Dreadnoughts.
Even A.J.B. is angry: 'I have three all–powerful, all–ignorant men sitting
there and partitioning continents with only a child to make notes for
them.' I have an uneasy suspicion that by the 'child' he means me. I
had better lie very low for a bit. Anyhow I have, I think, got my point.
But it was playing with gunpowder.

June 1, 1919
H.N. to Vita   *Paris*

I really feel that this bloody bullying peace is the last flicker of the old
tradition, and that we young people will build again. I hope so.

June 8, 1919
H.N. to his father   *Paris*

I have every hope that Lloyd George, who is fighting like a Welsh
terrier, will succeed in the face of everybody in introducing some
modifications in the terms imposed upon Germany. Now that we see
them as a whole we realise that they are much too stiff. They are not
stern merely, but actually *punitive*, and they abound with what Smuts
calls 'pin pricks' as well as dagger thrusts. Lloyd George is concentrating
upon Silesia, the cost of the Armies of Occupation, and the admission
of Germany into the League of Nations. Yet the real crime is the
reparations and indemnity chapter, which is immoral and senseless.
There is not a single person among the younger people here who is
not unhappy and disappointed at the terms. The only people who
approve are the old fire-eaters. I have tried, with the help of the
Treasury man [Maynard Keynes] who is first class, to water down the
Austrian financial clauses, but was told to mind my own business.

---

[1] Vita's pet–name for Harold.

Anyhow, I think we shall, provided Ll.G. wins his battle, get the Germans to sign. God help us if we can't. They will have us at their mercy.

June 28, 1919
Versailles

Diary

La journée de Versailles. We enter the Galerie des Glaces. It is divided into three sections. At the far end the Press are already thickly installed. In the middle is a horseshoe table for the plenipotentiaries. In front of that, like a guillotine, is the table for the signatures. '*Faites entrer les Allemands*', says Clemenceau. Through the door at the end appear two huissiers with silver chains. They march in single file. After them come four officers of France, Great Britain, America and Italy. And then, isolated and pitiable, come the two German delegates, Dr Muller, Dr Bell. The silence is terrifying. Their feet upon a strip of parquet between the savonnerie carpets echo hollow and duplicate. They keep their eyes fixed away from those two thousand staring eyes, fixed upon the ceiling. They are deathly pale. They do not appear as representatives of a brutal militarism, The one is thin and pink–eyelidded, the second fiddle in a Brunswick orchestra. The other is moon-faced and suffering. It is all most painful.

They are conducted to their chairs. Clemenceau at once breaks the silence. '*Messieurs*,' he rasps, '*la séance est ouverte*.' He adds a few ill-chosen words. 'We are here to sign a Treaty of Peace.' The Germans leap up anxiously when he has finished, since they know they are the first to sign. William Martin, as if a theatre manager, motions them petulantly to sit down again. Mantoux translates Clemenceau's words into English. Then St Quentin advances towards the Germans and with the utmost dignity leads them to the little table on which the Treaty is expanded. There is general tension. They sign. There is general relaxation. Conversation hums again in an undertone. The delegates stand up one by one and pass onwards to the queue which waits by the signature table. Suddenly from outside comes the crash of guns thundering a salute. It announces to Paris that the second Treaty of Versailles has been signed. Through the few open windows comes the sound of distant crowds cheering hoarsely.

Celebrations in the hotel afterwards. We are given free champagne at the expense of the tax–payer. It is very bad champagne. To bed, sick of life.

Harold remained in Paris for several months after the signature of the Versailles Treaty, to settle outstanding questions like the partition of Thrace and a separate treaty with Austria. He was seconded to the League of Nations' London and Paris offices from October 1919 to May 1920, and then returned to the Foreign Office under Lord Curzon, whom he accompanied to the Lausanne Conference (1922–3) to settle the differences between Turkey, Italy and Greece. He remained in London till 1925, when he was posted to the Legation in Teheran, Persia. He was rising fast in his profession, having been awarded the CMG for his work at the Peace Conference and promoted from Third Secretary to First.

It was during the first two years of this period, 1919–20, that Vita's love-affair with Violet Trefusis reached its climax. The two women eloped to France, determined to spend the rest of their lives together, and were retrieved by their husbands in a dramatic scene at Amiens, which Vita described in an autobiographical sketch which was published in Portrait of a Marriage *(1973). It was the crisis of their marriage, and paradoxically stabilised it, for having escaped this near-disaster, each relied absolutely on the other's support and love for the remainder of their lives.*

Both were already prolific writers. In these years Harold wrote biographies of Verlaine, Swinburne, Tennyson and Byron and a novel, Sweet Waters, *while Vita, also a novelist, wrote the history of her family,* Knole and the Sackvilles, *and began her long and most famous poem,* The Land. *They were very sociable, and Vita, after a brief affair with a man, Geoffrey Scott, discovered the most influential friend of her life, Virginia Woolf.*

November 4, 1919
H.N. to Vita *Paris*

I do envy you so your freedom and liberty[1] – but don't let yourself feel it is a right, this self-indulgence: it is merely a holiday. Oh darling, I am rather fussed about you – not about you or me, but about you

---

[1] Vita was staying with Violet Trefusis at Monte Carlo.

getting sloppier and sloppier, till even having to wear stays will become a *corvée* [unpleasant duty] – and your life will become one long sluttish slatternly muddle. That's why it annoys me that you should *always* lose your luggage. It's so slovenly. I loathe slov (rather a good word that). But I know you don't think you do a slov about your work. But that's no excuse, as you can sit down to that and not move, and it doesn't entail plans, arrangements, accounts, time-tables, arguments, accuracies, previsions, coming upstairs, telephoning, writing cheques, writing in the counterfoil of cheques, standing in queues, talking to servants, having to make up one's mind, pushing, having one's hair blown about in the wind – no, one just sits in a chair quite still and quiet with a cigarette, 2 tubes of lipsalve and a pot of powder. My darling, I want you back by Dec. 21 – and no mistake about it.

February 4, 1920
H.N. to Vita   *Paris*

My dearest, I thought of you so much last night. I am so worried about you. You are all wrong in thinking that I look upon you as my *légitime*. You are not a person with whom one can associate law, order, duty – or any of the conventional ties of life. I never think of you in that way, not even from the babies' point of view. I just look on you as the person I love best in the world, and without whom life would lose all its light and meaning. My darling, I do hope you can come over here – it would be bloody for you in a way, but I do so want to have you with me, and you can write. The [Hotel] Alexandre III is quite comfy, and very clean. I don't want to be here long – it is terribly dull if one hasn't got a lot of work, or doesn't plunge into debauchery.

January 12, 1921
Diary   *Foreign Office*

The P.M. [Lloyd George] says he won't come to Paris and that Curzon is to run the thing alone. This means that he sees it will be a failure and prefers not to be there. Exhausted and depressed. Chiefly by a look in Vita's face which shows that V. [Violet Trefusis] has been at her again.[1] Poor darling. I decide to go down to Knole.

Diary   *February 28, 1921*

At the [Foreign] Office I meet Vansittart who tells me that Winston has made a frightful row with the P.M. over the intercept of my interview with Sicilianos [head of a Greek delegation]. So even my own personal position has gone wrong now. No home. No affection. No money. No happiness. Oh Vita, Vita, what you have to answer for. I simply long to get abroad and away from them all. What a bloody thing it is to have so thin a skin! Last week was the worst week I have ever gone through. I am a harmless happy creature by nature. If only I didn't care for her it would help. But I love her so.

Diary   *August 11, 1921*

Lunch with the Eric Forbes Adams to meet [Chaim] Weizmann, head of the Zionist organisation. An attractive man: his idealism; his resemblance to Lenin. He tells me of a strange luncheon the other day at Mr Balfour's with Lloyd George, Churchill and Hankey. Weizmann asked Mr B. definitely what he had meant by 'a national home for the Jews'. B. said, 'I meant a Jewish state.' Lloyd George added, 'We all meant a Jewish state.' Churchill was disconcerted.

                                                             October 8, 1921
Diary   *Rome*

To the Palazzo Barberini to lunch with Princess Jane [Barberini]. A large shuttered room with a tiled floor. Slowly from the darkness emerges walnut furniture and a painted balustrade upon the ceiling. Eagles and peacocks perch over the big doorways in the centre of the balustrade. Princess Jane is dressed as a widow with a Marie Stuart hat

---

[1] They went together to Hyères, but the danger was past. The scene at Amiens had defused their affair.

and a white face. She had got drunk at Venice and had fallen down, and Ozzie [Dickinson] had fallen on top of her and broken two of her ribs. So she had gone to bed and been X-rayed. We went into the dining-room – a cool, grey room with a terracotta wall fountain, two armorial tapestries and a macaw. The arms of the San Faustino, the Bourbon lilies with a bar sinister, sprawled in stucco upon the ceiling, and from their edges hung two lamps in painted metal with a central glass globe. Gerry [Wellesley] didn't like the lamps. He told her so. He said he would have preferred wooden chandeliers gilded.

Diary   *February 16, 1922*

Curzon has come a big cropper over the Egyptian business.[1] Allenby had prepared a series of concessions and had telegraphed from Cairo to Curzon asking him to see them through the Cabinet. C. had telegraphed back promising his support, but when the proposals came before the Cabinet there was some slight opposition. C. immediately telegraphed to A. suggesting a compromise. A. replied that he would resign if his proposals were not accepted. C. then sent a long telegram with numbered paragraphs pointing out how wrong A. had been all along and how wicked of him it was to suggest resignation. A. replied by telegraph that he was coming home, and by despatch completely disposing of C's indictment. C. suppressed this despatch and A. on arrival insisted on it being circulated to the Cabinet. C. said it would create a bad impression. A. replied, 'On whom? Or rather, *of* whom?' C. then began to cry. The next day A. met the Cabinet and they agreed, not with C. but with A. The result is that C. (having a perfect case with the Cabinet) has shown them once and for all that he is a coward, and has shown A. that he is a shit. Not a very estimable man.

---

[1] Lord Allenby, the High Commissioner for Egypt, was eager to abolish the British protectorate and acknowledge her as a sovereign state. Harold's sympathies were with Allenby. His opinion of Curzon was soon to change remarkably in Curzon's favour.

Diary   *February 23, 1922*

To an evening party at Buckingham Palace. I wander into the Throne
Room, where a buffet is arranged down one side. Opposite are the
red sofas in tiers, and sitting there, a little shrunken and faded since I
last saw her ten years ago, is Ellen Terry [the actress]. She asks me to
get her some iced coffee. I do so, and in return, ask her to tell me
about Tennyson. She is vague at first and a little muddled in her head.
I try leading questions: 'Did he come to the rehearsals or the final
performances?' 'No, only the rehearsals. He was very kind. Very vain
and very gruff. But so simple. No, not rude. Just vain and simple. Like
a child.' I asked her about his reading aloud. She said *The Northern
Farmer* was the best. Her face lit up when she remembered it. 'You
see,' she said, 'he had the accent already. And he *acted* the thing. Oh,
it was very funny', and she shook her little old head and smiled. I asked
her about the other poems. Oh no, she had not heard him recite *Maud*,
but *Locksley Hall* – yes, she had heard that. And then she put back her
head and began a sort of recitative, humming the metre; and as she
went on she remembered Tennyson, how he had done it, and a faint
echo of his boom came into her voice and her legs began to work up
and down to the rhythm. At which her coffee cup upset on her black
jet lap, and I had to mop it up with my handkerchief. When this was
done, her face was vague again. 'Very simple,' she murmured, 'just like
a child. And I reverenced him so. We all reverenced him.'

Diary   *March 2, 1922*

I went to see Curzon. He was in bed on the top floor of Carlton
House Terrace. As I was taken up in the lift, his valet whispered, 'Very
troublesome, sir, his Lordship today.' I go into a little room like an 8/-
room at the Lord Warden Hotel [Dover]. Pink and white wallpaper;
maple washing-stand with cheap wash-basin; cornflowers; Pears soap;
a thin rather miffy shaving brush; maple dressing-table; half-empty
bottle of hair-wash; a large stained wooden hairbrush; a glass; electric
light shade above it all; by his bed a red silk and glass reading lamp; on
the wall cheap etchings of Belgian cathedrals; photographs of Lady C.
and the children in cheap blue leather frames; a washing bill on the

mantelpiece; an old Gladstone bag and a green suitcase in a corner; a brass bed with a pink silk eiderdown, and in it the Marquess in a flowered dressing-gown. His spine was hurting him and he winced as he bent over to write.

October 29, 1922
The Wharf

Diary

A long talk with Mrs [Margot] Asquith in the morning. She shows me her rooms and pictures and books. She talks about Gladstone. He told her that what he was most proud of was having conquered his natural stinginess. When the Asquith Cabinet fell [in 1916] and they were turned out of Downing Street, some of her letters were sent to No. 10 and were forwarded by Lloyd George's secretaries with 'Not known' written across them!! She will not like my book on Tennyson: she says he always spoke nicely about other poets and was not jealous. She hedged rather when I quoted to her instances of jealousy. She showed me a letter from Lloyd George to Asquith when he had formed his Government. It began, 'Dear Sir' and went on, 'The King has called upon me to etc ...', and ended with the request that he would not oppose. It was written in holograph and not typed. She also told me about Winston's vanity: but she admires and loves him all the same.

Sat next to old Asquith at luncheon. Someone said how odd it was that Lord Midleton was not included in the Cabinet. Mr A. snuffed a bit and then with his strange sucking-in smile said, 'They're afraid of his brains.' He also said that the Kaiser was the only royalty he had met who was of sufficient culture and intelligence to choose as a companion.

December 22, 1922
Lausanne

Diary

Curzon in a very curious mood in the morning. Almost hysterical. He had had a conversation the night before with Ismet, Barrère and

Garroni.[1] The latter two toady Ismet – calling him Excellence, and *ami et cher collègue*, and this makes Curzon nearly sick with disgust. He imitated to me the adulatory gesticulations of Garroni. He was half laughing at the imitation and half almost crying at it having all to begin again in half an hour. He is a very odd man. It was like Sarah Bernhardt in *Phèdre*. The conversation began at 11. Ismet, as is usual with him, goes back on all he had agreed to at the previous meeting. In despair Curzon leaves it to Barrère to achieve some firm agreement. Lunch with C. He is disheartened: he feels that if he were left alone to deal with Ismet, he could bring the thing off, but the intrusion of Barrère and Garroni makes it all impossible. I am sorry for him. In the evening Venizelos comes and we have a conversation *à trois* about the island of Imbros and the Patriarch. Curzon says, 'How impressive that man is.' I reply that I am very fond of him. But to myself I admit that V. is not quite the man he was. Dine with the Japanese. An awful function.

Diary

December 28, 1922
Lausanne

Lunch with the Marquess [Curzon]. He is in very good form, and I get him on to Tennyson. He embarks upon an imitation of Tennyson reciting *Tears Idle Tears*. It is far more effective than any other imitation that I have heard. The slight burr of the 'r's, the broad 'o's and 'a's, and the sudden drop on 'no more' with the 'r' pronounced as a consonant. He also tells us of [Oscar] Wilde and Monckton Milnes[2] as an old man, drunk at a ball at Norfolk House and sitting in a little alcove all flushed and asleep with his false teeth fallen out on his shoulder.

---

[1] Ismet Pasha was Foreign Minister of Turkey, Camille Barrère was French Ambassador in Rome. Marchese Garroni represented Italy at the Lausanne Conference.
[2] The poet, biographer and man of letters, who died in 1885.

December 30, 1922
Diary   *Lausanne*

I break to the Marquess that I am going on the basis of a final and not
a preliminary treaty. He gasps. He puts his head in his hands in an
agony of despair at having to rely on subordinates who are not only
incompetent (that he knew) but also insubordinate. At last he looks up
from his despairing position. 'You have done this?' he says. 'You have
done it, knowing, I suppose, that it was in direct contradiction to my
own decision and to the agreement I have reached with M. Barrère.'
'I knew that, sir, but on going into it, it seemed the only sensible thing
to do the opposite.' The Marquess leaned forward in his chair and his
eye glared. 'You thought that, did you? You thought that . . .' Then he
flung himself back. 'Well, I suppose you were right.' This is a moral
victory. Of course he'll blame me if it goes wrong and take the credit
for himself if it goes right. But still I WON.

Thus ends a perfect year. Best year since 1914. Happy year. I think
so much of my darling V.

January 4, 1923
Diary   *Lausanne*

Dine with the Marquess. He tells ghost stories. He believes absolutely
in ghosts which is odd in so unspiritual a person. He tells us that when
he was going out to India he was sent for to Balmoral. After dinner
they stood in the Tartan Room. His back was bad and Queen Victoria
asked him to sit down. He sat beside her on a little hard tartan chair.
While he was there a servant came in and handed her a telegram on a
salver. She fiddled for her glasses but could not read it. She handed it
to him. 'Read it,' she said, 'Mr Curzon.' He began to read. It was a
long telegram from Kitchener announcing the battle of Omdurman
[September 1898]. At the bottom of the first page were the words,
'His Royal Highness Prince Christian Victor [the Queen's grand-
son] . . .'. Turning over with terror of finding the words, 'was killed
this morning', he was relieved to find the words, 'comported himself
as befits a soldier and an officer in Your Majesty's army'.

H.N. to Vita   *January 9, 1923*
Telegram   *Lausanne*

Letter just received. Delighted to expect you at Lausanne on Friday
morning. Don't fail, as Marquis is counting on you to help him at
huge official dinner on Saturday. Lady Curzon comes today. I haven't
written lately in view of your arrival. Oh God I long to see you, so
bring pretty clothes and jewels. Keeping very snobbish about you and
want to show you off. Isn't this an extravagant sort of telegram to send.
Hadji.

                                                      January 24, 1923
H.N. to Vita   *Lausanne*

I am so angry that I am not in a fit state to write. I don't remember
having been so angry in my life. It is about the Turks. They had the
impudence to say that they must be allowed to dig up our graves at
Gallipoli and put them all in one cemetery. I simply saw red. I told
them that it was incredible that a beaten country should raise such a
question. Then they climbed down but they did not climb down far
enough and I refused to go on discussing. Really they are quite, quite
mad – and if they want war they will get it. I feel I won't speak to
them again. I told them that the British Empire would never, NEVER
evacuate Gallipoli until our graves were safeguarded.

                                                       February 1, 1923
H.N. to Vita   *Lausanne*

I really think now that we shall leave on Sunday *and with a Treaty.* I do
really. Of course it is *entirely* the Marquis, absolutely entirely. When I
thought he was wrong, he was right, and when I thought he was right,
he was much righter than I thought. I give him 100 marks out of 100
and I am so proud of him. So *awfully* proud. He is a great man and
one day England will know it.

   But you see, Britannia *has* ruled here. Entirely against the Turks,
against treacherous allies, against a weak-kneed Cabinet, against a
rotten public opinion – and Curzon has *won.*

All this is after an interview with Ismet, when he collapsed in spite
of [Raymond] Poincaré telling him not to collapse. And it was due
to the Marquis sitting there solid and *grand seigneur* and amused and
brutal.

February 4, 1923
Lausanne

Diary

Pack in morning. We are all tense and depressed awaiting the Turkish
move. At 1.30 it comes, in the form of a note. It accepts all the British
claims practically, but holds out over economics and capitulation. At
2.40 Bompard [assistant to Barrère] comes, and the Marquess decides
to give way over ships and Mosul ... Ismet comes at 5.40, and from
then on the scene is intensely dramatic. He twists about in his chair
and mops his forehead, dabs with his handkerchief and is very nervous.
Bompard speaks well, Garroni lamentably. Then the Marquess, unsur-
passed. He uses every tone – appeal, cajoling, despair, menace. At 6.30
Ismet retires with his colleagues. By then the passages are crowded
with experts and journalists, while our luggage is being wheeled off
to the train. At 6.45 he returns, and accepts *all* our things, but refuses
economics and capitulation, and insists on Greece not being allowed
its claim for reparations. I leave the room to telephone to Venizelos.
By the time I get back, the question has got off reparations to capitulation. The three allies bombard Ismet with appeals and menace. He
is obdurate. He loses his temper. He says, 'I shall return to Angora
[Ankara] and tell my people that the Conference under the Presidency
of Lord Curzon desires war.' 'No, No, No,' we all shout. The telephone
rings, and a little voice, 'Japanese delegation here', and I ring off, and
turn round to face the room and find Curzon looking at his watch.
'You have only half an hour, Ismet Pasha, to save your country.' Ismet
bounces about upon his chair and puts the tips of his fingers on his
damp forehead: '*Je ne peux pas. Je ne peux pas.*' Curzon looks across at
Bompard: 'Well?' It is no use, no use.

We get up to go. They leave the room sullenly, out into the crowds
of journalists and experts. Among them is [René] Massigli, with the
Treaty ready for signature. We decide to make one last attempt.
Bompard and Montagna [second Italian delegate] are sent after Ismet

to suggest a new capitulation formula. The train is stopped for half an
hour while we snatch a dinner. At 9.15 we leave. There is a crowd at
the station. Bompard arrives at the last moment. No good. Ismet won't
give way. And so we slip into the night.[1]

Diary

September 4–19, 1923
London

During this period I have been too rushed by the Greece–Italian
crisis to write my diary.[2] It entailed continual staying up in London,
sometimes at the Automobile Club, and sometimes with Gerry [Wel-
lesley] in Portland Place, and sometimes even in the office. I must have
telephoned at least 50 times to Paris and ten times to Kedleston
[Curzon's Derbyshire house]. It became apparent from the first that
Curzon and Tyrrell had only backed the League because they felt,
ignorantly, that it was a way out of the difficulty. When they realised
that it was not a way out but a way deeper in, they tried to back out
without saying so, and grasped eagerly at Poincaré's suggestion to have
the whole thing settled by the Ambassadors Conference. I tried in vain
to get them to see the issue in wider proportions and to realise that we
had a chance of calling the new world into being in order to redress
the balance of the old. They would not see it: Tyrrell because he is for
an arrangement at any price, and has no intellectual principle or moral
stability; Curzon, because of his inordinate vanity, was affected by the
Harmsworth Press attacks and by a certain jealousy of Lord R. Cecil.
The result was that we killed the League and fortified Poincaré. Terribly
depressed by this lack of strength and guidance.

---

[1] In his book *Curzon, The Last Phase* Harold reproduced long extracts from his diary
('by a member of Lord Curzon's staff'), but elaborated and further dramatised the
above text.

[2] Mussolini, provoked by the Greeks over another affair, bombarded and occupied the
Greek island of Corfu. The Greek Government appealed to the League of Nations,
whose first real test this was. Curzon at first agreed with them, but Raymond Poincaré,
the French Prime Minister, sided with Italy. Mussolini said that he would accept the
decision of the Ambassadors' Conference, which was entrusted with implementing
the Treaty of Versailles, but not of the League.

Diary   *January 23, 1924*

Curzon comes round in the morning to say goodbye.[1] He apologises
to his Private Secretaries for having been a 'hard task-master'. He
leaves before luncheon. [Ramsay] MacDonald meanwhile had telephoned that he would be across at 2.30. But he came at 2.15 – was
not recognised, and was taken for a journalist and up to the top floor –
was asked whom he wanted to see. Then he was taken into his room
by an office keeper and looked out onto a thick black fog. Then the
private secretaries appeared. Then [Sir Eyre] Crowe appeared. The
conversation was not very auspicious. MacDonald said he would see
neither papers nor Ambassadors. That [Arthur] Ponsonby [Under
Secretary of State] would do everything, and that Crowe must take his
orders from Ponsonby. Crowe said – not at all, that as S. of S. Mac-
Donald would have not only to see the Ambassadors, but would have
to write down afterwards what they said. MacDonald said he would
do neither. Crowe said he would have to. Then he went away.

Diary   *January 26, 1924*

I gather that an unexpected difficulty has occurred regarding the
recognition of Russia which MacDonald wishes to effect immediately.
It appears that the King [George V] absolutely refused to receive a
Soviet Ambassador as that would entail shaking hands with him. It was
then suggested that a Minister should be received – but here again the
King was adamant. He is an obstinate and outspoken little man.
Meanwhile, such minutes as MacDonald has written are sensible and
strong enough. But they are apt to be delayed, and a rather urgent
paper which I sent in on Wednesday has still not returned [Saturday].
This marks a great difference from the Curzon days.

---

[1] Stanley Baldwin's Government was defeated in the General Election on the previous
day, and Ramsay MacDonald, who succeeded him as Prime Minister, announced that
he would also take charge of the Foreign Office.

Diary   *March 7, 1924*

Have a long talk with Ramsay MacDonald in the morning regarding Anglo-Italian relations. He sits there puffing at a pipe and very dour and sad and disillusioned. He waggles his leg with impatience, perplexity or despair, and yet he does not seem to wish to hurry the conversation, but goes slowly, slowly. Rather tentative are his remarks and very Scotch in sound. He flares up once at the thought of Mussolini. His eyes give a sudden flash: 'The greatest rascal in the world.'

Diary   *April 4, 1924*

Put up a minute to the P.M. suggesting that the Elgin marbles be returned to Athens in connection with the Byron centenary. My real object was to try to get them to restore the column [caryatid] of the Erechtheum which has been taken away [to the British Museum]. But the minute is not a success and causes bad blood.

H.N. to Vita   *December 4, 1924*

I have been worrying all day about Violet [Trefusis]. I couldn't bear it in the end and sent you a silly telegram. I hope you weren't cross. But, my darling, I do so dread that woman. Her very name brings back all the aching unhappiness of those months, the doubt, the mortification and the loneliness. I think she is the only person of whom I am frightened – and I have an almost superstitious belief in her capacity for causing distraction and wretchedness. Of course I know that it's all over now, but what I dread is your dear sweet optiness [optimism] – 'Oh but it's quite safe – and rather fun' – and then she will mesmerise you and I shall get a telegram to say you are staying on in Paris. If I do, I shall fly over at once – I'm not going to trust to luck this time. Oh my darling – do please be very careful and take no risks. You don't know how anxious I am.

I lunched with Mrs [Margot] Asquith. What a splendid woman she is! I am really fond of her. It was a nice luncheon and she told me stories about Kitchener. But all the time I was thinking of that basilisk

[reptile] over there and my poor sweet opty at No. 53 Rue de Varenne.[1]
Oh how glad I shall be to hear you are coming back!

Diary   *January 6, 1925*

Vita meets me at Reading, and we drive on to the Wharf [the Asquith
house]. We arrive to find them all playing bridge. I read Mrs Asquith's
proofs of her new book *Personalities* – giving accounts of her visits to
Egypt, America, Spain and Italy. Atrociously written, carelessly revised,
incredibly indiscreet, embarrassingly vain – but they build up an
impression of her real character, her zest and liberalism. It is curious
to think that Posterity will misunderstand Margot. They will think her
a vulgar and disagreeable adventuress. She is nothing of the sort. She
is vain, of course, but it is no common vanity. She is observant rather
than intelligent. Above all, she is brave, affectionate, loyal. Her zest is
like champagne. Her generosity of thought and action is like a fresh
wind. The love that hangs about her house gives it all a spirituality
which is different from the ghoulish intellectualism of other circles.
Both V. and I feel it a real privilege to go to the Wharf and come away
with added sensitiveness to life.

The party are just bridge partners plus Violet Bonham Carter,
Elizabeth [Bibesco], and Ian Campbell-Grey [portrait painter]. We sit
up late. Margot tells us of a talk with the King. She prefers George V
to Edward VII, whom she found German and coarse. He had asked
her to tea. He said, 'Mrs Asquith, you are a great specialist in character.
What do you say of *me*?' 'Oh, I couldn't, sir.' 'Well – out with it.' 'But
you wouldn't like it, sir.' 'Oh no – go ahead.' 'Well, sir, you see, your
great fault is that you don't enjoy yourself.' The King was taken aback.
Finally, and quite simply, he said, 'Yes, I know: but, you see, I don't
like Society: I like my wife.' An attractive story. Margot does not like
the Queen [Mary]. Thinks her hard and stupid and sly. Says she loathes
her children. But then Margot's standard of parental affection is a high
one.

---

[1] The house in Paris of Walter Berry, where Vita and Violet were to meet again at a
lunch-party.

Diary   *January 22, 1925*

In the afternoon the Secretary of State [Sir Austen Chamberlain] has a meeting in his room which is attended by all the senior members of the Office. The purpose of the meeting is to discuss the future policy of the British Empire. [Owen] O'Malley, who speaks first, plumps for isolation. I, who speak second, have got a cold and plump for nothing except fulfilling our debts of honour. Gerry Villiers plumps for supporting France in any circumstances. Headlam Morley clamours for the reconstruction of 'the Concert of Europe'. And so on. Finally Crowe sums up by saying isolation is impossible. We must modify the Covenant [of the League of Nations] and the Protocol, and make thereunder a restricted understanding with France to protect the Channel ports. This is something, while not going too far. The real problem, which no one would face, is, 'Have we got a Dominion or a Downing Street Foreign Policy?' The two things are very different and cannot be fused without trouble.

Diary   *March 26, 1925*

Go up to Kedleston [for Curzon's funeral] ... At Derby there is a crowd and several motors. At Kedleston there is another crowd of local people. We enter the hall. There are wreaths against the columns and the coffin on a trestle; dark red velvet with brass nails in panels. We go on to the library where there is a fire and we sit about talking with bated breath. Then the undertaker hurries in. 'You better come now if you want a good place.' So we go into the hall and stand by the coffin. Then the choir files in and the Archbishop of York. Then Lady Curzon, erect, haggard, beautiful, comes and stands by the head of the coffin. *Rock of Ages* by a village choir, and the smell of roses and lilies. An address by the Archbishop, and then with shuffle and shove the undertakers seize the coffin, grasping the brass handles with their shaking black kid gloves, working their shoulders underneath. It lurches out into the cold March wind and down the stairway. Lady Curzon follows like Antigone. There is a crowd at the little church, and I can't see much. Afterwards I go into the chapel. They have moved one of the malachite slabs and let in the coffin a few feet below. They have sprinkled a handful of silver sand on it. We go back into the house. Baba Curzon and Cimmie Mosley [daughters] appear. Very upset. Very sweet. Lady C. says he has left me some papers. I get back to Derby. And travel for four hours talking to Maud Cunard. Then the lights of London and dinner at the Garrick.

Diary   *June 7, 1925*

Dine and sleep with the Churchills at Chartwell. Winston is delighted with his house, which he considers a paradise on earth. It *is* rather nice. Only Goonie [Lady Gwendeline Churchill] there, and a red-headed Australian journalist called [Brendan] Bracken. A most self-confident and, I should think, wrong-headed young man. We talk about Curzon. Winston is nice about him. *June 8.* Motor up with Winston. A rather perilous proceeding. We break down two or three times on the way.

Diary   *July 1, 1925*

On walking across the [Guards] Parade, I am accosted by a Tommy in uniform with an untidy tamoshanter on and a weather-beaten unshaven face. He says, 'Is [Rennell] Rodd in the Office?' On looking again I see that it is little Lawrence of Arabia. What an odd shifty charlatan that man is. A mixture of a brute and a schoolboy. He tells me that his book [*The Seven Pillars of Wisdom*] is so conceived as to mystify the bibliophiles – no two copies being quite the same.

Diary   *September 23, 1925*

Walford Selby comes in and asks whether I would be willing to go as Counsellor to Teheran or Peking. I refuse – on grounds of family affairs. My idea is (1) that we can't dump the children anywhere. (2) that Ben requires constant looking after by V. or me if he is not to go off the rails. (3) that we can't afford it if V goes backwards and forwards. (4) that with both father and B.M. ill, we can neither of us go so far away. On second thoughts, however, I realise (1) that it is a mistake ever to refuse a job. (2) that it would mean promotion and a good chance. (3) that I can't hope to stay here [London] for ever and might get something far worse. (4) that if V. stays at home in the summer it won't be so bad. Decide to consult [Sir Lancelot] Oliphant and father.

Harold Nicolson decided to accept the appointment of Counsellor to the Legation in Teheran, where he was born, and travelled to Persia (Iran) via Cairo, Jerusalem and Baghdad. He remained there for eighteen months, taking charge of the Legation between two Ministers, and writing his best-known book, Some People. *Vita twice visited him there and wrote two books about her travels,* Passenger to Teheran *and* Twelve Days, *the latter an account of her walk through the Bakhtiari mountains in southern Persia accompanied by Harold. They returned together to England in May 1927.*

Diary   *November 4, 1925*

Leave England. V. drives me to Victoria. An agonising farewell. Feeling absolutely wretched.

Diary   *November 16–26, 1925*
                                                         Jerusalem to Teheran

Go to the Cook's office. They tell me that none of the Nairn convoys [trans-desert cars] have got through lately, that they are all held up at Amman, that the one coming the other way [from Baghdad] got stuck and they had to live by eating sparrows, and that in any case, there is no chance, if I adopt this method of progression, of my reaching Baghdad in time for the Teheran connexion. I then proceed to the Wailing Wall, which fully expresses my feelings. It was like a hive of bees. We then go up to Government House. Lord and Lady Plumer [High Commissioner for Palestine]. Very old England. Lord P. says I would be a fool to motor. I must fly. So we telephone to the Ramleh aerodrome. They say I must take the Egyptian airmails. Hell. Dine with [Sir Ronald] Storrs and discuss vulgarity. *November 17.* I receive a message from the Air Force at Ramleh strongly advising me to go by Nairns and not by air. I therefore decide on Nairns. *November 19.* Nairns packed full. Never heard of me. *November 21.* I go with Storrs to see the Pavement in the Ecce Homo convent – undoubtedly that on which Pilate sat. Most impressive. At 6.30 the [Nairn] cars arrive. Yes, I have a place. At midnight we get to Amman. Sleep comfortably in a bell tent. *November 22.* On and on through the dark with white stars and the circle of the headlights. We reach the Euphrates. From there 70 mph across the desert, with mirages in front all the time, and then suddenly a factory chimney. We get into Baghdad about 3.30. *November 23.* We reach Kermanshah [Persia]. *November 25.* Get up at 5.30, expecting to start at 6. Walk about, furiously impatient till 9.45 when the car arrives. Reach Kasvin. *November 26.* Go on well enough, when crash go the back springs. No hope. At 3.30 a Ford car appears. We eat in the courtyard of the inn when suddenly a *gholan* comes in, salutes, and says the Minister is there. I dash out, and find Percy [Loraine][1] in the yellow Legation car. Bundle my things in and do the last 25 miles [to Teheran] in comfort – while an amazing sunset turns the hills to scarlet.

December 13, 1925
British Legation, Teheran

H.N. to his parents

I went with Percy Loraine to meet the Shah, Reza Khan.[2] He received us in a little pavilion in the garden of the house he built for himself. It is quite unpretentious: very clean; lots of new paint and ghastly new chairs of terrible shapes. A roaring fire. They went to tell him that we had arrived, and shortly a step of huge weight was heard on the pavement of the colonnade and two of the windows were successively darkened by a huge form walking past them. By the third window he entered. He must be six foot three, inclined to corpulence, simple khaki uniform with no decorations, high uncomfortable collar in

---

[1] British Minister to Persia, and Harold's immediate boss.
[2] Reza Pahlavi rose from the ranks to be Commander-in-Chief of the Persian army and then Prime Minister. In the autumn of 1925 he deposed the Shah, and was himself elected by the Majlis to the vacant throne. He was to be crowned in April 1926.

which he evidently feels ill-at-ease, high-peaked cap like a Greek general which adds to his height. Coarse red hands. Rather coarse nose. Fine chin. Clipped moustache turning up at the ends. Unshaven. Bushy eyebrows. Fine but rather bulging eyes. He looked tired and in ill health. At first his face seemed sullen and rather too much jowl. But after I had paid him some compliments he cheered up, laughed in a way that was half-shy and half-sly, I can't be sure which – pats his fat fingers over his unshaven chin and began to talk quietly and sensibly about the situation and his own prospects. I was frankly puzzled by him. At one moment he took off his hat, disclosing a tiny round skull (much better shaved than his chin) and making him look exactly like a Cossack. That, of course, is the dominant impression at first – a non-commissioned officer in the Cossack brigade: coarse humour, ungainly manner, latent brutality. But then his voice is so gentle, and at certain angles his face suddenly becomes fine and distinguished, and his simplicity is attractive. He teased me about looking so young, said he did not believe I was more than 28[1] and added that I must have had no trouble in love or politics. After a bit his sudden animation left him, and he talked listlessly and without much point. When we said good bye, he suddenly burst out into real cordiality. He begged Loraine not to let him become pompous when he becomes Shah and thanked him for all he had done to help him in a very simple and absolutely convincing way. In fact I am puzzled. There is certainly great force in him somewhere, but I am not sure whether it will survive the luxury of the throne, or whether it might not become mere brutality. I don't like that sly look.

H.N. to his parents

March 11, 1926
Teheran

I had a telegram to say that Vita was on her way from Baghdad in a good car and should reach Kermanshah by 6.30. 6.30 passed, and then 7 and I found the suspense intolerable. Only a fortnight earlier a car had been held up by brigands outside Kermanshah and both the occupants had been shot. By eight o'clock I could bear it no longer

---

[1] Harold was thirty-nine.

and went into the consulate garden where there is a little hillock
looking out over the town and the plain beyond. The moon hung
smaller than the night before and there were a few large stars. The
dogs in the town were howling at the moon and from the mountains
behind came the sharp yapping of jackals. I strained my ears to catch
the sound of a motor and my eyes to see the glow of its lamps. But the
night seemed empty of everything but my own anxiety. They told me
dinner was ready. I could eat nothing. Then the man came in and said
quite casually that a motor was coming up the drive. I dashed out, and
there were two head-lights flashing on the slim poplars on each side.
The dogs had stopped barking. I could make out two huddled figures
inside. With a wide sweep the motor swung round to the doorway –
and there was my Vita all in furs and with a new dog on her knee. We
almost cried with excitement. And we talked and talked and talked.
She had seen Egypt and Delhi and Agra but we talked about the garden
at Long Barn and about Ben and Nigel.

H.N. to his parents

April 29, 1926
Teheran

Yesterday was the Coronation of the Shah. We drove there in State –
a thing I particularly abominate. I never did like amateur theatricals,
and I loathe bumping along a street surrounded by escorts. My friendly
profile does not lend itself to such pro-consular antics and the collar
of my uniform cuts cruelly into my chubby neck. Then we arrived.
But Loraine, who has a weakness for the processional, insisted on our
continuing through the gardens of the palace. First stalk six guards in
solemn idiocy, then the Loraines in equal solemnity, and then I come
with Vita. At the main court of the palace there is a band. This is an
awful moment as Loraine springs rigidly to attention while they play
God Save the King. Lady Loraine bares her head as do the devout after
receiving Holy Communion, and I get hot and uncomfortable, longing
with a home-sick passion for my pipe. Finally, with much bowing on
the part of court officials, we climb the steep staircase. Under Vita's
orders this vast railway-station had been painted a simple apricot.
It looked very well. So did Vita. She wore in the centre of her
black toque the emeralds which Narr-id-Din-Shah had presented to

Mummy, feeling that it would be pleasant for them to revisit the scene of their youth. We were then ranged to the left of the throne. The rest of the palace was filled with Mullahs. Half an hour after it was supposed to have begun, there were a series of cries from the entrance signifying the approach of the Valiald.[1] This infant thereupon entered dressed as a general and surrounded by members of the Cabinet carrying the regalia on red velvet pads. Another pause and then another shrill cry at the entrance. Slowly the Shah, dressed in a blue mantle embroidered with pearls, slouched up the aisle and climbed onto the throne. The latter is not what you know as the Peacock Throne. The new throne was really magnificent. He sat on it – rigid, theocratic, rather superb – this Cossack trooper, the Ruler of the World, the King of Kings. When they had ceased intoning, the Minister approached with the regalia. Taking the vast diamond crown in both his red hands he clapped it firmly upon that Cossack pate, becoming instantly rigid again like an idol, the diamonds shooting points of fire. A vast and bulbous sceptre was then placed in his right hand, and in his left the carbon copy of the speech. Still rigid and motionless he read the speech in a toneless voice. The guns boomed distantly, and in a few minutes, bowing to right and left, the King of Kings slouched from the room followed by his little mosquito son.

Next night the Shah gave a party in the gardens of the Palace. They were beautifully illuminated and there was much champagne and many excellent fireworks. But for Vita and me God lay in wait preparing unfortunate incidents. Mine came first. We were dining with the opium commission and on climbing into the car my uniform trousers split across the seat. A trail of white shirt emerged from the aperture. I found safety pins at the commission and the tails of my coat hid what might otherwise have seemed ungainly. Vita's incident occurred at the end of the party. She was wearing her big emerald chain and the central drop fell off during the evening. It seemed hopeless to find it as she had been walking all over the garden. But on proceeding to the throne room to break the news to one of the palace officials, I found the Prime Minister and the Minister of Public Works anxiously going round the Peacock Throne trying to fit into it an emerald which had

---

[1] The Crown Prince of Persia, then aged eight. In time he became Shah himself, and was dethroned in 1979.

been found lying at its feet. So I reclaimed the emerald and put it in my pocket.

Vita leaves on Tuesday. I don't like to think about it.

H.N. to his parents

May 7, 1926
Teheran

I can't tell you what I have suffered by this severance.[1] I did not know that the human heart was capable of such mental agony. There have been moments when I felt that it was too much to be borne. I fainted this morning in my office. Of course I shall have recovered when you get this or I wouldn't tell you. But I now realise that nothing can be weighed in the scale of human relationships and that never again will I sacrifice my personal affairs to my career or my duty. I shall get through this summer somehow. In October Vita will return. If at the end of the year they won't transfer me, then I shall resign. I can easily make enough to live on by writing. Of course I shall do nothing impulsively. I have a whole year, damn it, in which to think it over. But on one thing I am quite determined – never again to expose V. and myself to such misery.

H.N. to Vita

May 12, 1926
Teheran

Tray is writing his article about alternatives to chastity.[2] It is very good – perfectly simple and closely reasoned. He concludes (having watched us and knowing how much we love each other) that the best

---

[1] He had said goodbye to Vita at Resht on the Caspian, whence she travelled home via Baku, Moscow, Berlin and Holland.

[2] 'Tray' was Raymond Mortimer, who remained in Teheran as Harold's guest after Vita's departure. Leonard Woolf thought the article was too frank for publication in the *New Statesman*. Vita's comment was: 'He leaves out the stipulation that the two people who are to achieve this odd unity must start with special temperaments. It is all very well to say that the ideal is "marriage with liaisons". But if you were in love with another woman, or I with another man, it would inevitably rob our own relationship of something. As it is, the [homosexual] liaisons which you and I contract don't interfere.'

life is marriage plus liaisons. Or rather his argument is: (1) Passion, i.e. being 'in love', can only last a certain number of years. (2) After that both sides instinctively search for variety. (3) If the doctrine of fidelity is too rigid, then they both have a sense of confinement and frustration, and irritation results. (4) But if there is mutual physical freedom, this sense of bondage does not arise. Good relations are maintained – and from this emerges community of life, and *love*, which is something quite different from passion, and far deeper than affection. He says that only really fine characters and determinedly intellectual people can attain to this. But that the confusion of 'love' and 'in love' – and the idea that love merely equals affection – leads to great confusion. There is something in all this, but I expect there is a snag somewhere. You see our love is something which only two people in the world can understand. The first and dearest of these two people is Viti. The second, poor man, is your own Hadji.

H.N. to his parents

May 26, 1926
Teheran

Lady Loraine left this morning. She is an odd ungainly dutiful creature. She doesn't understand either Vita or me, and without disliking us very acutely, thinks us odd. She thinks I ought to entertain the Colony. I'm damned if I will. The Counsellor is not supposed to entertain, not this one, anyhow. I try to see as few people as I can since they are all completely uneducated and uncivilised, and I don't know what to say to them. I like riding and bathing and reading – but I loathe tea-parties and won't do them. If they don't approve, they can get rid of me and I shall be delighted to have the excuse. After all it is bad enough to have to endure exile and separation from all those one loves without having to add to this the torture of dull society. I simply won't do it – and it is rubbish to talk of my 'duty'. My duty is to work and not to entertain Anglo-Indians. 'They don't', said one of these women, 'have punkahs [fans] in this country.' I said, 'Oh god!' She said, 'What did you say?' I said, 'What I remarked, Mrs Elgood, was "Oh god!"' She said, 'Oh Mr Nicolson, you do have a funny way of putting things.' Really, it is grotesque. All this bad temper comes from having been really upset by Vita's departure. I feel indignant that I should have to submit to such unhappiness. And for what? Anybody else could do my job as well as I can. Probably better. Damn! Damn! Damn!

July 1, 1926
H.N. to Vita   *Teheran*

Well, I have had my party. There were 36 people. I sat at one end of the table and Percy [Loraine] at the other. The whole staff was there plus the heads of the colony. There was a balalalalalaika orchestra on the lawn and a great number of little miffy Chinese lanterns. We had soup, trout, cutlets in aspic, turkey and an apricot ice. My wine had arrived two days before. I made a nice English-public-schoolboy sort of speech. Percy replied very slowly and with some emotion. I was rather pleased with my speech and when it was all over I went up to Tray and said, 'Well, how did it go?' – expecting praise. He said it had made him almost sick. He was really angry about it. Funny Tray. Because really the speech was quite moderate and devoid of undue sob-stuff. But I admit it was rather an Empire-builder's speech and aroused Tray's anti-virility complex. Also I think he thought it rather shaming. He said it had irritated him as much as I would be irritated if I saw him dressed up as a woman in some Paris dance-hall. I think this really was his attitude, and he is right in feeling that I loathe the *tapette* [gay] side of him as much as he hates the Kipling side in me.

Well, feeling rather crushed by this attack, I led the way to the second part of my party – which took place in my own house. It really looked rather well, and there was another band there and a good buffet and heaps of drink. It really *was* a success; people danced and drank and enjoyed themselves. It went on till 2 a.m. Oh my Viti, how I missed you! The Minister was impressed, I think – and I have at a stroke removed all criticism of my not entertaining. Also, whatever Tray may say, I think the colony were impressed by my noble uplifting patriotic sturdy homily. Perhaps it *was* a little revivalist in tone – Yes? No?

July 10, 1926
Gulahek, Teheran

H.N. to Vita

I have got two Virgins staying with me. They came in a Ford car from Isfahan. The smaller one is called Miss Richardson. She has an inquisitive little face like a ferret. She has lovely deep copper hair – all oily and smooth as women should. But like women should not, she has bobbed it, after the manner of the Sassanid dynasty, so that it looks like a hayfield which has been nibbled at by a small pair of blunt nail-scissors. The other is called Miss Winifred Eardley, known to her friends (of whom Miss Richardson is one) as Winnie. She has either got very acute indigestion or else an inferiority complex. Anyhow, she sniffs.

Now, how comes it that I, who loathe women in general and virgins in particular, should for three whole weeks have to entertain these types? How comes it that I who am rendered rather ill by the thought of the church, who doesn't like missionaries, and who hates society, should entertain these vestals of the Church Missionary Society? Will you please explain all this to me? Like Wordsworth, I 'wonder at myself like men dismayed'.[1] I suppose it is the white man's burden. And the maddening thing is that Trott [a Consular official], who rather likes them, being a white man all through, gets all the credit. And that I, who am bored stiff and have to make an effort to be polite, am just thought an amiable pagan. And last night Trott's motor broke down and I had them alone for dinner and I had toothache. They said, or rather Miss Richardson said, 'This is heavenly – one might be anywhere but in Persia.' She said it in a wistful way, poor little bitch, gazing at *The Field* spread out on the table under a lamp with a red silk fringe to it. One could see the poor little sparrow-mind fluttering back to the rectory drawing-room. 'Too, too, too' went the owls. The fountains splashed on the blue tiles, the durbar tent bulked billowy against the white hot stars. And yet that effect of red light on *The Field* took her away back to the Eversley [Surrey] rectory. I was touched by this, and went to bed with that evening-service feeling, trying to feel more hospitable about them – had I put Bromo for them? Would they like a book?

---

[1] The quotation should be: 'We wonder at ourselves like men betrayed'. Wordsworth, *The Borderers*.

But really I don't mind much. I see, as I write, a flash of white muslin going towards the tent. 'Winnie! Breakfast's ready – there's honey.' 'Coming, dear.' Oh England – my England – how I *love* you. That's why I don't mind having them.

July 16, 1926
Teheran

H.N. to Nigel (aged nine)

I do hope you won't make Mummy nervous by being too wild. Of course men must work and women must weep, but all the same I do hope that you will remember that Mummy is a frightful coward and does fuss dreadfully about you. It is a good rule always to ask before you do anything awfully dangerous. Thus if you say, 'Mummy, may I try and walk on the roof of the green-house on my stilts?', she will probably say, 'Of course, darling', since she is not in any way a narrow-minded woman. And if you say, 'Mummy, may I light a little fire in my bed?', she will again say, 'Certainly, Niggs'. It is only that she likes being asked about these things beforehand.

August 28, 1926
Teheran

H.N. to Percy Loraine

Where I think we see differently is about the Shah. You feel that he is something reliable and solid. I think him infinitely untrustworthy and sly. Again, you believe somewhere in the Persians. I think them the most contemptible race on earth. You believe in good relations as something positive: I only believe in them as something negative, i.e. they won't get us what we want, but they may prevent us being bothered by pin-pricks. The Persians have heaps of pins (Gulchek, Capitulations, Gulf) which they could use if they wanted to be nasty. Good relations prevent them from being nasty; but it doesn't make them nice.

November 7, 1926
H.N. to Vita   *Teheran*

Dearest, you don't know what *The Land* means to me![1] I read it incessantly – it has become a real wide undertone to my life. I forget absolutely that it is by you: it is such a lovely thing, darling, so beautiful a thing. It gives one a sense of permanence. It seems infinitely better each time one reads it. I keep on coming with surprise on lines I hadn't noticed:

'How delicate in spring they be/That mobled blossom and that wimpled tree'
'Some concord of creation that the mind/Only in perilous balance apprehends'
'She being beautiful, and Leah but tender-eyed'

lines which one could instance as the very stuff of poetry – lines which are as memorable as catching a swallow-wing of thought which would have been lost by the drudge of prose. Oh my dear, if there was ever a work of art about which I feel *certain* it is this. So certain that, except for fun, I don't care what other people say. So certain that I feel shy about it, like I feel shy about all my profounder feelings. My darling – it is so absurd – but I feel *grateful* to you for it. I don't mean to exaggerate, but it has added a pleasure to life. It is so firm, reliable. It never lets one down. Dearest, the fact that it is by you (a fact which is too incredible to be realised) really does not weigh with me. But I know that the side of you which wrote that poem is detached from all mundane things – that it is above all exterior connections. You will get outside it in the same way one day. You will think, 'Did I really write that?'

Of course naturally I want it to be a public success. But intrinsically I don't care. I simply know that it is a part of English literature, whereas all the other stuff is just like *Vogue* or the *Daily Mail*. Funny Mar!

---

[1] Vita had sent him the proofs of her epic poem. She added to it during her second visit to Persia in April 1927, and it was awarded the Hawthornden Prize for Literature in June.

November 19, 1926
H.N. *to Vita*   *Teheran*

I went to Clive's[1] opening reception for the Persians. Mrs Elgood told me that they had thrown Henry's [dog] body on to the dust heap outside the Russian Embassy. I don't think I have ever been quite so angry in my life. I absolutely saw red. I left the Legation and dashed across to my house. I quite unconsciously seized the two sticks you used for your ankle and called for Bogber [servant]. He must have thought his last hour had come – seeing me standing there in a frock-coat transfigured with rage and waving two sticks in my hand. He got as white as a sheet and dodged behind the table. I spoke to him in Persian at first. He said, of course, that it was the fault of the Dispensary people. He had told them exactly what to do, but had had to come back here because of his work. I then stopped talking Persian and spoke to him in English. I then sent him out with lanterns and a man to rescue that poor little corpse and bury it decently.

It is things like this that really exhaust me – I felt as though I had been beaten all over – like you, my sweet, after a scene with your mother. It is things like this also that show one what savages these people really are. I walked back to the Reception, and looked at all those polite frock-coated people with a feeling of loathing.

November 21, 1926
H.N. *to his parents*   *Teheran*

This is rather awful, isn't it, being 40. Good bye to middle youth! I simply hate it. All that I care for is youth and energy and striving. I don't want to have been successful. I want to go on trying. It is no fun being at the top of one's profession – the only fun is getting there. I wasn't made to be old. When God made me he forgot all about the fact that I should have to grow up sooner or later. I have had such a frightfully good time all these 40 years and have done exactly what I liked and done nothing meretricious at all, so God is sure to take notice soon and avenge himself on me.

---

[1] Sir Robert Clive, who, after an interval when Harold took charge, succeeded Percy Loraine as Minister in Teheran.

December 17, 1926
H.N. to Vita   *Teheran*

No, my sweet, it doesn't annoy me that you should write so much
about Virginia [Woolf]. From your point of view I know that the
friendship can only be enriching. I am of course a little anxious about
it from her point of view as I can't help feeling that her stability and
poise are based on a rather precarious foundation. I mean it would be
rather awful if you coming out here made her ill. That is my main
consideration. Attached to it, like a little ivy growing at the foot of a
castle, is the feeling that she will make me seem dull to you. Not
jealousy, darling – only an instinctive movement of self-defence. But
my dominant idea is one of pleasure that the rich ores of your nature
should be brought to light – I *know* that it does you mental and moral
good to be with her and be loved by her, and that is all that matters. I
think you are very akin – the marriage of true minds to which I will
not allow myself (even to myself or to you, which is the same thing)
to admit impediment.[1]

And as for *my* relations with Virginia – I shall never forget how kind
she was to me when I was smarting from Lytton's rudeness.[2] There
was no reason why she should have been nice about it except that she
saw I was flustered and in real pain. So at the bottom of my terror of
her glimmers a little white stone of gratitude which can only be
increased by her loving you.

January 7, 1927
H.N. to Vita   *Teheran*

Such a marvellous day yesterday. An absolute stillness. It is so odd that
cloudless days should differ so much from each other. I think this place
is excellent for training the observation. There is the vast uniformity
in space and even time: the feeling that it will all be the same colour
and contours right away to China: the feeling that it was the same

---

[1] The quotation is from Shakespeare's Sonnet 116. Harold was worried that Vita's affair
   with her might precipitate in Virginia Woolf a recurrence of her madness.
[2] Lytton Strachey had been disdainful at a Bloomsbury party in March 1921 about
   Harold's book on Tennyson, which was published on that very day.

colour and contour five thousand years ago: that is the first background. The second background is the climate. The fact that one really does get about 300 days in the year which are absolutely cloudless – and thus in appearance absolutely the same. The fact that there are no breezes in Persia – rare gales only, howling against an absolute stillness. All this produces a monochromatic background against which little changes – the sound of a dry leaf pattering on a tin roof, the trail of smoke against the umber plain, take a far intenser significance. I think that it is this that has made me so sensitive to nature sounds. Persia in effect is a great stillness that really is its charm. And darling, how immense that charm is. Now that my happiness has come back to me I savour it with joy. I ride out over the hills and look back on that amazing design of plain and mountain. And I shout – so that Bay Rum [horse] pricks his ears – 'Viti! Viti!'

H.N. to his parents

January 14, 1927
Teheran

I have finished my silly book [*Some People*], and sent it off to the publisher. It should be out by the time I get back, and if there is a row about it, I shall be there to face the music. There just might be trouble – though the book is harmless enough, only there is a sketch of the Lausanne Conference which, while it does not of course touch on actual politics, is technically a violation of the Foreign Office rule against publishing anything to do with one's official experiences. But I don't care: the book is not in the least malicious or indiscreet, and if other people wish to poke about for malice or indiscretions, it is not my fault. And the idea of the book is original. I take nine people and describe them in the manner I described Jeanne de Hénaut. You see, it is really an autobiography – only each person is made the centre of the picture and I only appear in the background. Most of the people are wholly imaginary, only real people and real incidents mix in with them. Everybody will be terribly puzzled as to who everybody else is, and there will be a great deal of identification going on. But as a matter of fact, they are all composite portraits except Jeanne who is of course drawn straight from life. There is a picture of Curzon which gives, I think, the side of him that was most attractive. The only thing that the

F.O. may resent is that I laugh a good deal at people and they may be
afraid it will be their turn.

March 12, 1927
Diary
                                                              Teheran

Wake up in the morning with a conviction that I shall chuck the
diplomatic service. I had been fussing and worrying about this problem
for months – and then this morning I woke with a calm and certain
conviction as if it had come to me from outside. Write to Cadman
[Chairman of the Anglo-Persian Oil Company] asking him to give me
a job.[1]

April 5, 1927
Diary
                                              Bakhtiari mountains, Persia

Wake up in a gale with black clouds scudding across the Zirreh pass.
The mules are gathered in the courtyard. Finally Vita, Lionel [Smith]
and I start off at 8.15 on foot, leaving the others to follow. We start to
climb. Weather improves. By the first patch of snow we find a drift of
purple crocuses. Reach the top of the pass at 10.45. Masses of aconites
but nothing else. Steep and perilous descent to a sort of downland over
which the wind howls which makes V. furious.

April 8, 1927
Diary
                                                  Bakhtiari mountains

V. and I start off down the gorge. The road is muddy and difficult, and
I slither along. Then it comes on to pour with rain and I have only a
flannel suit on. A terrible feeling of despair descends on me. I say that
I loathe the Bakhtiari mountains and wish I hadn't come. Vita is an
angel of comfort, and then the sun comes out and I cheer up. We see
masses of colchicum and some crown imperials in flower, some good
saxifrages and lichens, a few dull orchids – and that's all. On and on

---

[1] In the London office. This application came to nothing.

we go, and finally after about four hours we meet the guard riding
back to look for us. We are joined by Lionel and Gladwyn [Jebb]. It
then begins to hail, and we start again. Up and up – our feet slipping
in the sticky soil. We get to the top of the pass but there is no joy in
our hearts. We then descend, slipping and sliding. We are very
exhausted. At about 6.30 we see our tents, having been at it for eleven
hours. We recover. Light a fire. Dine. The weather clears a little, but
when we go to bed everything is rather damp and sticky. I have a
nerve-storm caused by a sudden loathing for Vita's hold-all.[1]

                                                     April 12, 1927
Diary   *Persian Gulf*

We come out of the trees to the top of the pass and suddenly the
mountains end and we look across rolling uplands to where a trail of
smoke, as if from some far-distant Vesuvius, hangs its feather the sky.
'*Edareh! Edareh!*' the porters exclaim. 'The Company! The Company!'.
They mean the Anglo-Persian Oil Company. V. and I are delighted to
recover the real Persian landscape and to get away from all that Tyrolean
business.

*They returned to England via Basra, Baghdad, Damascus, Alexandria,
Marseilles and Paris. In October 1927 Harold was posted to the British
Embassy in Berlin as Counsellor, and remained there until he retired from the
Diplomatic Service at the end of 1929. Between Ambassadors he was chargé
d'affaires, and found time to write the Life of his father, Lord Carnock, who
died in November 1928.*

---

[1] Of this day, Vita wrote in *Twelve Days*: 'Up till then, Harold Nicolson and I had very
carefully avoided making any comments to one another about our journey, but now
our tacit resolution broke down. "This damned country!" we said, almost in tears.
"Why did we ever come?" We agreed that we did not even think the scenery beautiful.
"I *loathe* mountains," he said, standing there in the wood, muddied up to the knees.
"I *hate* tents," said I. "We've got to go on with it, though," we said. We stared at each
other, so woebegone that we finally burst out laughing.'

Diary

May 8, 1927
Long Barn

Drive down on a wonderful spring evening to Long Barn. Reach it at 6.30. The garden is a different place — wide lawns and tidy edges, tulips, aubretia, phlox, black irises — a sea of colour. I am amazed at it. It is all so exciting that before dinner I am violently sick and have to be given brandy. I have never felt so happy in my life. All the weary months of exile are wiped out like a sponge. We plant out irises dug up in Persia.

Diary

July 17, 1927

Leonard and Virginia [Woolf] come in their new second-hand motor. I talk to Leonard about Imperialism. He says the question is not whether it is right or wrong, but that it is practically impossible. I fear he may be right. But it saddens me, as I feel our national genius lies that way and that way only. I do not share Raymond's [Mortimer] belief that we could be great again in international matters. Virginia had been interviewed by an American lady journalist who was collecting material for a lecture on figures in English literature. She had told her that she had vaguely heard about a set or group called The Bloomsbury Group. She said, 'At your group socials I suppose you read aloud and then have a discussion or debate?' I can see Bloomsbury doing that!

Diary

October 14, 1927

Get a letter from Walford Selby saying he can't manage to send me to Rome, but will I please go at once to Berlin. There are few things that I would dislike more — and it is bad luck on Vita. But I *won't* chuck it if I can possibly help. So I accept, gloomily.

Diary   *October 20, 1927*

Dine with Clive Bell. Virginia Woolf and T. S. Eliot there. Eliot was
in a white tie and waistcoat – not in the least like Bloomsbury, and for
that matter not in the least like a poet. He looked like a young and
successful doctor or lawyer. His mind does not work quickly.

                                                          November 3, 1927
H.N. to Vita   *British Embassy, Berlin*

I love foreign politics, and I get them here in a really enthralling form.
If I chucked them for merely emotional reasons I should feel a worm –
unworthy of what is one of the few serious and virile sides of my
nature. 'Yes', you say, 'that's all very well – but what about me?' I know,
my saint, and I am bothered by that consideration. But somewhere
right deep down you must realise that Hadji's willingness to do hard
grudging work merely because it is interesting is a very respectable
form of looniness. It should give you somewhere, somewhere deep
down, a twiddle of respect. Doesn't it? So bear with me, my sweet. I
won't undergo anything *intolerable* for this idea: but Berlin is not
intolerable and I can't pretend that it is.

                                                          November 7, 1927
H.N. to Vita   *Berlin*

I had Noël Coward to luncheon yesterday.[1] Then we went on to a
review in the big Music Hall here. It was rather an odd thing to do
but Coward has little time and is anxious to pick up something original
for the review which he is himself producing in London [*This Year of
Grace*]. I must say, he *is* rather remarkable. Completely self-educated
– and producing a review in which he acts, sings and dances himself
and of which he has written the plots, the words and the music.
When you add to this the fact that he also writes excellent social satire,
one can't help treating him with respect. He is a bounder of course –

---

[1] He was only twenty-seven, and had just achieved his first success with *The Vortex* and
   Hay Fever.

but I don't really mind that when combined with real talent and energy.

We left at about 4.30 and went to a party at Mrs Albert's. Mrs A. is the American wife of Dr Albert who was the man who invented poison gas. They are very rich and have a large house with damask, Dutch pictures, tapestry and very heavy Italian furniture. Mrs Albert turned to me: 'I didn't see you in church today, Mr Nicolson.' 'No – I hate church.' 'But the Bishop was there.' 'I loathe Bishops.' Complete consternation on the part of Mrs Albert. Change of subject. 'Don't you play bridge, Mr Nicolson?' 'No – not on Sunday afternoons.' Whereat Mrs Albert became so puzzled that she gave me up and returned to the subject of servants. Never, *never* will I set foot in that house again.

December 31, 1927
Diary   *Berlin*

Well, not a bad year. Persia, Bakhtiari, and then that lovely long holiday at home. The Hawthornden prize for Vita, and for me the very real success of *Some People*. Trouble with the F.O., however, about refusing to go back to Teheran, and some disgrace and disgruntlement for a bit – ending with my getting the excellent job of Counsellor in Berlin. But all this is nothing to the joy of my home life – Vita and the boys. Health good – and morals pretty bad – drink and indulgence a little exaggerated for my age. But not serious. Am definitely getting stout but still look about 35 though 41. Brain and energy unimpaired. A lucky man so far.

February 11, 1928
H.N. to Vita   *Berlin*

Sinclair Lewis[1] is an odd red-faced noisy young man, who called me Harold from the start, and wouldn't leave me. He insisted on me going to a bar with him and then he insisted on coming back to dinner with

---

[1] Sinclair Lewis (1885–1951), the American novelist, whose *Main Street* (1920) had been a major best-seller. He was awarded the Nobel Prize for Literature in 1930.

me. He talked the whole time, and drank and drank. At 9.30 he
remembered that he had got to take his fiancée to a ball, and off he
went dragging me with him as he said he was too tight to dress. He
then spoke of Anglo–American relations. What could be done? Were
we drifting into war? Good God – what was there to do? Would I
write a joint letter with him to the *Evening Standard*? And yet what
could we say? Perhaps it would be better to leave it alone? And yet he
did so love England. No wonder we hated America. And would I
come round with him to Edith Thompson's?[1] She might be annoyed
at his being so late. And of course I wasn't ill – why, he could feel my
pulse. Yes, I must come. And, oh yes, he was sleeping with Edith
tonight and must take his pyjamas round. And would I telephone for
a taxi? And did he look very tight? Because Edith minded.

I went to see Edith. She was a nice wise woman with charm and
good sense, and I packed them off together to a ball and went to bed.

April 10, 1928
Berlin

H.N. to Nigel (aged eleven)

Mummy says that you are an angel, but have got spots. Now, spots
come from picking – not just picking blackberries or strawberries. But
from picking spots. Also from not taking Eno's Fruit Salts when one
is bunged up. Also from eating sweets. I used to have spots something
dreadful at your age – and now I have got a complexion of which any
schoolgirl would be proud. How did I get that complexion? By Eno's.
So next time you see a spot, think of me, and say these words, 'My
father, although spotty as a youth, has now got a complexion which,
though mottled by age and drink, is to all intents and purposes that of
a schoolgirl. He knows. 'E knows. Eno's.' Then all will be well.

---

[1] In fact, she was Dorothy Thompson, the American journalist, whom Lewis married
as his second wife in 1928 and divorced in 1942.

April 14, 1928
H.N. to Vita   *Berlin*

I went to the Puccini Abend at the Staats Oper. It really was very
good. I enjoyed it hugely. In the intervals Ivor[1] and I ate more and
more sausages. I like him so much. He is completely unspoilt by his
success and absolutely *thrilling* about his life. He has contracts which
will bring him in £35,000 by November next year. He calculates that
if his health lasts he should be able to make about £500,000 before he
is forty. He is rather appalled by this – and is very sensible about it.
Says it makes one feel such a fool to be worth so much money solely
because of one's profile. He suffers dreadfully from the worship of
flappers. Every day there are two or three of them who wait outside
his house just to see him. There were twelve of them at the station to
see him off! All this must be terribly bad for a person – and he is
himself terrified of becoming fatuous about it.

May 16, 1928
H.N. to Vita   *Berlin*

Cyril [Connolly] came yesterday.[2] Like the young Beethoven, with
spots. And a good brow, and an unreliable voice. He flattered your
husband. He sat there toying with a fork and my vanity, turning
them over together in his stubby little hands. He tells fortunes.
Palmistry. But the main point is that he thinks *Some People* an
important book. IMPORTANT! And it was just scribbled down
as a joke. He was terribly interested in Mr Peabody, and we had a long
talk about him.[3] Mr Peabody is shaping slowly into a very strange
shape indeed. Like an hour-glass. I really am going to take trouble
with that book, and there is a lot of cerebration going on, conscious
and unconscious.

---

[1] Ivor Novello, the Welsh-born composer, actor and film star, then aged thirty-five.
[2] The author and literary critic (1903–74).
[3] *Mr Peabody* was the working title Harold gave to his second novel. He put it aside
to write *Lord Carnock*. He completed the novel in 1932 and published it as *Public
Faces*.

June 30, 1928
Berlin

H.N. to his parents

We had a small farewell luncheon with the President [Hindenburg]. Only the Chancellor and his wife, the von Schuberts, and the Lindsay two.[1] The President lives in the Palace in the Wilhelmstrasse which was formerly tenanted by the Minister of Court. It is a fine palace with a lovely garden – huge trees running in an avenue down to the Tiergarten, with lawns and fountains filling up the space between them. We were met at the door by the President's son who is also his adjutant and taken rather solemnly upstairs escorted by two beadles in cocked hats and by rows of footmen in lovely blue liveries. The contrast between all this formality and the immense simplicity of Hindenburg was very striking. He is enormous, straight as a lathe, not deaf in the least, and bearing his eighty years and the adoration of Germany with great simplicity and a sort of gentle humour like that of a nice old buffer in a club. He has a delicious way of raising his eyebrows and twinkling when he makes his little jokes. The luncheon was rather alarming as neither the Chancellor nor von Schubert dared speak in Hindenburg's presence and the old man himself was too intent on eating what I must say was a very exquisite luncheon with really wonderful wines. After luncheon we sat round a table and had coffee, the three ladies grouping themselves on a canapé at the end of the room. Hindenburg made me sit next to him, and became quite talkative. He asked me after father's health which I thought was polite of him since he added '*Er war nicht unserer Freund*,' but he said it without any trace of resentment, much as one would say 'So and so rowed against me in the Cambridge boat.' He also talked about his early years at Hannover and of how there still lingered many English words and customs, such as passing the port round from right to left. He then talked of the war quite naturally, speaking of the development of aviation and how the excellence of our air-force had taken the Germans rather by surprise.

---

[1] The Field Marshal, who had been elected President in 1925, was eighty-one. The Chancellor was Hermann Müller. Carl von Schubert was Foreign Secretary. Sir Ronald Lindsay was retiring as British Ambassador, leaving Harold in charge of the Berlin Embassy, and in 1930 was appointed Ambassador to the United States.

He asked me to 'Come and see me again' as if he were just an old retired General in Cheltenham.

H.N. to Vita

August 3, 1928
Berlin

At seven I had to get up in order to meet old [Sir Horace] Rumbold.[1] I put on my top hat and tails, and motored in on a lovely clear morning feeling rather cross and uncomfortable in my stiff clothes. There is no doubt moreover that I do *not* like Ambassadors arriving when I am in charge. They had opened the special waiting-rooms at the Friedrichstrasse [station] – and there was the whole staff there looking very lovely, and two representatives of the German Government. The train came in and old Rumby bundled out rather embarrassed with an attaché case in one hand and in the other a novel by Mr Galsworthy. I introduced him to the German representatives and to the staff, while the crowd gaped and gaped and the policemen stood at the salute. Photographs were taken, and then very slowly we passed through the waiting rooms preceded by the Oberbahnhofführer [station-master] to the waiting cars. I carried the attaché case. We drove round to the Adlon [hotel] where he is staying until the Embassy is in order. We were greeted by the whole Adlon family.

Rumby was confused. 'Never', he said, 'have I felt so odd.' You see, the last time the poor man was in Berlin was exactly fourteen years ago to the day almost – on August 4 1914 – when he was Counsellor and crept out of Berlin under cavalry escort and amid the booings of a crowd. It is odd thus to return. He is a nice old bumble bee – and I am quite happy with him. But he is not Lindsay – no, no.

H.N. to Vita

August 9, 1928
Berlin

We had a long argument last night on what was the test of intelligence. Cyril [Connolly] said that if a woman had *really* read through the whole of Proust he would think her intelligent. I said that was rubbish,

---

[1] Who succeeded Lindsay as Ambassador.

as I felt sure that Lady Gosford had read through the whole of Proust. I tested intelligence not by knowledge or culture but by imagination and ability to draw quick and original associations. Raymond [Mortimer] stuck up for culture: he said that one could tell by what a person had read how intelligent they were. The discussion, I felt, was about to become angry. The figure of strife stood gaunt and impatient at the next cross-road.

So I changed the subject to day-dreaming. Cyril and I agreed that we had both had day-dreams. I said I dreamt of doing brave things – of shooting ibex from a very great distance, of behaving with conspicuous courage at fires, or revolutions, or during a debate in the House of Commons. Cyril said that his day-dreams were largely stories in which he figured as the Sheik Senoussi and in which, disguised in white scarfs, he captured European tourists and put them all to death with the exception of Bobby Longden, who, on his side, would be grateful for this privileged treatment.[1] Raymond, for his part, said that he never day-dreamed: that he thought it 'shocking' to do so – a relaxation of intellectual fibre which was worse than drugs.

Again the figure of strife loomed in the distance, so the conversation was diverted once more, from personal experience to culture. Cyril said that the difference between Bloomsbury and Chelsea culture was that the former would think the *Oedipus Rex* better than the *Epictetus*, and the latter would prefer the *Epictetus* to the *Oedipus Rex*. Tray [Mortimer] was a little disconcerted by this and retreated into the French XVII century where he was fairly safe. I, for my part, said I must take Henry [dog] out to pee.

November 17, 1928
Berlin

H.N. to Vita

I have no desire whatever for fame, and would really be bored to feel that people in a Harrogate Hydro knew about me in the sort of way that they know about Hugh Walpole. 'There's H. Nicolson', they would exclaim as a ham-faced arthritic limped through the palm-

---

[1] Robert Longden was on a visit to Berlin from Magdalen College, Oxford, of which he was a Fellow. He became Master of Wellington College in 1937, and was killed by a German bomb in 1940.

court. No, thank you very much. I want *influence*, and to be esteemed
by the people I like.

H.N. to Vita

November 19, 1928
Berlin

Oh God, how I wish that life were twice as long and that the days
consisted of 100 hours each! Every morning I wake up thinking how
I want to write a book about Puritanism, and spend a winter in Tahiti,
and learn how to fish for salmon, and go on a walking-tour through
Patagonia, and try and get at the secret of Cézanne's landscapes (I am
really wild about Cézanne just now), and do nothing for six weeks
except visit the Greek islands with my darling and the boys, and build
a house in the Lebanon, and visit Australia, South Africa and America,
and do a fuller life of Byron, and Ludwig II, and through all this go
on being a diplomat, having Long Barn, and seeing every autumn the
wood-smoke drift across the dear remembered woods.

Diary

December 31, 1928
Berlin

Thus, in pain and fever, ends one of my worst years. A horrible year.
Lionel [Lord Sackville] dies, and I thus not only lose a great friend and
support, but my poor darling V. loses her adored house [Knole]. B.M.
behaves abominably and the whole year is occupied by squabbles with
her, which we loathe, and by attendant financial difficulties. My old
father dies, thus breaking a link with my youth. The whole year has
been spent in Berlin, separated from Vita, my home and the boys. I
am distinctly older. Feeling bald and fat. I have written nothing this
year of any importance and done no diplomatic work of the slightest
value.

So much for the dark side. On the light side, there are compensations.
Both my and V.'s literary reputations have much increased and I can
now command big sums for magazine articles. We have all been well.
Ben and Nigel are getting on splendidly, the former having got a
scholarship at Eton. Then I have made some really nice new friends –

the Lindsays, Noël Coward, Cyril Connolly, Bob Boothby, Maurice Bowra, John Sparrow, Francesco Mendelsohn, Dan Lascelles, Christopher Sykes. Not really a wasted year, but a dark one.

March 15, 1929
H.N. to Vita   *Cologne*

After writing to you yesterday I went to see the Oberbürgermeister. His name is Adenauer, and he is a rather remarkable figure in modern Germany.[1] There are some who say that if Parliamentarianism really breaks down in Berlin, they will summon Adenauer to establish some form of fascismo. For the moment he rules Cologne with an iron hand, and is responsible for such things as the new Rhine bridge and the Presse exhibition. There was some sort of fuss going on round his room when I got there, private secretaries dashing about, people opening doors, squinting in, then shutting them again rapidly. I was asked to sit down while bells buzzed and people hurried in and whispered to each other, and then hurried out again. I am to this moment unaware what had happened, but the contrast between the scurrying and whispering outside, and the sudden peace of his own large study, was most effective, and this strange Mongol, sitting there with shifty eyes in a yellow face, sitting with his back to the window, talking very slowly and gently, pressing bells very slowly – 'Would you ask Dr Pietri to come here' – snapping with icy politeness at the terrified Dr Pietri when he arrived – possessed all the manner of a Dictator. It is not a manner which I like, but it is a manner which once seen is never forgotten. I feel I could adopt it at once. I shall try to do so. One of the main stunts is to create an atmosphere of rush and flurry around one and be oneself as calm as the hollow in the centre of a typhoon. Another stunt is to talk to subordinates in a very gentle voice but with a sudden flash of a shifty eye.

He was very expansive on the subject of town-planning. I told him how impressed I had been by the garden-suburbs of Frankfurt, and he was not pleased at this, knowing that his garden-suburbs were not up

---

[1] Konrad Adenauer, who was to become Chancellor of Germany 1949–63, was Lord Mayor of Cologne 1917–33, when he was dismissed by Goering and temporarily imprisoned.

to the same level. He said that the Frankfurt people had lost a great
deal of money by extravagance in garden-suburbs, and that his own
aim was not to bring the town into the country but the country into
the town. It was at that stage that he summoned the agitated Dr Pietri
and told him to show me all there was to be seen.

H.N. to Vita

April 12, 1929
Berlin

I dined with H. G. Wells and Moura Budberg.[1] Towards the end of
the evening, Wells ceased to flirt with the lady, and talked intelligently.
He spoke of his young life, of a grandfather who had been a gardener
at Penshurst, of his father who had had very small feet and hands and
bowled at cricket, of his mother who lived well into his success but
was always anxious about the insecurity of a writer's profession. One
day he showed her a cheque for £6,000 which he had just received
from America. She sighed deeply, 'Oh dear, how I wish you could get
something permanent.' He said that on looking back, his life seemed
a very short one, 'although some things in it seem a very long way
away'. He is a wrong-headed but amusing little man. He believes in
the new world very thoroughly, I think. He did not think very much
of Lenin as a personality, but realised that he must have been one.
What was funny was that he was embarrassed about going out to pee.
We teased him about it, and he admitted that this was one of his
conventions.

H.N. to Vita

April 16, 1929
Berlin

I went to H. G. Wells's lecture in the Reichstag. One simply could
not hear a word. Not a single word. It was rather a disaster. After that
there was a dinner at the Adlon. [Albert] Einstein presided. He looks
like a child who for fun has put on a mask painted like Einstein. He is
a darling. He made a little speech for Wells which I then translated. I

---

[1] Baroness Budberg, born a Russian, was formerly the mistress of Maxim Gorki, then
Wells's, and an exotic figure in London society.

began by saying, 'I have been asked to translate Professor Einstein's speech. I may add that it is the first thing of his that I have ever understood.' They thought that a funny joke.

May 18, 1929
H.N. to Vita   *Berlin*

Cyril [Connolly] is not perhaps the ideal guest. He is terribly untidy in an irritating way. He leaves dirty handkerchiefs in the chairs and fountain pens (my fountain pens) open in books. Moreover it is rather a bore having a person who has *nothing* of his own – not a cigarette or a stamp. In fact the poverty of this colony is heart-rending. Christopher and David are both absolutely bust.[1] But I really am firm about it, and won't take them all to Pelzer's [restaurant] to eat plover's eggs. In other ways, however, Cyril is a pleasant guest, easily amused, and interesting about things. I don't trust him a yard and think he makes mischief. He is very thick with Violet Trefusis, and I imagine that he is very disloyal about me when with her. I rather mind that, as she is so unscrupulous and appears never to have got over the desire to revenge herself on me. But what does it all matter so long as none of these people can make trouble between you and me?

May 25, 1929
H.N. to Vita   *Berlin*

We motored the Yorks out to the golf-course for luncheon.[2] She is really a delightful person, incredibly gay and simple. It is an absolute tragedy that she should be a royalty. Moreover she is no fool. She talked to me so intelligently about *Some People*, whereas he had clearly read only the Arketall story and had got it wrong. But she and Cyril Connolly are the only two people who have spoken intelligently about

---

[1] Harold gave sanctuary in his flat in north-west Berlin to Cyril Connolly, aged twenty-six, Christopher Sykes (an attaché at the British Embassy), aged twenty-two and David Herbert (son of the Earl of Pembroke), aged twenty-one.

[2] The Duke and Duchess of York, later King George VI and Queen Elizabeth (still later, Elizabeth the Queen Mother).

the 'landscape' element in *Some People*. She said, 'You choose your colours so carefully – that bit about the palace in Madrid was done in grey and chalk-white, the Constantinople bits in blue and green, the desert bits in blue and orange.' Of course, that may be second-hand, but I don't think so – and even if I am making a mistake about her intelligence, I am making no mistake about her charm. It is quite overwhelming. He is just a snipe from the great Windsor marshes. Not bad-looking – but now and again there is that sullen, heavy-lidded, obstinate dulling of the blue eyes which is most unattractive.

July 7, 1929
H.N. to his mother   *Berlin*

I think you are right in insisting that the book[1] should be a biography and not a history of European diplomacy. There is a danger that my interest in the political and historical side may tempt me beyond the actual frame of father's life and lead me into controversial discussions. On the other hand, you must admit that father was such a central figure in the foreign politics of his time that it is almost impossible to avoid giving some outline of what was happening beyond. For instance, there is a German theory that he was one of the authors of the Encirclement Policy. One must show that there was at the start no idea of encirclement. To do this one must also show that when we looked for alliances we looked first to Germany. We gave her the first refusal of our friendship and she refused it. Why? It is only fair on Germany to show that she refused it because of our treachery and duplicity about the Portuguese colonies. I want this book to be a monument to a man whom I loved and admired more than I have or ever shall admire any man. But if it is to be a monument conspicuous and desirable (as I wish it to be) it must not be built of the lath and plaster of nationalism but in the firm marble of internationalism. I must write like a European and not like a member of the Junior Carlton.

I don't want this book to be a memorial volume which will be read only by friends and relations. I wish it to be a book which brings home

---

[1] *Lord Carnock*, the biography of his father, who had died in November 1928. Harold worked on the book for as much as seven hours a day, before and after his Embassy work, and always considered it the best of his books.

to ordinary people that unless one thinks war horrible, war will come again. It was merely because millions of people in 1913 imagined that there was something more dreadful, such as loss of national honour, than war, that five million young men were butchered in the mud. I feel myself that war is the worst evil that can happen to a country, and that this jargon about national honour is dangerous jargon. I feel this deeply and honourably. There is no tinge in what I feel of my irritation against diplomatists and generals. On the whole, the people at the top were less to blame than the *Daily Mail* and other sensational journals. I myself, in 1914, was burning for war. So was Fred and so was Eric [his brothers]. It was quite natural with the ideas to which we had been educated. But they were false ideas. No system of thought can be right which considers it 'honourable' to gash the bodies of men with fire and steel and allow them to be gnawed by rats in the mud. I do not forget for one moment that people in 1913 did not realise what war was. It was not their fault. It took my generation five years of hell to learn the lesson. But having learnt that lesson one must, one MUST, pass it on to others.

July 22, 1929
Berlin

Diary

Get a letter from Bruce Lockhart asking me whether I would like a job under Beaverbrook on the *Evening Standard*. I reply that I am prepared to consider the offer but must know first what salary I should get and how much of my time it would take up. I also say that I will not voice Tory opinions or attack my own radical tenets. I write to Vita and to Leonard [Woolf] asking their advice.[1]

August 8, 1929
Berlin

H.N. to Vita

Today, for all I know, may be a decisive date in my life. I feel rather wretched. Whatever happens – whether I get this [Beaverbrook] job or not, I shall feel rather gloomy. If I fail to get it, then I shall feel

---

[1] They both advised acceptance of the offer.

blamiert [ridiculous]. If I get it, then I shall feel depressed at leaving diplomacy. Gloom in either case. But it may simply be liver.

I daresay that the main cause of my gloom is fuss about money. My poverty is really getting on my nerves. I mean it is awful not to have any money in the bank. Of course I have got enough to go on with and I am not in serious difficulties. But it is just the feeling of having spent so much money here and having absolutely nothing to show for it. Anyhow, I funk all bills. *J'ai peur des notes comme d'une abeille* [I fear bills as much as a bee].

I heard from the Ambassador that there are five Legations to be filled – Mexico, Athens, Belgrade, Bucharest and Oslo. Now it is *quite* likely that they will offer me Athens, Belgrade or Bucharest. If they don't, then I shall have no qualms at all about resignation. But if, a week after accepting Beaverbrook's offer, I get appointed to Athens, then I admit that I shall think that fate has played me a scurvy trick. Five years in Athens, and then an Embassy. I should probably think of it in those terms. Poor Hadji – not much of a success in life. Everybody will think me quite, quite looney.

You see, my darling, supposing I hear, after I have resigned, that they really were about to offer me Athens. Supposing that, having become a hack journalist cadging interviews from people, I think of the man who got my job at Athens sailing from Aegean island to Aegean island. Supposing that when Beaverbrook has chucked me out after four years, I hear that my successor at Athens has been appointed to Rome. But perhaps I am doing a White Queen [in *Alice in Wonderland*] and getting all my regrets over in anticipation.

August 11, 1929
H.N. to his mother   *Berlin*

I have been busy on Russia all the last fortnight. It is very interesting. Goodness how Father worked! His dispatches are really miles ahead of those that are written today. I can't quote all those dispatches as there is no room, and the general effect is what is so impressive rather than the individual report. But it strikes one that the whole level of the Petersburg Embassy was far above that which we have here today. I do hope that I am able to succeed in conveying what father really was. It is a difficult task. Continually I am bothered by the problem of the 'audience'. On the one hand I want to appeal to as wide an audience as possible, to make known to people who never heard of him, to show to future generations how it came that the war arose. On the other hand I want the book to appeal to scholars and specialists, and to be regarded as a serious contribution to history. Between these two objects I may fail. But in any case, I am doing my best and working harder than I have ever worked at any book.

August 26, 1929
H.N. to Vita   *Berlin*

You say in your letter that Ernest Gye[1] must have upset me by telling me not to leave the [diplomatic] service. No, my sweet. My perplexities and hesitations are deeper than that. You see, diplomacy really does give me leisure to do literary work of my own and it *does* have advantages such as leave, nice people etc. Moreover (and this is the essential point) if I stay in diplomacy I am certain of being 'successful', or, in other words, of getting to the top. You say, with justice, that it is not a very glorious top. I quite agree. Yet I have sufficient knowledge of human nature to realise that it is more satisfactory to succeed on a small scale than to fail on a big one. If I end up as an Ambassador, I shall always feel (and say) what a wonderful career I could have made for myself in the open market. But if I climb down into the open market and then fail to make good there, I shall regret bitterly not having remained in my armchair and ended as an Ambassador. I shall feel that I was absolutely mad to chuck a certainty for an uncertainty, and at an age when my supply of violent energy must shortly begin to give out.

I don't think I shall be affected by the present [Foreign Office] moves, but I shall certainly be affected by the new ones. There is even a prospect, if I stay on, of my being a Minister next year with £4,000 a year.

Naturally I put against this (1) B.M.[2] (2) Being separated from you.

---

[1] Gye entered the Foreign Office in 1903 and became Minister in Tangier 1933–6.
[2] Lady Sackville threatened to cut the annual allowance to which Vita was legally entitled, and one motive for Harold's resignation was to earn sufficient money as a journalist to enable them to renounce it.

In the end, these two factors will probably be determinant. But you must understand, my love, that the decision is a grave one to have to take, and you can't quite expect me to chuck my job at my age [forty-three] in a spirit of light-heartedness. I feel *very* heavy-hearted about it, and whatever decision I do take will not have been taken without hours and hours of very anxious thought. If I were ten years younger, the whole thing would be different.

December 16, 1929
Berlin

H.N. to Vita

At the Buccaneers [Club] dinner there were nearly 40 people – including old Rumbie [Rumbold] and the American Ambassador. Speech by Rumbie which gave me a lump in my throat. Speech by me – very restrained but gulpy. Musical honours. All went off very well. It is quite extraordinary how nice people are to me here. They really are sorry I am going.

Rumbie made a rather provocative speech saying that the Foreign Office ought to have been able to keep me 'had they possessed more imagination'. As all the Press were there, this was rather odd.

I was exhausted by the whole thing, and sank into my bed with relief. Luncheon with the [Carl von] Schuberts today. Tomorrow dinner at the Embassy – and then my farewells are over.

Tomorrow will be my last letter.

December 19, 1929
Berlin

Diary

Leave Berlin. A *beau départ*. I am presented with a cactus. The end of my diplomatic career.

PART II

LITERATURE AND POLITICS
1930–1939

At the beginning of 1930 Harold Nicolson, having resigned from the Foreign Office, joined the staff of Lord Beaverbrook's Evening Standard. *There he collaborated with Robert Bruce Lockhart in writing the* Londoner's Diary — *about twelve paragraphs a day of social, political and literary gossip. He found the job degrading. He also began broadcasting a series of talks for the BBC under the title* People *and* Things, *and wrote book reviews for the* Daily Express.*

In January 1930 he was forty-three years old. Vita Sackville-West was thirty-seven, and their sons, Benedict and Nigel, were fifteen and thirteen. Harold lived for most of the week at 4 King's Bench Walk, Inner Temple, and at weekends went to Long Barn, their house near Sevenoaks. In May of this year Vita bought Sissinghurst Castle, a decrepit house near Cranbrook, Kent, and they moved there permanently in 1932.

Diary   January 1, 1930

I am glad that 1929 is over. Not a very happy year for me, since it has entailed being separated from Vita and living a rather hugger-mugger existence in Berlin. But there have been compensations. In the first place I have worked hard at father's book [*Lord Carnock*], and completed it before the year was out. In the second place, I was able to perfect my knowledge of the German character: in other words, to make quite certain that I did not understand them in the least.

Diary   January 8, 1930

Work fruitlessly superficially futilely upon the Londoner's Diary. The difficulty is that the only news I get is from friends and that is just the news that I can't publish.

Lunch with Sibyl Colefax.[1] The Rudyard Kiplings there. Rudyard

---

[1] One of London's leading hostesses, who lived at Argyll House, Chelsea.

Kipling's eyebrows are really very odd indeed! They curl up black and furious like the moustache of a Neapolitan tenor. He has a slightly Anglo-Indian voice, with notes of civil service precision in it, and his conversation is twisted into phrases like his writing. He spoke of Cecil Rhodes and [Theodore] Roosevelt. Admired them both.... He assured me that Rhodes did not drink: he looked as if he did, but that was due to a weak heart.

Diary   *January 23, 1930*

I was summoned by Lord Beaverbrook. I arrived at Stornoway House to find him alone writing a cross letter to his son about bills. In a few minutes Winston Churchill slouched in. Very changed from when I last saw him. A great round face like a blister. Incredibly aged. Looks like pictures of Lord Holland. An elder statesman. His spirits also have declined and he sighs that he has lost his old fighting power.

They talked the whole time about Empire free trade. Winston says that he has abandoned all his convictions and clings to the conviction of free trade as the only one which is left to him. But he is clearly disturbed at the effect on the country of Beaverbrook's propaganda. He feels too old to fight it. 'Thirty years ago,' he said, 'I should have welcomed such a combat: now I dread it.' He seems to think [Stanley] Baldwin [Leader of the Conservative Opposition] absolutely hopeless, and no instructions have been given to the provincial candidates and agents as to the line that decent Conservatives will adopt. Beaverbrook uses every wile to secure if not his support then at least his agreement not to oppose. I must say, he is rather impressive. Young [fifty] and nervous he walks about the room piling argument on argument and statistic on statistic. There is no question but that he is passionately sincere and has really studied his subject.

Diary   *March 8, 1930*

Down to Long Barn. We go round the field at Westwood [the neigh-bouring farm] with Mrs Taylour the lady who owns Cookes [poultry farmers]. She will sell us the ridge fields at £150 an acre when they

are only worth £50. She will sell us the whole of Westwood for
£21,000. Now this is absurd and beyond the dreams of possibility. She
is erecting huts and cottages on the field that overlooks our garden.
The view from Long Barn – its best point – will be spoilt. Very
gloomily we discuss migrating to Dorset.

Diary   *March 26, 1930*

On to the *Daily Express* office about books. I see an intolerable man
who treats both me and literature as if they were dirt. I am so depressed
by the squalor of this interview that I return home in a nerve-storm.
To make it worse, I am sent out to represent the *Standard* at the Knights
of the Round Table dinner. There is no seat for me and I creep away
in dismay and humiliation. I never foresaw that writing for the Press
would be actually so degrading. What I dread is that I might get to
like it: the moment I cease to be unhappy about it will be the moment
when my soul has finally been killed.

Diary   *April 4, 1930*

Vita telephones to say she has seen the ideal house – a place in Kent
near Cranbrook, a sixteenth-century castle [Sissinghurst].[1]

Diary   *April 5, 1930*

Go down to Staplehurst with Ben. We are met, after some delay, by
Vita, Boski [Audrey le Bosquet, Vita's secretary], Niggs [Nigel], and
all the dogs. We then drive to Sissinghurst Castle. We get a view of
the two towers as we approach. We go round carefully in the mud. I
am cold and calm but I like it.

---

[1] Vita wrote in her diary that night, 'Fell flat in love with it'.

H.N. to Vita   *April 24, 1930*

My view is:

(a) That it is most unwise of us to get Sissinghurst. It costs us £12,000 to buy and will cost another good £15,000 to put it in order. This will mean nearly £30,000 before we have done with it. For £30,000 we could buy a beautiful place replete with park, garage, h. and c., central heating, historical associations, and two lodges r. and l.

(b) That it is most wise of us to buy Sissinghurst. Through its veins pulses the blood of the Sackville dynasty.[1] True it is that it comes through the female line – but then we are both feminist and after all Knole came in the same way. It is, for you, an ancestral mansion: that makes up for the company's water and h. and c.

(c) It is in Kent. It is in a part of Kent we like. It is self-contained. I could make a lake. The boys could ride.

(d) We like it.

Diary   *May 6, 1930*

After dinner we are rung up by Beale [the land-agent]. He says that they accept our price. I sit there while Vita answers the telephone: 'Quite' ... 'Yes, of course' ... 'Oh naturally!' She puts down the receiver and says, 'It is ours.' We embrace warmly....

Diary   *June 6, 1930*

I go to William Rothenstein [the portraitist] to have a drawing done. He tells me that Oscar Wilde had a red face, grey lips and very bad teeth. He was so ashamed of his teeth that he used to put his hand over them when he spoke giving an odd furtive expression to his jokes. Rothenstein did a drawing of Wilde which the latter always took with him. He lost it in Naples after the trial. It was probably stolen. That was about the only portrait of Wilde ever made.

---

[1] Cecily Baker, daughter of Sir Thomas Baker, who owned Sissinghurst in the reign of Henry VIII, married Sir Thomas Sackville, first Earl of Dorset, to whom Queen Elizabeth gave Knole in 1566.

Diary   *June 22, 1930*

Talk to Stephen Spender. He is an intelligent young man [aged twenty-
one] with wild blue eyes and a bad complexion. He takes his work and
poetry with immense seriousness, and talks for hours about whether he
is more fitted to be a poet than a novelist. He is not conceited so much
as self-preoccupied. He is absolutely determined to become a leading
writer. A nice and vital young man whom we both liked.

Diary   *July 2, 1930*

Dine at Sovrani's with Bob Boothby [Conservative MP]. Bob tells me
that when someone asked Ramsay MacDonald whether he, Bob, was
about to join the Labour Party, Ramsay replied, 'No, Bob is no Labour
man: it is merely that he has a deep personal admiration for myself.'
That is characteristic of the man's diseased vanity. I talk to [Harold]
Macmillan. He says that the old party machines are worn out and that
the modern electorate thinks more of personalities and programmes
than of the pressure put upon them by an electoral agent. He thinks
that the economic situation is so serious that it will lead to a breakdown
of the whole party system. He foresees that the Tories may return with
a majority of 20 and then be swept away on a snap vote. No other
single party will form a Government and then there will be a Cabinet
of young men. He was kind enough to include me in this Pitt-like
Ministry.

Diary   *July 6, 1930*

Winston [at Wilton, the Pembrokes' house in Wiltshire] talks long and
sadly about Beaverbrook's Empire Free Trade campaign which he sees
is ruining the country. He says it will hand over South America to the
Yanks, split the Empire for ever, and shatter the Conservative Party
into smithereens. He is writing three books – one a last volume of
the *World Crisis* – one a life of the Duke of Marlborough – one

reminiscences of his own.[1] He is in gentle and intelligent form. He goes for a long walk with Vita and tells her his troubles and hopes. He spoke of his American tour. The difficulty of drink and food. One never got real food, only chicken.

Diary   *July 10, 1930*

Dine with Sir Henry Norman – a man's dinner.[2] I sit next to Bernard Shaw. He is amazingly young looking [he was seventy-three]: his shoulder blades at the back stick through his dinner jacket like those of a boy who has not finished growing. His hair is dead white but thick. His cheeks as pink as a girl's. His eyes as simple and unmalicious as those of an animal. And yet behind their simplicity is a touch of reserve. He talks with a faintly effeminate voice and a soft brogue. He had a special menu of excellent vegetables.

He talked of Laurence [Olivier]. Said he was a born actor. Spoke of him with real admiration. Afterwards we went upstairs and there were some young girls to amuse the old man. Simon was charming about my book [*Lord Carnock*]. Ned Lutyens was even sillier than usual.

Diary   *October 5, 1930*

We start off at 10 to motor to Chequers. On passing through Bromley we half-see a poster blown by the wind which looks like 'Airship destroyed'. We stop later and buy a paper. We find that the R.101 has crashed near Beauvais,[3] and that [Lord] Thomson with 43 other people have been burnt alive. We then drive on to Chequers.

When we arrive we find that the P.M. [Ramsay MacDonald] is up in London and is expected back later. Ishbel [his daughter] says he will

---

[1] An abridged and revised edition of *The World Crisis*, published in 1931; *Marlborough*, published in four volumes, 1933–8; and *My Early Life*, published in 1930.

[2] Norman was a businessman, journalist, traveller and briefly a Liberal MP. The other guests were Bernard Shaw, Sir John Simon, Sir Edwin Lutyens, Lord Dawson and A.A. Milne.

[3] The airship, R.101, crashed that morning on a hillside in France, killing forty-six people including Lord Thomson, the Minister for Air. There were only seven survivors.

be in a dreadful state. He arrives about 1.30. He looks very ill and worn. [Richard] Bennett, the Prime Minister of Canada, is there. Ramsay begins to introduce him to Vita but forgets his name. He makes a hopeless gesture – his hand upon his white hair – 'My brain is going,' he says, 'my brain is going.' It is all rather embarrassing. He then tells us that the bell beside his bed had rung that morning and he had lifted the receiver. He was told it was the Air Ministry. He was told of the disaster. He dashed up to London in 55 minutes and went to the Air Ministry. There were only a few clerks about. Salmond [Air Marshal Sir Geoffrey Salmond] was got hold of and sent across to France. Baldwin came to see him. They agreed that no man's health could stand being Prime Minister. The King was in a dreadful state. Ramsay seemed more worried about the King's dismay than about anything else.

We then go in to luncheon. All very beautifully and excellently done. Afterwards we go up to the long gallery. The women look at Cromwell's head [life-mask]. The P.M. pours out to Vita the miseries of his soul: he cannot sleep: two hours a night is all he gets: he can do no work: 'the moment I disentangle my foot from one strand of barbed wire it becomes entangled in another. If God were to come to me and say "Ramsay, would you rather be a country gentleman than Prime Minister?", I should reply, "Please God, a country gentleman."' He is a tired exhausted man. Bless him.

Diary   *October 18, 1930*

Feeling very depressed with life. Can't make out whether it is mere middle-aged depression or that I loathe journalism so much that it covers all my days with a dark cloud of shame. I feel that I have no time to add to my reputation by doing serious work and that my silly work day by day diminishes the reputation I have already acquired. I have become 'famous' as a radio comedian,[1] and I shall never be able to live down the impression thus acquired. I would give my soul to leave the *Standard* but I daren't risk it because of the money. Middle age for a hedonist like myself is distressing in any case but with most

---

[1] For his weekly BBC broadcasts, *People and Things*.

people it coincides with an increase of power and income. With me I
have lost all serious employment, sacrificed my hopes of power, and
am up against the anxiety of having not one penny in the world beyond
what I earn. I have never been unhappy like this before.

In the afternoon we go to Sissinghurst. A lovely evening. We sleep
in the top room of the tower, on two camp beds.

Diary   *November 27, 1930*

To Noël Coward's *Private Lives* with Vita and on to supper with Noël
at 17 Gerald Road. An elaborate studio. Noël very simple and nice.
He talks of the days when his mother kept lodgings in Ebury Street
and he himself had a top back room. Gradually he began to make
money and took the top floor for himself, finally descending to the
first floor and ejecting the lodgers. 'As I rose in the world I went down
in the house.' Completely unspoilt by success. A nice eager man.

Diary   *November 30, 1930*

Tom Mosley tells me that he will shortly launch his manifesto practically
creating the National Party. He hopes to get Morris [later Lord
Nuffield] of Oxford to finance him. He hopes to get [Maynard] Keynes
and similar experts to sign his manifesto. He hopes that [Oliver] Stanley
and [Harold] Macmillan will also join. He hopes to get the support of
Beaverbrook. I doubt whether many of these hopes will be realised,
but his conversation is convincing enough to decide me to write to
[Sir John] Tudor Walters declining his offer to stand for Falmouth.[1]
That is one boat burnt.

Diary   *December 22, 1930*

Bertram Mills gives a luncheon for 1,100 people at Olympia. I am
about to enter when I hear a voice behind me. It is Ramsay MacDonald.
He says, 'Well, this is my one holiday in the year. I love circuses.' At

[1] The Liberal seat from which Walters was resigning.

that moment they hand him a telegram. He opens it. He hands it to me with the words, 'Keep this, my dear Harold, and read it if ever you think you wish to be Prime Minister.' It is a telegram from some crank society abusing him for attending a luncheon in honour of a circus proprietor – since performing animals are cruel. He is disgusted and his pleasure spoiled.

Diary   *December 31, 1930*

Thus ends the year 1930. Such an odd year. We buy Sissinghurst; we make a vast sum of money from our books; we increase our fame and lower our reputation; we prepare for the future. Viti has been very well and happy except for her back. . . . I have quite found my feet in the *Standard* office – and Beaverbrook likes me. But that is all very well. I was not made to be a journalist and do not want to go on being one. It is a mere expense of spirit in a waste of shame. A constant hurried triviality which is bad for the mind. Goodness knows what I shall do next year. I am on the verge of politics. I am on the verge of leaving the *Evening Standard* and either writing books of my own or sitting in the House of Commons. 1931 assuredly will be the most important year, for good or ill, in my whole life.

Harold's dislike of journalism increased as his ambition to enter politics mounted. He joined Oswald Mosley's New Party in face of Lord Beaverbrook's disapproval and Vita's conviction that the whole Mosley venture was insane.

Diary   *January 28, 1931*

Walking across St Stephen's Yard I observe a small figure in front of me with collar turned up. He turns to see who is behind him and I see it is Ramsay MacDonald. I say, 'Hullo, sir. How are you?' He greets me warmly. We walk across to Downing Street and people take off their hats as he passes. The traffic is stopped. He talks about Vita's broadcast on Persia: the best he has ever heard. He asks me to come in and have a drink. We reach the door of No. 10. He knocks. The porter opens and stands to attention. Ramsay asks him, 'Is Berry in?' 'No, sir, he has gone.' 'Is Ishbel in?' (not 'Miss Ishbel'). 'Yes, sir.' 'Would you ask her to bring two glasses to my room?' We then go upstairs. The room has an unlived-in appearance. Turners over the fireplace. Ishbel is there. He asks her to get us a drink. She goes out and returns with two tooth-glasses and a syphon. She says she can't find any whisky. Ramsay says it is in the drawer of his table. He finds it. 'What about some champagne,' he says, 'to celebrate the victory?' [an unexpected Government majority on the Trade Disputes Bill]. I say I will not have champagne. Malcolm [MacDonald] comes in. 'A cigarette?' I say I will. 'Malcolm, we have got cigarettes, haven't we – in that Egyptian box?' Malcolm goes to search for the Egyptian box. Then there are no matches.

He complains of overwork and bother. He sees me out. Nothing will convince me that he is not a fundamentally simple man. Under all his affectation and vanity there is a core of real simplicity.

Diary   *February 15, 1931*

At Savehay [the Mosleys' country house]. Oliver Stanley, Harold Macmillan and other MPs come over including [David] Margesson [later Conservative Chief Whip]. Play rounders. I fall into the stream. Tom is organising his New Party. Poor Cimmie [Mosley] cannot follow his repudiation of all the things he has taught her to say previously. She was not made for politics. She was made for society and the home. He wants me to sit on the Party's publicity committee. I say that he must ask Beaverbrook, but as the latter is so busy with his East Islington Election he will not listen.

                                                   March 4, 1931
H.N. to Sir Oswald Mosley   *Evening Standard*

I spoke to Max [Beaverbrook] about joining your party. He was most appreciative. Striding about the room he explained to me how far, far more remunerative it would be for me to attach myself to some more established machine. He became eloquent on the constituencies and jobs which could be conquered and acquired under the tattered banners of the old parties. And when I, sitting there glum and obstinate, remarked that I did not care for the old parties, he said, 'Go to Hell with ye – and God bless ye.'

After which he expressed admiration for yourself and deep sympathy with me in my obstinacy and wrong-headedness. He said I had his blessing (his sorrowed blessing) in joining you. I might serve on any of your committees if I wished. I must not boost you unduly in the *Evening Standard*. Nor must I devote to the New Party the time that I ought to devote to the *Standard*. Nor must I proclaim on the housetops my conversion to the faith. But short of that I might do what I liked.

Diary   *April 29, 1931*

... H. G. Wells talks to me after lunch about Beaverbrook. He says that he is really alarmed lest B. should have hardening of the brain. He contends that he is showing the first symptoms, namely a dislike of contradiction and an avoidance of all people who are likely to contest anything that he says. Wells had been down there lately and stated that he had returned with the determination never to visit Cherkley [Surrey] again, since one came away with a vague sense of humiliation and an acute sense of disquiet.

I drove back with Margot Oxford who, as usual, is very bitter about everything. She is furious with me for joining the New Party and tries to imply that this is a personal disloyalty to the memory of old Asquith [her husband]. When I said that it would be equally disloyal to my affection for that old man to have joined Lloyd George, she merely pinched me very hard with a long, claw-like hand and tells me not to become tiresome. 'People,' she said, 'of your age get into the habit of saying tiresome things. You must break that habit.'

Dined with Clive Bell and Keynes. Keynes is very helpful about the economics of the New Party. He says that he would, without question, vote for it. The attitude of the Labour Party on the Sunday Cinema Bill, as well as that on Free Trade, has disgusted him. He feels that our Party may really do an immense amount of good and that our Programme is more sound and certainly more daring than that which any other party can advance.

Diary   *May 19, 1931*

Go to the Chelsea Flower Show. The rock gardens are pretty poor
owing to the late season, but the herbaceous plants are extremely good.
We take notes of all copper and orange plants for our walls. Have tea
in McLaren's tent. Harry McLaren [later Lord Aberconway] is president
this year and Christabel [his wife] has been spending the afternoon
taking over the King [George V] and Queen [Mary]. She said that ten
minutes before the King arrived, an agitated equerry telephoned from
the Palace to warn them that H.M. was in a furious temper. This did
not diminish her anxiety at the prospect of taking a walk round the
garden with him for over an hour. When he arrived, however, he
appears to have quieted down and to have quite enjoyed himself. His
remarks on being confronted with various plants are characteristic of
the Royal mind. He was shown one hybrid of extreme delicacy and
importance and after gazing at it for a minute in heavy-eyed silence,
remarked: 'What a large quantity of moss they have put round the
roots. I wonder how they manage to get so much moss.' At another
point he was shown some very rare plants for which explorers have
risked their lives. 'Yes,' he said, 'people risk their lives for many curious
objects. What, for instance, would happen to us if this tent came down
upon our heads?' Christabel, unaware whether this was Royal humour
or merely Royal sense of association, hedged by replying, 'That, Sir,
would indeed be terrible.' 'It would indeed,' the King answered.

Diary   *May 28, 1931*

Shaw was at luncheon. He talked a great deal. He said that when he
started to write a play, he never worked out the plot beforehand. What
happened was that he had an idea for a play and started at once writing
the first act. Subsequently, of course, he was aware, while writing, of
the limitations of the stage and he presumed that some censor was at
work within him modelling what he wrote into dramatic form. After
Methuselah, he had determined to write no further plays, but one day
he said to his wife that he was feeling growing pains and a desire to
write further. 'Why,' she said to him, 'do you not write about Joan of
Arc?' He replied, 'I will,' and started writing immediately. In the same

way, *The Doctor's Dilemma* was taken entirely from a chance visit to a London hospital and a conversation with Dr Almroth Wright [originator of anti-typhoid inoculation]. He then spoke a great deal about St Joan saying that she was the first Protestant and the first nationalist in Europe.

Diary   *June 13, 1931*

Down to Sissinghurst. Discuss future plans with Vita and decide that we shall make an enormous tree border run down to the lake. Also decide to run a lime-walk around the top of the moat. Draw designs in the evening for our new wing [eventually abandoned]. Our difficulty is that we do not wish to fake a Tudor reproduction and yet anything 18th-century must look too grand for the rest of the building.

Mosley offered Harold the editorship of the New Party journal Action *— a post which he felt he could not accept because he was bound by contract to Beaverbrook until the end of 1932. Beaverbrook retaliated with the suggestion that if Harold were to leave the New Party, he could edit the* Evening Standard.

Diary   *June 18, 1931*

After dinner, I discuss with V. the situation raised by my luncheon with Beaverbrook. Clearly I am likely to fall between two stools. Were I to enquire further into Beaverbrook's offer, I might well be put in a position of authority on the *Evening Standard* which would mean not merely a very high salary, but also an opportunity of making a decent and influential paper out of it. There is no limit to the possibilities opened by such a prospect. Alternatively, there is a chance that the New Party within five years would be in such a position as to force a coalition upon one of the other two parties. In such a coalition, I should certainly be able to ask for the Foreign Office, and here again, there is no limit to the avenue of extensive power. For some time V.'s responses had become fewer and far between. When I reach the point where I picture myself riding on an elephant at Delhi, I find that for the last half-hour she has been asleep.

Lord Beaverbrook to H.N.

June 25, 1931
Cherkley, Leatherhead

I am very sorry to hear that you are getting more deeply involved in the New Party.

I think the movement has petered out. It might be saved by immense sums of money, and brilliant journalistic support, but of course there is a conspiracy of silence in the newspapers, except for the particular newspapers I am connected with.

I hope you will give up the New Party. If you must burn your fingers in public life, go to a bright and big blaze.

Diary   *July 17, 1931*

I think that Tom at the bottom of his heart really wants a fascist movement, but Allan Young [secretary to the New Party] and John Strachey think only of the British working-man. The whole thing is extremely thin ice and I raised it purposely to see whether the ice had become any thicker. I talk to him afterwards about the paper and we decide we must start immediately and go ahead within the next ten days.

Diary   *July 23, 1931*

I am working at the *Evening Standard* office when, at about 11 a.m., Tom rings me up and says will I come round at once. He had, at that moment, received letters from John Strachey and Allan Young resigning from the Party. I go round at 12.30 and find the Council gathered together in gloom. We try to get hold of our two delinquents but they are out and will not return till 6.0. As 6.0 is the hour at which they announced their intention of communicating their resignation to the Press, that is not of much value. We adjourn for luncheon.

Back to the office. I begin drafting statements to the Press in order to meet John's impending announcement. While thus engaged a letter comes in containing that announcement. It says that they have resigned because Tom, on such subjects as The Youth Movement, Unemployment Insurance, India and Russia, was adopting a fascist tendency. On all these points except Russia (where John's memo was idiotic) they have had their way. I draft another statement.

At 5.30 we at last find they have returned to 7 North Street. Bill Allen [New Party member] and I dash round in a cab. John is at the House but Allan Young is upstairs with Esther. He descends to the dining room looking pale and on the verge of a nervous breakdown. We say that Tom suggests that they should not openly resign at this moment, but 'suspend' their resignation until December 1, by which date they will be able to see whether their suspicions of our fascism are in fact justified. Allan might have accepted this, but at that moment John Strachey enters. Tremulous and uncouth he sits down and I repeat my piece. He says that it would be impossible for him to retain his name on a Party while taking no active direction of that Party's affairs. He would feel that in his absence we were doing things, with his name pledged, of which he would deeply disapprove. He then begins, quivering with emotion, to indicate some of the directions in which Tom has of late abandoned the sacred cause of the worker. He says that ever since his illness Tom has been a different man. His faith has left him. He is acquiring a Tory mind. It is a reversion to type. He considers socialism a 'pathological condition'. John much dislikes being pathological. His great hirsute hands twitched neurotically as he explained to us, with trembling voice, how unpathological he really was.

Undoubtedly the defection of John and his statement that we are turning fascist will do enormous electoral harm to the Party. Politically, however, it will place Tom in a position where, with greater ease, he can adhere to Lloyd George and Winston. I think that John and Allan are inspired with passionate sincerity. Subconsciously, however, Tom's autocratic methods and biting tongue have frayed their vanity and their nerves. I see us from this moment heading straight for Tory Socialism.

Diary   *July 30, 1931*

To luncheon with the Huntingtons[1] to meet James Joyce. We await the arrival of this mysterious celebrity in a drawing-room heavy with the scent of Madonna lilies. Suddenly a sound is heard on the staircase. We stop talking and rise. Mrs Joyce enters followed by her husband. A young looking woman with the remains of beauty and an Irish accent so marked that she might have been Belgian. Well dressed in the clothes of a young French bourgeoise: an art-nouveau brooch. Joyce himself, aloof and blind, follows her. My first impression is of a slightly bearded spinster: my second is of Willie King [authority on Sèvres porcelain] made up like Philip II; my third of some thin bird, peeking, crooked, reserved, violent and timid. Little claw hands. So blind that he stares away from one at a tangent, like a very thin owl.

We go down to luncheon. Gladys Huntington in her excitement talks to Joyce in a very shrill voice on the subject of [Italo] Svevo. She bursts into Italian. I catch the fact that Joyce is contradicting Gladys pretty sharply, and withal with bored indifference, Desmond [Mac-Carthy] weighs in with a talk about Charles Peace and the Partridge murder. I describe the latter with great verve and acumen. 'Are you,' I say to Joyce, hoping to draw him into conversation, 'are you interested in murders?' 'Not,' he answers, with the gesture of a governess shutting the piano, 'not in the very least.' The failure of that opening leads to Desmond starting on the subject of Sir Richard and Lady Burton. The fact that Burton was once consul at Trieste sends a pallid but very fleeting light of interest across the pinched features of Joyce. It is quickly gone. 'Are you interested,' asks Desmond, 'in Burton?' 'Not,' answers Joyce, 'in the very least.' He is not a rude man: he manages to hide his dislike of the English in general and of the literary English in particular. But he is a difficult man to talk to. 'Joyce,' as Desmond remarked afterwards, 'is not a very *convenient* guest at luncheon.'

On August 22 Harold left the Standard *to edit Mosley's* Action. *The first number appeared some six weeks later. On August 24 Ramsay MacDonald abruptly formed a Coalition Government, with himself as Prime Minister,*

---

[1] Constant Huntington, an American, Chairman of Putnam, the publishers.

to the consternation of the Labour Party, most of whose members split from him.

H.N. to Vita

September 8, 1931

Action, 5 Gordon Square, WC1

Madam,

I understand that you are prepared to contribute to this journal a weekly article containing hints to the amateur gardener.

This article should contain 650 words, and the ms of the first article should be received at this office not later than September 22nd.

The fee payable to you for this contribution will be £0.0.0.

Diary

September 22, 1931

Party meeting at 11.30. We discuss *fascismo*. Tom says the young Tories are forcing on an Election for October. He is being approached on all sides to join some combination. The increase in communism will be rapid and immense. But can we counter this by fascism? And will not the Conservative element be represented not by dynamic force but by sheer static obstruction? The worst of it is that the communists will collar our imaginative appeal to youth, novelty and excitement. We decide to call the Youth Movement the Volts (Vigour-order-loyalty-triumph).

Diary

October 1, 1931

Lunch with Sibyl Colefax. A good party. Lady Castlerosse, Diana Cooper, Charlie Chaplin, H.G. Wells, Tom Mosley. We discuss fame. We all agree that we should like to be famous but that we should not like to be recognised. Charlie Chaplin told us how he never realised at first that he was a famous man. He worked on quietly at Los Angeles staying at the Athletic Club. Then suddenly he went on a holiday to New York. He then saw 'Charlie Chaplins' everywhere – in chocolate, in soap, on hoardings, 'and elderly bankers imitated me to amuse their children'. Yet he himself did not know a soul in New York. He walked through the streets where he was famous and yet unknown. He at once went to the photographer and had himself photographed as he really is.

Polling Day in the General Election of 1931 was on October 27. Ramsay MacDonald asked the country to return him as the head of the National Government. He won the Election overwhelmingly.

The New Party's showing was abysmal. All of their twenty-four candidates lost, and twenty-two forfeited their deposits. Harold stood as the New Party candidate for the Combined English Universities; he came last of five candidates, with a vote of 461. Mosley was also defeated, at the bottom of the poll. Soon afterwards Action *ceased publication.*

Diary   *November 2, 1931*

Life is a busy but I am glad to say a mottled business. Hell! Heaven! I am going through a bad period. A period of ill success. I am so used to being successful that failure gives me indigestion. This does not arise from my forfeiting my deposit in the Election. I had foreseen that. It arises from my having been unable to control Hamlyn [General Manager of *Action*] or run the paper in a really efficient manner. The fact is that I am not a journalist and as such not well suited to be a man who runs a weekly. I see both sides of every question. That is a mistake. Yet I should like to make something of this paper. The difficulty is that I am backed and financed by a political party. And even then it is not a party but rather a sly little movement. I am loyal to Tom since I have an affection for him. But I realise that his ideas are divergent from my own. He has no political judgement. He believes in fascism. I don't. I loathe it. And I apprehend that the conflict between the intellectual and the physical side of the New Party may develop into something rather acute.

Diary   *November 24, 1931*

Lunch with Tom and Cimmie over their garage. I beg Tom not to get muddled up with this fascist crowd. I say that in the first place fascism is not suited to England. He says he feels no resentment: that he had expected that the effect of his defeat would be to throw him into a life of pleasure: on the contrary, he feels bored now with night clubs and more interested than ever in serious things. I say that he must now acquire a reputation of seriousness at any cost. That he is destined to lead the Tory Party (at this, Cimmie, who is violently anti–Tory screams aloud) – and that he must rest in patience till that moment comes, and meanwhile travel and write books.

We go on to a Party Meeting. The accounts disclose that we have £1,000 left. That this sum will not suffice to pay the lease and other commitments due in March, and that therefore the Party will have to borrow or steal from the Newspaper fund. As our own circulation has dropped to 30,000 and we are running at a loss of £1,000 a month, the prospect is gloomy.

Diary   *December 23, 1931*

A gloomy day spent in giving notice to the [*Action*] staff. I only hope there will be money enough to pay them good compensation. Vita visits my bank and extracts an unwilling loan from them. My future financial prospects are so black that I groan to gaze into the abyss. I feel irreparably shallow.

Diary   *December 31, 1931*

Of all my years this has been the most unfortunate. Everything has gone wrong. I have lost not only my fortune, but much of my reputation. I incurred enmities: the enmity of Lord Beaverbrook; the enmity of the BBC[1] and the Athenaeum Club; the enmity of several stuffies. I left the *Evening Standard*, I failed in my Election, I failed over

---

[1] Reith, Director General of the BBC, had terminated Harold's contract for a series of talks on modern literature, because Harold praised Joyce's *Ulysses*.

Action. I have been inexpedient throughout. My connection with Tom Mosley has done me harm. I am thought trashy and a little mad. I have been reckless and arrogant. I have been silly. I must recapture my reputation. I must be cautious and more serious. I must not try to do so much, and must endeavour to do what I do with greater depth and application. I must avoid the superficial.

Yet in spite of all this – what fun life is!

In January 1932 Harold and Mosley went to Rome to study fascism at close quarters, and Harold went on alone to Berlin. He was horrified by what he saw, but Mosley was greatly stimulated. The New Party was approaching its transformation into the British Union of Fascists.

Diary

January 1, 1932
Paris

A fine cold morning. Walk up to the Arc de Triomphe through the Tuileries gardens. Memories of my past life: the toy shop in the Rue de Rivoli when we stayed at the Embassy in 1891[1]: the time that Reggie [Cooper, Harold's oldest friend] and I stayed at Versailles and bicycled into Paris every morning leaving our bicycles at the Gare St Lazare: then the successive times at Jeanne's [de Hénaut]: the walk along the Avenue des Acacias learning French vocabularies: the Peace Conference. Thinking of these things I see little children scudding little chips of ice over the round pond. They swirl and tinkle. The fountain clears a space for itself on the pond, blowing sideways. *J'ai plus de souvenirs que si j'avais mille ans* [Baudelaire].

I walk thus, *parmi les avoines folles*, to the Hotel Napoleon. I am taken up to Tom's room. He is in blue pyjamas having only just arisen from sleep. He had spent *réveillon* at the Fabre-Luces and been kept up doing *jeux de société* till 8 a.m. He looks pale. Walk down again the Avenue Friedland and the Faubourg St Honoré. Again these incessant memories – the insistence of which show me how much I now regret the past. The tricolor in the January sun. The swept courtyard of the Embassy. The tug always at my heart of diplomacy in all its forms.

---
[1] When he was five, and his uncle, Lord Dufferin, was British Ambassador to France.

To the Gare de Lyons. The Rome Express, magnificently aligned, waits to receive me and me alone. I occupy the whole of one coach and a very little Frenchman occupies the whole of another coach. Read. Dine lonelily and well. Sleep.

Diary

January 5, 1932
Rome

Tom talks to me about his impressions. He feels that one of our disadvantages as compared with these people is actual costs. In Italy you can run even a daily paper at a little loss. Our own compositors' union is so exacting that we can never compete with the great combines. He believes therefore in the future of our clubs. He feels that we should have two categories: one the Nupa [Youth Movement] clubs, and the other Young England clubs. The latter would be wholly unpolitical. The former would correspond to the S.S. or *Schutzstaffel* organisation of the Nazis. Christopher [Hobhouse, the author] insists that the movement should be working-class. I insist that it should be constitutional and that Tom should enter Parliament. He thinks he could do so with the backing of Winston and the Harmsworth press.

Diary

January 6, 1932
Rome

Spend most of the day reading *fascisti* pamphlets. They certainly have turned the whole country into an army. From cradle to grave one is cast in the mould of fascismo and there can be no escape. I am much impressed by the efficiency of all this on paper. Yet I wonder how it works in individual lives and shall not feel certain about it until I have lived some time in Italy. It is certainly a socialist experiment in that it destroys individuality. It destroys liberty. Once a person insists on how you are to think he immediately begins to insist on how you are to behave. I admit that under this system you can attain to a degree of energy and efficiency not reached in our own island. And yet, and yet ... The whole thing is an inverted pyramid.

Tom cannot keep his mind off shock troops, the arrest of MacDonald

and J.H. Thomas [Secretary of State for the Dominions], their intern-
ment in the Isle of Wight and the roll of drums around Westminster.
He is a romantic. That is his great failing. . . .

                                                        January 7, 1932
Diary   *Rome*

Tom off to Mussolini. He finds him affable, but unimpressive. He
advises Tom not to try the military stunt in England.

                                                        January 9, 1932
Diary   *Rome*

Lunch with the Schuberts at the German Embassy, a bad villa near the
Lateran Palace. They think that Hitler will agree to confirm Hindenburg in his presidency. This will give them another year free from
internal disturbance and may lead to a coalition. I am glad to find
myself again in the old diplomatic atmosphere – so calm, so quiet, so
distinguished. Frau von Schubert stands for all that is best in the old
life, and makes me homesick for it. This homesickness is increased by
another bludgeon attack upon me in the *Times*. . . . I loathe publicity
in any form, as much as father loathed it, yet I seem always to be thrust
into publicity of the most unenviable and damaging nature. I know
that I have been reckless the last two years and that caution is not
among my virtues. But I am not quite so scatter-brain as all that.

                                                       January 18, 1932
Diary   *London*

Go to see Tom on his return from Italy. He was much inspired by
Milan which he found Greek and bracing. He says that Mussolini sent
him a message telling him to call himself Fascist. He does not want to
do anything at present. What he would like would be to lie low till
the autumn, write a book, then rope in Winston Churchill, Lloyd,
Rothermere and if possible Beaverbrook, into a League of Youth. Then

launch an autumn campaign. He fears, however, that the Harmsworths, being restless folk, cannot be 'kept on ice' for so long as the autumn and that we may be forced to do something violent in the spring. It is a bore being thus dependent on the prima donnas of the Press.

Diary

January 27, 1932
Berlin

There was a moment when Hitler stood at the crest of national emotion. He could then have made either a coup d'état or forced a coalition with Brüning. He has missed that moment.[1] The intelligent people feel that the economic situation is so complicated that only experts should be allowed to deal with it. The unintelligent people are beginning to feel that Brüning and not Hitler represents the soul of Germany. In Prussia it is true Hitler is gaining ground. But he is losing it in Bavaria and Württemberg which are comparatively prosperous. Hitlerism, as a doctrine, is a doctrine of despair. I have the impression that the whole Nazi movement has been a catastrophe for this country. It has mobilised and coordinated the discontented into an expectant group: Hitlerism can never satisfy these expectations: the opinion they have mobilised may in the end swing suddenly over to communism. And if that be a disaster (as to which I am still not certain), then Hitler is responsible. The Ambassador [Sir Horace Rumbold] feels that anything may happen and that the only certain thing is uncertainty.

Diary

January 31, 1932

Plant wistaria upon dead apple trees. Feeling depressed. Why? Is it merely that after the debauchery of Berlin I have a liver reaction? Or is it that while at Berlin I have been able to push from myself the realisation of my own practical difficulties and these have swung back upon me with sudden vigour?

There is a dead and drowned mouse in the lily-pond. I feel like that

---

[1] Heinrich Brüning was Chancellor of Germany. Harold had reached Berlin on the very day when Hitler announced that he intended to stand against Hindenburg for the Presidency.

mouse — static, obese and decaying. Viti is calm, comforting and considerate. And yet (for have I not been reading a batch of insulting press-cuttings?) life is a drab and dreary thing. I had a great chance. I have missed it. I have made a fool of myself in every respect.

> Surely there was a time I might have trod
> The sunlit heights, and from life's dissonance
> Struck one clear chord to reach the ears of God?[1]

Very glum. Discuss finance. Vita keeps on saying that we have got enough to go on with. But when one goes into it, that enough represents only two months. I must get a job. Yet all the jobs which pay humiliate. And the decent jobs do not pay. Come back to Long Barn. Arrange my books sadly. Weigh myself sadly. Have put on eight pounds. Feel ashamed of myself, my attainments, and my character. Am I a serious person at all? Vita thinks I could make £2,000 by writing a novel. I don't. The discrepancy between these two theories causes me some distress of mind.

Diary   *March 2, 1932*

Lunch with T.S. Eliot. He is very yellow and glum. Perfect manners. He looks like a sacerdotal lawyer — dyspeptic, ascetic, eclectic. Inhibitions. Yet obviously a nice man and a great poet. My admiration for him does not flag. He is without pose and full of poise. He makes one feel that all cleverness is an excuse for thinking hard. He does one good.

Diary   *March 6, 1932*

In the evening Vita and I discuss finance. Our discussion is interrupted by a sudden desire on her part to take the Blue Train to Biarritz, or why not Syracuse, or why, if one has got so far as that, not go to Greece, or the Lebanon? I point out that we CANNOT AFFORD IT – THAT WE ARE POOR PEOPLE THESE DAYS – she

---

[1] Oscar Wilde's lines prefixed to the Paris edition of his *Poems*, 1881.

says she will make so much money in America [on a lecture tour], and she wants the sun. I long also to go off before I am chained again to an office stool, but it would be madness. We work out that our life costs us no less than £240 a month. That at present we have £600 and about £1,000 owing from America. We do not want to use the latter because of income tax.

Meanwhile Louise [Vita's lady's-maid] during the day has been spreading out the carpets Viti brought from Streatham [one of Lady Sackville's houses]. They are moth-eaten but superb. It is typical of our existence that with no settled income and no certain prospects, we should live in a muddle of museum carpets, ruined castles, and penury. Yet we know very well that all this uncertainty is better for us than a dull and unadventurous security. After dinner we discuss the front of Sissinghurst. We decide to plant a wall of limes, framing the two gables and the arch, and following on to a poplar avenue across the fields. That is our life. Work, uncertainty, and huge capitalistic schemes. And are we wrong? My God! we are not wrong.

Diary   *March 14, 1932*

Feel more happy and healthy than I have felt in my life. This is due to the violet rays at Sissingbags [*sic*], plus lack of unsuccessful occupation. I am doing nothing, therefore I do not fail. I am about to do many things, therefore I am on the verge of success. I know that this verge will not be a very sharp or productive verge. But until I reach it, I feel it will be magnificent, remunerative and calm.

Thus ended Harold's connection with Mosley's New Party and Mosley himself. At the beginning of April he began his novel Public Faces, *set in the not too distant future of 1939. It is a satirical account of a political crisis, involving many of his friends in new roles. It took him three months to write, at the rate of 5,000 words a day. As soon as he had finished it, he began to write* Peacemaking.

Diary   *April 11, 1932*

I have been thinking during the last few days about my book. I have now had three good months of quarantine, and feel that I have at last got the poison of journalism out of my system. I can now settle down to write a book. What book? It comes down to doing either a sequel to *Some People* or a novel on a grand scale. I have toyed with the former idea. Yet I am not happy about it. Sequels are in every case bad things. I expended upon *Some People* the best of my autobiographical experience, and the sense of development which gave unity to that book could not be reproduced again in a book dealing only with my middle life. Again, the note of *Some People* is good-humoured irony plus a certain youthful irreverence: I could not, at my age, recapture the exact mood in which it was written, and if I did, the repetition of that mood might prove ungainly and false. In the third place, I have nothing to write about which interests me on the same scale of *Some People* things.

I shall try, therefore, to write a novel. About what? I think that it should be dramatic, even a romantic, novel. Dealing with diplomacy and character. A central figure, intense as Charles Siepmann [Director of Talks at the BBC], who might be a Private Secretary. A dispute, say in Persia. A Secretary of State such as Joynson Hicks [Home Secretary 1924–9, later Lord Brentford] – unctuous, evangelical, and insincere. A woman Under-Secretary of the type of Hilda Matheson [recently Director of Talks, BBC]. All this could work up into a play eventually. So much for the scaffold: but I must choose a material and a design. There must be a central intellectual theme: and a central emotional theme. I must choose one out of many 'ideas' and concentrate on that: the individual versus the democratic machine; something like that. But apart from all this, it is the *key* which I find difficult – whether ironical or romantic or angry.

Diary   *April 19, 1932*

I go to the New Party meeting in Great George Street. Tom says that he has been asked by Margesson to rejoin the Tory Party, and that he has been asked to lead the Labour Party. He will do neither of these

Harold and Vita at Sissinghurst in 1932

things. He wishes to coordinate all the fascist groups with Nupa and thus form a central fascist body under his own leadership. I say that I think this is a mistake. He says that it would be impossible for him to re-enter the 'machine' of one of the older parties. That by doing so he would again have to place himself in a strait-waistcoat. That he has no desire for power on those terms. That he is convinced that we are entering a phase of abnormality and that he does not wish to be tarred with the brush of the old regime. That he thinks, as leader of the fascists, he could accomplish more than as a party back-bencher, and that in fact he is prepared to run the risk of further failure, ridicule and assault, than to allow the active forces in this country to fall into other hands. I again say that I do not believe this country will ever stand for violence, and that by resorting to violence he will make himself detested by a few and ridiculed by many. He says that may be so but that he is prepared to take the risk. I say that on such paths I cannot follow him. We decide to think it over.

The argument, though painful, is perfectly amicable. The ice cracks at no single moment. Nor do I think that Tom was hurt or imagined for one moment that I was deserting him.

Yet I hated it all, and with battered nerves returned to Cannon Street and took the train home.

Diary   *July 19, 1932*

This lovely summer is amazing. Work hard at Chapter 12. Finish *Secretary of State* [altered to *Public Faces* after the lines by W.H. Auden] at 10.40 p.m.

Diary   *July 29, 1932*

Rains. Start my book on the Peace Conference [*Peacemaking*].

Diary   *October 6, 1932*

Paving across the courtyard finished. They begin upon the windows in the porch. Viti and I plant lupins at the end of the moat walk. *Public Faces* published.

Diary   *October 19, 1932*

A lovely day. Round to the *New Statesman*. Kingsley Martin [editor, 1930–60] indicates that he wants me to become literary editor. That is all very well. But I get £600 a year already from my articles and could not expect to make more than £1,000 a year as Lit. Ed. This would mean that I should gain only £400 a year net and that sum would be absorbed by loss of time and the need to live in London for four days a week. Besides, I think that Raymond [Mortimer] should have that £1,000 a year.

On to Constable's to see Michael Sadleir. He talks about my Peace Conference book. He agrees that it should be in two parts and that the second part should be my diary as it stands. He says that *Public Faces* is going very well. I say, 'How well?' He says that it sold 1,600 copies before publication. I say that Viti's *Family History* [published this year] sold 6,000 copies before publication. He says, 'But then she has broken through.' I say, 'Broken through what?' He says, 'The middle-class belt.' Buy a pair of shoes at Fortnum and Mason.

Diary   *October 21, 1932*

Over to Churt to see Lloyd George. Motor there with Copper [chauffeur] at the wheel. Arrive at 1.0. Gate-piers with Welsh emblems. Cystus and rosemary. A small house. A parlour-maid. A puff of hot air as I enter. Ll.G.'s study. Ceiling up to the roof. Comfortable arm-chairs. Photograph of A.J. Balfour on his writing table, and an engraving of Bonar Law above it. He rises from his hard Windsor chair. He waddles powerfully as of old.

He talks of Tom Mosley. His lack of judgement, his wasted opportunities, his courage. He talks of his early speeches. 'Nobody listened

to him, but I did. I knew that that young man always had something
to say.' About fascism in England, he is not so sure it may not be
possible. One doesn't know. 'I do not know at this moment what our
condition really is. On the surface all seems right enough. But what is
happening underneath?'

We go into luncheon. He discusses bores: he says that a man who
finds any other man a bore is a fool: no man, once you are alone with
him, is a bore: he has always something which he knows better than
other people: it is only when he interrupts other and more vital
informants that he becomes a bore. He talks of Asquith; his inability
to face facts except under pressure. Of [Sir Edward] Grey; his sham
honesty. Of Edward VII; his dignity and his shrewdness; how he never
treated Ll.G. as monarch to subject, but as old man to young man. 'He
was irresistible.' Of Gladstone; his terrifying eyes. We talk Peace
Conference. I go with him back to the study. I produce my thirty
questions which I have prepared. He answers glibly. His answers will
all be embodied in my book. Main new thing is that he thinks President
Wilson had something like a stroke in March [1919]. After April 1 he
fell entirely under the influence of Clemenceau.

Ll.G. is on the surface as hearty and brilliant as ever. But one feels
it is an effort. I felt he was glad that I did not stay long.

*During the first three-and-a-half months of 1933, Harold and Vita went
on a lecture tour of the United States and Canada. For Harold it was the
first of many visits; for her it was the first and last. Their schedule was
exhausting, and it coincided with a grave economic crisis in America. They
visited fifty-three cities, spent sixty-three nights in the train and covered over
30,000 miles.*

                                                    December 31, 1932
Diary   *On board* Bremen *in Atlantic*

A fine sun–swept day with great towers of waves hurtling past us and
mantling on the horizon. Too rough to work. We lie on our beds and
read. Eat huge meals. It gets calmer in the evening. An attempt at
réveillon – consisting mostly of balloons.

A lovely year for which I thank life heartily. I have got rid of both journalism and politics. All the horrors of 1931 are behind me. I enjoyed writing *Public Faces* and it has had a certain success. I have enjoyed my articles for the *New Statesman* which have also helped my reputation. I have loved working on my book on the Peace Conference. Vita, except for overwork in the summer, has been well and happy. Rebecca has entered our life.[1] Ben has left Eton, having recovered his self-esteem there. Niggs is as sensible and hard-working and sweet as ever, and Sissinghurst has become for us the real home which we shall always love. I do not expect that I shall ever love a year so much as this year. And I render thanks.

Diary

January 5, 1933
New York

Wake up at 5.30. Dress and go on deck. It is warm with a faint rain. We are in the East River. By 7.30 it is quite light and two tenders come alongside. We file up for the medical examination and the passports. Having finished the passports we dash out to see the entry into New York. We are intercepted by reporters. We take them to the writing room and sit around a table. They ask us questions. What do we think of American women? What do we think of the future of marriage?

We drive through Brooklyn in a car. A lovely morning. All very like Berlin. Suddenly as we reach Manhattan Bridge the skyline indents itself for us. Up Broadway and Madison to this hotel. Rooms 1852 and 1853. Nesting boxes. As we enter the room the telephone rings. Press people arrive. Bootleggers ring up. Social hostesses ring up. There are two telephones, one in each room, and three publicity agents, that of the hotel, that of Doubleday and that of Colston Leigh [lecture agent].

The afternoon is a further succession of journalists, flowers, bell-hops, photographs, telephones. We have no time to unpack and change our clothes.

---

[1] A wire-haired terrier.

We go to a suite at the Waldorf Astoria where we dine. Charles Lindbergh and his wife are there.[1]

Lindbergh is a surprise. There is much more in his face than appears from photographs. He has a fine intellectual forehead, a shy engaging smile, windblown hair, a way of tossing his head unhappily, a transparent complexion, thin nervous capable fingers, a loose-jointed shy manner. He looks young with a touch of arrested development. His wife is tiny, shy, timid, retreating, rather interested in books, a tragedy at the corner of her mouth. One thinks of what they have been through and is shy to meet them.

We go on to the Empire State Building. The lights of the great avenues sparkle like fire-flies. But there are great dark patches where there are no fire-flies at all. The great water spaces. The shadows of huge buildings. Little cabs creeping like lice. To bed at 1.0. Not tired. Oh brave new world!

Diary

January 8, 1933
New York

Lunch with Elizabeth Marbury,[2] at 13 Sutton Place. Find Mrs Vanderbilt there representing society. [Hendrik] Van Loon [the historian] representing literature. Wylie representing journalism – he is editor of the *New York Times*. Miss Marbury is enormous, emphatic, civilised, gay. She says she is 76 and has never been so happy as in the last fifteen years. All passion spent. She abuses all other agents. She wants [Vita's] *Seducers in Ecuador* put into a play. Van Loon is Dutch but very Americanised. Wylie is pure American.

Now, here were three people corresponding roughly to [James] Garvin, Ethel Smyth and Maynard Keynes. And this, with infinite slowness, was one of the many stories that Wylie told: 'That,' he said, 'reminds me of a story I heard the other day down town. A man is taken from speak-easy to speak-easy. He returns to his wife after having music of negro orchestras drummed into his ears. She says, "How are

---

[1] Since his solo transatlantic flight in 1927, Lindbergh had been America's hero. His fame was increased by the kidnapping of his baby son, whose body was found in a wood a month later.

[2] The author and literary agent, who died a fortnight after this meeting.

you feeling?" He says, "Rather syncopated." She looks up "syncopated" in the dictionary and finds it says "passing rapidly from bar to bar".' We laugh politely. But it is incredible that such a story should be told by people and to people who are really educated. It is this that I find so trying. They are so slow in conversation that it is like being held up by a horse-dray in a taxi. And then they never listen to what one says oneself.

The depression is dreadful. All the hotels are bankrupt. Most apartments are empty. The great Rockefeller buildings, and the two theatres, are to close down. Rockefeller will lose some £3,000,000 a year by this venture. Four thousand architects out of work in New York alone.

January 27, 1933
Washington

Diary

Viti and I drive out to Mount Vernon [George Washington's house]. We stop on the way to see the Lincoln memorial and the statue. It is impressive with its sunken eyes and heavy working-man hands. But there is a look of angered despair in the face by which I am not surprised. The dramatic effect is heightened by flood lighting in the roof. Then along the grey Potomac in a gathering snow storm. Mount Vernon is impressive in its simple magnificence. There is a park-like farm with a big estate feel about it. The ceilings and the furniture indicate a high level of culture and taste.

Lunch at the Embassy. Then on to the Senate. The Vice President [Charles Curtis] presides. A bleary, tobacco drugged looking man. He has a wooden mallet which he holds by the hammer end tapping irritably with it against the wood of the desk. Around the tribune sit little boys like the elder sons of peers on the steps of the throne. They wear black plus fours with black woollen stockings and shoes. They giggle and pick their noses. From time to time a Senator beckons to them and they run messages giggling back at their fellows. The desks for the Senators are arranged in a rough semicircle with a gangway down the middle. The room itself is rectilinear and scarcely decorated at all. Two brown-wood roll-top desks are pushed against the wall. There is a hard top light from the glass ceiling and busts along the cornice. Under each desk is a spittoon of green glass. The Senators, when they speak, turn their back upon the President and address each other walking away from their desks. They all look stout, solid, blear-eyed and sulky. [William E.] Borah [Dean of the Senate] is there. He is not what I expected. I expected an ascetic, arrogant, enfevered face: it is just an untidy rather unimportant sort of face, shaking his invincible locks.

We are picked up there by Elizabeth Lindsay[1] and she and Vita drive on to the White House. Negro footmen in dark livery with silver buttons. Aides-de-camp in white gloves and cigarettes. They are given tea. Two negroes stand behind President Hoover at attention like eunuchs.

January 28, 1933
British Embassy, Washington

H.N. to his mother

Since I last wrote we have been all over New England and have given some eight or ten lectures each. We have stayed with private people, at hotels, at girls' schools, at women's colleges. It is not as exhausting as I had expected. I fear however that once the novelty has worn off we shall find it almost intolerably boring. The same people, the same questions, the same food, the same iced water. It is all rubbish saying that one gets drink in the United States. I daresay that the young men about town manage to have their flasks, but the elderly school ma'ams who seem to constitute our major clientele never see or offer anything except iced water – and for days on end we have had no other beverage to quicken our exhausted minds. I daresay it is a good thing. I do not find I really miss it.

I have been over Harvard and Yale and many women's colleges. The whole standard of comfort is fifty times higher than our own and the standard of culture about fifty times lower. But they are all terribly in earnest and gradually they may get to know the difference between teaching and learning. All the houses are comfortable and all the people kind. Too kind, too kind ...

---

[1] Sir Ronald Lindsay, who had been Harold's Chief in Berlin, was now British Ambassador in Washington.

Diary

February 7, 1933
Chicago

Wake up to find a blizzard proceeding outside. The whole place howls and whirls and boils. It is like smoke blowing upwards. Lake Michigan is frozen right up to the beach and in ridges in the shape of breakers. The lake further out, where it has always been frozen, is a dark scabby colour. A few cars struggle along Lake Shore Drive, twist and stagger and then get stuck. The snow banks against their mud guards and radiators. Vita has to catch the 11.30 for St Louis. She will not let me go to the station. She disappears into a revolving snow landscape through a revolving glass door.

H.N. to Vita (in Wisconsin)

February 16, 1933
British Embassy, Washington

Lunched with Alice Longworth [eldest daughter of Theodore Roosevelt]. My word! How I like that woman! There is a sense of freedom in her plus a sense of background. That I feel is what is missing in this country – that sense of background. Nobody seems to have anything behind their front. Poor people, they feel it themselves and hence all those pitiful gropings after manor-houses in Wiltshire and parish registers and the Daughters of the Founding Fathers. But Alice Longworth has a world position and it has left her simple and assured and human. Yes, there at least is an American who is unquestionably a woman of importance.

H.N. to Vita (in Columbus, Ohio)

February 17, 1933
Charleston, South Carolina

I feel rather guilty as I have been enjoying myself these days and you must have been having an absolutely foul time. My poor sweet. It isn't fair. That's what comes of being a celebrity and having a husband and two children to support.

I went to the train [in Washington] having stolen a large bottle of brandy.

February 18, 1933
H.N. to Vita   *Charleston, South Carolina*

Charleston really is delightful. It has personality – which is a thing most American towns and people lack. The whole place is old in character and southern. The old atmosphere of lazy, untidy, dignified, lotus-eating, anti-noise and rush. Even their voices are soft. They loathe 'taste' which they call *Lady's Journal*, and they keep old Victorian things in their houses so as not to 'become period'. Their servants are all black nannies like in magazine stories, but they refuse to sentimentalise about them. They are infinitely less affected, more proud, than the denizens of Rye and Broadway.

Dubose Heywood – author of *Porgy* [1925] – picked us up. A very thin, quiet, interesting man. He motored us out to Middleton Place, some fifteen miles away. We drove through avenues of huge ilexes draped in Spanish moss. It isn't moss in the least but a hanging creeper like old man's beard. The effect is as if every tree were draped in widow's weeds of grey. In detail it is ugly and untidy: in the mass it is strange and impressive.

Middleton Place was one of the great plantation seats. It is as romantic in its way as Sissinghurst. Enormous ilexes, eighteen feet round in the trunk, flank a wide lawn cut up into high beds of camellias in flower. . . .

We came back and I came face to face with Elizabeth Lindsay. We fell into each other's arms. I said I had been to Middleton. She said, 'Now what did it remind you of?' I said it had reminded me strangely of something but I could not say what. She said, 'Well, it's Vita's poem *Sissinghurst*.' Of course it was. She is no fool, that Elizabeth.

I gave my lecture in a lovely Adam hall with old pictures. The whole thing is so effortless and unaffected here. No strain. No noise. I delight in it. We MUST come. They are all longing to see you. Great passion-spenters.[1]

---

[1] Vita's novel *All Passion Spent* was as great a best-seller in America as it had been in England.

February 23, 1933
H.N. to Vita (in Newark, Delaware)   *Cincinnati, Ohio*

I confess that I myself find all this slushy adulation very trying – and irritating in the sense that all unrealities are irritating. Of course I know that you and I are very gifted and charming. Only we are not charming in the sort of way these people suppose.

One should remember, however, that if we were lecturing at Cheltenham, Roedean College, Bath and Harrogate we should be faced with just the same vapidity of compliment, by just the same uniformity of faces. I try to concentrate on the really nice people we have met. It is not that these people are really less civilised than similar sorts of people in England. It is just that at home we should be bored stiff by that sort of person, and that here we have the feeling (which may or may not be justified) that there simply does not exist the sort of other person whom we like. If you cut out the territorial aristocracy and the types which have gathered round them in England, and also cut out our scholars and our intellectuals – one would be left with a residue which would be no better than, and possibly worse than, our audiences.

March 4, 1933
Diary   *Toledo, Ohio*

We have luncheon with a Women's Club. Daffodils and wallflowers on the table. The rest of the guests at little tables all around. I sit next to a woman in purple silk. 'Well, Mr Nicolson, and are you going right out to the coast?' 'Yes, Mrs Scinahan, we go to San Francisco, Los Angeles and Pasadena. We then visit the Grand Canyon.' 'That is swell for you, Mr Nicolson. When I first saw the Grand Canyon I said, "My, if only Beethoven could have seen this." You see, I am very musical. I do not know how people can see life steadily unless they are musical. Don't you feel that way, Mr Nicolson?'

Meanwhile the inauguration of President Roosevelt was proceeding in Washington and a huge voice was braying out across the daffodils in their art-ware. '*And now,*' yelled the voice, '*the historic moment is about to arrive. I can see the President-Elect . . .*' The band strikes up at that moment *Hail to the Chief.* My neighbour pauses for a moment while we have the President's inaugural address. It is firm and fine. 'It is such a pity,' twitters Mrs Scinahan beside me, 'that you are only staying such a short time in Toledo, Mr Nicolson. I would wish to have you see our museum here. We have a peristyle of the purest white marble – a thing of utter simplicity but of the greatest beauty. I always say that the really beautiful things in life such as the Sistine Madonna are beautifully simple.' '*Small wonder*,' boomed the voice of President Roosevelt, '*that confidence languishes, for it thrives only on honesty, on honour, on the sacredness of obligation, on faithful protection, on unselfish performance . . .*' 'You see,' whispered Mrs Scinahan, 'the peristyle is lit by hidden lights in the cornice. And they change colour, Mr Nicolson, from the hues of sunrise to those of midday and then to sunset. And at night it is all dark blue. Very simple.'

I strive to catch the historic words of Roosevelt. 'You see, Mr Nicolson,' whispered Mrs Scinahan, 'our peristyle is a dream in stone. Now I mean that literally. The architect, Mr J.V. Kinhoff, dreamt of that very peristyle. And one day . . .' 'Mrs Scinahan,' I say firmly, 'do you realise that your new President has just proclaimed that he will, if need be, institute a dictatorship?' 'My,' she said, 'now isn't that just too interesting? Not that I care for the radio, Mr Nicolson. We have one, of course, at home above the bathing-pool. It sounds so much better out of doors.'

Afterwards, Viti and I have to stand up to say a few words. I get back on them by stating that they have just listened to the most important announcement in American history. We then go to the station and entrain for Detroit.

Diary

March 18, 1933
San Francisco

We are met on the landing by Mr Gaer of the *San Francisco Forum*, a representative of the *San Francisco Examiner*, and a stout gentleman with a carnation who I discover afterwards is the manager of the William Tylor Hotel. We drive off. Vita is silent, looking to right and left in order to catch sight of an earthquake up a side street before it reaches us. She holds her bag tightly in one hand and me in the other in order to jump out quickly with her two possessions once the tremors begin.[1] We reach the hotel. A facade of brick. Now Vita had been told especially that we must go to a steel and not brick hotel. The porter begins to take off our bags, and the second taxi with the manager and his carnation arrives. I murmur feebly, 'Is this hotel built of steel?' 'Steel and brick,' they answer. Dumb victims of an impending earth catastrophe, we enter the hotel. We are taken up to the thirteenth floor where there is a lovely view from a corner window. From there I observe the Pacific. Vita, however, has only observed that we are terribly far off from the ground. 'Isn't,' she says, 'this very high up?' Being a tactful man, and having a bad cold, I do not press the two points which have arisen in my consciousness. I do not say 'there is the Pacific' since that would have suggested stout Cortez and Vita at the moment is not feeling stout in the least. Nor do I suggest that it is very questionable whether in an earthquake it is better to be high up or low down. In the former case there is less to fall on top of one, in the latter case there is less distance for oneself, if it comes to the point, to fall. I avoid these controversial topics and seize the telephone. 'Couldn't we have a room lower down?' We can have a room on the fifth floor if we want. I am thus robbed of my view of the Pacific Ocean, but we leave it at that, and the rooms are larger and nicer.

March 28, 1933
Smoke Tree Ranch, California

Diary

We reach Smoke Tree Ranch and are shown our cottage – an asbestos hut with bedrooms, shower room and kitchenette. Mr Doyle, the owner of the ranch, comes to visit us. The desert is all around us with sage bush and verbena in flower. The hills across the plain are pink and crinkled as in Persia. We are very happy. Unpack and write up this diary. We then go across the sand between the little tamarisk hedges and enter Mr Doyle's house. We are given mint julep. We then cross to dinner in the main cottage. Good food. I do not sleep well as the desert air is too exciting. The coyotes howl in the hills.

---

[1] There had been a severe earthquake in San Francisco a few weeks previously.

April 1, 1933
Diary   *Grand Canyon, Arizona*

... The train reaches the Grand Canyon at 8.10 mountain time. We walk to the hotel a few yards away and go on to the terrace from which the Grand Canyon opens before us. It is very like the Devonshire Cliffs near Dawlish only without the sea. It gets less like Dawlish as one looks at it after breakfast, and becomes more like the Grand Canyon in Arizona – twenty Matterhorns blazing with alpine glow and situated many thousand feet below one. We walk on further for a bit and sit under the pines. We find some seeds of unknown plants and a saxifrage. We then walk back to the hotel just in time for a dance of Hopi Indians.

A fat chief in feathers explains in that flat voice assumed by orientals when they know English very well, that the Hopis are a very peaceful tribe and as such have no war dance, but that he will show us the sort of war dance that they would have had had they been a less peaceful tribe. Having given us this bright explanation he starts to yell aloud and shake a cardboard shield and a bow and arrow. Being a stout man, and his assistant brave not being very well, the dance is defective in vigour. There is also an eagle dance and a cow dance – neither of which carry much conviction. A good deal of shuffling in moccasins and shaking of bells and feathers. Vita is deeply impressed by the Grand Canyon.[1] So am I.

They returned home in the Bremen *in mid-April to the domestic felicities of Sissinghurst. Harold began writing his book on Lord Curzon, and finished it by November. They were still worried by their financial problem, and by the continuing problems of Harold's future. Which was he to be – a writer who dabbled in politics, or a politician who enjoyed writing?*

---

[1] In 1942 she wrote a novel, *Grand Canyon*, based on this visit.

Diary   *May 9, 1933*

Storm and sun. Ben goes to Brighton to see B.M., who behaves with
devilry by telling him things to put him against his mother and me.
Luckily it doesn't work – but it will have been a shock to him and
might have had very serious consequences. Feel sick with anger.[1]

Diary   *May 27, 1933*

Go to tea with the Drummonds. [Lord] Eustace Percy there. He walks
back with me. He says that the world does not realise how far the
capitalist system has really broken down. I say that it is not the old
question of rich versus poor, but of man versus the machine. He says
that it is merely the old thing of consumption and production in
another form. I say, 'Is it, Eustace, seriously now?' He says, 'No,
Harold, it isn't. It is a new factor.' We discuss whether economics are
a science or an art. We agree that the Victorians regarded it as pat as
Latin grammar. Now there is the something unknown. That has
rendered economics more dynamic and far less respectable.

I ask him whether he thinks I am lotus-eating by living in the
country and doing what I love. He says that serious people ought to
withdraw from life nowadays as it is so transitional as to entail insin-
cerity. I feel comforted by him: I am worried about Ben: I am worried
about life: and this old friend is calm and sincere. He says what he likes
is administration. He should be head of a great university.[2] In spite of
his pessimistic views I leave him feeling more confident. As long as we
keep our intellectual integrity we shall be all right. I lost it in 1931: I
have got it back today.

---

[1] Lady Sackville had told Ben about his mother's affairs with Violet Trefusis and Virginia
Woolf. Ben described the incident in *Portrait of a Marriage*, pp. 180–1.
[2] Later he was. He was Rector of the Newcastle Division (King's College) of Durham
University, 1937–52.

Diary *June 16, 1933*

Work hard at *Curzon* [*Curzon, The Last Phase*]. Lady Curzon writes that she is going to write the life herself. That means that she will do his personal side and use all the letters she promised me. This is really not such a blow as it sounds since the book will be mainly a study of post-war diplomacy and I do not wish to cram it with personal detail. Moreover it leaves me free to say what I like. We decided yesterday quite suddenly at luncheon to go off to Italy for three weeks. These improvised excursions are the best. We shall leave on the 25th.

Diary *June 21, 1933*

Have a long talk with Gladys Marlborough [the second wife of the ninth Duke of Marlborough] about Proust. She had known him for years. She said that his snobbishness was just snobbishness and that there was little more to say about it. He would repeat names to himself succulently. Once she said to him that she thought the Duke of Northumberland had a lovely name. He was very excited. '*Tiens,*' he exclaimed, '*je vais l'annoncer.*' And up he got, flung the door open and yelled, '*Madame la Duchesse de Northumberland!*' This brought on a fit of coughing and wheezing. She also said that Albert ['Albertine'] was not, as I had been told, a Syrian waiter, but a boy at the Lycée Condorcet. He deliberately made Proust jealous. Proust loved Hardy. He said that *A Pair of Blue Eyes* was of all books the one which he would himself most gladly have written.

Diary *August 4, 1933*

Wystan Auden reads us some of his new poem in the evening. It is in alliterative prose and divided into Cantos.[1] The idea is Gerald Heard as Virgil guiding him through modern life. It is not so much a defence of communism as an attack upon all the ideas of comfort and complacency which will make communism difficult to achieve in this

---

[1] An unpublished, untitled, poem of some 2,000 lines, of which a copy is in the Swarthmore College library, PA, USA.

country. It interests me particularly as showing, at last, that I belong to an older generation. I follow Auden in his derision of patriotism, class distinctions, comfort, and all the ineptitudes of the middle classes. But when he also derides the other soft little harmless things which make my life comfortable I feel a chill autumn wind. I feel that were I a communist, the type of person I should most wish to attack would not be the millionaire or the imperialist, but the soft, reasonable, tolerant, secure, self-satisfied intellectual like Vita and myself. A man like Auden with his fierce repudiation of half-way houses and his gentle integrity makes one feel terribly discontented with one's own smug successfulness. I go to bed feeling terribly Edwardian and back-number, and yet, thank God, delighted that people like Wystan Auden should actually exist.

Diary   *August 26, 1933*

After luncheon at Lympne [Sir Philip Sassoon's house] Colonel T.E. Lawrence, the uncrowned king of Arabia, arrives. He is dressed in an Air Force uniform which is very hot. Unlike other privates in the Air Force he wears his heavy uniform when he goes out to tea. He has become stockier and squarer. The sliding, lurcher effect, is gone. A bull terrier in place of a saluki.

Diary   *October 11, 1933*

Go to see Tom Mosley at Ebury Street. He has had a bad back and is lying down. One of his fascist lieutenants is there but leaves us. He says he is making great progress in town and country alike. He gets very little money from the capitalists but relies on canteens and subscriptions. His aim is to build up from below gradually, and not to impose construction from above as we did in New Party days. Whenever anything happens to remind him of Cimmie,[1] a spasm of pain twitches across his face. He looked ill and pasty. He has become an excellent father and plays with the children. Cimmie's body is still at Cliveden in the chapel, and he visits it once a week.

---

[1] Cynthia Mosley had died five months earlier, aged thirty-four.

Then to the London Library. H.A.L. Fisher [the historian] in the chair. He talks to me afterwards about Curzon. He says he was above all a *savant* and an historian and not a man of action. That he would bore the Cabinet by endless discourses, and when asked for his policy would look disconcerted and astonished. Fisher never once knew Lloyd George to be rude to Curzon.

Diary   *October 27, 1933*

Viti gets a letter from her French bank saying she has a balance there of £2,600. We decide on this that I shall NOT have to sell myself to Beaverbrook. I am immensely relieved. The dread of the ordeal and humiliation had been hanging over me like a sullen cloud. Work hard and cheerfully at Chapter IX [of *Curzon*]. Very cold and damp. In the afternoon plant irises and mark out the path in the kitchen garden.

Diary   *November 23, 1933*

Read through the whole of *Curzon*. A most disappointing book. It falls between two stools. It is too detailed and historical for the ordinary reader, and not documented enough for the student or as a work of reference. If I could be certain of getting the papers out of Lady Curzon I should write the whole thing over again. She is a most tiresome and inconsiderate woman.

Diary   *December 24, 1933*

I have got into the way of taking my happiness for granted. Yet Viti is not a person one can take for granted. She really does not care for the domestic affections. She would like life to be conducted on a series of *grandes passions*. Or she thinks she would. In practice, had I been a passionate man, I should have suffered tortures of jealousy on her behalf, have made endless scenes, and we should now have separated, I living in Montevideo as H.M. Minister and she breeding Samoyeds in the Gobi Desert.

Diary   *December 31, 1933*

A year coloured by two anxieties, some disappointments and much
pleasure. The first anxiety was Niggs' illness [appendicitis], which
caused us agony at the time but which has left no traces. The second
has been money worry. By giving up what B.M. ought to pay us under
settlements we are flung back upon what we can make. It is quite clear
that as long as B.M. lives and unless we begin to make more money
by books, we are in for a very difficult time. This for me is a constant
anxiety. Vita takes it more calmly. B.M. is likely to live five more years
at least[1] and to become more and more paranoiac. No job that I could
get in London would really make the difference unless I sold myself to
Beaverbrook which I cannot face. Thus at the back of all our life is a
sense of worry and possible disaster.

   In addition to all this there is the sad feeling that I have not made
the best of my life. I cannot write better than I write now, and my best
is little more than hack-work. My three books on diplomacy will have
a certain value since they represent experience, study, and a certain
amount of practical reflection. But they are not good enough to justify
my having cut adrift from public service. Had I remained in diplomacy
I should have had at least the illusion of progress. The horrors of age
would have been compensated for by material rewards. I should have
been soothed by the fallacy that 'Minister', 'Ambassador' etc. did
represent some sort of progression, some rising scale of achievement.
Yet would I *really* have been lulled by such a fallacy? I do not think so.
The constant work might have given me the illusion of creative activity,
whereas the self-centred work that I do now seldom gives me that
illusion. On the other hand, I should have ruined my domestic happiness and sacrificed much personal enjoyment. It would not be true
to say that I 'regret' having left diplomacy. What I regret is that I did
not from the first devote my energy to some profession which could
have been combined with my present sort of life.

*Vita, and Harold's sister Gwen, went to Italy, where Harold joined them, and
from there to Morocco, where he had spent much of his childhood. He conceived*

---
[1] Lady Sackville died two years later, in January 1936.

*the idea of a six-volume autobiography, but did not pursue it. After a severe
but short illness, he returned to Sissinghurst for the summer.*

                                                  February 1, 1934
H.N. to Vita   *4 King's Bench Walk, EC4*

Your telegram arrived saying that you have taken the Castello [at
Portofino]. Well, I am all for that sort of thing, as you know. I liked
being turned out of my dear little suburban home [Long Barn] and
made to sleep in a ruined tower on a camp-bed [Sissinghurst]. And I
see no reason why, in the present state of our finances, you did not
buy the Castello outright. You might also lease the Carnarvon Villa in
case Olive Rinder comes to stay with us. But I am glad all the same.
It all comes from Gwen reading the Tauchnitz edition of the works of
Elizabeth Russell.[1] I hope you are both very uncomfortable and happy.
Bless you both.

                                                  February 4, 1934
H.N. to Vita   *Munich, en route to Portofino*

I found that Jim Lees-Milne[2] was going over to Paris on the Friday . . .
He had never been to Versailles so we went out there to lunch. It was
quite empty and very cold and magnificent. We lunched at the Trianon
Palace where the Treaty was presented to the Germans in 1919. Very
odd it was after all these years. We walked to the Trianon and then up
through the park to the Chateau. I picked up several hints for Sissinghurst. The *Basin de Neptune* would do well in Mr Nicolson's
rondel.

   Jim is such a charming person. He has a passion for poetry and
knows masses about it. I like my friends to be well-read and well-bred.
Jim is such an aristocrat in mind and culture. You would like him
enormously.

   I walked to [James] Joyce's flat in the Rue Gallilée. It is a little

---

[1] Her famous novel, *The Enchanted April*, was set in the Castello.
[2] The architectural historian who acquired many historic houses for the National Trust.
In 1934 he was aged twenty-five.

furnished flat and stuffy and prim as a hotel bedroom. The sitting room was like a small salon at a provincial hotel, and the unreal effect was increased by there being florists' baskets about with arranged flowers. Joyce glided in. It was evident that he had just been shaving. He was very spruce and nervous and natty. Great rings upon little twitching fingers. Huge concave glasses which flicked reflections of lights as he moved his head like a bird, turning it with that definite insistence to the speaker as blind people do who turn to the sound of the voice. Joyce was wearing large bedroom slippers in check, but except for that one had the strange impression that he had put on his best suit. He was very courteous as shy people are. His beautiful voice trilled on slowly like Anna Livia Plurabelle [in *Finnegans Wake*]. He has the most lovely voice I know – liquid and soft with undercurrents of gurgle.

He told me how the ban had been removed from *Ulysses* (Oolissays, he calls it) in America. He had hopes of having it removed in London also and was in negotiation with John Lane. He seemed rather helpless and ignorant about it all, and anxious to talk to me. One has the feeling that he is surrounded with a group of worshippers and that he has little contact with reality. This impression of something unreal was increased by the atmosphere of the room, the mimosa with its ribbon, the bird-like twitchings of Joyce, the glint of his glasses, and the feeling that they [Joyce and his son] were both listening for something in the house – a shriek of maniac laughter from the daughter along the passage. He told me that a man had taken Oolissays to the Vatican and had hid it in the cover of a prayer book, and that it had been blessed in such a disguise by the Pope. He was half-amused by this and half-impressed. He saw that I would think it funny, and at the same time he did not think it wholly funny himself. It was almost as if he had told me the story in the belief that it might help to lift the ban in England.

My impression of the Rue Gallilée was the impression of a very nervous and refined animal – a gazelle in a drawing-room. His blindness increases that impression. I suppose he is a real person somewhere, but I feel that I have never spent half-an-hour with anyone and been left with an impression of such brittle and vulnerable strangeness.

February 9, 1934
Diary   *Portofino*

Drive up to Max Beerbohm's villa [at Rapallo]. He meets us. It is a
shock. He is quite round; his cheeks have chubbed round a scarlet nose
like two melons with a peppercorn between them. And his head has
sunk sideways a trifle – a very different thing from the neat slim
seductive person I first remember. Mrs Beerbohm appears straw-
coloured and *affairée*. Then Gerhart Hauptmann [the German drama-
tist] and his wife. He is more magnificent than ever. A huge grey
frock-coat of which the waistcoat buttons up almost to the chin
disclosing a little black stock from which hangs a huge *catena* of
tortoiseshell at the end of which is (as I later observe) a flat gold watch.
    We go up to the little house for luncheon. It is almost unbearably
hot, but the food and wine are excellent. Hauptmann talks a great deal
and very simply. He talks about the lack of harmony in the German
character. 'But you,' I say to him, 'seem to be harmony personified.'
'Yes,' he answers, '*aber nach siebzig jahre bestrebungen* [but after exerting
myself for seventy years].' Max, who speaks no German, says little, and
in fact I scarcely had a word with him.

February 10, 1934
Diary   *Cap Ferrat*

I leave the Castello; Vita and Gwen remaining on till tomorrow. I take
the train for Genoa and at Genoa I take a Pullman car which provides
an excellent luncheon and lands me at Beaulieu at 2.45 or so. Met by
Gerald Haxton [Somerset Maugham's secretary]. The King of Siam is
expected and there are people in uniform in front of the waiting room
and a red carpet. Drive to Villa Mauresque [Maugham's villa]. Willy
Maugham plays billiards with Gerald for a bit and I read my beloved
Proust. The house is all white and furnished with Chinese things of
great value and therefore very few. A lovely house. We motor into
Nice and then on to Cannes where at the Carlton bar we meet Michael
Arlen and his wife. Dine with them. Willy Maugham tells me two
stories about Lillie Langtry.[1] They were crossing to America together

---

[1] Mistress of Edward VII.

and one night on deck she mentioned a man called Eckmühl, or something like that. Willy said he had never heard of Eckmühl. 'But,' said Mrs Langtry, 'he was famous on two continents.' 'And why was he famous?' asked Willy. 'I loved him,' she answered quite simply. Then there was another story. She had an affair with the Crown Prince Rudolf or Archduke Leopold or someone – anyway a potent potentate to be. They were sitting in front of the fire and had a row. She took off a huge emerald ring which he had given her and cast it into the flames. He immediately dropped down on his knees and began to rummage in the ashes. 'Naturally,' said Mrs Langtry, 'I couldn't love him again.'

Michael Arlen is one of the few writers who have had the sense to realise that his great vogue was not permanent, and that he must treat his income as capital. Thus although he was at one time making about £20,000 a year, I doubt whether he actually earns today more than £1,200. But he has investments. He is a decent companionable person, clever and intelligent. The two so seldom go together.

February 11, 1934
Cap Ferrat

Diary

Since I left Munich – and in this sunshine – an idea has been forming in my mind. 'I shall,' I said suddenly to myself, 'write an autobiography in six volumes. It will be called F.A. or *Fictional Autobiography*. It will be dedicated to Vita.'

Since then the thing has seldom been absent from my mind, and I see the whole scheme as a vast undertaking stretching over ten years. Primarily it will be a study in mutations. But I shall try and give to it a serious philosophical shape. I may be wrong, but I feel in the last year I have found myself. And if my present mood of energy and confidence persists, then I shall bring the whole thing off.

Curiously enough, the idea has shown me one thing clearly. I have been toying with the theory that when B.M. dies I shall go into politics, and many of my day-dreams have centred upon the picture of my returning to the Foreign Office as Secretary of State. But now that I am obsessed by the IDEA all of this seems perfectly trivial, and is disclosed as an attempt to solace myself for not writing better by the illusion that I am really a man of action. Thus I now see six volumes ahead of me – *à la recherche du temps perdu*. Tangier fits in beautifully for this.

February 18, 1934
Marrakesh, Morocco

Diary

Begin taking notes for my *magnum opus*. Rather appalled by its hugeness. After luncheon we go down to the town. The [Atlas] mountains are visible and it is very warm. Walk about the market. There are story tellers and snake-charmers and conjurers. The whole atmosphere is unchanged since thirty years ago. A lovely new moon in the evening. Please God make me able to do my *magnum opus*.

February 19, 1934
Marrakesh

Diary

Is the book to be fictional or accurate? There is much I do not mind saying about myself but much which would, if truly told, cause trouble to other people. The only standard, I think, is to expose myself to any amount of shame but to disguise other people so that they will not get involved in my humiliations. Yet the book will be nothing if it is not true.

Proust was not honest enough. If I do not possess his talent, I do possess far more courage. I have a good memory, an observant nature, and have lived through one of the most interesting fifty years in the history of human civilisation. If I can reproduce those years in a really sincere form I shall have contributed something to human understanding. But can I be sincere without wounding people less pachydermatous than myself? The only thing about which I know anything is myself. Yet I was not alone.

March 10, 1934
Diary   *Tangier*

My ear, which was stung at Fez, has begun to suppurate. I do not
know how to treat it and send for the doctor. Spend the morning
working on my proofs [of *Curzon*, published on May 10].

March 19, 1934
Diary   *London*

Go to see Knuthsen [Harold's doctor, Sir Louis Knuthsen]. As I enter
he says, 'You're ill!' 'No,' I answer, 'I am not ill. In fact I have just
eaten the largest luncheon I have ever eaten.' 'Sit down,' he says, taking
my pulse and at the same time thrusting a thermometer into my
mouth. 'Thought so,' he says, releasing the pulse. 'Over 100.' 'Thought
so,' he says, glancing at the thermometer, '101. Now let's look at the
ear.' He thinks I have got staphylococcus poisoning and tells me to go
straight to bed. In the early morning my temperature goes down to
98°. I therefore get up intending to see him at 2.30. But by then I feel
groggy, take my temperature again, and find it nearly 104. I telephone
to Knuthsen saying this. He fixes me up with a room in a nursing-
home in Manchester Street where I am to go at 4 p.m.
    Spend the interval writing my Will, instructions to Christopher
Hobhouse etc. These may be the last words I ever type on my beloved
Tikki [typewriter]. I am not really jumpy, which is strange, rather
excited and amused. I wish V. were here, but it would fuss her terribly
to telegraph tonight when she is so far away [motoring home through
Provence]. If I am not well, I shall telegraph to her tomorrow morning.
But even if I am a corpse before she arrives, I have nothing to say to
her which she doesn't know – immortal love, immortal gratitude.
These cannot die.

Diary   *March 24, 1934*

In the night the crisis comes. I am sick and feverish and pour with
sweat. Very apprehensive and nightmarey. Dim edges of consciousness

flickering like a battlefield. Very horrible. In the morning I recover.
My temperature drops to normal.

*At the end of June, he was invited to write the life of the American Dwight
Morrow (1873–1931), lawyer, financier, and diplomat, whom Walter
Lippmann described as 'a public figure of the first magnitude'. Harold had met
him once at the London Conference in 1930. To gather material for the book,
he went to America in September and stayed with Mrs Morrow, whose daughter
had married Charles Lindbergh.*

Diary   June 26, 1934

Lunch at Morgan, Grenfell.[1] After luncheon Teddy Grenfell takes me
into another room and shows me a letter to him from Mrs Dwight
Morrow. 'Will I write the biography of her husband?' I reply that the
idea appeals to me. However, it will entail visiting New York and
Mexico. This means loss of income here and expenses there. I should
have to be indemnified for these expenses. He asks me to think it over.
I am attracted to the idea, as I admired Morrow and want to write a
book about an American. It will have a small success here but should
go well in America. But he was a fine man and I should like to do it.
The difficulty is that if I have my expenses paid I shall lose something
of my independence and that unless I have my expenses paid I can do
nothing.

Diary   August 13, 1934

Finish the main skeleton of my Morrow notes. I can now begin on
the bricks.

---

[1] The finance house associated with J.P. Morgan & Co., New York, of which Morrow
was a partner.

Diary   *August 22, 1934*

Dread going to America and being parted from Viti. It is like a dark
cloud ahead. Yet if I say so, she will feel she ought to come with me
which is impossible. Depressed also about the Morrow book. At the
Garrick I met Constant Huntington who, as an American, gave me
glum advice. He says I shall never be able to capture the American
background and that if I try to do so they will think I am being
patronising. I must expect great prejudice in the USA against my
doing it at all. I felt diffident about that side from the first. God grant
that I make a good book of it – mainly for Mrs Morrow's sake. It is so
bold of her to suggest me and I know all too well that her friends and
family will reproach her for it. I must try and make this the best book
I have written.

I have left active life too soon. I could have done this biography
business when 60, and devoted these thirteen years to real active work.

H.N. to Vita   *September 16, 1934*
                                              Berengaria, *one day out*

It was slightly foggy as we approached Cherbourg. We swung into the
outer harbour and I watched the tender approaching. I remember how
in the *Bremen* I had leaned over and seen Ben and Niggs on that tender.
J'avais pitié de moi. I entered the bar and ordered a martini. That made
me feel better, and when I felt the throb of engines again I faced my
departure with emotion but not in despair. For half an hour I paced
the deck seeing the lights fling out sudden appeals. And then I said
goodbye to my really beloved continent and retired to my cabin.

H.N. to Vita   *September 23, 1934*
                               Deacon Brown's Point, North Haven, Maine

I pinched the blind [in the train] and pulled it up. A Scotch mist and
by the railway embankment masses of stunted golden rod with rain
drops hanging. We were met by the captain of the Morrow's [launch]
St Michael, by a man I could not make out, by another man I could

not make out and by a third man I could not make out. Anyhow I shake hands all round and if I include a chauffeur here and there what does it matter in this egalitarian country?

I walked across to the cable office and sent B.M. a many happy returns cable. The man there was helpful in the best American way. 'Now see here,' he said, 'when exactly do you wish this dame to receive your message.' I said that her birthday was September 23. 'Is that so?' he commented. 'But you see,' I said, 'I am not sure whether in England they deliver telegrams on a Sunday.' 'Is that so?' he said. 'Well now you just leave it to me. With our deferred rate, we can make certain sure that the lady gets her message before she retires for the night.' I must say, there is something about this side of American manners which attracts me strongly. It has nothing about it of the prim self-consciousness of the English petty official.

We went down to the little pier where something between a yacht and a steam launch awaited us. The Scotch mist hung over the little harbour and the spars and the rigging of a little yacht at anchor was hung with heavy drops. We hummed out into a satin sea, accompanied by a soft circle of fog. The islands are some eight miles from the mainland and I enjoyed the forty odd minutes which it took to creep cautiously towards them. We swung between two islands and across to a third where there was a landing stage. A station car was waiting for us. We drove in and out of little bays with pines down to the water and eventually the pines became tidier and there were sweeps of mown grass between the plantations. Then we swept on to the house. It was built by [Chester] Aldrich and is charming. It is of wood and has shingle sides. Rocks and islands at every angle and the sea splashing in and out of the dahlias.

Mrs Morrow advanced to meet us at the gate. A little woman, neat and ugly. She was in quite a state of excitement at my arrival. She had not slept all night. I feel that this book means so very much to her. I pray that I shall not disappoint her. She worships her husband's memory, but is intelligent enough not to wish to control what I write.

The Lindberghs are in California and are coming back shortly. I gather they will be at Englewood [New Jersey] all through the time I am there.

September 30, 1934
H.N. to Vita   *Next Day Hill, Englewood, New Jersey*

As we approached Epping Forest (since it is in such terms that you must visualise this place), a man at the gate waved us on with an electric torch. To be accurate, there is no gate, only two piers and a little hutch in which the detectives group and grouse. Banks, the butler, was waiting. 'Mrs Morrow,' he said, 'is dining out with Mr Lamont [Chairman of J.P. Morgan and Co.]. Colonel and Mrs Lindbergh are here.' He led the way through the Home and Garden Hall to the Home and Garden boudoir. There was Anne and Charles. Anne like a Geisha – shy, Japanese, clever, gentle – obviously an adorable little person. Charles Lindbergh – slim (though a touch of chubbiness about the cheek), schoolboyish, yet with those delicate prehensile hands which disconcert one's view of him as an inspired mechanic. They were smiling shyly. Lindbergh's hand was resting on the collar of a dog. I had heard about that dog. He has figured prominently in the American newspapers. He is a police dog of enormous proportions. His name is Thor. I smiled at him a little uncertainly. Not for a moment did Lindbergh relax his hold on the collar. It is this monster which guards Lindbergh baby No. 2.

'What a nice dog!' I said.

'You will have to be a little careful at first, Mr Nicolson,' he answered.

'Is he very fierce?'

'He's all that. But he will get used to you in time.'

'Thor is his name is it not? I read about him in the papers.'

I stretched a hand towards him. 'Thor!' I said, throwing into the word an appeal for friendship which was profoundly sincere. He then made a noise in his throat such as only tigers make when waiting for their food. It was not a growl, it was not a bark. It was a deep pectoral regurgitation – predatory, savage, hungry. Lindbergh smiled a little uneasily. 'It will take him a week or so,' he said, 'to become accustomed to you.' He then released his hold on the collar. I retreated rapidly to the fire place, as if to flick the ash away from my cigarette. Thor stalked towards me. I thought of you and my two sons and Gwen and Rebecca [his terrier], and my past life and England's honour. 'Thor!' I exclaimed. 'Good old man!' The tremor in my voice was very tremulous.

Lindbergh watched the scene with alert, but aloof, interest. 'If he wags his tail, Mr Nicolson, you need have no fear.' Thor wagged his tail and lay down.

I had a stiff whisky-and-soda and talked to Anne. Feeling better after that, I turned to Lindbergh. 'What happens,' I asked, 'if Thor does not wag his tail?' 'Well,' he said, 'you must be careful not to pass him. He might get hold of you.' 'By the throat?' I asked – trying, but not with marked success, to throw a reckless jollity into my tone. 'Not necessarily,' he answered. 'If he does that, you must stay still and holler all you can.'

By the time you get this I shall either be front page news, or Thor's chum. I have a lovely suite here. Large sitting-room, superb bathroom, large bedroom. I shall be supremely comfortable. I am here all safe with a super police dog to protect me against gangsters and detectives behind every bush.

H.N. to Vita

October 1, 1934
Englewood

Lindbergh has an obsession about publicity and I agree with him. He told me that when Coolidge presented him with a medal after his Paris flight he had to do it three times over – once in his study which was the real occasion, and twice on the lawn of the White House for the movie people. 'The first time,' he said, 'I was kind of moved by the thing. After all I was more or less a kid at the time and it seemed sort of solemn to me to be given that thing by the President of the United States. But when we had to go through the whole damned thing again on the lawn – me standing sideways to the President and looking an ass – I felt I couldn't stand for it. Coolidge didn't seem to care or notice. He repeated his speech twice over in just the same words. It seemed a charade to me.'

An odd thing. We have breakfast together. The papers are on the table. The Lindbergh case is still front-page news.[1] It *must* mean something to him. Yet he never glances at them and chatters quite

---

[1] The arrest of Bruno Hauptmann, for kidnapping the Lindbergh baby.

happily to me about Roosevelt and the air-mail contracts. It is not a pose. It is merely a determined habit of ignoring the Press. I like the man. I dare say he has his faults, but I have not yet found them. She is a little angel.

H.N. to Vita

October 9, 1934
Englewood

Yesterday Hauptmann was identified by Lindbergh as possessing the voice he had heard calling in the cemetery.[1] Yet this dramatic event did not record itself upon the life here. Lindbergh was at breakfast as usual and thereafter helped me to unload my Leica camera. He is very neat about such things and I am clumsy. He then said, 'Well, I have got to go up to New York – want a lift?' I said no. Then I worked hard at my files and at luncheon there was only Anne and me. Towards the end of the luncheon Lindbergh arrived and we chatted quite gaily until coffee came. We had that in the Sun Parlour, and when it was over I rose to go. The moment I had gone I saw him (in the mirror) take her arm and lead her to the study. Obviously he was telling her what happened in the court. But they are splendid in the way that they never intrude this great tragedy on our daily lives. It is real dignity and restraint.

At 3 p.m. I went out for my walk in the garden. Anne and Jon [two years old] join me. Jon is bad at going down steps and has to turn round and do them on his tummy. He is a dear little boy with the silkiest fair curls. I think of his brother. It is a ghastly thing to have in one's life and I feel profoundly sorry for them. The best way I can show it is by manifesting no curiosity. But it is awkward and rather farcical when I take up the paper at breakfast and it is full of nothing else. 'Things seem to be getting rather dangerous in Spain,' I say. But I am sure that is the best attitude.

---

[1] Where the ransom money was handed over in April 1932.

October 26, 1934
H.N. to Vita   *Englewood*

My God! What a difficult job I have taken on. It seems more and more difficult as I get deeper. And therefore more and more fascinating. Morrow is a Protean figure. There was about him a touch of madness, or epilepsy, or something unhuman and abnormal. Very difficult to convey, but certainly there. He had the mind of a super-criminal and the character of a saint. There is no doubt at all that he was a very great man.

November 7, 1934
H.N. to Vita   *Englewood*

There was a reception for the Englewood neighbours. In they poured, about eighty of them, and I was introduced to each single one. I got an ache in my face. But how undiscriminating are Americans! A sickly looking dotard in huge glasses assured me of the immense interest taken by Morrow in music. 'But surely,' I suggested, 'he was not really musical.' 'So people have said, Mr Nicolson; but I assure you that is not true. He would come to our glee-club evenings and beat time with his hand. There was a song called *So Let's Have Another* – it went like this': (dotard sings drinking-song in undertone with gestures of his right hand as if clinking tankard against tankard). 'Not of course that Dwight was in favour of excessive drinking, but he liked the swing of the thing.' (Further spectacle of dotard humming and carousing.) 'And then he felt that it made people feel human, Mr Nicolson. He was always one for the human side. So that always at *alumni* dinners he would ask the glee-club to sing that song and he would always keep time with it with his fork and knife. I can tell you he was a real man right through.' This sort of thing makes me loathe Morrow.

Finally they began to drift away. They went. Mrs Morrow, Miss Shiff [secretary], Anne and I were left alone in the big room. We agree that it had all gone very well. A sepulchral voice broke in on us from outside the window. 'Have they all gone?' And in vaulted Lindbergh who had been watching outside. Miss Shiff gazed at him with lustre eyes. He handed her what remained of the caviare sandwiches. 'You look all in, Miss Shiff. Have a bite.' She bit lovingly.

November 25, 1934
H.N. to Vita   *Englewood*

In the afternoon I sat with Anne in the Sun Parlour and she went through the notes she had prepared for me. You know, Viti, there is a great difference between an observant and non-observant person. 97% of humanity is non-observant. Anne is observant. She noticed every detail about her father and remembered it. She sat there graceful and shy upon the chintz sofa reading her notes slowly with precision. 'He would rub his right forefinger over the back of his left hand as if feeling a lump. When he threw away his newspaper it never fell flat upon the carpet but always remained standing upwards.' 'He would tear off little bits of paper while talking, roll them into spills, and then work the spills into his ear. These spills would lie about the floor. We hated them.' 'On Sunday evenings we used to have family prayers. As we got older these prayers became more and more embarrassing and therefore fewer.' And then there was a description of family breakfast which was so good that I told her to write it down and I shall produce it in the book just as I did your piece in father's book [*Lord Carnock*].

During the two months between his return to England in December 1934 and his next visit to America in February 1935, Harold wrote ten of the eighteen chapters of Dwight Morrow, *and on board ship completed a further five. He reached Englewood on the very day when Hauptmann was found guilty of the murder of the Lindbergh baby. Later he went with Mrs Morrow to Mexico, where her husband had been American Ambassador. He returned to England at the end of March, but was summoned back to America in June to deal with criticisms of his book.*

H.N. to Vita　　　　　　　　　　　　　　　　*Englewood*

Dinner yesterday evening was rather strained. You see, that morning
Judge Trenchard had summed up in the Hauptmann trial. He did
it very well and his statement was one of which even an English
judge need not have been ashamed. Lindbergh tells me that it reads
more impartial than it sounded. The jury had been in consultation for five hours when we sat down to dinner and a verdict was
expected at any moment. They knew that the first news would
come over the wireless, so that there were two wirelesses turned
on – one in the pantry next to the dining-room and one in the
drawing-room. Thus there were jazz and jokes while we had dinner,
and one ear was strained the whole time for the announcer from
the courthouse. Lindbergh had a terrible cold which made it
worse.

Then after dinner we went into the library and the wireless was on
in the drawing-room next door. They were all rather jumpy. Mrs
Morrow, with her unfailing tact, brought out a lot of photographs and
we had a family council as to what illustrations to choose for the book.
Then Dick Scandrett [Morrow's nephew] came to see me. It was about
10.45. The Lindberghs and Morgans with Mrs Morrow left us alone.
We discussed Dwight for some twenty minutes. Suddenly Betty [Mrs
Morrow] put her head round the huge Coromandel screen. She looked
very white. 'Hauptmann,' she said, 'has been condemned to death
without mercy.'

We went into the drawing-room. The wireless had been turned on
to the scene outside the court-house. One could hear the almost
diabolic yelling of the crowd. They were all sitting round – Miss
Morgan with embroidery, Anne looking very white and still. 'You
have now heard,' broke in the voice of the announcer, 'the verdict in
the most famous trial in all history. Bruno Hauptmann now stands
guilty of the foulest . . .' 'Turn that off, Charles, turn that off.' Then
we went into the pantry and had ginger-beer. Charles sat there on the
kitchen dresser looking very pink about the nose. 'I don't know,' he
said to me, 'whether you have followed the case very carefully. There
is no doubt at all that Hauptmann did the thing. My one dread all
these years has been that they would get hold of someone as a victim

about whom I wasn't sure. I am sure about this – quite sure. It is this way . . .'

And then, quite quietly, while we all sat round the pantry, he went through the case, point by point. It seemed to relieve all of them. He did it very quietly, very simply. He pretended to address his remarks to me only. But I could see he was really trying to ease the agonised tension through which Betty and Anne had passed. It was very well done. It made one feel that there was no personal desire for vengeance or justification; there was the solemn process of law inexorably and impersonally punishing a culprit.

Poor Anne – she looked so white and horrified. The yells of the crowd were really terrifying. 'That,' said Lindbergh, 'was a lynching crowd.'

He tells me that Hauptmann was a magnificent-looking man. Splendidly built. But that his eyes were like the eyes of a wild boar. Mean, shifty, small and cruel.

February 16, 1935
H.N. to Vita   *Englewood*

I went through the book yesterday and am terribly discouraged. It is as heavy as lead. What was interesting about Morrow was his character and his method. But the actual things he did were very dull. I fear that the book falls between two stools. I have tried to make it the same sort of thing as my book on my father, but whereas father was dealing with great historical and dramatic events, Morrow was dealing with the New York Underground Railways. I am very disappointed in the book now that I read it *en masse*. I fear it will have largely to be re-written. I console myself by thinking that one always goes through a stage of gloom and that re-writing is never as serious a business as it seems. The real work is getting the facts down on paper. It is not very hard work titivating them up a little once they are in some sort of form. It is odd, really; I was not conscious that the book was dull when I was writing it. I never felt stale or bored with it. But the resultant effect is something which does not live at all. It just crawls along in prose.

February 22, 1935
H.N. to Vita   *Casa Mañana, Cuernavaca, Mexico*

I cannot tell you the beauty of the mornings and the evenings in this place. My little cottage, which is only one room really and a bathroom, is at the bottom of the garden and the main house is three terraces higher. I have two little windows with blue shutters and little blue wooden bars. The centre of the room is taken up by large folding doors, which, when opened, turned the room into a loggia. I shut them at night.

When I wake I see a square of sunshine from the little east window upon my wall. I then look at the clock. 7.30. I then wait till 8.15. I then rise, open my two doors. That is the excitement. The first impression is a puff of cool datura smell – not hot datura smell. The second is of ringing sunshine and blue sky. The third is tropical creepers tumbling up into that sky – magenta and scarlet and blue. In my own little walled garden there is a tree called Jacaranda, which is quite naked of leaves, but from which burst huge plumes of blue-like enormous wistaria blooms. On the wall, which must be twenty feet high, is a vast *Thunbergia* with blue morning-glory flowers. On the higher terrace I see plumbago, white oleander and hibiscus.

I put on my dressing-gown and soon I hear flip-flap on the steps and Carmencita appears carrying my shaving water in a tin cruche. I then shave and dress, walking towards the door the whole time and gazing out upon this piled and terraced Gauguin. (Bananas when fruiting are very rude. They hang like a stallion.) I then climb up the several flights of staircase, past the pool, to the upper loggia where there is breakfast. I then come down again to find my room swept and garnished and heavy with the scent of Bermuda lilies. I then write to you. I then work. I then lunch. I then sleep. I then work again. I then have tea. I then work again. I then have a bath. I then dine out on the terrace. I then play nap which is a good game. I then go up on the Mirador and look out over the view. I then go to bed.

I should like never to move out of this enchanted garden but I suppose I will have to. It is incredible that this should be in the New World. I cannot believe that I am not in Spain. But there is also a Tahiti flavour about it.

March 8, 1935
H.N. *to Vita*   *Cuernavaca*

I have FINISHED THE BOOK! Morrow is dead. I have had to
leave a tiny gap in the chapter on the Naval Conference as I cannot
finish that part until I have seen Massigli. But it is only about 3,000
words of a gap in a book of 110,000. Yes – it is done. I am relieved.

Diary   *May 16, 1935*

Betty telephones at noon to ask me to come over at once. Evidently
the House of Morgan are raising difficulties. Very annoyed and
depressed – but I shall have to go. Book a berth on the *Aquitania*
May 29.

June 1, 1935
H.N. *to Vita*   Aquitania, *two days out*

Well I tackled a large section of the Lamont [House of Morgan] dossier
yesterday. It is easier to meet them on points of fact. But it is points of
interpretation which will be difficult. It all boils down to the difference
between my conception of banking and theirs. There was one
comment which amused me. I had written, in describing the immense
expansion assumed by Morgan's bank at the outbreak of the war, 'It
ceased to be a private firm and became almost a Department of
Government.' I meant that as a compliment. Old J.P. Morgan appears
to have regarded it as an insult. He has added a little note on his own,
'I have no right to ask you to alter this, but it will be interpreted as if
we were reduced to the status of a department subordinate to the
Government.' This is characteristic of both of us. *I* feel it the highest
compliment to compare Morgan's to the Foreign Office. *They* regard
it as an insult to suggest that they have any connection with the
Government, or any Government. But, you see, the whole point of
view is different. I regard bankers and banking as rather low-class
fellows. They regard officials as stupid and corrupt. Anyhow I continued my emendations this morning and should finish the whole
Lamont dossier before I reach New York.

June 4, 1935
Diary   *Englewood*

In the car I discuss the thing with Betty. I find on arrival a memorandum
by Reuben Clark [legal adviser to the State Department who accompanied Morrow to Mexico] bitterly attacking the whole Mexican
chapters and saying the thing will do harm. He has evidently been put
up to this by Lamont. The result is that Betty has lost all confidence
in the book and in me. I shall either have to withdraw the book or
insist on its being printed as it stands. We sit up talking till 1.40 a.m.
and I retire to my room only to lie awake in torments of rage. How
seldom do I get as angry as this and how seldom do I feel unable to
sleep! A horrible night.

June 7, 1935
Diary   *Englewood*

Devote today to revising the whole book in the light of final criticisms.
As I read it again, it seems to me to be very sugary sort of stuff. The
influence of American caution and sentimentality has pervaded my
style. My fear of hurting Betty's feelings has made me a trifle sloppy.
And then the excisions have removed from the book any tang it may
have had. Thus the result is soft and flabby. But in spite of all this
Morrow does emerge as a real person, not as a legend. I am not really
discontented with the book.

June 19, 1935
Diary   *London*

Christopher [Hobhouse] tells me that I have 'not got a political mind'.
I ask him to explain what he means. He says that I am too fastidious
and too critical to have the essential faculty of belief in democracy. He
is right.... With his usual insight he realises that my desire to go into
politics is motivated by feelings other than real political ambition or
aptitude. He knows that I wish to enter public life partly from a sense
of curiosity, partly from a feeling of duty, and partly because I have not
sufficient confidence in my own literary gifts.

Now all this coincides with a real perplexity. I think it odd that I who have worked so hard and have written so many books should not have a serious literary position. I have been thinking that this must be due to the fact that I do not possess essentially a literary gift. I therefore desire politics as a sort of alibi from literary failure. . . .

In July Harold went to America for the fourth time in less than a year, this time accompanied by his son Ben. Dwight Morrow *was published in October.*

July 12, 1935
H.N. to Vita   *North Haven, Maine*

Already by breakfast it was very hot and the flag on the mast hung limp in a cloudless sky. We returned to our cottage and worked hard. Ben really does work when he gets to it. Four hours at a time without a word and with neat and careful notes entered in a *cahier*. At 12.30 there was a knock at the door. Charles Lindbergh appeared. 'It is a perfect day for flying: would you like to go up, Ben?' Ben said that he would, and we walked out to the front where the flying field had been cleared. There was a little aeroplane scarlet as sealing-wax. Ben was quite calm and brave and aloof and slow and distant and drawly and incompetent. They climbed in. Off they went over the sea and islands and then high, high up in the ringing air. I watched my poor son and heir up there, a tiny point in the stratosphere. In half-an-hour they came down and there was Ben safe and aloof and lethargic and drawly and incompetent. But even he expressed something which in some-one else would have been indicative of slightly aroused interest but which in him was passionate enthusiasm. I did so envy him, damn you.[1] That perfect summer's day, that lovely island-studded sea, those distant mountains and that vault of blue above the scent of pines. Damn you.

---

[1] After a near-escape in 1923, Harold promised Vita that he would not fly again. Later, he found it impossible to keep this promise, but he always went to America by sea, never by air.

July 17, 1935
H.N. to Vita   *North Haven*

I worked and worked and at four-thirty there was the whole thing
beautifully finished and at five-thirty there was the beach-wagon going
down to the village with my final proofs for Harcourt, Brace. I watched
it turning the corner with deep relief. No book has caused me such
fuss and worry as this one. It is a relief to see it turn tail and go.

Ben leaves tomorrow for Boston, Washington and Philadelphia. He
has got museums opened for him all along the route. He gets on very
well with Lindbergh who seems to enjoy talking to him. Lindbergh
has a reputation for being an extremely silent man, yet with us he
chatters the whole time.

Anne told me a story which I find strange. They were asked formally
to the White House after their flight to China. Much against their will
they went. Mr and Mrs Hoover were very polite. But Mrs Hoover
called them 'Mr and Mrs Lingrün' throughout. Now isn't that very
odd indeed? What would Freud have said to that? That is the sort of
story I really enjoy. An insoluble problem in human conduct. Now
you see, that's what comes of foreign travel. Had I stayed at Sissinghurst
I should never have learnt that Mrs Hoover called Lindbergh Lingrün.

Diary   *August 16, 1935*

I dreamt that Vansittart wrote and asked me to join the F.O. again. My
disappointment when I woke up and found that this was only a dream
is a measure of how much I really mind having severed my connection
with the F.O. I must seriously consider, now that I have finished my
diplomatic books, and now that politics offer no opening and journalism is horrible to me, if I could not creep back somehow into the
Service.

Diary   *August 21, 1935*

I drive to Grosvenor Square to lunch with Emerald Cunard. Then a
lovely lady arrives whom I afterwards identify as Lady Jersey. Then in

comes Sir Arthur Wauchope, High Commissioner in Palestine. And
then a slim young man of the name of Davison. And then Emerald
herself very glad about everything. Then Anthony Eden.[1] Then Walter
Elliot [Minister of Agriculture]. We go into luncheon.

Emerald is at her best. She well knows that Anthony Eden and Elliot
are not able to disclose what happened at the Cabinet this morning.
Yet she also knows that by flagrant indiscretion she may get them to
say something. 'Anthony,' she says, 'you are all wrong about Italy. Why
should she not have Abyssinia? You must tell me that.' As the only
guest I have not mentioned was de Castellane of the French Embassy,
Eden's style was cramped. He just reacted flippantly. They therefore
discussed English women and how they were no help to their husbands
whereas the merest French cocotte at Toulon moved heaven and earth
in favour of her *commandant de frégate*.

As I was one off Eden I was able from time to time to ask leading
questions: e.g. 'What attitude will Switzerland adopt?' 'She has her
constitutional difficulties, but we do not think that land frontiers
matter very much.' He then said that Lloyd George had been
summoned that morning into conference. He had explained that
Italy in 1919 had been offered far more than she could absorb. This
is true about Eregli, Adalia and Albania. Eden asked me whether
this was true. I said it was. I asked what other people had been
called into consultation. He said old Lansbury, Herbert Samuel, and
Winston. Also Bruce of Australia and other High Commissioners.
He said that Winston was all out for blood and thunder. I referred
to the unhelpful attitude of the French press, instancing the *Figaro*
of yesterday. He said, 'Yes, it would be simple enough if the French
were really with us.' From which I gather that he himself and the
F.O. are out for sanctions but that the French and the Beaverbrook
and the Rothermere Press over here are a doubtful quantity. Walter
Elliot hinted that we might remove the embargo on the export of arms
to Abyssinia and I suggested that this would not be understood in the
USA.

I felt that I had touched the fringe of the centre of the problem. But

---

[1] He was then Minister without Portfolio for League of Nations Affairs, with a seat in
the Cabinet, and was to become Foreign Secretary in December in succession to Sir
Samuel Hoare. He was aged thirty-eight.

I also felt that in the F.O. I should have been in the centre of the problem. I was very sad.

Then back by the 5.42 to Sissinghurst. The posters of the evening papers bear headlines, 'Ramsay MacDonald says, "Worst crisis since 1914" ' 'Ll.G. and Lansbury summoned to F.O.' 'Opposition consulted' etc. etc. A general crisis atmosphere. It is very hot in the train. I read the silly books I collected at the *Daily Telegraph*. A guidebook to Morocco. A book on English phonetics for foreign readers. I feel more out of it all than ever.

Diary   *October 3, 1935*

Buck De La Warr[1] telephones to say that if I will agree to contest West Leicester in the National Labour interest he thinks he can give me a safe seat. I answer that I must think it over.

West Leicester had been represented by a National Liberal since 1931. A few months after the Election, he crossed the floor and became an Opposition Liberal — an act that displeased his constituents. They were determined to replace him. Harold agreed to stand as a National Labour candidate, with Conservative support.

Mussolini had invaded Abyssinia on October 3, and the General Election took place during the height of the crisis. Both major parties backed the policy of League of Nations sanctions against Italy.

Harold defended the National Government's home policy, of which he knew little, and his own peculiar political past. His ignorance of Leicester added to his dislike of electioneering, and Vita refused to make a single appearance at his side. Harold said that she was ill.

---

[1] Vita's cousin, Parliamentary Secretary to the Ministry of Agriculture, and the National Labour Minister in charge of Parliamentary candidates.

H.N. to Vita (in France) October 11, 1935

I went to see Buck yesterday. Jarvis [Chairman of the West Leicester Conservative Association] was there. He is aged about 35; high colour; high morals. He began by saying that it is most important that I should stand as 'The National Government Candidate' and not as 'National Labour'. I let Buck answer that point as I am all at sea about these labels. Buck said he agreed. I said, 'But supposing people ask me what party I belong to, what am I to say?' Buck said that I must say that I was a follower of Ramsay MacDonald. The conversation went on this way with me sitting all good and quiet on the sofa. Then I realised that something must be done. I said that it was no use asking me about these things, but that what was important was that I should not get a single vote under false pretences. I would be anything they liked except all things to all men. I would not pretend to be a Tory to catch the Tory vote and so on. I would get muddled if my own position was not quite clear and straight from the start. 'I am very bad,' I said, 'at *prolonged* deception.' Anyhow they agreed and told me not to fuss about MY HONOUR.

As regards expenses, headquarters will pay one third, local organisation one third, and (what may strike you as unexpected) V.S-W. one third. [She does it by raising a mortgage on Long Barn.] I shall ask for £500 from you under this head, pay you interest on it, and repay the mortgage when I become First Lord of the Treasury. I made it quite clear you could take no part. I said that I much objected to the 'Candidate's Wife' stunt, that you were not interested in politics and that it would be humbug to pretend that you were. They said that would be all right. It would go down very well if I explained that in advance.

November 5, 1935
H.N. to Vita *Leicester*

... It is not a pleasant experience. There are always two or three women who sing out the whole time 'That's a bleeding lie' or 'You ought to be ashamed of yourself' and remarks like that. These interruptions, which are organised, and constant, do in fact force one to concentrate against getting angry and are therefore exhausting.

The discouraging thing about it all is that one feels that what one says is not believed and that in any case only about 8% of the electors ever hear one.

November 7, 1935
H.N. to Vita *Leicester*

I think that we may say that the position is more or less as follows:

(1) I have about a 48% chance – just a little below even chances. In other words, the odds are really against me, but there is just a chance I may scrape in.

(2) If I fail, I shall not feel that it was due to any mistakes on my part, to any lack of organisation or lack of energy.

(3) If I succeed, it will be a great personal triumph.

Were I a young man, it would be worth it. But of course I cannot pretend at my age it is pleasant to have a failure and to spend all this money and energy for nothing. Generally in experiences such as this there is something, some isolated moment, which one enjoys. I hate and loathe every moment of this Election. The evening meetings are such absolute HELL that they hang on one's soul all day like a lump of lead.

November 14, 1935
Diary *Leicester*

Polling Day. One of the strangest days of my life. It pours, the rainwater sluicing down the dark streets. At about 10 p.m. we go on to the de Montfort Hall and find the counting in progress. Long trestle tables with people counting in rows. The voting papers are separated into little bundles of fifty and I and my supporters stroll around the tables watching the size of the piles. By about 11.30 p.m. it is clear to us that Morgan [Labour] will be first, I second, and Crawfurd [Liberal] third. I go out into the lobby and listen on the wireless for other results. I return to the main rooms and find my supporters very glum and sad. Morgan is triumphant. 'It's a bad system of counting this,' he exclaims, 'the first thing I shall do is to get some alteration in the ballot law.' He says this openly, assuming that he will get in. Then come the announcements for East and South Leicester. Lyons and Waterhouse [Conservative] both in. Applause and cheers, plus two short speeches. By that time my own tables are handing their bundles up to the platform. Jarvis comes to me in the hall and says 'You ought to be up on the platform by now.' So up I go. There is a group round the central counting table, including the returning officer and my agent Tuthill. Morgan sees me, and comes up to me. 'Well,' he says, 'you have done splendidly – a rare fight for a first election – but do not be discouraged – we want men like you in the House of Commons.' 'What,' I ask him, 'is your majority?' 'My tellers,' he answers me, 'estimate it at between 1,200 and 1,500.' I shake his hand in congratulation.

I then walk to the back to think out my speech for seconding the vote of thanks. I catch Tuthill's eye as he stands there at the table. He winks at me and jerks his head. I imagine that he wants to ask me some question and go up to him. 'You're in,' he whispers, 'by 150.' My first thought is 'Poor Morgan – I must show no sign of triumph.' I return again to the back and I hear Morgan's voice, almost hysterical, 'I claim a recount, I claim a recount.' The bundles are then handed down again to the main room. I stand there looking up at a sea of excited faces, including my Benzie, my Niggs and Sam [his brother-in-law, Francis St Aubyn]. I give them a slight affirmative motion of the head and see the colour rush to Niggs' face. Never shall I forget that second. The recount goes quickly. Waterhouse, imperturbable as always, comes up slowly to me smoking a cigarette in a long holder. 'Well,' he says, 'you must be feeling pretty proud. The greatest fight of the whole election.' The bundles are then returned and the Socialists query many defective papers. I give them all they want. That leaves me with [a majority of] 87. Tuthill moves away from the table very quietly. 'Well,' he says, 'we're in.'

The news communicates itself to the crowd in the hall below and there is a hum rising like a swarm of bees. The Press buzz round me. The Clerk to the Council steps forward and makes his announcement. As my majority is announced, a wild yell goes up from the hall. People rush towards the platform. I step forward and make a short speech. Morgan follows, then Crawfurd. Then photographs outside and on to the Constitutional Club. They are waiting for me in the street in the rain and as I draw up there are shouts of 'Here he is!' Out they drag me and hoist me up the stairs. Pandemonium let loose. I am dumped on the staircase and say a few words. Then back to the hotel — champagne with Waterhouse. To bed at 2.30 a.m.

Vita to H.N.

November 15, 1935
Sissinghurst

I am *so* glad. What a triumph! My heart stood still when I heard 'Leicester West' on the wireless. Oh darling. I do congratulate you.

Harold retained his seat for the next ten years. The National Government under Baldwin had won the Election with a huge majority. The National Labour Party, led by Ramsay MacDonald, held eight seats, but excluding MacDonald himself, and his son Malcolm, who had lost their seats.

Soon after the Election, the Foreign Secretary (Sir Samuel Hoare) made a secret pact with the French (Laval) to surrender a large part of Abyssinia to Italy. This caused a crisis and the dismissal of Hoare. It was on this subject that Harold made his maiden speech on December 19.

H.N. to Vita

December 4, 1935

There is something very strange about Stanley Baldwin. At first sight he is a solid English gentleman, but then one observes odd nervous tricks. He has an extraordinarily unpleasant habit of smelling at his notes and licking the edges slightly as if they were a flap of an envelope. He scratches himself continuously. There are russet patches across his head and face. And a strange movement of the head, with half-closed eyes, like some tortoise half-awake smelling the air — blinking, snuffy, neurotic.

I went to the smoking-room, which was an unwise thing to have done. I wanted to see if I could find [Sir] Ralph Glyn with whom I was supposed to be lunching today. But the smoking-room was full of old boys sitting round tables and drinking whisky. It is not in the least

like the smoking-room at the Travellers Club. It is far more like the
bar of a pub. Shouts and laughter and an almost complete absence of
decorum. Having got in, I could scarcely get out, and I tried that
business of walking rapidly through with head turning right and left
and eyes bearing that far-away look which signifies, 'I am not in the
very least bit shy. I am merely looking urgently for someone of immense
importance.' Then to my horror from the extreme end of the room
came yells of 'Harold!' – and there was Winston Churchill and [Sir]
Robert Horne and Oliver Stanley waving at me. I had to go towards
them feeling stared-at and conspicuous.

Winston rose tubbily and stretched out great arms. 'Welcome!
Welcome!' he yelled. You know how overwhelming his charm can be,
but I would rather it had occurred in greater privacy. 'Well,' he shouted,
'when I saw your result on the tape, I said to myself, "That means he
goes straight into the Cabinet", and then I remembered that all your
Party were already in the Cabinet and that they must have at least one
follower on the back benches. So I realised that you would be chosen
as the single follower.' This amused people all around and there was
general laughter while I stood there looking a fool. But I do not
suppose I really looked so foolish as I felt, and then I sat down with
them for a moment and nothing could possibly have been so delightful
as they were.

H.N. to Vita   *December 10, 1935*

After luncheon I went round to the Privy Council Office for a meeting
of our National Labour Party. It is a lovely room with a huge sculptured
fireplace and many Queen Anne inkstands. Ramsay sat there in front
of the fire and we others sat on either side. We discussed the future
organisation and policy of our Party. It was a ridiculous and rather
painful discussion. It boiled down to the question of Party funds. We
had so much in hand which would enable us to keep on for such and
such a time. How were we to get more money? Ramsay dismissed that
question as secondary. 'One can always get money,' he said, 'for great
political purposes.' Kenneth Lindsay, who is an impatient and able
man, suggested that we might discuss what those purposes were. We
all winced at that. 'We shall,' said Ramsay, 'be neither red, white nor

blue. We stand for Labour within the Baldwin organisation. We shall further the aims of the organisation but we shall remain OUR-SELVES.' Having said that, he struck the arm of his chair with a clenched fist and gazed upwards to where, above the mantelpiece, God was most likely to be found. 'OURSELVES,' he repeated fervently, like a Covenanter dedicating his sword and buckler. We did not even like to look at each other so awkward were our feelings. It was by then 3.30 p.m., and in acute embarrassment we broke up.

H.N. to Vita   *December 12, 1935*

I am really fussed about this Abyssinian business. It seems to me that Sam Hoare has completely and absolutely let us down. I feel very deeply about it and shall certainly not vote with the Government unless I am convinced that they have not done what they seem to have done. But I believe they have. It is really disgraceful – Sam Hoare was certified by his doctors as unfit for public business, and on his way to the sanatorium he stops off in Paris and allows Laval to do him down. My God! Were I on the other side of the House what a chance for a crushing speech.

Diary   *December 13, 1935*

Dine with Sibyl Colefax. Diana Cooper, Mr and Mrs [Ernest] Simpson, Bruce Lockhart and the Prince of Wales there. The latter is very thin; his complexion has gone and he is brick-coloured, against which background his fair eyelashes rise and fall. He talks a great deal about America and diplomacy. He resents the fact that we do not send our best men there. He knows an astonishing amount about it all. 'What can I do?' he says. 'They will only say, "Here's that bloody Prince of Wales butting in".' One finds him modest and a good mixer.

Diary   *December 19, 1935*

After questions Sam Hoare comes in with his nose plastered [broken while skating] and sits on the third bench below the gangway. He makes his [resignation] statement in a precise voice. It is excellent. His voice just breaks at the end: 'I trust that my successor will have better luck than myself.' Then Attlee moves a vote of censure, and while he does so Hoare creeps out a broken man. I do not like the man but my whole sympathy went out to him.

The Speaker's Secretary taps me on the shoulder and says that I will be called after Macpherson and Maxton. It is getting near the dinner hour. I must confess that waiting is torture to me and I am afraid that my knees will knock together when I rise. But eventually Maxton finishes his speech and I find myself on my feet and beginning, 'I crave the indulgence ...' It all goes well enough and members crowd in from the dining-rooms. Baldwin remains on the front bench and leans forward appreciatively. Very friendly of him. When I sit down there is much applause and Eustace [Percy] comes and says it was the best maiden speech he has ever heard. He is followed by J.H. Thomas [Secretary of State for the Dominions] who sits down beside me: 'You did fine, 'Arold, you did fine!' Thereafter many Members cross the House and congratulate me, and one way and another it is rather a sort of demonstration. Duff Cooper is particularly polite. Yet I know that I could have done it better if I had been less nervous. The manner was right enough but the matter was too thin. But it is good enough for a start.

Diary   *January 13, 1936*

Meet Sibyl Colefax at the Apéritif, then on to the Phoenix Theatre for the first night of Noël Coward's play [*Tonight at Eight-Thirty*]. Sibyl breaks to me the fact that the other two members of our party are the Prince of Wales and Mrs Simpson.

Mrs Simpson is bejewelled, eyebrow-plucked, virtuous and wise. I had already been impressed by the fact that she had forbidden the Prince to smoke during the entr'acte in the theatre itself. She is clearly out to help him. Our supper party at the Savoy Grill goes right enough,

but I find the Prince gazing at my tie and [soft] collar in a mood of
critical abstraction – the eye of Windsor blue surrounded by jaundice.
Nobody pays any attention to him, and what is odd is that the waiters
do not fuss unduly. The Prince is extremely talkative and charming. I
have a sense that he prefers our sort of society either to the aristocrats
or to the professed high-brows or politicians. Sibyl imagines that she
is getting him into touch with Young England. I have an uneasy feeling
that Mrs Simpson, for all her good intentions, is getting him out of
touch with the type of person with whom he ought to frequent.

Go home pondering on all these things and a trifle sad. Why am I
sad? Because I think Sibyl is a clever old bean who ought to concentrate
upon intellectual and not social guests. Because I think Mrs Simpson
is a nice woman who is flaunted suddenly into this absurd position.
Because I think the P. of W. is in a mess. And because I do not feel at
ease in such company.

*On January 19, Harold went to Dingwall, Scotland, where Malcolm Mac-
Donald was standing as National Labour candidate at a by-election. There he
learned of King George's death, on January 20, 1936.*

Diary   *January 28, 1936*

The King's funeral. I stay in at K.B.W. [King's Bench Walk] all morning
and do not hear more than the minute-guns firing dolefully in the
distance.

Go to see Buck De La Warr and we discuss the future of National
Labour and agree that there is none. Now that the two MacDonalds
[Ramsay and Malcolm] have fought [by-elections] with the aid of the
Tory Central Office we cannot claim any independence. He says
that Baldwin is really keen to maintain the semblance of a National
Government and wants us to help.

Diary *February 5, 1936*

Ramsay MacDonald takes his seat amid much booing on the part of the Labour Opposition and only perfunctory cheers on our side of the House. I receive a chit to go down and see him. He asks me if I will be his Parliamentary Private Secretary. I suggest that were I to do this I should limit my freedom of action in the House. He says that on the other hand it would give me enormous insight into the working of the Parliamentary machine, and into the functioning of the Privy Council Office, and into such schemes as Radium research; apart from this it would be very useful to our own group to have a Secretary (i.e. Whip) who would keep him in touch with lobby opinion and enable the group as a whole to put up a continuous and combative fight. I suggest that the group as at present constituted is not capable of putting up such a fight. Its able men are on the front bench; its back-benchers are not able, with the possible exception of [Richard] Denman. He says he is astonished at the amount of National Labour feeling in the country. Now this is simply dealing in unreality. There is no National Labour feeling in the country; there is only progressive conservatism. But Ramsay would sooner die than enter into a real alliance with the Tories based on any system of fusion.

Diary *February 10, 1936*

Dine with the De La Warrs in their mews. We are all very sorry for old MacDonald but feel that he is too vain to have any sense of reality. I tell them how he imagines his own election is a proof that the country believes in National Labour and that we have the ball at our feet. 'And we know——' I say, 'that it isn't a ball at all; it is only a Carters Little Liver Pill.' Then back to the House.

Diary *February 13, 1936*

Go to see Anthony Eden in his room; he is very frank. He says that his aim is to prevent another German war. To do that he is prepared to make great concessions to German appetites provided they will sign a disarmament treaty and join the League of Nations. I am all in favour of such a far-sighted plan.

H.N. to Vita   *February 18, 1936*

I went to see Ramsay MacDonald. I told him I would not be his P.P.S. but would be glad to help him unofficially in any way I could. He asked me to 'drop in on him' every morning. Well if it is only a drop, I don't mind. But I dread an orgy of vain outpourings. I fear that Ramsay is a vain and slightly vindictive old man. Why is it, darling, that I who am the least combative person on earth seem always to be attached to battle-cruisers – Curzon, Tom Mosley, B.M. – but I daresay it is good for me.

H.N. to Vita   *February 20, 1936*

My new pal [Lady] Maureen Stanley asked me to come round and meet her father who is just back from hobnobbing with Hitler. Now I admire [Lord] Londonderry [Secretary of State for Air, 1931–5] in a way, since it is fine to remain 1760 in 1936; besides he is a real gent. But I do deeply disapprove of ex-Cabinet Ministers trotting across to Germany at this moment. Anyhow, when I got in, there was a dear little woman in black sitting on the sofa, and she said to me, 'We have not met since Berlin.'[1] I sat down beside her and chattered away all friendly, thinking meanwhile, 'Berlin? Berlin? How odd. Obviously she is English, yet I do not remember her at all. Yet there is something about her which is vaguely familiar.' While thus thinking, another woman came in and curtsied low to her and I realised it was the Duchess of York.[2] Did I show by the tremor of an eyelid that I had not recognised her from the first? I did not. I steered my conversation onwards in the same course as before but with different sails; the dear old jib of comradeship was lowered and very gently the spinnaker of

---

[1] See this volume, May 25, 1929.
[2] By the end of the year she would be Queen Elizabeth, wife of George VI, and after his death, Queen Mother.

'Yes Ma'am' was hoisted in its place. I do not believe that she can have noticed the transition. She is charm personified.

Italy's continued invasion of Abyssinia, culminating in the capture of Addis Ababa in May, partly overshadowed the drama of Hitler's occupation of the Rhineland in March. He was acting in violation of the Treaty of Versailles and the Locarno Pact. Both Britain and France were outraged, but neither had the determination to act, and Hitler won the first of his bloodless victories.

Diary　　　　　　　　　　　　　　　　　　　　　*March 9, 1936*

Vita's [44th] birthday. Great excitement about Hitler's coup. House crowded. Eden makes his statement at 3.40. Very calm. Promises of help if France attacked, otherwise negotiation. General mood of the House is one of fear. Anything to keep out of war.

H.N. to Vita　　　　　　　　　　　　　　　　　*March 12, 1936*

The French are not letting us off one jot or tittle of the bond. We are thus faced either with repudiation of our pledged word or the risk of war. The worst of it is that in a way the French are right. We know that Hitler gambled on his coup. If we sent an ultimatum to Germany she ought in all reason to climb down. But then she will not climb down and we shall have war. Naturally we shall win and enter Berlin. And what is the good of that? It would only mean communism in Germany and in France and that is why the Russians are so keen on it. Moreover the people of this country absolutely refuse to have a war. We shall therefore have to climb down ignominiously and Hitler will have scored. But it does mean the final end of the League and that I do mind dreadfully. Quite dreadfully.

Diary   *March 17, 1936*

Meeting of the Foreign Affairs Committee in the House of Commons.
It is packed. The debate is opened by [Victor] Raikes who urges that
sanctions against Germany in any form would mean war and that the
country is not prepared to fight for France. I reply by saying that we
are bound morally by Locarno and that while we must restrain France
from any rash demands we must never betray her.

Diary   *March 23, 1936*

The feeling in the House is 'terribly pro-German', which means afraid
of war.

Diary   *April 2, 1936*

I dine with Mrs Simpson to meet the King. Black tie: black waistcoat.
A taxi to Bryanston Court: an apartment dwelling; a lift; butler and
maid at door; drawing room; many orchids and white arums. The
guests consist of Lady Oxford, Lady Cunard, Lady Colefax, Kenneth
Lindsay, the Counsellor of the US Embassy at Buenos Aires plus
wife, and Alexander Woollcott [American playwright and critic]. Mrs
Simpson enters bringing in the King. We all bow and curtsey. King
looks very well and gay. It is evident that Lady Cunard is incensed by
the presence of Lady Colefax and that Lady Colefax is furious that Lady
Cunard should also have been asked. Lady Oxford appears astonished to
find either of them at what was to have been a quite intimate party.
The King passes brightly from group to group. Sibyl makes the mistake,
to my mind, of talking very close to his ear, thus indicating that she
knows how deaf he is. He asks me to tell Lindbergh to come and see
him.[1] I bow. Then dinner.

Something snobbish in me is rather saddened by all this. Mrs
Simpson is a perfectly harmless type of American but her husband is
an obvious bounder and the whole setting is slightly second-rate.

---

[1] Charles and Anne Lindbergh had taken a two-year lease of Long Barn, to escape
publicity in the United States.

Sibyl's excuse is that she makes him happy and that should be enough. But I do not myself want to be drawn into that set if I can help it.

Harold gained in reputation. He played an active role in the House, wrote the main policy statement for his Party, was elected Vice-Chairman of the Foreign Affairs Committee, and meanwhile continued to write book reviews for The Daily Telegraph.

Vita was no less active. Her Joan of Arc *was published in June, and she had started* Pepita. *The house at Sissinghurst was finished, and the garden continued to expand.*

H.N. to Vita   *April 28, 1936*

Luncheon alone with Robert Vansittart [Head of the Foreign Office] at his house. Van was extremely pleasant and friendly. His view is that a German hegemony in Europe means the end of the British Empire and that we have no right to buy Germany off for a generation by offering her a free hand against the Slav countries. Once she has established herself in an unassailable position she will turn round upon us and we shall be too weak to resist her. I think he is right in theory but in practice it would be quite impossible for us to get the British people to fight Germany for the sake of the Czechs.

Tell Gwen I do not need Sanatogen at present. What I need is a feeling that we shall avoid a war. And that feeling I do not have at the moment.

H.N. to Vita   *May 5, 1936*

Eden made such a dramatic statement yesterday. Nobody knew exactly what had happened to the Emperor [of Abyssinia], and Attlee asked a private-notice question. Eden replied at length, ending by the statement that HMS *Enterprise* had been sent to take him to Palestine. 'He embarks,' he added, glancing at the clock, 'at quarter-to-four.' It was then twenty minutes to four, and we had a sudden picture of the steaming heat of Djibouti, the untidy French officials, and the strange black family being saluted by midshipmen in white ducks and sailing away from Africa five minutes later.

H.N. to Vita   *May 13, 1936*

The gentian-bed sounds very professional. I am all for gentians. What fun we are going to have! I do so love the garden. It is a sort of still backcloth to my rattley ruttley rottley (those words are meant to convey the impression of an elderly Ford lorry bumping along a pavé road. I am a master of language) life.

Diary   *May 21, 1936*

There are rumours that the Government is to be reconstituted after Whitsun. *The Star* last night stated apparently that I should be given a Ministerial job if [J.H.] Thomas goes. Obviously this is being talked about in the lobbies, as when Winston came in and sat beside me in the House he grinned and said 'I gather you are about to leave this comfortable bench.' I have heard no direct news of any such offer, but my first inclination is to refuse it on the grounds (1) that it is not fair on older members that I should be given a Government job after only six months in the House, and (2) that it is not really fair on the Conservative back-benchers that a Government job should be given to National Labour. I may find that if the proposal is put to me it will be almost impossible to refuse it.

Diary   *May 28, 1936*

Nancy Astor is terribly indignant at the King for having invited to his first official dinner Lady Cunard and Mr and Mrs Simpson. She says that the effect in Canada and America will be deplorable. She considers Lady Cunard and Chips Channon as 'disintegrating influences', and she deplores the fact that any but the best Virginian families should be received at Court. I stick up both for Emerald Cunard and for Mrs Simpson, but I refrain from saying that after all every American is more or less as vulgar as every other American. Nancy Astor, herself an American, by her vain and self-conscious behaviour in the House, cannot claim to be a model of propriety. In any case she is determined to tell the King that although Mrs Simpson may appear at Court, she must not appear in the Court Circular. I suggest to her that any such intimation would be regarded by H.M. as a gross impertinence. She says that when the dignity of the United States and the British Empire is involved, it is her duty to make such sacrifices.

Diary   *June 10, 1936*

Dine with Sibyl Colefax. It is rather tragic, since we all feel that it represents the last big party she will ever be able to give.[1] I arrive to find the Lamonts,[2] the Stanleys, the Brownlows, the Vansittarts, Bruce Lockhart and Buck De La Warr. After keeping us waiting for half an hour, the King [Edward VIII] arrives and we go into dinner almost at once.

After the women have gone out, the King talks at length to Tom Lamont about American conditions and impresses him deeply with his wide knowledge and intelligence. The King told me about his dinner with the Lindberghs. He said that Anne Lindbergh had been rather shy at first, but that 'old S[tanley] B[aldwin] and I, with our well-known charm, quickly put her at ease'. There is no doubt about it that he has infinitely improved since the old Prince of Wales days. He seems almost completely to have lost his nervousness and shyness, and his charm and good manners are more apparent than ever.

After dinner Rubinstein[3] plays some Chopin and a few extra people come in. After Rubinstein has played three times, the King crosses the room towards him and says, 'We enjoyed that very much, Mr Rubinstein.' I am delighted at this, since I was afraid that Rubinstein was about to play a fourth time. It is by this time 12.30 and the King starts saying good-bye. This takes so long that at our end of the room we imagine that he has departed, and get Noël Coward to sing

---

[1] Her husband had died on February 19, and she was leaving Argyll House in Chelsea.
[2] Thomas Lamont, Chairman of J.P. Morgan & Co.
[3] Arthur Rubinstein, the Polish pianist, then aged forty-eight. Harold was tone-deaf.

us one of his latest songs. The King immediately returns on hearing this, and remains for another hour, which is not very flattering to Rubinstein.

H.N. to Vita

June 28, 1936
Cliveden, Taplow

Cliveden [the Astors' home], I admit is looking lovely. The party also is lavish and enormous. How glad I am that we are not so rich. I simply do not want a house like this where nothing is really yours, but belongs to servants and gardeners. There is a ghastly unreality about it all. Its beauty is purely scenic. I enjoy seeing it. But to own it, to live here, would be like living on the stage of the Scala theatre in Milan.

H.N. to Vita   *July 1, 1936*

When the House of Commons gets to know me better, they will know that I am a good old tea-cup really. I do not mind that for the moment they should suppose I am dynamite disguised as vitriol. I cannot maintain the position I have now acquired. My present reputation is fallacious and transitory. It is a March flower. But I shall bloom all right in June. And my roots are deep in energy and faith. You know that – and that is where you help me. Politics I can look after myself. But my faith (in life and integrity and human nature) is something which you alone really understand, and to replenish which I rush to you like a petrol-filling station. We never talk about it, since we never talk about the really vital links between us. But that is where you help.

Diary   *July 13, 1936*

See Ramsay MacDonald. He is busy already with papers regarding the Coronation, and was trying to work out whether stands could not be erected in Hyde Park. This brings him to the problem of the King's appalling obstinacy and to the unfortunate Court Circulars in which Mrs Simpson's name figures as a guest. He says this is making a bad effect in the country. 'The people', he says, 'do not mind fornication, but they loathe adultery.' The only person who can remedy this situation is Mrs Simpson herself, but there is always the possibility that her head (which as a head is not exceptional) may become turned.

Diary *July 16, 1936*

Foreign Affairs Committee. Winston argues from the premise, which everyone accepts, that our main duty is to defend the British Empire and the Rhine frontier. What we have got to ask ourselves is whether that task would in the end be facilitated by our telling Germany she could take what she liked in the east. Were we to say this, Germany, within the course of a single year, would become dominant from Hamburg to the Black Sea, and we should be faced by a confederacy such as had never been seen since Napoleon.

Just before the House rose for the summer recess at the end of July the Spanish Civil War broke out. During the recess Harold travelled to Northern Ireland and Scotland to do research for Helen's Tower, *his biography of the first Marquess of Dufferin and Ava, and later to Austria, Venice and the French Riviera.*

Diary *August 8, 1936*

The Spanish situation is hell. Philip Noel-Baker writes to *The Times* pretending that the Madrid Government is one which should command the support of all democratic liberals. In fact, of course, it is a mere Kerensky Government at the mercy of an armed proletariat. On the other hand, Franco and his Moors are no better. The Germans are fussing outside Barcelona with their pocket-battleships 'making themselves felt'. It is serious in that it emphasises the division of Europe between left and right. Which way do we go? The pro–German and anti–Russian tendencies of the Tories will be fortified and increased.

September 8, 1936
Diary   *Sissinghurst*

The Lindberghs, Betty Morrow and Constance [Morrow] come over from Long Barn in the afternoon. Lindbergh has just returned from Berlin where he has seen much of German aviation. He has obviously been much impressed by Nazi Germany. He considers that they possess the most powerful air-force in the world, with which they could do terrible damage to any other country, and could destroy our food supplies by sinking even convoyed ships. He admits that they are a great menace, but he denies that they are a menace to us. He contends that the future will see a complete separation between Fascism and Communism and he believes that if Great Britain supports the decadent French and the red Russians against Germany there will be an end to European civilisation. He does not see any real possibility of our remaining in the centre between the right and the left. I point out to him that we are on this point a disunited nation, and that to go wholly red or wholly swastika would split our opinion from top to bottom. He contends that we cannot continue to remain on the hedge. That the old political divisions have ceased to count. That the severance today is between fascism and communism and that we cannot possibly find a middle way between these two opponents. I very much fear that he is correct in this diagnosis, and that our passion for compromise will lead us to a position of isolation, internal disunity and eventual collapse. Yet I cannot bring myself to envisage any adherence either to right or to left. Isolation seems our only policy. But it is not really feasible. Never have we been faced before by so appalling a problem, since always before we have had a comparatively united public opinion.

September 22, 1936
H.N. to Vita   Schloss St Martin, Upper Austria

Chips[1] is not really a snob in an ordinary way. I suppose everyone has
some sort of snobbishness somewhere just like everybody has a few
keys somewhere. What makes Chips so exceptional is that he collects
keys for keys sake. The corridors of his mind are hung with keys which
open no doors of his own and no cupboards of his own but are just
other people's keys which he collects. There they hang – French
keys, English keys, American keys, Italian keys and now a whole
housekeeper's truss of Central European keys.

September 27, 1936
Diary   Villa Mauresque, Cap Ferrat

To Monaco, where I am met by Willy [Somerset] Maugham's enormous car and vast chauffeur. It starts with a loud snort as of six
horsemen of the Apocalypse and roars through Monaco, through
Villefranche, through Cap Dail, shrieking round precipices, hurtling
through caverns, thundering through village streets. I sit back and pray
to God in heaven. Miraculously we arrive.

Diary   October 5, 1936

Dine with Bernard Berenson [the art historian] at Lady Horner's
house. He is very interesting about London in the 'nineties. He used
to dine regularly with Oscar Wilde. He said that when alone with him
the mask of affectation gradually (but only gradually) dropped off. But
that in public he posed deliberately. Mrs Berenson says that, having
met him five nights in succession, he said to her 'Now you have
exhausted my repertory. I had only five subjects of conversation prepared and they have run out. I shall have to give you one of the former
ones. Which would you like?' They said they would like the one on
evolution. So he gave them the one on evolution.
   Berenson asks whether there are any conversationalists of my

---
[1] Sir Henry Channon, Conservative MP and fellow-diarist.

generation. I am bound to say there are not. Not that I know of. We have no time.

H.N. to Vita   *October 6, 1936*

I went to my Party Meeting. Ramsay was in great form, and he chaffed me for being a friend of Wallis Simpson's. I do not know how he learnt that I ever knew her. I walked away with him and he spoke seriously about it. It seems that the King drove himself to Aberdeen to meet the lady and then drove her out to Balmoral. It is a real infatuation. What would his dear great grandmother [Queen Victoria] have said! But Ramsay thinks it will do harm. It irritates me that that silly little man *en somme* should destroy a great Monarchy by giggling into a flirtation with a third-rate American.

Diary   *November 4, 1936*

Go to see Parliament opened. It pours with rain. The King's accent is really terrible. He speaks of Ammurica. I then lunch at the snack bar and thereafter change into my [Diplomatic Corps] uniform. At three I go to the House where I join Florence Horsburgh in Margesson's room.[1] She is in brown velvet. We then go and sit behind the P.M. He is very nice to us. Then the Speaker reads the speech and Miss Horsburgh rises. She is very calm and does it quite beautifully. I then get up and start off not feeling nervous. When I get to the part when I refer to Winston not having been elected for W. Leicester he shouts out 'They also rejected the Rt Hon Member for the Scottish Universities [Ramsay MacDonald].' This leads to a howl from the Opposition, and when I go on to praise Ramsay MacDonald they hoot and interrupt. The rest of my speech goes off all right.

---

[1] She was to move the Address in reply to the King's speech, and Harold was to be her seconder.

Diary   *November 7, 1936*

Many press cuttings come in which suggest to me that my speech on Tuesday was really more of a floater than I had imagined. It is most unfortunate, as I gather that they really did mean to give me a job in the Government when the reshuffle comes in the spring and I may now lose the chance forever. Three minutes of blindness and a ruined career! But I do not seriously believe this, although I could kick myself for having exaggerated the Ramsay part. I could have easily fulfilled the requirements of loyalty and courage by a fleeting reference which would not have provoked the outburst it did.

Diary   *November 18, 1936*

Have a long talk with Sibyl [Colefax]. She had been spending last Sunday down at the Fort [Belvedere] with nobody else beyond a new naval equerry and Mrs Simpson. She had a heart-to-heart talk with the latter and found her really miserable. All sorts of people had come to her reminding her of her duty and begging her to leave the country. 'They do not understand,' she said, 'that if I do so, the King will come after me regardless of anything. They would then get their scandal in a far worse form than they are getting it now.' Sibyl then asked her whether the King had ever suggested marriage. She seemed surprised and said 'of course not'. Sibyl then suggested that it would be a good thing if certain Cabinet Ministers were told of this and were in a position to deny the story of the impending marriage. Mrs Simpson readily agreed to this, and authorised Sibyl to see Neville Chamberlain [Chancellor of the Exchequer]. Unfortunately Neville was ill in bed with gout, but Sibyl was able to send him a message through Mrs Chamberlain and derived the distinct impression that Baldwin had been told by the King that he was determined to marry Mrs Simpson after the Coronation. Sibyl agrees with me that Mrs Simpson is perfectly straightforward and well-intentioned, and that it is quite possible for the King to have spoken to Baldwin before raising the matter with Wallis herself. Sibyl wants me to do something more about it; but I refuse mainly because I dislike gossip but also because I remember how badly everybody burned their fingers over Mrs Fitzherbert [wife of George IV].

Diary   *November 30, 1936*

Ramsay MacDonald talks to me in deep sorrow about the King. 'That man,' he says, 'has done more harm to this country than any man in history.' It seems that the Cabinet are determined that he shall abdicate. So are the Privy Council. But he imagines that the country, the great warm heart of the people, are with him. I do not think so. The upper classes mind her being an American rather than her being divorced. The lower classes do not mind her being an American but loathe the idea that she has had two husbands already. Ramsay is miserable about it. The effect on America, the effect on Canada, the effect on our prestige. And in particular he is furious because Malcolm [MacDonald] had almost succeeded in persuading [Eamon] de Valera to accept Edward VIII as King, and now the whole thing is torn to pieces. I am distressed since I feel sorry for Wallis Simpson and hoped that she was a decent person. But after her having lied like that to Sibyl and allowing Sibyl to make a fool of herself in going to see Chamberlain – I cannot feel that she can be anything better than a fool or a minx.

H.N. to Vita   *December 7, 1936*

You will be wanting to hear the news, so I will write tonight instead of waiting until tomorrow morning. All is settled for the King's abdication, but Baldwin has given the King 'a few more days' to think it over. In the House today, Winston (whose line is, 'let the King choose his girl') suffered an utter defeat. He almost lost his head, and he certainly lost his command of the House. It was terribly dramatic.

Oliver Baldwin came to see me this morning. He told me that his father and the King walked round and round the garden at Fort Belvedere discussing the business, and then returned to the library having agreed that H.M. must abdicate. Stanley Baldwin was feeling exhausted. He asked for a whisky-and-soda. The bell was rung: the footman came: the drink was produced. S.B. raised his glass and said (rather foolishly to my mind), 'Well, Sir, whatever happens, my Mrs and I wish you happiness from the depths of our souls.' At which the King burst into floods of tears. Then S.B. himself began to cry. What a strange conversation-piece, those two blubbering together on the sofa!

Diary   *December 10, 1936*

The House is crowded and rather nervous and noisy. I am glad to have got my front row of the stalls so early. The Prime Minister comes in, pushing past the encumbered knees of his colleagues, and finds his place. He has a box with him, and on sitting down, at once discovers that he has lost the key. He probes and rummages for a bit and then finds the key. He unlocks the box, extracts some sheets of paper with the royal monogram in red, and with it some flimsy notes of his own, more squalid than a young Labour candidate would dare to produce at a Wapping by-election. He collects them hurriedly and the next minute seizes the red-monographed sheets, walks firmly to the Bar, turns round, bows, and advances to the Chair. He stops and bows again. 'A message from the King,' he shouts, 'signed by his Majesty's own hand.' He then hands the papers to the Speaker.

The latter rises and reads out the message of Abdication in a quavering voice. The feeling that at any moment he may break down from emotion increases our own emotion. I have never known in any assemblage such accumulation of pity and terror.

The Prime Minister then rises. He tells the whole story. His papers are in a confused state. He confuses dates and turns to Simon, 'It was a Monday, was it not, the 27th?' The artifice of such asides is so effective that one imagines it to be deliberate. There is no moment when he overstates emotion or indulges in oratory. The tragic force of its simplicity. It was Sophoclean and almost unbearable. There was no question of applause. It was the silence of Gettysburg.

On leaving the library, I bumped straight into Baldwin in the corridor. It was impossible not to say something. I murmured a few kind words. He took me by the arm.

'You are very kind,' he said, 'but what do you really think about it?' I detected in him that intoxication which comes to a man, even a tired man, after a triumphant success. 'It was almost wholly unprepared. I had a success, my dear Nicolson, at the moment I most needed it. *Now is the time to go.*' I made no answer.

'You see,' he went on – still holding me by the arm, 'the man is mad. *MAD.* He could see nothing but that woman. He did not realise that any other considerations avail. He lacks religion. I told his mother so. I said to her "Ma'am, the King has no religious sense." I do not mean by that his atheism. I suppose you are either an atheist or an agnostic. But you have a religious sense. I noticed it the other day. (That meant my sticking up for Ramsay.) You realise that there is something more than the opportune. *He* doesn't realise that there is anything beyond. I told his mother so. The Duke of York has always been bothered about it. I love the man. But he must go.'

Then he got on to Winston. He said, 'Do you know, my dear Nicolson, I think Winston is the most suspicious man I know. Just now I said that the King said to me, "Let this thing be settled between you and me alone. I don't want outside interference." I meant to indicate by that the reason I had not made it a Cabinet question from the start. But Winston thought it was a thrust aimed at him, and has been at my Private Secretary within the last five minutes. What can one do with a man like that?'

I suggested that Winston had put himself in a false position. The P.M. flung up his hand. 'We are all in false positions!'

No man has dominated the House as he dominated it tonight, and he knows it.

Diary   *December 31, 1936*

So ends a full and historic year. I have been well and happy. A happy year, a useful year, but clouded by menace on the Continent. I reach the age of fifty. That is a deep sorrow to me. I should not mind it so much. But I have dispersed my energies in life, done too many different things, and have no sense of reaching any harbour. I am still very promising and shall continue to be so until the day of my death. But what enjoyment and what interest I have derived from my experience! I suppose I am too volatile and fluid. But few people can have extracted such happiness from fluidity, and when I look back upon my life, it is as gay as an Alpine meadow patinated with the stars of varied flowers. Would I feel happier if I had stuck to a single crop of lucerne or clover? NO.

At the end of the year, Harold left England for Uganda, as a member of a Parliamentary Commission to study and report on African education. He was away ten weeks. This experience confirmed his view that civilisation existed only in a few Western European cities, but he was fascinated by the journey, and described it at great length in his diary, from which only very few passages are reproduced here.

Diary

January 13, 1937
Entebbe, Uganda

After dinner last night we discussed the capacity of the African brain. Kauntze [the Director of Medical Services] said that it had been proved by Windt that the cells of the African brain were undeveloped. What he wanted to find out was whether these cells developed in the educated African. So we must cut up a Makerere [College] student and see.

Diary

January 23, 1937
Ujiji, Tanganyika

Drive in procession to Ujiji, the big native centre where Stanley met Livingstone [in 1871]. We go direct to the spot where this famous meeting took place. An old man is brought up in a net and deposited upon the spot – marked as it now is by a monument, the old mango tree having died – and is given an ebony and silver walking-stick by H.E. [Sir Harold MacMichael, Governor]. The reason for this is that as a boy he was Livingstone's servant. We ask him about Livingstone. He raises bleared eyes to us and fumbles in his purple toga, producing a stained piece of paper. It is only a news–cutting from some African paper saying that he (Jumbee Heri) is the sole survivor among Livingstone's servants. We can get no more out of him, and he is put back in his grass net and hoicked up on to a pole and carried off swaying slightly and grasping his stick between the meshes of his net.

Diary

February 8, 1937
Kampala, Uganda

Get up at dawn, the freshest dawn I have ever felt outside of Switzerland. Great miles of dew and early sunshine. We motor to Nakuru [Kenya] aerodrome. The famous flamingo lake is quite near and we fly over it. It looks at first as if it had been edged in a coral necklace, but as we swooped down, the necklace dissolved into a million pelicans flying in wedges. Below us the lake, with this screen of pink flamingoes flying across it, and through them the wake of a vast hippopotamus. And around us plain and mountain in the early light. Probably the loveliest thing I have seen. We then turn west and after an hour we leave Rift Valley and drop down to Lake Victoria. We land at Entebbe at 10.30, having accomplished a two-day journey in two hours.

Diary

February 13, 1937
Entebbe

I talk to the boys in the Big School. I am tired and feel a gap between my mind and my words. This missing on two cylinders is increased by the fact that the boys laugh at the wrong time. My jokes, poor little things, are met in black blank silence. My few patriotic allusions arouse a flash of white teeth and a cacchination throughout the hall. At the end they ask questions which are sensible and indicate that they really did understand the whole time.

Diary

February 22, 1937
Khartoum

... Sanders, the Private Secretary, realising our interest in Gordon, manages to unearth some photographs of the Palace as it then was. He produces Gordon's old servant who happened to have gone off the day before the Dervishes entered [Khartoum, March 1884], and who thus escaped alive. He was quite good on the subject of the photographs. He showed us that what we took to be a flowering shrub or something (since the photographs were really very faded) was in fact Gordon's elephant tied up to a palm tree. He then took us to the place where Gordon was murdered. He says that there is no doubt at all that he was murdered on the steps. He showed us exactly how the present steps and the original steps differ from each other. He says that the picture 'The Death of General Gordon' is almost wholly accurate. He added that they did not find Gordon at first, not because he was in hiding, since he was in the dining room, but because they were chasing Coptic clerks in the garden, murdering them and making them squeal. Then they came to the Palace itself. Gordon came out from the dining-room on to the verandah and shouted to the Sudanese guard below in very bad Arabic, 'Kill them! Kill them!' He was leaning over the rail of the balcony shouting, 'Hit them! Hit them!' when a dervish flung a spear which made him spin round and stand for a moment on the top of the stairs before he toppled down. Then they cut off his head and almost cut him to pieces. The remains 'were thrown into the river at the place where the soldiers used to wash', i.e. opposite the Palace gate. The old man was not in the least gaga and became quite excited in explaining it all. But he had small sense of proportion and seemed more anxious to explain to us that there were three lavatories on each floor of the Palace than to tell us the details of Gordon's death. He said that although he did not witness the scene, he had obtained full details the next day from someone who had. I expect that this is the most authentic account that can be derived.

Despite his promise to Vita, Harold flew home to England on March 7. She was touring Algeria with Gwen St Aubyn and returned to Sissinghurst in the middle of the month. The Coronation of King George VI was on May 12.

Diary   *March 17, 1937*

It is quite possible, without undue shame, to arrive at Buckingham Palace in a taxi even though one's taxi driver (in an orgy of democracy) insists upon throwing his cigarette down upon the red carpet of the steps; but it is difficult when the outer hall is filled with Beefeaters, Gentlemen-at-Arms, and Royal Watermen to dash past duchesses in their tiaras and to say to someone (who for all one knows, may be the Lord Chamberlain or the Master of the Horse) 'please, do you think I could get a taxi?'

The dining table is one mass of gold candelabra and scarlet tulips. Behind us the whole of the Windsor plate is massed in tiers. The dinner has been unwisely selected since we have soup, fish, quail, ham, chicken, ice and savoury. The wine on the other hand is very excellent and the port superb. I discuss with David Cecil the reasons why we have been asked. He says, 'I know why I have been asked. I have been asked as a younger member of the British aristocracy.' I say that I have been asked as a rising politician, and I regret to observe that David is not as convinced by this explanation as I might have wished.

Afterwards the Queen goes the rounds. She wears upon her face a faint smile indicative of how much she would have liked her dinner party were it not for the fact that she was Queen of England. Nothing could exceed the charm or dignity which she displays, and I cannot help feeling what a mess poor Mrs Simpson would have made of such an occasion. It demonstrated to us more than anything else how wholly impossible that marriage would have been. The Queen teases me very charmingly about my pink face and my pink views in exactly the same words as Mr Baldwin had used previously . . .

I go back to the Stanleys' house and have some beer while we discuss the strange legend of monarchy.

Diary   *April 4, 1937*

Victor [Cazalet] is very excited by hearing that instructions have been issued from Buckingham Palace that members of the Royal Family are in future to cut Emerald Cunard. This is apparently due to (a) her having encouraged Mrs Simpson to become Queen of England and (b) to her having denied Mrs Simpson thrice when the crash came.

Diary   *May 12, 1937*

The Coronation. We breakfast in the House, and then ... I go to see Ramsay MacDonald for a moment and find him sitting in his room punching a hole in his sword belt and looking very distinguished in a Trinity House uniform. I tell him how well he looks: 'Yes,' he answers, 'when I was a visitor to a lunatic asylum I always noticed how well the worst lunatics looked.' I then go across to the Abbey and find my seat in the South Transept. Almost before we are aware what is happening the ceremony begins. I am not going to describe it since the newspaper accounts are full and accurate and since I shall write something for the *Figaro* myself. I get away about 2.40 and have an excellent lunch at the House. The carriage arrangements for the Abbey have broken down completely, and the guests were stranded until nearly 7.

Diary   *May 27, 1937*

I arrive at the House just in time to hear Baldwin make his last statement amid loud applause.[1] With characteristic subtlety he does it in the form of an answer to a question on Parliamentary salaries, so that his final words are to give us all £200 a year more. This means a lot to the Labour members and was done with Baldwin's usual consummate taste. No man has ever left in such a blaze of affection.

Ramsay also has to answer a question and does it well. He is greeted with cheers. I go to see him afterwards. He had had an interview that morning with the King and had been offered and refused an Earldom. He had also seen the Queen. Poor old boy, he was pleased by the kindness they had shown him. He had told the Queen that the King had 'come on magnificently since his accession'. She had been pleased. 'And am I doing all right?' she asked. 'Oh you ...' Ramsay had answered with a sweep taking that all for granted. The King had told him that for long periods at the Coronation ceremony he was unaware of what was happening. There is no doubt that they have entered upon this task with a real religious sense.

---

[1] Stanley Baldwin was succeeded as Prime Minister by Neville Chamberlain on May 28.

Diary   *July 27, 1937*

The Foreign Affairs Committee is addressed by Anthony Eden. He gives a general review of the problems from Tokyo to Washington. He says that the French really did take the initiative on Non-Intervention [in Spain] and were not put up to it by us. He admits that Non-Intervention has largely failed, but he says that it has prevented the dispatch of organised consignments of men and that those who have indulged in it are now sorry that they spoke. He makes a great point of the fact that whereas the difficulties of the dictator states are hidden behind a steel curtain, all our own cards are on the table. We must never bluff. But in fact the position is better than formerly since both Germany and Italy are abating their former truculent attitude. The foundations of peace, he says, are firmer than we suppose, and our diplomatic position with the neutral countries in the Eastern Mediterranean and in the United States is stronger than ever before. In private conversation with him afterwards he says that he thinks the Spanish War will last another year, and he hopes it will end in a deadlock out of which some middle government will emerge. He points out that if Franco wins he will be able to hold Spanish Morocco but that if he loses the Government will not be strong enough to turn him out, and a very difficult situation will arise.

Diary   *November 10, 1937*

Take the 8.53 to London [from Leicester]. The porter tells me as he puts in my luggage that Ramsay MacDonald is dead, and I am so shocked by this information that I tell the man to go to the Central Station instead of the L.M.S.

Otto Kyllman [of Constables] asks me to go and see him urgently and then suggests that I should do the official biography of MacDonald. I say that I don't admire him either morally or intellectually sufficiently to justify so much labour. One can never write a biography of anyone for whom one did not have real enthusiasm.

Diary   *November 15, 1937*

Have a long talk in the smoking room with Winston Churchill. He congratulates me on my intervention in the Foreign Affairs Committee on Thursday, saying that he has seldom seen so short a speech make so much effect in so short a time. I say that I feel terribly hampered in making up my mind about foreign politics, since I have actually no conception whatsoever as to our real defensive power. Obviously, if it is a question between complete defeat and the surrender of the German colonies, there can be no question whatsoever. But if we are in fact able to defend ourselves, I see no reason why we should make concessions without receiving something in return. Winston says that it is of course impossible for the Government to disclose our exact strength at the moment, but that 'he takes it' Germany's air force is a little stronger than the French and British air forces combined. If you add to that the Italian air force, which is a very excellent striking machine, we are indeed not in a position to go to war without very active Russian assistance. He is in a very quiet, sensible and chastened mood.

Diary   *November 25, 1937*

Henry [Chips] Channon asks my advice about his diaries which he has kept at great length since 1917. He says that they are very outspoken and scandalous, but that they record the lives of important people for the last twenty years. He has made a Will leaving them to me plus £500. I say that he must make another Will leaving them plus £1,000 to Christ Church Library, with instructions that thirty years after his death the four youngest fellows of the time should consider their publication.[1]

---

[1] They were, in fact, bequeathed to his son Paul, and edited for publication by Robert Rhodes James.

Diary   *December 8, 1937*

Go to breakfast with Lord Baldwin at 69 Eaton Square. I arrive to find
him seated at the breakfast table opening his letters. He is rather lame
with arthritis but otherwise looks well. He said that he only got out
just in time and that a few weeks more would have led to a real collapse
similar to that of Ramsay MacDonald's. He said that he had always
looked forward to his retirement to be able to read and think, but that
for the first three months he had been quite unable to think and only
able to read detective novels. He was now beginning to recover and
was reading Froude on Erasmus.

   He goes on to talk about his mother's family and the Burne Jones–
Kipling circle. He said that when Morris died at 63, the doctor said
'He has died of being William Morris.' We then talk about the
Abdication, and he says that there were patches in the King's brain
which were those of a child of thirteen. He considers Mrs Simpson to
be an admirable woman within her circle of conscience, but to have
no conception of proportions outside that circle. He showed me the
original of the little pencilled note that King Edward had sent him
after the Abdication.

   He talked of Winston Churchill and said he lacked soul. I suggested
that Winston is very sympathetic to misfortune in others. He answered,
'I don't deny that Winston has a sentimental side.' He then goes on:
'And what is more, he cannot really tell lies. That is what makes him
so bad a conspirator.'

   I was alone with him for over an hour, and nothing could have
exceeded his mellow charm.

Diary   *December 31, 1937*

I have been conscious that my political career has suffered a decline. I
do not possess sufficient combative instincts to impose my personality
upon the House of Commons. Although I am a good platform speaker
and a better lecturer, I am not at my ease in the Chamber.

   The difficulty is that Foreign Affairs, which are my special subject,
are not a subject on which I wish to speak. It only does harm. Thus I
have remained largely silent and the impression is that I have 'dropped

out'. By one good speech I could destroy that impression and recover the general expectation which they had of me before my unfortunate speech on the Address in 1936. But I feel somehow that I am not sufficiently virile to force myself upon the House and that I am too old to create a gradual impression as Baldwin did.

How much do I mind this? Probably more than I realise. I am so happy in my domestic and ordinary life that I do not notice much that I have not fulfilled high hopes.

Almost from the moment when he succeeded Baldwin, Neville Chamberlain assumed increasing control of Foreign Affairs. He bypassed the Foreign Office by sending his own emissaries to appease the Dictators. Anthony Eden, his Foreign Secretary, protested that this private diplomacy flattered enemies and offended allies. In January, when Eden was on holiday, Chamberlain brushed aside President Roosevelt's offer to mediate between the European powers, and Eden returned too late to repair the damage. At the moment when Hitler was openly threatening the independence of Austria, Chamberlain proposed to open discussions with Mussolini. The timing and tactics of these negotiations were the main cause of the disagreement between the Prime Minister and Foreign Secretary; their mutual distrust lay behind it. Eden resigned on February 20 and was succeeded by Lord Halifax. Harold spoke up strongly for Eden in the House and in the Foreign Affairs Committee. The National Labour Party virtually disowned his conduct, but his Leicester constituents gave him a unanimous vote of confidence.

H.N. to Vita   *January 7, 1938*

I went to Wandsworth Jail yesterday morning. The Governor was a splendid type of person. He took me round himself through every cranny of the place. It is rather ghastly – not that they could make it better, but imprisonment is a ghastly thing. What is so touching are their little possessions which they deliver up when they enter the prison. They take off their clothes and never see them again until they come out. But what is nice is that they clean and press the clothes for them before they are coming out so as to give them back their self-respect. I do not quite see how it could be more humane, but of course I went away feeling a beast and a brute.

January 20, 1938

Diary   *Leicester*

... To the Club where I meet Bertie Jarvis. We go over future
engagements and I see that he is rattled by [Barnett] Janner.[1] He thinks
he will turn me out, but does not express it in that way. The way he
expresses it is to say, 'We will give him a fine run for his money.' In a
way, I think that Janner will make a better Member than I am.

Diary   *February 3, 1938*

Dine at St James' with Gladwyn Jebb. Characteristically we do not
touch on the centre of Foreign Affairs. Here I am, Vice Chairman of
the Foreign Affairs Committee of the House, and there he is, Private
Secretary to the Permanent Under Secretary of State [Sir Alexander
Cadogan] — and friends of long standing — yet such is the tradition of
discretion that I dare not ask him a single question nor even why it is
that he has to return to the Office after dinner. That would not be so
in France.

Diary   *February 17, 1938*

Meeting of the Foreign Affairs Committee. I open the discussion by
indicating that Hitler has now reestablished his legend and imposed
the will of the party on the army. The cautious people have been
proved wrong. I discuss the implication of the Austrian agreement[2]
and indicate that Mussolini must have known in advance and must
have been bought with certain promises. What were those promises
and why has he now 100,000 men in Libya? I conclude by suggesting
that we should keep a stiff upper lip, not throw sops or slops about,
wait, and above all arm. Winston takes a far more truculent attitude

---

[1] Labour candidate for West Leicester, who eventually defeated Harold in the General
Election of 1945, and his son Nigel in the Election of February 1950.
[2] Hitler had made a pact with Schuschnigg, the Austrian Chancellor, that while Austria
would retain nominal independence, in effect control of her affairs would pass to
Berlin. Mussolini temporarily disappeared in order to avoid replying to Schuschnigg's
appeal for help.

than I do. The whole feeling of the meeting is very different from that of a year ago. They no longer believe that we can buy Germany off with concessions.

Diary   *February 20, 1938*

The Cabinet meet three times today, and on the late news it is put out that Eden has resigned. We spend much of the morning listening to Hitler's Reichstag speech on the wireless. It is meant to be moderate, but his references to foreign countries, his talk of 'steel and iron', are received with wild demonic yells.

Diary   *February 21, 1938*

Party meeting at Tufton Street. Malcolm [MacDonald] takes the chair and tells us what happened. He spoke calmly and quietly. He states that in his opinion Eden made a mistake. He goes on to say that Eden was his best friend in the Cabinet and in fact dined with him when he drafted his letter of resignation. He then explains that there was no difference as to the objectives of policy, and that Eden agreed with the Cabinet as to the necessity of talks with Italy and Germany. His recent disagreement with the P.M. turned upon a question of method. His resignation, owing to the gradual accumulation of these small differences, was inevitable sooner or later. He felt that assurances regarding Spain and propaganda should precede any official conversations. The P.M. felt that we should make a gesture, open negotiations and hope that the good feeling thus established would lead the Italian to behave kindly to us. Hence the split.

I say that I shall speak in favour of Anthony and against the P.M. They say that will be all right so long as I disassociate the Party. I then go down to the House. There are large crowds. Towards the end the P.M. comes in and is loudly cheered. I do not join in. Then Anthony and Bobbety Cranborne[1] come in shyly across the bar and sit in the famous seat below the gangway. They are cheered wildly by the Opposition. He [Eden] looks very pale and a trifle nervous. He makes

---

[1] Under Secretary of State for Foreign Affairs, who resigned with Eden.

a speech which was not really very good. There was just a sufficient note of recrimination to spoil the dignified effect and not enough to constitute an appeal.

Bobbety follows and is far more effective. He speaks of Italian blackmail which arouses vociferous cheers. The P.M. follows – he is halting, precise and grim. It goes very badly. Then the debate opens. I am called about 7.15. I speak for about twenty minutes. The House crowds in. That is very flattering. I attack Italy and the P.M. and defend Anthony – 'butchered to make a Roman holiday'. I am loudly cheered by the Opposition. Afterwards there is that scurry which one knows accompanies a successful speech. Lloyd George says, 'A fine Parliamentary performance.' Winston Churchill says, 'You spoke wonderfully. I envy you your gift.'[1] The others fiddled about.

H.N. to Vita   *February 25, 1938*

When I arrived at Leicester station I was met by Jarvis who informed me that the opinion in the Conservative Association was all on the side of Chamberlain and that I had better say nothing at all. I said 'Not at all. I have come up here to explain my action to my constituents and explain it I shall.'

My speech in fact went well. They did not understand most of it but they agreed. They passed a unanimous vote of confidence with real enthusiasm. I was, as the papers say, 'visibly moved'. And this morning I got a note from Bertie Jarvis: 'Sorry, Harold. You were right and I was wrong. The speech was triumphant.'

We had a most unpleasant meeting of the Foreign Affairs Committee. We heard that they were going to ask for our resignation as Chairman and Vice Chairman. Or at least that Nancy Astor was going to ask. Paul Evans [Chairman] and I therefore agreed that we should resign on our own initiative. Thus when the meeting opened, Paul got up and said that he and I and Jock McEwan [Secretary] had

---

[1] In the course of his speech Harold had said: 'I regret that the great principles of our policy should now lie tattered at our feet. Above all, I regret that we should see "their sire, butchered to make a Roman holiday."' The quotation was from Byron's *Childe Harold*.

determined to resign. The room was packed and there was one great
shout of 'No!' That sounds splendid, but what it really meant was that
they thought our resignation would embarrass the Government, as
indeed it would. Several people got up quite shamelessly and suggested that we should not resign at once but merely do so later
when feeling had diminished. At this Winston in all his majesty rose
and said that they were being mean and petty. They were not treating
us fairly and he must insist on a vote, either Yes or No. They then
voted. Those in favour of our not resigning were unanimous except
for one little vicious hand against. That hand was the hand of Nancy
Astor.

We then adjourned in some excitement. In the corridor a friend of
mine called Alan Graham came up to Nancy and said, 'I do not think
you behaved very well.' She turned upon him and said, 'Only a Jew
like you would *dare* to be rude to me.' He replied, 'I should much like
to smack your face.' I think she is a little mad.

Diary   *March 8, 1938*

I work away with Richard Law.[1] He is a great friend of Eden's. He
said that the P.M. had of late been definitely rude to Eden and that the
latter had derived the impression that he was wanting to drive him
out. The P.M. had returned a snubbing message to President Roosevelt. Eden had much resented this since it ruined his policy of close
relations with America. The P.M. is bitterly anti-Russian and also anti-
America. The soul of the ironmonger is not one which will save
England.

*On March 12 German troops crossed the Austrian frontier and entered Vienna
unopposed. Austria was declared annexed and Schuschnigg was arrested. Hitler
was triumphantly received in Vienna on March 14, the very day when
Chamberlain told the House that only the combined forces of Europe could
have prevented it.*

---

[1] Son of the previous Prime Minister, Bonar Law. He was one of the pro-Eden MPs
who voted against the Munich Agreement, and was created Lord Coleraine.

Diary   *March 15, 1938*

This sense of danger and anxiety hangs over us like a pall. Hitler has completely collared Austria; no question of an Anschluss, just complete absorption.

Dine with Sibyl. Desmond [MacCarthy] is in despair and says that the Government have betrayed the country and that the Tories think only of a Red danger and let the Empire slide. I am in grave doubts about my position. How can I continue to support a Government like this?

Diary   *March 16, 1938*

Go to Pratt's [Club] with Winston Churchill. He doesn't fully agree with us about Spain[1] but mainly because of his personal friendship with Spanish grandees. He says that never before has a man inherited a more ghastly situation than Neville Chamberlain, and he places the blame wholly on Baldwin. He says that in his long experience he has never known a Conservative Party composed of so many blind and obstinate men. He says that he will wait for a day or two in the hope that the negotiations which are now going on between Chamberlain, Attlee and Sinclair [a fact denied by Attlee] for a formula of policy which will command the assent of the whole House have either failed or come to fruition. But if no clear statement is issued between now and Wednesday next, he will refuse the whip and take some fifty people with him. This threat should in itself suffice to determine the Government. He says that the situation is worse than in 1914. 'We stand to lose everything by failing to take some strong action. Yet if we take strong action, London will be a shambles in half-an-hour.'

Diary   *April 7, 1938*

Paul Emrys-Evans tells me that the Foreign Affairs Committee wish me to resign my post as Vice Chairman. I say I shall do so. I know that

---

[1] Earlier that day Harold had advised the Prime Minister to occupy Minorca.

I cannot possibly continue since I disagreed with the Chamberlain policy. But I do not like being turned out.

In April Harold went on a British Council speaking tour of the Balkans, with a secret mission from the Foreign Office to attempt to restore some confidence among the Eastern Europeans. His visit was used in the Balkan capitals as an excuse for pro-Western demonstrations.

April 17, 1938

H.N. to Vita   *British Legation, Bucharest*

I lunched with the King. At 12.30 I said that I must dress for luncheon. As I walked upstairs I felt strangely giddy. The staircase seemed to shift and wobble. I was appalled. Suppose I came over faint during my luncheon? That would be hell. I arrayed myself miserably in the tail-coat of Rex Hoare [the British Minister] which would not, I regret, meet in front. But it looked all right. Then I espied the bottle of Sal Volatile. I corked it tightly and put it into my pocket, in fact the only pocket which I could call my own, my trouser pocket. Then off I went.

At the Palace an aide-de-camp in stays and aiguillettes arrived and made polite conversation. Then a lift hummed and two pekinese darted in barking followed by the King [Carol] in naval uniform. I bowed. He greeted me with affection and respect. We passed into the dining-room. I sat on his right. The aide-de-camp sat on his left. The pekinese sat on his knee. We started conversation.

He had ordered, he said, a purely Rumanian luncheon. God, it was good! In spite of my feeling so faint, I gobbled hard. We talked agreeably. He is a bounder but less of a bounder than he seemed in London. He was more at ease. His Windsor blue eyes were wistful and he had something behind them. He spoke with intelligence about Chamberlain and Eden and the Italian Agreement and the French Cabinet and the League of Nations. He was well-informed and most sensible. We kept all debating topics away.

I was beginning to enjoy my conversation when I was aware of a cold trickle and the smell of ammonia. I thrust my hand into my pocket. It was too late. The Sal had indeed proved Volatile and my trousers were rapidly drenched. I seized my napkins and began mopping surreptitiously. My remarks became bright and rather fevered, but quite uninterrupted. I mopped secretly while the aroma of Sal Volatile rose above the smell of *gruzhenkoia*.

This was agony. I scarcely heard what he was saying. 'Have you,' he was asking, 'recovered your land-legs yet? After three days in the train one feels the room rocking like after three days at sea.' So that was it! Why on earth had he not told me before, and now it was too late. I recovered my composure and dropped my sodden napkin. The conversation followed normal lines. At 2.45 he rose abruptly. I rose, too, casting a terrified glance at the plush seat of my chair. It bore a deep wet stain. What, oh what, will the butler think? He will only think one thing.

April 22, 1938
Sofia

H.N. to Vita

I went to write my name upon the King [Boris of Bulgaria]. There were four books to write in: the King's; the Queen's; the Princess's; and the *Prince héritier*, who is eighteen months. I wrote my name very distinctly in the last as he must have difficulty, being so young, in reading foreign hand-writings.

Then to see the Prime Minister [Keosseivanoff] in the Foreign Office. It is the same as in my day and I thought how often father must have waited in that waiting-room.[1] The Prime Minister was not an attractive man. An ex-diplomatist with those over-polished manners, that *boulevard extérieur* elegance, which always faintly annoys me.

Then came the Press in a band. I sat there and they fired questions at me. I was as discreet as I could be. Here again I am front-page news. It is pathetic how these people long for British friendship and how they exaggerate my importance and the meaning of my visit.

---

[1] Lord Carnock was British Agent in Sofia in 1894–5, when Harold was eight.

Diary *May 6, 1938*

Lunch with H.G. Wells at 13 Hanover Terrace. The other guests are
Bernard Shaw and Mr Brendan Bracken, Penelope Dudley Ward, and
Moura Budberg. Shaw looks very frail and jaunty. We talked about
T.E. Lawrence and Shaw says that his mistake was that he always tried
to hide in the limelight. He says that he had a boyish mind and that
his smile remained that of a public school boy. Wells teases him about
his love of publicity and he is none too pleased. He talks about Barrie.
Shaw says that Barrie would talk quite a great deal but it was always
dull. He was not an attractive man. Like a spinster.

H.N. to Vita *May 17, 1938*

We had an excitement yesterday, Swinton [Air Minister] sacked. But
how silly the whole thing is! Here we are in the gravest crisis in our
history, with a genius like Winston doing nothing and Kingsley Wood
as our Minister for Air with Harold Balfour (a mere lickspittle) as his
No. 2. It is all due to David Margesson [Chief Whip]. I admire David,
since he is strong and efficient and kind. But I do not believe that
he is a good Cabinet-maker. Much sickness left behind. Nobody
understands why Euan Wallace is sent to the Treasury. Nobody understands why on earth Stanley (who is amiable but stone deaf) is given
the Dominions. Nobody understands anything. There is a real impression that the whole show is going to crack up.

Diary *May 18, 1938*

On my way back I stop at Pratt's where I find three young Peers who
state that they would prefer to see Hitler in London than a Socialist
administration. I go to bed slowly, pondering upon the Decline and
Fall of the British Empire.

Diary   *May 22, 1938*

Charles and Anne Lindbergh and Mrs Morrow come over from Long
Barn. Lindbergh is most pessimistic. He says that we cannot possibly
fight since we should certainly be beaten. The German Air Force is
ten times superior to that of Russia, France and Great Britain put
together. Our defences are simply futile and the [barrage-]balloons a
mere waste of money. He thinks that we should just give way and then
make an alliance with Germany. To a certain extent his views can be
discounted, (a) because he naturally believes that aeroplanes will be the
determinant factor in war; (b) because he believes in the Nazi theology,
all tied up with his hatred of degeneracy and his hatred of democracy
as represented by the free Press and the American public. But even
when one makes these discounts, the fact remains that he is probably
right in saying that we are outmastered in the air.

Diary   *May 26, 1938*

Lunch with Maureen Stanley. The Halifaxes are there. Lord Halifax
tells me that Goebbels said to him 'You must realise how sensitive we
are. You have a three hundred years tradition behind you. We have
only four.' That means that they regard themselves as something quite
new. We regard them as a development of Prussian history. They regard
themselves as a revolution. They are thus enraged when we suggest
that Hitler might go to a better tailor. We are rather arrogant and
insensitive regarding that aspect.

We discuss the question of conciliating Goering. Halifax says that
he would be pleased by an invitation to Sandringham. I say that we
should resent any such thing. It would affect American opinion. It
would lower our dignity. No – ask Goering to Nepal as much as you
like: but do not expect the Queen to shake hands with him. Halifax is
rather startled by our vehemence.

Diary   *June 6, 1938*

Chamberlain (who has the mind and manner of a clothes-brush) aims
only at assuring temporary peace at the price of ultimate defeat. He
would like to give Germany all she wants at the moment, and cannot
see that if we make this surrender we shall be unable to resist other
demands. If we assuage the German alligator with fish from other
ponds, she will wax so fat that she will demand fish from our own
ponds. And we shall not by then be powerful enough to resist.

Yet if we provoke Germany now (when our defences are in a pitiable
state), she will or may destroy us utterly. We all know that at the
moment Germany is not prepared for a European War. But if we really
oppose her, she may drive us into it. And if we do not oppose her she
will become so strong that we cannot face it. There is some truth in
the idea that every month gained is a month gained. The Italians are
already distrusting Mussolini, and after our Czechoslovak success the
Germans are distrusting Hitler. The spell may have been broken, and
I know that it is little more than a spell. But what happens if the
Japanese involve America in an Asiatic war, involve Russia as well,
detach some of our ships – then Germany can strike in Europe.

We have lost our will-power, since our will-power is divided. People
of the governing classes think only of their own fortunes, which means
hatred of the Reds. This creates a perfectly artificial but at present most
effective secret bond between ourselves and Hitler. Our class interests,
on both sides, cut across our national interests. I go to bed in gloom.

H.N. to Vita   *June 17, 1938*

I met an Austrian yesterday who had just got away from Vienna, and
what he said made me ill. There is a devilish sort of humour in their
cruelty. For instance, they rounded up the people walking in the Prater
on Sunday last, and separated the Jews from the rest. They made the
Jewish gentlemen take off all their clothes and walk on all fours on the
grass. They made the old Jewish ladies get up into the trees by ladders
and sit there. They then told them to chirp like birds. The Russians
never committed atrocities like that. You may take a man's life; but to
destroy all his dignity is bestial. This man told me that with his own

eyes he had seen Princess Stahremberg washing out the urinals at the Vienna railway-station. The suicides have been appalling. A great cloud of misery hangs over the town.

Dearest, what unhappiness there is in the world. I am glad I am in a position to do something, however slight, to help. I simply could not just remain idle and do nothing.

Diary   *June 27, 1938*

Anthony Crossley takes me to task for being so anti–Chamberlain.[1] He says that I am working for his fall. He says that the Conservatives realise this and simply hate me. I say, 'But surely, Anthony, they are always so polite when I meet them?' 'Yes,' he answers, 'that is part of their technique.'

                                                                         August 5, 1938
H.N. to Vita   *Villa Mauresque, Cap Ferrat*

I came down to the villa, had a bath, shaved, put on my best clothes. Because the late King of England was coming to dinner. Willy Maugham had prepared us carefully. He said that the Duke [of Windsor] gets cross if the Duchess is not treated with respect. . . . Recently some old friend of the Duchess had opened the conversation at luncheon by saying 'How lovely Wallis is looking, Sir!' '*WHO???*' snapped the Duke. In all innocence the poor trout repeated 'I said, Sir, how lovely Wallis was looking.' He turned his back on her and never spoke to her again throughout the meal. 'Oh dear,' said Sibyl [Colefax], 'what then am I to call her?' 'D-D-D-uchess,' said Willy. 'I shan't,' said Sibyl. Then followed a long pause. 'I-I-I-think I shall ask Eliza [his daughter] to c-c-c-urtsey to her,' said Willy. 'You won't get me curtseying,' said Sibyl. 'W-W-W-ell,' said Willy, 'perhaps if Eliza comes to the door with me, then she can get her curtsey over outside.' 'Yes,' said Sibyl, 'I don't mind that.'

Thus when they arrived Willy and his daughter went into the hall.

---

[1] Nevertheless, Crossley joined the anti-Chamberlain Eden Group and abstained in the vote of confidence after Munich.

We stood sheepishly in the drawing room. In they came. She I must say looks very well for her age. She has done her hair in a different way. It is smoothed off her brows and falls down the back of her neck in ringlets. It gives her a placid and less strained look. Her voice has also changed. It now mingles the accent of Virginia with that of a Duchess in one of Pinero's plays. He entered with his swinging naval gait, plucking at his bow-tie. He had on a *tussore* dinner-jacket. His face and the back of his neck are burnt brick red and his fair hair shows up against it as if it were stuck on with glue or were a wig or something. His eyes looked less like fried eggs than formerly. He was in very high spirits. Cocktails were brought and we stood round the fireplace. There was a pause.

'Oim sorry we were a little loite,' said the Duke, 'but Her Royal Highness wouldn't drag herself away from the Amurrican orficers.' He had said it. The three words fell into the circle like three stones into a pool. Her (gasp) Royal (shudder) Highness (and not one eye dared to meet another).[1]

Then we went into dinner. I sat next to the Duchess. He sat opposite. They called each other 'darling' a great deal. I called him 'Your Royal Highness' a great deal, and 'Sir' the whole time. I called her 'Duchess' sharplike.

We chattered a great deal. You know that tiresome way royalties have of pretending everything is being very amusing when it isn't. I do not think that ex-Kings are very good company. But of course one cannot get away from his glamour and his charm and his sadness. Though I must say he seemed gay enough. They have a villa here and a yacht and go round and round. He digs in the garden. But it is pathetic the way he is sensitive about her. I heard him say, 'I think that must have been when I was King.' A strange remark to overhear at dinner.

She was loaded with magnificent jewels. It was quite clear to me from what she said that she hopes to get back to England. She was very bitter about the French, very bitter about the 'politicians' by which I suppose she meant Baldwin. I should imagine she has great social ambitions and wants to return to England to play some sort of part. I derive this from the fact that when I asked her why she didn't

---

[1] King George VI had refused to allow his sister-in-law the title of Royal Highness.

get a house of her own somewhere, she said 'One never knows what may happen. I don't want to spend all my life in exile.'

August 22, 1938
Diary   *London*

Lunch with the Russian Ambassador [Maisky] alone. I ask him what Russia would do if Germany pressed on to the Black Sea. He says that the old pan-Slav feeling is dead, that Russia has no sympathy for the semi-fascist systems, and that she is profoundly disillusioned with the western democracies. If we and France went to war on behalf of the Czechs, then Russia would help. But if we abandon Czecho-slovakia, then Russia will become isolationist. She is unconquerable and has her own unlimited territory and resources. But she would not consent to Germany establishing her influence over Turkey.

Diary   *August 23, 1938*

I explain to Vita, Ben and Nigel that this diary, of which they know the industry and persistence, is not a work of literature or self-revelation, but a mere record of activity put down for my own reference only.

The month of September 1938 culminated in the Munich settlement, by which Hitler gained most of what he had demanded. He claimed that the western territories of Czechoslovakia (the Sudetenland) were ethnically German, and he demanded their secession to Germany. Chamberlain was determined to avoid war, and put pressure on the Czech Government to give way. He had two meetings with Hitler at which he attempted to modify the German claims, but at the last moment it seemed that Hitler was too intransigent even for Chamberlain. Czech troops moved to the German border, and the British fleet was mobilised. On September 28 war was averted by Hitler's invitation to the leaders of Britain, France and Italy to meet him in Munich. An agreement was signed which ended the crisis, and Chamberlain was hailed on his return as a great peace-maker. Harold, and many others like him, took a different view. He regarded the Munich Pact not only as a betrayal of the Czechs, but as an irremediable surrender to Hitler. He spoke up strongly against it both in Parliament and in his constituency. It was his finest hour.

Diary   *September 1, 1938*

We may just squeak through. On the other hand we may get into the same mess as in 1914 – namely, give the Czechs the impression that we shall fight for them, and the Germans the impression that we shall not.

Diary   *September 4, 1938*

Work at my [BBC] talk for tomorrow. I try to tell people why it is vital that we have to fight for Czechoslovakia. I say (1) Because it is of vital interest to the British Empire to prevent Germany dominating Europe, becoming invincible and holding us at her mercy. (2) Because it is a test case in the spiritual conflict between liberty and the Nazi theory.

Bob Boothby told me how he persuaded Winston to see Halifax and urge that some show of friendship or solidarity should be made with Russia. Halifax made no great objection. The P.M. regards it as a bitter pill but is prepared to swallow it. He [Boothby] regrets bitterly that Anthony [Eden] should remain away during this time and do nothing. He thinks he has 'sunk himself' by so doing. He also thinks that Duff Cooper has sunk himself by going yachting in the Baltic at a moment of crisis. Here I agree.

Diary   *September 11, 1938*

Several people ring me up during the day begging me 'to do something'. They have no idea what they want me to do but they are getting hysterical and it is some relief to them to bother other people on the telephone.

Oliver Stanley's [Secretary for the Dominions] point of view is typical I suppose of the better type of Cabinet opinion. What the worst type of opinion may be passes my comprehension. Thus Oliver on the one hand agrees that the conflict has nothing really to do with Czechoslovakia but is the final struggle between the principle of law and the principle of violence and that the two protagonists in this struggle are Chamberlain and Hitler. He also agrees that if Germany were to make an attack on Czechoslovakia and if France were to be drawn in it would be practically impossible for us to abstain. Yet his incidental remarks show me that at heart he is longing to get out of it. At the same time any reference to Russian assistance makes him wince, and at one moment he sighed deeply and said, 'You see, whether we win or lose, it will be the end of everything we stand for.' By 'we' he means obviously the capitalist classes.

Diary   *September 14, 1938*

The news is even worse. Japan and Italy have announced that they stand by Germany. The Russian fleet is mobilised. The Sudetens refuse to negotiate and maintain their ultimatum. We feel we are on the very edge of the railings lining the cliff. I have not the heart to listen to the 9.40 news. Then Viti comes in and says the P.M. is flying tomorrow to [see Hitler at] Berchtesgaden. My first feeling is one of enormous relief.

Diary   *September 15, 1938*

How difficult it is to decide! Vita takes the line that the Sudeten Germans are justified in claiming self-determination and the Czechs would be happier without them in any case. But if we give way on this, then the Hungarians and the Poles will also claim self-determination, and the result will be that Czechoslovakia will cease to exist as an independent state. Vita says that if it is as artificial as all that, then it should never have been created. That may be true, although

God knows how we could have refused to recognise her existence in
1918. . . .

Diary   *September 19, 1938*

I go to see Anthony Eden in Fitzhardinge Street. I find him in the
depths of despair and ask him what attitude he will adopt. He says that
it is very difficult to make any formal decision until the full facts are in
his possession. He says that probably if he had been in Halifax's place
he might have done the same as he did. Only he adds, with a smile,
'but I do think I should not have put myself into Halifax's place'. He
says that it is very difficult to criticise one link in the chain of events
when the whole chain is in itself vicious. He doesn't wish to lead a
revolt or to secure any resignations from the Cabinet.

We then discuss the effect of our surrender.[1] He takes the very
gloomiest view, feeling the leadership has now passed completely from
our hands into that of Germany.

We talk of what small comfort it is to have been proved right, and
how terrible has been the influence of the Cliveden set. As I leave him
he says, 'Well, we shall not be able to avert war now.'

I dine at the Marlborough with Buck De La Warr and Walter Elliot
[Minister of Health]. The latter very ingeniously states the Government
point of view. He makes a great point of the desertion of France, saying
that when one army runs away the other army can scarcely maintain
its position. He denies absolutely that the Prime Minister was given
an ultimatum at Berchtesgaden and in fact he says that Chamberlain
told Hitler that if, pending negotiations, the Czech frontier were
violated he would himself regard it as 'an intolerable affront'. He claims
that the Russians never promised really to help and that we could not
have asked the country to go to war merely to prevent a few Germans
joining their fellow citizens. He is very charming and plausible but my
heart is no lighter and my anger in no way diminished as I make my
way to the BBC.

---

[1] The Anglo-French plan for handing over to Hitler the German-speaking area of
Czechoslovakia.

Diary   *September 21, 1938*

The news is gloomy. Poland and the Hungarians have asked for similar secessions. The Berlin Press say that what remains of Czechoslovakia must adopt a more 'positive' attitude to Berlin. That means she must subordinate her foreign policy to that of the Wilhelmstrasse. Chamberlain goes to Godesberg tomorrow. I pity him.

Diary   *September 22, 1938*

Winston Churchill telephones. Would I come up to London for a meeting at 4.30 in his flat? I say that I shall be there.

I go to 11 Morpeth Mansions. As I approach the door, I see the vulture form of Bob Cecil slipping into the flat. While I wait for the lift to descend Winston appears from a taxi. We go up together. 'This,' I say, 'is hell.' 'It is the end of the British Empire.'

Winston had just been to Downing Street. He says that the Cabinet are at last taking a firm stand. Chamberlain is to demand from Hitler (a) early demobilisation (b) agreement that the transfer of the Sudeten territories should be undertaken gradually by an international commission (c) that there must be no nonsense about the Polish and Hungarian claims (d) that what remains of the Czechs shall be guaranteed. We say at once 'But Hitler will never accept such terms.' 'In that case,' says Winston, 'Chamberlain will return tonight and we shall have WAR.' We suggest that in that event it will be inconvenient having our Prime Minister in German territory. 'Even the Germans,' flashes Winston, 'would not be so stupid as to deprive us of our beloved Prime Minister.'

We then get down to business. It is interrupted, first by a telephone message from Jan Masaryk [Czech Ambassador in London] saying that the Germans have occupied Asch and that the Czechs are withdrawing gradually from the Sudeten areas. Also [Prime Minister] Hodza has resigned, and a 'Ministry of Concentration' has been appointed. Secondly, by a telephone call from Attlee saying that the Opposition are prepared to come in with us if we like. That is vague.

We continue the conversation. We conclude (a) that we shall support the P.M. if it means war or a firm line (b) that if he runs away again

we shall join with the Opposition (c) that we shall be summoned by
Winston again if things go wrong.

Dine at the Beefsteak. This is, I suppose, a more or less Tory Club
and they are all in despair about their Government. They admit that
at the moment half of the Cabinet will resign. I believe no such thing.
The fact remains that they feel Chamberlain has behaved with great
optimism and some conceit. The Berchtesgaden visit has been shown
to have been a gesture of weakness. Then there is the secrecy side.
Everybody was prepared to agree to Chamberlain's secret diplomacy,
provided that it would let us out: they are furious with it now that it
has let us in. My opinion is that these Tories are appalled by the force
of opinion in the provinces.

Diary   *September 23, 1938*

I finish my book [*Diplomacy*] at 4.45. So that's done. But I doubt
whether it will be published. We listen to the 6 o'clock news. Chamberlain has not resumed negotiations with Hitler: all they have done is
to exchange letters. Meanwhile Reuter reports that the *Freikorps* have
begun to invade Czechoslovakia. War is almost on us.

At 9 the telephone rings. It is Bob Boothby. 'I have just come back
from Geneva and I thought you might want a word.' 'What were they
feeling there?' 'Complete demoralisation, but I had a good talk with
Litvinov [the Soviet Foreign Commissar]. The Russians will give us
full support.' 'Well, what about Godesberg?' 'Haven't you heard?
Chamberlain is returning.' 'That means war?' 'Yes, it has taken the
Germans in their idiocy to push us into this. We gave them all they
asked for. Now they go to the point where they will push even us into
it, and we are in for four years.'

I suppose that Ribbentrop has convinced Hitler that whatever
happens we shall stay out. We cannot stay out now that Chamberlain
has sacrificed everything (even our honour) to secure a peace which
he has broken. How sorry I feel for the German people! All the
Cliveden set and *The Times* people prevented us from taking a strong
line while it could have made for peace. But we must support the
Government without vituperation or criticism. We are all in the same
boat now.

Diary   *September 26, 1938*

Winston gathers that the memorandum or letter which Horace Wilson [Chamberlain's emissary] is to give to Hitler is not in the least a retreat. It is merely an attempt to save Hitler's face if he wants to climb down. It offers a conference to decide the means of carrying out the Franco-British plan. It warns him that we do not accept his own post-Godesberg plan and that if he insists, we shall go to war. He had urged the P.M. to mobilise the Fleet at once and call up all reserves. He says he will do so at 9 p.m. this evening if Hitler's speech at 8 p.m. tonight is not conciliatory.

Winston says (and we all agree) that the fundamental mistake the P.M. has made is his refusal to take Russia into his confidence. Ribbentrop always said to Hitler, 'You need never fear England until you find her mentioning Russia as an ally. Then it means that she is really going to war!' We therefore decide that Winston shall go at once to Halifax and tell him to put out some notice before Hitler's speech. 'We have only got till nine,' says Winston grimly.

My first sight of the War of 1938 was a poster in the Strand: — 'City of Westminster: Air Raid Precautions: Gas Masks Notice', followed by instructions where to get yourself fitted for masks. My second sight was workmen digging trenches feverishly in Green Park.

Diary[1]   *September 28, 1938*

Hitler has announced that unless he gets an affirmative reply by 2 p.m. today he will mobilise tomorrow. I presume it means that he will try to cross the [Czech] frontier some time this evening. President Roosevelt has issued an eleventh hour appeal for a conference. We have mobilised the Fleet.

I walk down to the House at 2.15 p.m. passing through Trafalgar Square and down Whitehall. The pigeons are clustered round the fountains and children are feeding them. My companion says to me 'Those children ought to be evacuated at once, and so should the

---

[1] Harold dictated the whole of this entry, and broadcast it that night on the BBC Empire Service.

pigeons.' As we get near the House of Commons there is a large shuffling, shambling crowd and there are people putting fresh flowers at the base of the Cenotaph. The crowd is very silent and anxious. They stare at us with dumb, inquisitive eyes.

The Speaker began by announcing the death of previous Members, and he had hardly finished with the obituary list before the Prime Minister entered from behind his chair. He was greeted with wild applause by his supporters, many of whom rose in their seats and waved their order-papers. The Labour Opposition, the Liberal Opposition and certain of the National supporters [among them Harold] remained seated.

Chamberlain rose slowly in his place and spread the manuscript of his speech upon the box in front of him. The House was hushed in silent expectancy. From the Peers' Gallery above the clock the calm face of Lord Baldwin peered down upon the arena in which he himself had so often battled. Chamberlain began with a chronological statement of events which had led up to the crisis. He spoke in calm measured tones and the House listened to him in dead silence. The only interruption was made by the Messengers of the House who, as always happens, kept on passing along the benches the telegrams and pink telephone slips which were pouring in upon Members. Winston Churchill who sits at the end of my row, received so many telegrams that they were clipped together by an elastic band. Attlee sat opposite Chamberlain with his feet on the table looking like an amiable little bantam. The first burst of applause occurred when Chamberlain mentioned Lord Runciman's great services, and as he did so, he removed his pince-nez between his finger and thumb, raised his face to the skylight and spoke with friendly conviction. Being an experienced Parliamentarian, he would abandon his manuscript at moments and speak extempore.

The chronological method which he adopted increased the dramatic tensity of the occasion. We all knew more or less what had happened in August and the early weeks of September, and we were waiting for his statement of what had occurred during the last few hours. He reached the point where he described the fourth plan of President Benes. The mention of this plan was received with loud cheers, and he described it in precise terms, having taken off his pince-nez and holding them between his finger and thumb. 'On Friday, 23rd September,' he said, 'a Cabinet meeting was held again ...' The House leant forward, realising that he was passing from that part of the story which we already knew to the part that had not yet been divulged. He went on to describe his negotiations with the Czechs and the French and to tell us how he felt it necessary himself to visit Herr Hitler 'as a last resort'. When he said these words, 'as a last resort', he whipped off his pince-nez and looked up at the skylight with an expression of grim hope. He then described his visit to Berchtesgaden. 'It was,' he said with a wry grin, 'my first flight,' and then he described the whole visit as 'this adventure'. He said that his conversation with Hitler had convinced him that the Führer was prepared, on behalf of the Sudeten Germans, 'to risk world war'. As he said these words a shudder of horror passed through the House of Commons.

'I came back,' he added, 'to London the next day.' The House was tense with excitement. He then told us how the Anglo-French plan was described by Hitler at Godesberg as 'too dilatory'. 'Imagine,' he said, 'the perplexity in which I found myself.' This remark roused a murmur of sympathetic appreciation from all the benches.

'Yesterday morning,' began the Prime Minister, and we were again conscious that some revelation was approaching. He began to tell us of his final appeal to Hitler and Mussolini. I glanced at the clock. It was twelve minutes after four. The Prime Minister had been speaking for exactly an hour. I noticed that a sheet of Foreign Office paper was being rapidly passed along the Government bench. Sir John Simon interrupted the Prime Minister and there was a momentary hush. He adjusted his pince-nez and read the document that had been handed to him. His whole face, his whole body, seemed to change. He raised his face so that the light from the ceiling fell full upon it. All the lines of anxiety and weariness seemed suddenly to have been smoothed out; he appeared ten years younger and triumphant. 'Herr Hitler,' he said, 'has just agreed to postpone his mobilisation for twenty-four hours and to meet me in conference with Signor Mussolini and Monsieur Daladier at Munich.'

That, I think, was one of the most dramatic moments which I have ever witnessed. For a second, the House was hushed in absolute silence. And then the whole House burst into a roar of cheering, since they knew that this might mean peace. That was the end of the Prime Minister's speech, and when he sat down the whole

House rose as a man to pay tribute to his achievement. [Later H.N. added: I remained seated. Liddall behind me, hissed out, 'Stand up, you brute!']

Diary *September 29, 1938*

The papers are ecstatic about Chamberlain. Raymond [Mortimer] rings me up and says, 'Isn't this ghastly?' Eddy [Sackville-West] rings me up and says 'Isn't this hell?' Margot Oxford rings me up and says 'Now Harold you must agree that he is a great man?' I say 'Not at all.' 'You are as bad as Violet [Bonham Carter],' she snaps. 'He is the greatest Englishman that ever lived.'

It seems that my refusal to stand up yesterday when all the rest of the House went hysterical has made an impression. Everybody has heard of it. I was ashamed of the House yesterday; it was a Welsh revivalist meeting.

I had meant to go down to Sissinghurst but Winston asked me to stay on in London. At 7 p.m. we meet again at the Savoy. The idea had been to get Winston, Cecil, Attlee, Archie Sinclair and Lloyd to join in a telegram to the P.M. begging him not to betray the Czechs. We had been busy at that all afternoon. But Anthony [Eden] had refused to sign on the grounds that it would be interpreted as a vendetta against Chamberlain. Attlee had refused to sign without the approval of his party. There was thus no time. We sat there gloomily realising that nothing could be done. Even Winston seemed to have lost his fighting spirit. Afterwards I go to Brooks' to look at the tape. So far as I can see, Hitler gets everything he wants.

Diary *September 30, 1938*

Wake up feeling wretched. Usually I wake up feeling life is worth living. Today I woke up with iron in my soul. The terms as published seem to me to be little better than Godesberg although one must wait to see the map before deciding. Violet Bonham Carter rings me up. She had been seeing Jan Masaryk. He told her that our Minister in Prague had presented the Munich scheme to Benes and demanded an

acceptance in two hours. Benes and the Government will resign. So
Hitler has achieved even that. A terrible humiliation.

Diary   *October 1, 1938*

I go back to London [from Manchester]. The posters say 'Cabinet
Minister Resigns'. I assume that it is Buck – but not at all. It is Duff
Cooper and his resignation is accompanied by a nasty letter. He has
no money and he gives up £5,000 a year plus a job he loves.

Diary   *October 5, 1938*

I keep on rising in my place from 3 p.m. till 9.25. This is a good thing.
I have achieved a prominence in the House which is unjustified by my
juniority. Thus when I am called, there is a burst of applause and
people flock in. My speech goes well. I get approbation and notes
from many people. I know that it made its effect.

Diary   *October 6, 1938*

Our group decide that it is better for us all to abstain, than for some
of us to abstain and some to vote against. We therefore sit in our seats,
which must enrage the Government, since it is not our numbers that
matter but our reputation. Among those who abstained were Eden,
Duff Cooper, Winston, Amery, Cranborne, Wolmer, Roger Keyes,
Sidney Herbert, Louis Spears, Harold Macmillan, Richard Law, Bob
Boothby, Jim Thomas, Duncan Sandys, Ronald Cartland, Anthony
Crossley, Brendan Bracken and Emrys-Evans. That looks none too
well in any list. The House knows that most of the above people know
far more about the real issue than they do.

It was clear that the Government were rattled by this. In the first
place, the P.M. gave a pledge that there would be no General Election.
In the second place he made the astounding admission that his phrase
about 'peace in our time' was made under the stress of emotion. The
House breaks up with the Tories yelling to keep their spirits up. But

they well know that Chamberlain has put us in a ghastly position and that we ought to have been prepared to go to war and smash Hitler. Next time he will be far too strong for us.

Harold found himself out of sympathy not only with the Government, but with his party (and its leaders Malcolm MacDonald and Lord De La Warr). He considered resigning. Instead he allied himself with thirty other Members led unofficially by Anthony Eden.

He also began to write his weekly 'Marginal Comment' for the Spectator, *and would continue to do so for the next fourteen years.*

H.N. to Vita   *November 9, 1938*

I went to a hush-hush meeting with Anthony Eden. Present: Eden, Amery, Cranborne, Sidney Herbert, Cartland, Harold Macmillan, Spears, Derrick Gunston, Emrys-Evans, Anthony Crossley, Hubert Duggan. All good Tories and sensible men. This group is distinct from the Churchill group. It also includes Duff Cooper. We decided that we should not advertise ourselves as a group or even call ourselves a group. We should merely meet together from time to time, exchange views, and organise ourselves for a revolt if needed. I feel happier about this. Eden and Amery are wise people, and Sidney Herbert is very experienced. They are deeply disturbed by the fact that Chamberlain does not seem to understand the gravity of the situation. Unless we pull ourselves together and have compulsory registration [for military service] in the next few years, it will be too late. It was a relief to me to be with people who share my views so completely, and yet who do not give the impression (as Winston does) of being more bitter than determined, and more out for a fight than for reform.

H.N. to Vita   *November 11, 1938*

Anthony Eden's speech last night created a sensation. Nobody quite knew what he was talking about. Was he trying to split the Government? Or angling for a Coalition? Or what? I know what he is doing. He is trying to wake up the country to real energies and sacrifice.

Diary   *December 5, 1938*

Winston starts brilliantly and we are all expecting a great speech. He accused Hore-Belisha [Minister of War] of being too complacent. The latter gets up and says, 'When and where?' Winston replies, 'I have not come unprepared,' and begins to fumble among his notes, where there are some press cuttings. He takes time. The ones he reads out excuse rather than implicate Hore-Belisha. Winston becomes confused. He tries to rally his speech, but the wind has gone out of his sails, which flop wretchedly. He certainly is a tiger who, if he misses his spring, is lost.

Diary   *December 29, 1938*

I read *Childe Harold* with more appreciation than before. I feel happier after I have read it, having been so depressed these weeks. A gloomy anxiety has brooded over my apparent business. I wonder what is the real nature of that anxiety? Is it dread of war and a terror lest Ben and Niggs may be taken from me? Is it horror of violence and an impersonal wincing-away from the thought of whole families devastated in Bermondsey? Is it loathing of the thought that this evil *Mein Kampf* theory, this vulgar violence, may triumph over the gentle elegancies which we and France have evolved? Or does my depression come from the fact that I have no power and so little influence? That my lack of combative instincts makes me merely write comments upon statesmanship without being able to influence or to grasp it? Or is it just that Sissinghurst is not a winter resort, that I am overworked and know in my inside that I shall never be a good writer or a forceful politician? Or is it merely low physical depression at not being young, at being an old asthmatic buffer?

I wonder sometimes whether my activity, my ceaseless passion for work, is not merely a device for evading thought. Such is the fate of a frivolous and self-indulgent person who reaches autumn and observes how recklessly he has flung his seed.

Diary   *December 31, 1938*

It has been a bad year. Chamberlain has destroyed the Balance of
Power, and Niggs got a third. A foul year. Next year will be worse.

*On March 15, 1939 Hitler invaded Czechoslovakia and occupied Prague
without a fight. It was the virtual end of Chamberlain's policy of appeasement.
On March 31 he announced that Britain and France would guarantee Poland
against German attack. It was a sad triumph for Harold. He was still very
active, speaking frequently in Parliament and abroad, as well as broadcasting
and writing weekly for the* Spectator *and* Daily Telegraph.

Diary   *January 15, 1939*

Wind and rain. Finish my reviews and my article. V. and I go to the
new cuttings and examine the willows which Niggs and I planted.
Freya Stark [the traveller] comes to dinner. She is anti-Chamberlain
and thinks we should intervene in Spain at once. It is too late. Franco
is almost within sight of Barcelona and once he gets there he will cut
communications with France and obtain the munitions works of the
Republicans. I fear it is all over. Chamberlain announces that 'he is
returning from Rome convinced of the good faith and of the good
intentions of the Italian Government'. How can he say such a thing at
a moment when Italian troops are advancing on Barcelona? It is as bad
as his 'peace with honour' after Munich. Either he believes it, in which
case he has no conception of the real proportions of the situation, or
else he does not believe it in which case he is lying. How can he be so
obstinate?

Diary   *January 17, 1939*

The tragedy of Europe seems to come closer to us in ever diminishing
circles. Dear little Giles [St Aubyn, Harold's fourteen-year-old
nephew] chatters about Sir Humphrey Davy for whom he has a
passion. His sensitive nervous face and his intelligence make me even

more unhappy. What will that delightful boy have to create in the world which will be his adult world? To me it does not matter. I can just die. But he and Niggs and Ben have got to live, and all the delicacy of life will have gone. All the truthfulness, all the outspokenness, all the easiness of life will have gone. They will never know *la douceur de vivre*.

Diary   *January 25, 1939*

Lunch at Bedford Square with Margot Oxford and Elizabeth Bibesco. An incongruous party. Emil Ludwig [the biographer], Attlee, Leon Blum's nephew and a Harley Street doctor. Attlee is very silly and charming. A delightful man of course, but not a pilot in a hurricane. Ludwig almost cuts me dead. I avoid him. He says he is writing a book about the Windsors. Margot says, 'Dear me, that's very vulgar of you.' He is much taken aback.

Diary   *February 4, 1939*

V. and I go round to the Beales' [farmer at Sissinghurst] where there is a Television Set lent by a local radio-merchant. We see a Mickey Mouse, a play and a Gaumont British film. I had always been told that the television could not be received above 25 miles from Alexandra Palace. But the reception was every bit as good as at Selfridge's. Compared with a film, it is a bleary, flickering, dim, unfocused, interruptible thing, the size of a quarto sheet of paper such as this on which I am typing. But as an invention it is tremendous and may alter the whole basis of democracy.

H.N. to Vita   *February 7, 1939*

Really Chamberlain is an astonishing and perplexing old boy. This afternoon (as you will have heard) he startled the House and the world by proclaiming something like an offensive and a defensive alliance between us and France. Now that is the very thing that all of us have been pushing for, working for, writing for, speaking for, all these months. And the old boy gets up and does it as if it were the simplest thing on earth. The House was absolutely astounded. It could not have been more definite.

Now what does it all mean? Is he really so ignorant of diplomacy as to assume that this means little? I cannot believe that. He spoke so resolutely and so deliberately. The House cheered loudly. It was superb. I felt happy for the first time in months. But this is a complete negation of his 'appeasement' policy and of his Rome visit. He has in fact swung suddenly round to all that we have been asking for. What does it mean? I think that it can only mean that he realises that appeasement has failed. It is at this stage that his value as a diplomatic asset becomes operative. No ordinary German or Italian will ever believe propaganda telling him that Chamberlain is a 'war-monger'.

Diary   *February 9, 1939*

Lunch at the Russian Embassy. A strange party. Bob Boothby, Dick Law, Vernon Bartlett and J.B. Priestley. We start by talking rather shyly about food. Gradually, as the vodka circulates, we approach the less sure ground of politics. Maisky [Russian Ambassador] asks us (with his little Kalmuk eyes twinkling round the table), 'What is going to happen now?' We all hope that someone else is going to answer. I suggest gaily that the moment may be approaching when Russia will be forced to join the anti-Comintern Pact. Maisky says that Russia was obviously much wounded by Munich and that we can expect no advances from her side. But (and here he becomes serious) if *we* made approaches, we should not find Russia as aloof or offended as we might have supposed. Bob Boothby and I have an eye-meet like a tennis-ball across a net.

Diary   *March 15, 1939*

Frederick Voigt [Editor, *Nineteenth Century*] telephones to say that Hitler has occupied Prague. Go round to Mark Patrick's house for a meeting of the group. Eden says that he is going to speak today, and what is he to say? We all agree that the one thing not to do is hoot and jeer. We agree that we must support the Government, and that Anthony should speak, and that only our lesser fry should speak also. The rest to keep silent.

The *Manchester Guardian* today carried a leader headed 'The Gift of Prophecy'. There is a passage from my Munich speech.

Diary   *March 31, 1939*

Down to the House. The P.M. says he will make a statement shortly before three. The general feeling is that he will announce that if Poland and Rumania are attacked we shall go to war. There is some uneasiness about in the corridors. People fear lest Chamberlain may not stay put.

Chamberlain arrives looking gaunt and ill. The skin above his high cheek bones is parchment yellow. He drops wearily into his place. David Margesson proposes the adjournment and the P.M. rises. He begins by saying that we believe in negotiation and do not trust in rumours. He then gets to the centre of his statement, namely that if Poland is attacked we shall declare war. That is greeted with cheers from every side. He reads his statement very slowly with a bent grey head. It is most impressive.

Diary   *April 3, 1939*

The House rises at 10.50 p.m. and I am seized upon by Winston and taken down to the lower smoking-room with Maisky and Lloyd George. Winston adopts the direct method of attack. 'Now look here Mr Ambassador, if we are to make a success of this new policy, we require the help of Russia. Now I don't care for your system and I never have, but the Poles and the Rumanians like it even less. Although they might be prepared at a pinch to let you in, they would certainly want some assurances that you would eventually get out. Can you give us such assurances?' Lloyd George, I fear, is not really in favour of the new policy and he draws Maisky on to describe the deficiencies of the Polish Army. Apparently many of their guns are pre-Revolution guns of the Russian Army. Maisky contends that the Polish soldiers are excellent fighters and that the officers are well-trained. Winston rather objects to this and attacks Lloyd George. 'You must not do this sort of thing, my dear. You are putting spokes in the wheel of history.' The relations between these two are very curious. They have had bitter battles in the past and have emerged from these combats with great respect for each other's talents and an affectionate sharing of tremendous common memories. It is curious that little way that Winston has when he speaks to Lloyd George of calling him 'my dear'.

Diary   *April 9, 1939*

In the afternoon Viti and I plant annuals. We sow them in the cottage garden and then in the border and then in the orchard. We rake the soil smooth. And as we rake we are both thinking, 'What will have happened to the world when these seeds germinate?' It is warm and still. We should have been so happy were it not for the thought which aches at our hearts as if some very dear person was dying in the upstairs room. We discuss whether we might be defeated if war comes. And if defeated, surely surrender [suicide] in advance would be better? We ourselves don't think of money or privilege or pleasure. We are thinking only of that vast wastage of suffering which must surely come. All because of the insane ambitions of one fanatic, and of the vicious theory which he has imposed on his people.

The Western attitude was stiffening. The Anglo-Polish Pact of mutual assistance was signed in response to Germany's threat to Danzig. Britain and France signed equivalent guarantees to Greece and Rumania after Mussolini invaded Albania on April 7.

Diary   *April 10, 1939*

The Mediterranean Fleet has been assembled. Italy warns us that if we attack by sea she will drive towards Salonica through the Vardar Valley. Does Mussolini seriously suppose that he could defeat ourselves and France? Or is he still relying upon the defeatist and the pampered group in London who have for so long been assuring him that the capitalists of England are on his side? I do not believe that an intelligent man such as Grandi [Italian Ambassador in London] could have left him under any illusion that the will-power of this country is concentrated in Mrs Ronald Greville. The harm which these silly selfish hostesses do is really immense.[1] They convey to foreign envoys the impression that policy is decided in their own drawing-rooms. That is always what happens with us. The silly people are regarded as representative of British opinion and the informed people are dismissed as 'intellectual'. I should be most unhappy if I were Lady Astor. She must realise that her parrot cries have done much damage to what (to do her justice) she must dimly realise is the essence of her adopted class and country.

Diary   *April 11, 1939*

Harold Macmillan is enraged that Chamberlain should remain on. He thinks that all we Edenites have been too soft and gentlemanlike. That we should have clamoured for Chamberlain's removal. That no man in history has made such persistent and bone-headed mistakes, and that we still go on pretending that all is well.

There is a theory that the appeasers (Simon, Hoare and Horace Wilson) have regained their influence and that Chamberlain is preparing to overlook the rape of Albania and to enter into a new Mediterranean pact with Mussolini, under which we agree not to make an alliance with Greece and Turkey in return for Mussolini agreeing all over again to withdraw troops from Spain and Libya. I do not believe that Halifax would agree to anything so nonsensical, and if Halifax resigns the Government will fall.

---

[1] He was also referring to Lady Astor's Cliveden set. Elsewhere he wrote of Mrs Greville, the hostess who entertained lavishly in London and at her country house, Polesden Lacey, 'How come it is that this plump and virulent little bitch should hold such social power?'

Diary   *April 21, 1939*

The *Spectator* this week suggests that I should be sent as Ambassador to Washington. It amuses me to observe my own reactions to such a suggestion. My first fear is that it will expose me to ridicule, since all we Nicolsons are morbidly sensitive to being placed in a false position. My second impulse is to realise how much Vita would hate it. My third is to feel how much I should loathe the pomp and publicity of an Embassy. My fourth is to agree with the *Spectator* that I might do the job rather well. But it will not occur.

Diary   *April 23, 1939*

I talk to Gafencu [the Rumanian Foreign Minister]. He had been thrilled by his visit to Berlin. He said that Hitler had been quite polite and had not tried to bully him in the least. He had spoken quite calmly at first, but when he touched on ideology he began to scream. He had spent the whole time abusing this country. He had complained that there was no British statesman of sufficient magnitude or vision to agree with him to divide the world between them. He had no desire to possess the British Empire. All that he wanted was that we should not thwart his destiny in Eastern Europe. It was at this stage that he began to scream. He had said that it was grotesque to imagine that he wanted to invade Holland or Belgium. The only small countries that he wants to dominate were those of the East. Gafencu asked him whether these included Rumania, and then he stopped screaming and began to be polite. He said that if war came we might be able to destroy three German towns, but that he would destroy every single British town.

Diary   *April 29, 1939*

I feel pretty glum and devote myself to reviewing. There is Joyce's *Finnegans Wake*. I try very hard indeed to understand that book but fail completely. It is almost impossible to decipher, and when one or two lines of understanding emerge like telegraph poles above a flood, they are at once countered by other poles going in the opposite direction. I see that at the back of it all there is some allegory turning around the Tristan saga. But the research involved in working out this loose mosaic is greater than any ordinary reader can possibly undertake. I truly believe that Joyce has this time gone too far in breaking all communication between himself and his reader. It is a very selfish book.

Diary   *May 31, 1939*

Jack Macnamara told me an interesting thing. He is an intimate friend of one of the more decent Whips and had discussed with them the Eden Group. It seems that they respect Eden, Duff Cooper, Amery and the big bugs. But they are terribly rattled by the existence and the secrecy of the group itself. They know that we meet, and what they do not like is that we do not attack them in the House. If we came out in the open they would know where they stood. What they hate is this silent plotting. They start from the assumption that we wish to upset the present Government, to force them to take our leaders in, and that we juniors imagine that we shall get some pickings from the victory of our leaders. They regard me, it seems, as an able man gone astray. They do not understand how I can be National Labour, regarding that as treachery to my class.

Diary   *June 14, 1939*

Dine with Kenneth Clark. The Walter Lippmanns are there: also the Julian Huxleys and Winston Churchill as the guest of honour.[1] Winston is horrified by Lippmann saying that the American Ambassador, Jo Kennedy, had informed him that war was inevitable and that we should be licked. Winston is stirred by this defeatism into a magnificent oration. He sits hunched there, waving his whisky-and-soda to mark his periods, stubbing his cigar with the other hand.

'It may be true, it may well be true,' he says, 'that this country will

---

[1] Kenneth Clark was Director of the National Gallery, Walter Lippmann America's most distinguished journalist and Julian Huxley Secretary to the London Zoo.

at the outset of this coming and to my mind almost inevitable war be exposed to dire peril and fierce ordeals. It may be true that steel and fire will rain down upon us day and night scattering death and destruction far and wide. It may be true that our sea-communications will be imperilled and our food-supplies placed in jeopardy. Yet these trials and disasters, I ask you to believe me Mr Lippmann, will but serve to steel the resolution of the British people and to enhance our will for victory. No, the Ambassador should not have spoken so, Mr Lippmann; he should not have said that dreadful word. Yet supposing (as I do not for one moment suppose) that Mr Kennedy were correct in his tragic utterance, then I for one would willingly lay down my life in combat, rather than, in fear of defeat, surrender to the menaces of these most sinister men. It will then be for you, for the Americans, to preserve and to maintain the great heritage of the English-speaking peoples. It will be for you to think imperially, which means to think always of something higher and more vast than one's national interests. Nor should I die happy in the great struggle which I see before me, were I not convinced that if we in this dear dear island succumb to the ferocity and might of our enemies, over there in your distant and immune continent the torch of liberty will burn untarnished and (I trust and hope) undismayed.'

We then change the subject and speak about the Giant Panda.

H.N. to Vita   *June 19, 1939*

Why can we not be left alone? We are doing no harm. We care for fine and gentle things. We wish only to do good on earth. We are not vulgar in our tastes or cruel in our thoughts. Why is it that we are impotent to prevent something which we know to be evil and terrible? I would willingly give my own life if I could stop this war. I am so unhappy about the outside, and so happy in my own little orbit.

Diary   *July 24, 1939*

Go to tea at the Russian Embassy and find a strange collection of left-wing enthusiasts sitting round in the Winter Garden with a huge

tea-table spread with delicious cakes and caviar sandwiches, plus a
samovar. The Ambassador is however so interested in convincing them
how right is the Soviet definition of 'indirect aggression' that he forgets
to offer them any tea and they all go away casting regretful glances at
the untouched table. Maisky asks me to go into his study where I have
a long talk, plus a large quantity of the sandwiches which the other
guests have not been offered.

He says that he believes that Chamberlain hopes to get a compromise
on the Danzig question, and that if he does that, he will allow the
[Anglo-]Russian negotiations to lapse. He says that he has a definite
impression that the Government do not really want the negotiations
to go through.

Diary   *August 2, 1939*

To the astonishment of the House the Prime Minister gets up and after
saying that he will not give way an inch [on adjourning the House for
the summer recess], he adds that certain Members had thanked the
Whips for not putting on a three-line whip, but that he wished it to
be clearly understood that he regarded the vote as a vote of confidence
in himself. Ronnie Cartland says that the Prime Minister has missed a
great opportunity by not showing his faith in this great democratic
institution. He goes on, 'We are in the situation that within a month
we may be going to fight and we may be going to die.'[1] At this
Patrick Hannon laughs, and Cartland turns upon him with a flame of
indignation and says, 'It is all very well for you to laugh. There are
thousands of young men at this moment . . .' The effect is galvanic and
I have seldom felt the temperature rise so rapidly. He is then followed
by Macmillan who extracts some sort of promise from the Prime
Minister that he will call Parliament should a situation arise similar to
that which arose in September last year.

---

[1] Cartland himself was killed in action in May 1940.

H.N. to Vita   *August 2, 1939*

We have a debate today about whether we should adjourn or not. I
had hoped that Anthony Eden was going to take a strong line, but he
is now suggesting that we should all toe the line. I would do so were
it not that Winston refuses, and I cannot let the old lion enter the
lobby alone. But apart from this I do feel very deeply that the House
ought not to adjourn for the whole of the two months. I regard it as
a violation of the constitutional principle and an act of disrespect to
the House.

Why is it that I am always in a minority? Is it wrong-headedness? I
simply don't know. Or is it really that I am not a trimmer by nature
and hate discipline?

*As a result of Britain's (and France's) hesitation, Stalin approached Berlin and
negotiated the Russo-German non-aggression pact which provided that neither
country would attack the other or come to the help of a Third Power which
attacked them. It was signed by Ribbentrop on August 23.*

*During the first weeks of the Adjournment, Harold was sailing to France
on his yacht 'Mar'. On returning to Plymouth he heard of the emergency
meeting of Parliament on the 24th. He immediately rushed to London.*

                                                       August 22, 1939
Diary   'Mar', *Plymouth*

I have a feeling that I shall not have much more of my beloved yacht.
At six I listen to the News. The Germans and Russians have announced
that they propose to sign a non-aggression pact and that Ribbentrop
is on his way to Moscow for the purpose. This smashes our peace-
front and makes our guarantees to Poland, Rumania and Greece very
questionable. How Ribbentrop must chuckle. I feel rather stunned by
this news and sit on the deck in bewilderment with the fishing smacks
around me. I fear that it means that we are humbled to the dust.

Diary   *August 23, 1939*

Round to the Travellers and meet Archie Sinclair there.[1] He asks me
to dine with him and the Bonham Carters. We discuss what the Russo-
German agreement really means. There are those who take the view
that the Russians have been extraordinarily clever and are forcing the
Axis Powers to lay their cards upon the table. These people imagine
that Ribbentrop (who has already arrived in Moscow) will be kept
hanging about and will be humiliated. I doubt it. I doubt whether
Ribbentrop would have been such a fool as to go to Moscow unless
he was pretty certain that he would be exposed to no humiliating
delays. Archie had seen the Prime Minister this morning and found
him very depressed and resolute. He leaves us to ring up Winston
Churchill. The latter has just returned from Paris and is in high fettle.
The French are not at all perturbed by the Russo–German Pact and
are prepared to support Poland nonetheless. They are half-mobilising.
Winston has just rung up [Minister of Finance] Paul Reynaud, who
asserts that all is going well: by which he means war, I suppose.

As I drive back to the Temple, I pass a motorcyclist in a steel helmet.
A sinister sight.

H.N. to Vita   *August 24, 1939*

Just a scribble in the intervals of this debate. The P.M. was dignified
and calm, but without one word which could inspire anybody. He was
exactly like a coroner summing up a case of murder.

I see mighty little chance of peace. It may be that Colonel Beck
[Polish Foreign Minister] will lose his nerve and fly to Berchtesgaden.
But even that would be a bad catastrophe.

I gather that the P.M. has offered to resign, but the King won't
accept it.

---

[1] Sir Archibald Sinclair was Leader of the Liberal Party in the House of Commons, and
became Air Minister in Churchill's wartime Government.

Diary   *August 28, 1939*

All international train traffic has been stopped. All British ships have
been told to leave Italian and German ports. Lights are to be extin-
guished in aerodromes. The pound is falling on the New York
Exchange. The *Europa* has scuttled back to Hamburg and the *Bremen*
is taking refuge in New York. It looks as if war would burst upon us
tomorrow.

Again the curious contrast with August 3, 1914! Then we were
excited by all these events and there was a sense of exhilaration. Today
we are merely glum. It is not merely my age and experience which
silences me under this leaden cope of gloom.

Diary   *August 30, 1939*

Lunch with Sibyl Colefax. Lady Cunard and Ivone Kirkpatrick [First
Secretary in Berlin, 1933–8] there. He is interesting about Hitler. He
says that to meet socially, and when he is host in his own house, he
has a certain simple dignity, like a farmer entertaining neighbours. All
very different from the showy vulgarity of Mussolini. But that once
one begins to work with him, or sees him dealing with great affairs,
one has such a sense of evil arrogance that one is almost nauseated.
Evil and treachery and malice dart into Hitler's mystic eyes. He has a
maddening habit of laying down the law in sharp, syncopated sentences,
accompanying the conclusion either with a sharp pat of his palm upon
the table, or by a half-swing sideways in his chair, a sudden Napoleonic
crossing of his arms, and a gaze of detached but suffering mysticism
towards the ceiling. His impatience is terrific. We asked Kirkpatrick
what gave him a sense of actual evil. He said that after Hitler had flown
from Godesberg to Munich to murder Roehm [in 1934], he returned
in the very highest spirits, mimicking to his secretary the gestures of
fear which Roehm had made. This was told to Kirk by one of those
who were present.

Diary   *August 31, 1939*

The *Bremen* has left New York after having been held up for twenty-four hours by American customs. The *Europa*, after disguising itself and creeping round by Iceland, has reached Bremerhaven. The 1 o'clock news announces that we have decided to evacuate three million mothers and children tomorrow from menaced areas. It is rather grim. Historic names such as Rochester, Chatham, Southwark come over at us in the calm cultured voice of the announcer. The flag hangs limply on its flag-staff. It is odd to feel that the world as I knew it has only a few hours more to run.

Diary   *September 1, 1939*

I take a deck-chair and sit at the door of the South Cottage so that I can hear the telephone if it rings. Viti comes along the path walking quickly. 'It has begun,' she says. It seems that last night Förster [Nazi Gauleiter of Danzig], with Hitler's approval, announced the incorporation of Danzig in the Reich, and that hostilities between Germany and Poland have already begun. The House has been summoned for 6 o'clock tonight. It is exactly 10.45 that I get this news. Miss Macmillan [secretary] appears with my gas-mask in a box.

Motor up to London. There are few signs of any undue activity beyond a few khaki figures at Staplehurst and some schoolboys filling sand-bags at Maidstone. When we get near London we see a row of balloons hanging like black spots in the air.

Go down to the House at 5.30. They have already darkened the building and lowered the lights. The lobby is extremely dark, and the Chamber, which generally seems to be a dim aquarium, appears quite garish by comparison. The Speaker arrives punctually at 6 and we all bow to him. Lloyd George and Winston are already in their places facing each other. We have prayers. The Chaplain adds a little special prayer saying, 'Let us this day pray for wisdom and courage to defend the right.' The Prime Minister and Greenwood [Leader of the Opposition] enter together and are received with a loud cheer. People crowd into the Distinguished Strangers Gallery. The Polish and Russian Ambassadors find themselves next to each other. I grin up at Maisky and he grins back. The Dukes of Kent and Gloucester sit above the clock.

Chamberlain rises immediately. He begins by saying that the time has arrived when action rather than speech is required. He then, with some emotion, reminds the House how he prayed that it would never fall upon him to ask the country to accept the 'awful arbitrament of war'. 'I fear,' he continued, 'that I may not be able to avoid that responsibility.' He then goes on to say that we have neglected no means of making it crystal clear to the German Government that if they use force we should reply by force, and he raises his voice and strikes the box with a clenched fist as he says, 'The responsibility for this terrible catastrophe lies on the shoulders of one man, the German Chancellor, who has not hesitated to plunge the world into misery in order to serve his own senseless ambition.' This met with a loud cheer from all benches. He then continues calmly explaining the recent course of negotiations, resting the back of one hand upon the palm of the other, and every now and then pinching off his pince-nez between his finger and thumb. When he reveals the fact that the sixteen points which Hitler claims to have been rejected were never even communicated to the Poles, a gasp of astonishment rises and Lady Astor exclaims in ringing tones, 'Well, I never did!' He then reaches the climax of his speech, and after saying that the two Ambassadors have been instructed 'to hand to the German Government the following document,' he fiddles with his papers for some time and then produces a document which he reads very slowly.[1] He is evidently in real moral agony and the general feeling in the House is one of deep sympathy for him and of utter misery for ourselves.

I am afraid that the Lobby opinion is rather defeatist and they all realise that we have in front of us a very terrible task. The Prime Minister's speech is generally approved, although the Opposition mind very much his having brought in that friendly reference to Mussolini.

---

[1] The document, handed that evening to the German Government in Berlin, read: 'Unless the German Government are prepared to give satisfactory assurances that the German Government have suspended all aggressive action against Poland ... His Majesty's Government will without hesitation fulfil their obligation to Poland.'

Diary   *September 2, 1939*

The House is packed and tense and we wait there exactly like a court
awaiting the verdict of the jury. At 7.42 the Prime Minister enters with
Greenwood.[1] He gets up to speak. He begins with the chronological
method: 'On Wednesday night Sir Nevile Henderson, our Ambassador
in Berlin, handed to Herr von Ribbentrop ...' – that sort of thing.
His voice betrays some emotion as if he were sickening for a cold. He
is a strange man. We expected one of his dramatic surprises. But none
came. It was evident when he sat down that no decision had been
arrived at. The House gasped for one moment in astonishment. Was
there to be another Munich after all? Then Greenwood got up. The
disappointment at the P.M.'s statement, the sense that appeasement
had come back, vented itself in the reception of Greenwood. His own
people cheered, as was natural; but what was so amazing was that their
cheer was taken up in a second and greater wave from our benches.
Bob Boothby cried out, '*You* speak for Britain.' It was an astonishing
demonstration. Greenwood almost staggered with surprise. When it
subsided he had to speak and did so better than I had expected. He
began to say what an embarrassing task had been imposed on him. He
had wanted to support and was obliged to criticise. Why this delay?
We had promised to help Poland 'at once'. She was being bombed and
attacked. We had vacillated for 34 hours. What did this mean? He was
resoundingly cheered. The tension became acute, since here were the
P.M.'s most ardent supporters cheering his opponent with all their
lungs. The front bench looked as if they had been struck in the face.

The House adjourns. The lobby is so dark that a match struck flames
like a beacon. There is great confusion and indignation. We feel that
the German ships and submarines will, owing to this inexplicable delay,
elude our grasp. The P.M. must know by now that the whole House
is against him. He might (had he been a more imaginative man) have
got out of his difficulty. It was not his fault but that of Georges Bonnet
[French Foreign Minister]. But he is too secretive by nature to be able
to create confidence. In those few minutes he flung away his reputation.
I feel deeply sorry for him.

---

[1] Arthur Greenwood, Deputy Leader of the Labour Party, spoke for his Party in the
absence of Clement Attlee through illness.

Diary   *Sunday, September 3, 1939*

The papers announce that we are sending an ultimatum which expires at 11 this morning.

To Ronnie Tree's house. The usual members of our group are enlivened by the presence of Bob Boothby and Duncan Sandys of the Churchill group. We discuss first whether Anthony [Eden] is to accept the offer to join the Cabinet, although he is not included in the inner Cabinet. Some people think that he must refuse to join except as a member of the War Cabinet. Anthony rather writhes and wriggles, from which I gather that he has already committed himself to join and does not relish these suggestions.[1] I watch the minute hand of my watch creeping towards 11 a.m., when we shall be at war. When the watch reaches that point, we pay no attention. The Prime Minister is to broadcast at 11.15 and we have no wireless. The housemaid has one and she comes and fixes it up in a fumbling way. We listen to the P.M. He is quite good and tells us war has begun. But he puts in a personal note which shocks us. We feel that after last night's demonstration he cannot possibly lead us into a great war. At the end of his speech are official announcements and notably one which says that from this moment no factory sirens are to sound and that any we hear are to be taken to be air-raid warnings. One of the group who had come back into the Chamber after the adjournment says that Chamberlain remained on the bench with Margesson. The latter was purple in the face, and the former was white as a sheet. It must be clear to them that if it had come to a vote at the time, he would have been defeated.

At noon we return to the Chamber [after an air-raid warning]. The Speaker takes his seat with the usual calm procedure. We have prayers. The Prime Minister then makes a speech which is restrained and therefore effective. He looks very ill. Winston intervenes with a speech which misses fire since it is too like one of his articles. The sirens continue during the debate, but we pay no attention to them. They are sounding the all-clear. We learn afterwards that the whole air-raid warning was a mistake. But the effect of this alarm was that nobody

---

[1] In the afternoon he was, in fact, offered the Dominions Office without a seat in the Cabinet.

was really attuned to listen with any real receptiveness to the speeches
that were made.

At 1.50 I motor down with Victor Cazalet to Sissinghurst. There
are many army lorries along the road and a few pathetic trucks evacuating East End refugees. In one of those there is an elderly woman
who shakes her fist at us and shouts that it is all the fault of the rich.
The Labour Party will be hard put to it to prevent this war degenerating
into class warfare.

When I reach Sissinghurst I find that the flag has been pulled down.

PART III

THE WAR YEARS
1939–1945

The outbreak of war found Harold Nicolson in a gloomy mood. He feared defeat. When Hitler conquered Poland in less than a month, he and his colleagues in the 'Eden Group' were convinced that the British war-effort would only stiffen if Winston Churchill succeeded Chamberlain as Prime Minister.

Diary   *September 4, 1939*

... Two things impress themselves upon me. (1) Time. It seems three weeks since yesterday morning and it is difficult to get one's days of the week in chronological order. (2) Nature. Even as when someone dies, one is amazed that the poplar should still be standing quite unaware of one's own disaster, so also when I walked down to the lake to bathe I could scarcely believe that the swans were being sincere in their indifference to the Second German War.

Up to London. The posters carry the words 'British Liner Torpedoed'. It is the *Athenia* out from Liverpool to Canada or the United States which was torpedoed off the Hebrides [112 lives were lost; twenty-eight of them American]. Many Americans must have been drowned. How insane the Germans are at the very moment when Roosevelt has put out his neutrality proclamation. It is a bad proclamation from our point of view. He says that nothing on earth will induce the Americans to send forces to Europe. But he also says that no man can remain neutral in mind and that he knows where the right lies.

Diary   *September 5, 1939*

I am in a mood of deep depression. I do not really see how we can win this war, yet if we lose it, we lose everything. It may be that I am old [fifty-two] and sad and defeatist. But one thing I do know and it comforts me. I would rather go down fighting and suffering than creep out after a month or two at the cost of losing our pride. That may be the only thing left to us.

H.N. to Vita   *September 14, 1939*

The Opposition are getting somewhat restive, especially about the Ministry of Information. The latter has been staffed by duds at the top and all the good people are in the most subordinate positions. The rage and fury of the newspapermen passes all bounds. John Gunther [the American war correspondent] for instance, told me that he had asked one of the censors for the text of our leaflet which we dropped over Germany. The request was refused. He asked why. The answer was, 'We are not allowed to disclose information which might be of value to the enemy.' When Gunther pointed out that two million of these leaflets had been dropped over Germany, the man blinked and said, 'Yes, something must be wrong there.'

Diary   *September 16, 1939*

My appalling depression may be due to the fact that I am living my former life with all the conditions altered. Rob Bernays told me yesterday that all the front-bench people keep exclaiming, 'I wish I were twenty. I cannot bear this responsibility.' What they really mean is, 'I wish I did not know how bad things are!' The whole world is either paralysed or against us.

Diary   *September 17, 1939*

Write my *Spectator* article. At 11 a.m. (a bad hour) Vita comes to tell me that Russia has invaded Poland and is striking towards Vilna. We are so dumbfounded by the news that there is a wave of despair over Sissinghurst. I do not think that the Russians will go beyond her old frontier or will wish to declare war on us. But of course it is a terrific blow and makes our victory even more uncertain.

Let me review the situation. It may be that within a few days we shall have Germany, Russia and Japan against us. It may be that Rumania will be subjugated and that the Greeks and Yugoslavs will succumb to Germany. The Baltic and the Scandinavian states will be too frightened to do anything. Holland, Belgium and Switzerland will have to capitulate. Thus the Axis will rule Europe, the Mediterranean and the Far East. Faced by such a combine, France may make terms. Hitler is then in the position of Napoleon after Austerlitz, with the important difference that whereas we were then in command of the seas, our command of the seas is not now absolute. It is not so much a question of them encircling and blockading us; it is a question of us encircling and blockading them. Japan might threaten our position in Australia and the Far East. Russia might threaten us in India. Italy might raise the Arab world. In a few days our whole position might collapse. Nothing could be more black.

And yet and yet, I still believe that if we have the will-power, we might win through. The Germans, who are diffident by nature, can scarcely believe in this fairy-tale. A single reverse and they will be overcome with nervous trepidation. Our position is one of grave danger. A generous offer of an immediate truce with the prospect of an eventual conference might tempt us sorely. But we will not have a generous offer. What will happen? I suppose there will be a German ultimatum and a Coalition Cabinet. Chamberlain must go. Churchill might be our Clemenceau or our Gambetta. To bed very miserable and alarmed.

Diary   *September 20, 1939*

Lloyd George [then seventy-six] says that he is frankly terrified and does not see how we can possibly win the war. He contends that we should insist immediately upon a Secret Session of Parliament in which we should force the Government to tell us exactly how they estimate the prospects of victory. If our chances are 50/50, then it might be worthwhile organising the whole resources of the country for a desperate struggle. But if the chances are really against us, then we should certainly make peace at the earliest opportunity, possibly with Roosevelt's assistance. He indulges in a fierce onslaught on the stupidity and lack of vigour of the present Government. He contends that to have guaranteed Poland and Rumania without a previous agreement with Russia was an act of incredible folly and one which was due to the essential weakness of Chamberlain's character.

The House is in one of its worst moods. The Prime Minister rises to make his weekly statement. He reads it out from a manuscript and is obviously tired and depressed. The effect is most discouraging and Members drop off to sleep. The Prime Minister has no gift for inspiring anybody, and he might have been the Secretary of a firm of undertakers reading the minutes of the last meeting.

Diary   *September 25, 1939*

Allen Lane [Chairman of Penguin Books] comes to see me, and it is agreed that I do a Penguin Special for him on why Britain is at War.[1]

Diary   *September 26, 1939*

The Prime Minister gets up to make his statement. He is dressed in deep mourning relieved only by a white handkerchief and a large gold watch-chain. One feels the confidence and spirits of the House dropping inch by inch. When he sits down there is scarcely any applause. During the whole speech Winston Churchill[2] had sat hunched beside him looking like the Chinese god of plenty suffering from acute indigestion. He just sits there, lowering, hunched and circular, and then he gets up. He is greeted by a loud cheer from all the benches and he starts to tell us about the Naval position. He began by saying how strange an experience it was for him after a quarter of a century to find himself once more in the same room in front of the same maps, fighting the same enemy and dealing with the same problems. His face then creases into an enormous grin and he adds, glancing down at the Prime Minister, 'I have no

---

[1] Harold wrote this 50,000-word paperback in three weeks. It was published on November 7 and soon sold over 100,000 copies.

[2] Churchill was now First Lord of the Admiralty, with a seat in the Cabinet.

conception how this curious change in my fortunes occurred.' The whole House roared with laughter and the Prime Minister had not the decency to raise a sickly smile. He just looked sulky. His delivery was amazing. One could feel the spirit of the House rising with every word. In those 20 minutes Churchill brought himself nearer the post of Prime Minister than he has ever been before. In the lobbies afterwards even Chamberlainites were saying 'we have now found our leader'. Old Parliamentary hands confessed that never in their experience had they seen a single speech so change the temper of the House.

Diary   *September 27, 1939*

Lunch with Sibyl Colefax. The people are H.G. Wells, G.M. Young [the historian], Victor Cazalet and Jan Masaryk. The Duke and Duchess of Windsor appear although I had imagined that he was over in France. He is going there shortly. He is dressed in khaki with all his decorations and looks grotesquely young. H.G. Wells, who is a republican with a warm sympathy for the Duke of Windsor, refuses to bow to him but treats him with great friendliness. The Duchess tells me that on the day before war he sent a private telegram to Hitler urging him to do his best for peace. At 2 a.m. the next morning they were rung up by the night watchman saying that a most important telegram had arrived. The local postmaster insisted upon delivering this telegram in person and when it arrived they discovered that it was merely an acknowledgement by Hitler in perfectly polite terms of the telegram the Duke had sent. The postmaster was so impressed by the signature that he had felt it necessary to rouse the household.

I have seldom seen the Duke in such cheerful spirits and it was rather touching to witness their delight at being back in England. There was no false note.

Walking away with H.G. Wells I said to him, 'You must admit the man has got charm?' 'Glamour,' he said. 'Charm,' I said. 'Oh very well,' he said, 'have it your own way.'

Diary   *October 3, 1939*

I go with Duff Cooper to the Carlton Grill, where Diana [Cooper] has a supper party in honour of Burckhardt, the former League of Nations High Commissioner in Danzig. He is rather a dapper, smart, fresh-coloured Swiss aristocrat speaking the most beautiful French. I sit next to him and find him most intelligent and amusing. He talks a great deal about Hitler. He says that Hitler is the most profoundly feminine man that he has ever met, and that there are moments when he becomes almost effeminate. He imitates the movements of his white flabby hands. He says that Hitler has a dual personality, the first being that of the rather gentle artist, and the second that of the homicidal maniac. He is convinced that Hitler has no complete confidence in himself and that his actions are really governed by somnambulist certainty. He says that the main energy in Hitler is an energy of hatred, and that he never met any human being capable of generating so terrific a condensation of envy, vituperation and malice. Yet now and then there is a pathetic side to him. For instance, he once heard Hitler say, 'It is a great sorrow to me that I have never met an Englishman who speaks German well enough for me to feel at ease with him.' It was evident to Burckhardt that he was fascinated, 'as so many Germans are fascinated', by the problem of our easy-going self-assurance.

On October 28, Harold, with eight other back-bench MPs, flew to Paris to visit the Maginot Line, which impressed them greatly, and to exchange views with French politicians.

The closing months of 1939 only increased the strain of the war by inactivity; there was no fighting on land. The only major incident was Russia's invasion of Finland on November 30, following Finland's rejection of Soviet territorial demands. To everyone's astonishment, the Finns repulsed the Russian advance.

Diary   *November 2, 1939*

The Prime Minister makes his weekly statement. It is dull as ditchwater. I admit that there was little for him to tell us but he need not have done it in so glum and gloomy a form. I hear that Halifax said recently,

'I wish the P.M. would give up these weekly statements. It is as if one were in East Africa and received the *Times Weekly Edition* at regular intervals.' It is certainly very bad. Archie [Sinclair] and Attlee are little better. I am ashamed, as there are Dominion representatives recently arrived who are crowded in the Gallery. They had come expecting to find the Mother of Parliaments armed like Britannia. They merely saw the old lady dozing over her knitting, while her husband read the evening paper aloud.

Diary   *November 25, 1939*

How curious are the moods through which one passes! I sit here in my room at Sissinghurst thinking back on the days since September 3. The acute depression and misery of the first weeks have passed. I have accepted the fact that we are at war and I suppose that I am physically relieved by the fact that there are not likely to be any raids during the winter upon London and that the Germans have not made a dash through Holland. Yet the fact that this war is costing us six million pounds a day and that I am not really certain that we shall win it fills me with acute sadness at times. We shall keep up a brave face and refuse to admit that defeat is possible. But my heart aches with apprehension.

Diary   *November 30, 1939*

The Russians send an ultimatum to Finland and start bombing Helsinki and Vyborg. The P.M. makes a statement. The Labour Party are enraged with Russia. There are cries of 'Shame!' from all the benches. I was amused at Question time to watch a discussion between the Whips as to whom they should put up from the back-benches to answer [Hugh] Dalton. I saw them pointing at me, at which Margesson[1] shook his head in fierce negation. He never forgives nor forgets.

---

[1] David Margesson, the Chief Whip, deeply deplored Harold's opposition to Chamberlain during the Munich crisis.

Diary   *December 9, 1939*

Read Cyril Connolly's new paper *Horizon*. The editorial note says
that in this war we are not inspired by 'pity or hope' as in the Spanish
war. No pity. No hope. Glum. Glum. Glum. All this business about
our having lost what we used to describe as 'patriotism' must be
thought out carefully. The old national theory has been cut horizontally
by class distinctions. We used to cut it like a cake in perpendicular
wedges. Now we cut it sideways. This is a difficult alteration.

Diary   *December 14, 1939*

... Talk to Paul Evans.[1] He agrees that yesterday's sitting [the first
Secret Session] was a great blow to the Party machine. They must have
realised the underlying force of the opposition on our side. The effect
of the Secret Session was not to divulge secrets which could not have
been divulged in public. It was to show the Whips what their supporters
really felt. The tremendous reception given on our benches to Archie
Sinclair's speech must in itself have shown the Whips how precarious
is their hold on their own party. This marks a stage in the end of this
administration. They will try to placate us by appointing Amery
Minister of Economics. But our implacability remains. We have got
them.

Diary   *December 31, 1939*

Cyril Joad [the philosopher and broadcaster] expounds pacifism after
dinner. His line is that the ordinary person in England would be less
unhappy after a Nazi victory than if he or she lost their sons, lovers,
or husbands. He thinks only of the greatest unhappiness of the greatest
number, and accuses me of national and spiritual pride. It is a pleasure
talking to him. He stirs up the mind. He is extremely imaginative
about physical pain, and the picture of young men being gored by
bayonets is so terrible to him that he would prefer sacrificing liberty
to prevent it happening.

---

[1] Conservative MP for South Derbyshire.

I do not stay to watch the New Year in or the Old Year out. I write this diary at 11.45 and shall not wait. The old year is foul and the new year terrifying.

As a speaker, writer and member of many Committees, Harold was very active in what Churchill called 'these months of pretended war'. Aid to the Finns was under discussion when the Russians broke their resistance in mid-March. Chamberlain's leadership was still reluctantly accepted, until great events revealed its inadequacy.

Diary _January 1, 1940_

A pleasant dinner with Cyril Joad and Vita. We listen to Lord Haw Haw.[1] Joad does not think that he will have any effect on his young pacifists. It is upon the middle, uncertain people that he will have an effect, the untrained mind. He simply must be answered. Joad teases me for being self-depreciative. He says that I lack the competitive instinct and that I never throw the whole of myself into what I believe. He is, in a way, right about this. But what does it come from? Do I lack courage? But in the House I have been brave enough. It cannot be fear of responsibility or hard work, since I enjoy both. It is, I suppose, a profound disbelief in myself coupled with a rather self-indulgent and frivolous preference for remaining an observer.

Diary _January 3, 1940_

In the evening we hear Roosevelt's message to Congress. He begins by saying that the United States will never enter this war, and having said that, he delivers the most crushing attack upon our enemies that I have ever heard. It is superb. What a great man!

---

[1] William Joyce, called Lord Haw Haw after his supercilious voice, broadcast anti-British propaganda from Germany. After the war he was captured and executed as a traitor.

Diary   *January 6, 1940*

We dine with Victor Cazalet who has Eddy [Sackville-West] and the
Anthony Eden family staying with him. Anthony is in good form. I
can see that he still loathes the Prime Minister whom he regards as
obstinate, opinionated, rather mean, and completely ignorant of the
main issues involved. He also dislikes Sam Hoare [Lord Privy Seal],
whom he calls 'Aunt Tabitha'. He feels that Kingsley Wood [Secretary
of State for Air] is a help since he is truthful.

Diary   *January 7, 1940*

I am amused by the effect of Hore-Belisha's dismissal [as Minister of
War]. We in the House would assume that it was due to the fact that
having told so many lies he had sacrificed the confidence of the
country. But not at all. It seems that the country regard him as a second
Haldane and a moderniser of the Army. The line is that he has been
ousted by an intrigue of the Army chiefs, and there is a general uproar
about being ruled by dictators in brass hats. The Germans could make
great capital of this consternation, were it not that Belisha is a Jew. Yet
the general effect will be (a) among the unknowing that Belisha has
been sacked because he supported the private against the officer; (b)
among the *cognoscenti* that he has been ousted because he told lies, but
that Chamberlain managed the thing clumsily; (c) a vague suspicion
that the press are really anti-Chamberlain and are exaggerating this
incident in order to attack him. My own feeling is that this is less a
pro-Belisha than an anti-Chamberlain outburst.[1]

Diary   *January 13, 1940*

A great and angry tide is rising against the governing classes. I have
always been on the side of the underdog, but I have also believed in
the principle of aristocracy. I have hated the rich, but I have loved

---

[1] The true reason for Belisha's dismissal was that he had lost the confidence of the
Commander-in-Chief, General Gort, on questions of strategy.

learning, scholarship, intelligence and the humanities. Suddenly I am faced with the fact that all these lovely things are supposed to be 'class privileges'. When I find that my whole class is being assailed, I feel part of them, a feeling I have never had before.

Diary   *January 20, 1940*

We listen to Winston Churchill on the wireless after dinner. He is a little too rhetorical and I do not think his speech will really have gone down with the masses. He is too belligerent for this pacifist age, and although once anger comes to steel our sloppiness his voice will be welcome to them, at the moment it reminds them of heroism which they do not really feel.

Get a letter from Walter Lippmann. He says that the American people want us to win but wish to keep out. Thus there is a conflict in their desires, and they want to be assured that they OUGHT to keep out. It is this gap between one desire and the other which offers so wide a fissure for German propaganda.

Diary   *February 20, 1940*

The P.M. makes a statement about Finland which is loudly applauded. Also one about Norway and the *Altmark*.[1] Winston, when he comes in, is loudly cheered. I talk to Roger Keyes who was in the Admiralty while it was all going on. He says that our flotilla commander was assured by the Norwegians that there were no prisoners aboard the *Altmark*. He was shaken by this and telegraphed home. Winston replied, 'Well, find out from the Captain of the *Altmark* what he has done with the prisoners.' They tried to get the Norwegians to play up and to examine the ship themselves but they were too frightened of Germany. Finally, it was clear that the Norwegians would not cooperate and the final decision had to be made. Winston rang up Halifax and said, 'I

---

[1] The German merchant ship, with 300 British prisoners on board, took refuge in a Norwegian fjord where it was intercepted by HMS *Cossack* and the prisoners liberated.

propose to violate Norwegian neutrality.' Halifax replied, 'Go ahead.' The message was sent and they waited in the Admiralty anxiously for the result. What a result! A fine show. Winston, when he walks out of the House, catches my eye. He gives one portentous wink.

Diary   *February 29, 1940*

I see Vansittart. He is very worried by the return of Jo Kennedy, the American Ambassador. He says that Kennedy has been spreading it abroad in the USA that we shall certainly be beaten and he will use his influence here to press for a negotiated peace. In this he will have the assistance of the old appeasers of Maisky and the left-wing pacifists . . .

On March 6, Harold went to France for twelve days, lecturing on British war aims for the Ministry of Information. He visited Chalon-sur-Saône, Grenoble, Lyons, Besançon and Paris.

                                                          March 10, 1940
H.N. to Vita   *Grenoble*

I am introduced by the senior tutor in literature. I ascend the tribune. I make my speech, or rather I give my talk, which lasts fifty minutes. Again I abandon my prepared text, and talk just as if I were speaking in English. The audience listen with evident attention. At the end there is applause. The people in the front rows clap and murmur discreetly, 'Well done.' Suddenly, from the gallery where the students are seated, comes a second wave of applause accompanied by the stamping of feet. Everyone takes it up. It becomes a demonstration. I say a few words of thanks. And then the young people in the gallery rise to their feet and begin to shout. It becomes an ovation. I was much moved.

They talked about you at the meeting. Professor Blancagard said that you were one of the most admired poets in England. That gave me great pleasure and produced in me a wave of vague nostalgia. I leave for Lyons tomorrow.

                                                              March 14, 1940
Diary   *Paris*

Finland appears to have surrendered completely, and loses one-tenth of her territory and her strategic independence. I go to see Georges Mandel [Minister for the Colonies] at the Colonial Ministry. I find him seated at his desk on which the papers are piled as if they had just been spilled out of a suitcase. He asks me about the effect of the Finnish collapse upon British opinion. I say that I cannot tell from the newspapers and must wait till I get back to the lobbies. He says the effect on France will be tremendous. 'You see,' he says, 'our government decided upon war as the only alternative to admitting German domination. Yet when one decides on war one also decides to sacrifice many lives, to run many risks, and to endure many defeats. We are at present trying to conduct a war of appeasement which means that Hitler may win.' He asks me what they think of the French Government in England. He also is very anxious to know about our coming men. What of Eden? Is he a strong man? What about Herbert Morrison? '*Il nous faut des hommes!!*' he says.

Diary   *March 19, 1940*

The House is very crowded. Chamberlain makes a good debating speech, putting the whole blame for the Finnish collapse on the Scandinavian powers.[1] He is a remarkable man: there is no doubt about that. There is also no doubt that he wants to win the war. He gave the impression of great obstinacy and has enhanced his reputation. One thing that strikes drama is that he announces that at that very moment we are attacking the German air-bases at Sylt.

---

[1] Norway and Sweden had refused to allow British troops to pass through their territories to aid Finland.

Diary   *March 26, 1940*

Vita and I discuss the war. She says that she sees no logical reason why
we should retain Gibraltar, Malta, India or Aden. This enrages me
since it is due to loose thinking. People do not understand that it is
our independence and not imperialism which depends on such areas
of communication. I go to bed with a sad heart.

Diary   *April 2, 1940*

Dine with Kenneth Clark. Willie Maugham, Mrs Winston Churchill,
and Leslie Howard are there.[1] We have an agreeable dinner and talk
mostly about films. Leslie Howard is doing a big propaganda film
and is frightfully keen about it. We discuss the position of those
English people who have remained over in the United States. The
film stars claim that they have been asked to remain there since they
are more useful at Hollywood, but we all regret bitterly that people
like Aldous Huxley, Auden and Isherwood should have absented
themselves. They want me to write a *Spectator* article attacking them.
That is all very well, but it would lose me the friendship of three
people whom I much admire. I come back with Leslie Howard and
he continues to talk excitedly about his new film. He seems to
enter into such things with the zest of a schoolboy and that is part
of his charm.

Diary   *April 5, 1940*

I lunch at the Beefsteak. Harold Macmillan tells us Peter Fleming's
[the writer and traveller] *mot* about the Cabinet reshuffle: 'I do not
understand why they bothered to exchange Ministries; surely it would
have been simpler to exchange names?'
     It is curious to think back upon my moods since September 3. I

---

[1] Clark was then Director of the Film Division of the Ministry of Information.
Leslie Howard, the film star, was producing *The First of the Few* for the Ministry
and played the leading part. He was killed in June 1943 when his aircraft was shot
down.

recognise the first stage of acute depression, due I suppose to fear of the immediate Blitzkrieg and to hatred of war. Then there comes the second stage, trying to sort out my own ideas in order. And now there comes a third stage when I feel we CAN win the war but that we may fail to do so. My attitude towards the future is one of acute interest rather than acute dismay. My fear about what may happen to Nigel and Ben remains as an ulcer which winces at the thought. But my anger is increased. I want to win. I want to win. My God! I am prepared to sacrifice my whole happiness to victory. I feel resolute and well. I shall have my chance. I feel that in my odd fiddling, marginal, way I am helping. The *Spectator* articles have their effect. I feel combatant.

Diary   *April 8, 1940*

Come up in the early train with Walter Elliot [Minister of Health], Rob Bernays, Raymond Mortimer and Paul Hyslop [the architect] who have been staying at Swifts [Victor Cazalet's house]. We do not for once discuss politics, but we do discuss why I should hate T.E. Lawrence so much. After all, he was a friend of mine and our personal relations were never strained. I say that I feel for him that distaste that I feel for Sir James Barrie and John Galsworthy, namely that he acquired a legend without deserving it: he was fundamentally fraudulent. Walter Elliot asks did I really think the Arab campaign fraudulent? I say 'no' but the whole after-time. The *Pillars of Wisdom* book and that inane translation of Homer. He says that I must be jealous of a man of action who achieved more than I did and a man of letters who attempted more than I did. That may be true. But I am not a jealous person and I feel that there must be some other explanation of my antipathy.

Two tremendous months followed. April was the month when German troops overran Denmark and Norway; May the month of Hitler's attack in the West. As a consequence of the first campaign, and almost coincident with the second, Neville Chamberlain fell and Churchill became Prime Minister on May 10.

Diary   *April 9, 1940*

I go down to the House. The Prime Minister, who is looking very
haggard, makes a statement. It is rather well done and he admits quite
frankly that the Fleet is out and that we do not exactly know what is
happening. He discredits the rumour that Narvik has been occupied.[1]

The House is extremely calm and the general line is that Hitler has
made a terrible mistake. I feel myself that I wish that we could
sometimes commit mistakes of such magnitude. . . .

H.N. to Vita   *April 10, 1940*

I think the general opinion is that it is a bore but not a disaster. It
means of course that Hitler gets Sweden as well and all the other
neutrals will be terrified out of their lives. But it also means an
advantage for us in so far as the blockade is concerned, and extension
of the front.

Diary   *April 11, 1940*

To the House. It is packed. Winston comes in. He is not looking well
and sits there hunched as usual with his papers in his hand. When he
rises to speak it is obvious that he is very tired. He starts off by giving
an imitation of himself making a speech, and he indulges in vague
oratory coupled with tired gibes. I have seldom seen him to less
advantage. The majority of the House were expecting tales of victory
and triumph, and when he tells them that the news of our reoccupation
of Bergen, Trondheim and Oslo is untrue, a cold wave of disappointment passes through the House. He hesitates, gets his notes in
the wrong order, puts on the wrong pair of spectacles, fumbles for the
right pair, keeps on saying 'Sweden' when he means 'Denmark', and
one way and another makes a lamentable performance. He gives no

---

[1] Denmark was overrun by the Germans in a few hours. The Norwegian ports of
Narvik, Trondheim and Bergen were seized on April 9 from the sea, and Oslo was
captured by a German airborne force on the 10th.

real explanation of how the Germans managed to slip through to Narvik.

Diary   *April 23, 1940*

Lord Salisbury tells us that he had been to see Winston Churchill and had asked him quite frankly whether he believed he could carry on concurrently the job of First Lord and Co-ordinator of Defence [he had been appointed on April 4]. Winston told him that he is feeling in perfect health, that he would die if the Admiralty were taken away from him, and that the Press had much exaggerated his role as Co-ordinator of Defence, which was little more than Chairman of a Committee of the fighting services. He had no right to initiate suggestions or make decisions.

Diary   *April 30, 1940*

The news begins to creep through that the Germans have occupied Storen [thirty miles south of Trondheim]. That means that we are done. I talk to Harold Macmillan who has heard that we shall begin to evacuate Norway this evening. My Committee[1] think that this will be the fall of Chamberlain, and Lloyd George as P.M. The Whips are putting it about that it is all the fault of Winston who has made another forlorn failure. This is hell.

Diary   *May 4, 1940*

I find that there is a grave suspicion of the Prime Minister. His speech about the Norwegian expedition has created disquiet. The House knows very well that it was a major defeat. But the P.M. said that 'the balance of advantage rested with us' and that 'Germany has not attained her objective'. They know that this is simply not true. If Chamberlain

---

[1] It was known as the Watching Committee, composed of peers and MPs, including the majority of the Eden Group, meeting under the chairmanship of Lord Salisbury.

believed it himself, then he was stupid. If he did not believe it, then he was trying to deceive. In either case he loses confidence. People are so distressed by the whole thing that they are talking of Lloyd George as possible P.M. Eden is out of it. Churchill is undermined by the Conservative caucus. Halifax is believed (and with justice) to be a tired man. We always say that our advantage over the German leadership principle is that we can always find another leader. Now we cannot.

Diary   *May 5, 1940*

I read Dylan Thomas' *Portrait of the Artist as a Young Dog*. I am slightly disgusted by all the urine and copulation which occurs. I have a feeling that these people do not believe that they can write powerfully unless they can drag in the latrines. And yet it is quite clear that this young Thomas is a writer of great merit.

   The lovely day sinks to sunset among the flowering trees. The Italian news is bad. It seems incredible to us that Italy should really come in. If she does it means that Mussolini is convinced of our early defeat. He is no fool and must have reasons for this belief. That is what fills me with such depression. Not Italy as an enemy, but Italy convinced as an intelligent and most admirably informed nation that Germany is going to win this war.

Diary   *May 7, 1940*

The House is crowded [for the Norwegian debate], and when Chamberlain comes in, he is greeted with shouts of 'Missed the bus!'[1] He makes a very feeble speech and is only applauded by the Yes-men. He makes some reference to the complacency of the country, at which the whole House cheers vociferously and ironically, inducing him to make a little, rather feminine, gesture of irritation. Attlee makes a feeble speech and Archie Sinclair a good one. When Archie sits down, many people stand up and the Speaker calls on Page Croft. There is a loud moan from the Labour Party at this, and they practically rise in a

---

[1] In a speech on April 4, referring to the lack of a German offensive, Chamberlain had said, 'One thing is certain: Hitler missed the bus.'

body and leave the House. He is followed by [J.C.] Wedgwood who makes a speech which contains everything he ought not to have said. He gives the impression of being a little off his head. At one moment he suggests that the British Navy has gone to Alexandria since they are frightened of being bombed.

A few minutes afterwards [Admiral Sir] Roger Keyes comes in, dressed in full uniform with six rows of medals. I scribble him a note telling him what Wedgwood has just said, and he immediately rises and goes to the Speaker's chair. When Wedgwood sits down Keyes gets up and begins his speech by referring to Wedgwood's remark and calling it a damned insult. The Speaker does not call him to order for his unparliamentary language, and the whole House roars with laughter, especially Lloyd George who rocks backwards and forwards in boyish delight with his mouth wide open. Keyes then returns to his manuscript and makes an absolutely devastating attack upon the naval conduct of the Narvik episode and the Naval General Staff. The House listens in breathless silence when he tells how the Naval General Staff had assured him that the naval action at Trondheim was easy but unnecessary owing to the success of the military. There is a great gasp of astonishment. It is by far the most dramatic speech I have ever heard, and when Keyes sits down there is thunderous applause.

Thereafter the weakness of the Margesson system is displayed by the fact that none of the Yes-men are of any value whatsoever whereas all the more able Conservatives have been driven into the ranks of the rebels. A further terrific attack is delivered by [Leo] Amery, who ends up by quoting from Cromwell, 'In the name of God, go!'

Diary   *May 8, 1940*

Winston winds-up [the Norwegian debate]. He has an almost impossible task. On the one hand he has to defend the Services; on the other, he has to be loyal to the Prime Minister. One felt that it would be impossible to do all this after the debate without losing some of his own prestige, but he manages with extraordinary force of personality to do both these things with absolute loyalty and apparent sincerity while demonstrating by the brilliance of his personality that he has really nothing to do with this confused and timid gang.

Up to the last moment the House had really behaved with moderation, and one had the sense that there really was a united will to win the war. During the last twenty minutes, however, passions rose, and when the Division came there was great tensity in the air. Some 44 of us, including many of the young Service Members, vote against the Government and some 30 abstain. This leaves the Government with a majority of only 81 instead of a possible 213, and the figures are greeted with a terrific demonstration during which Joss Wedgwood starts singing *Rule Britannia*, which is drowned in shouts of 'Go, go, go, go!' Margesson signals to his henchmen to rise and cheer the Prime Minister as he leaves, and he walks out looking pale and angry.

Diary   *May 9, 1940*

Lunch at the Beefsteak and find that all are unanimous in feeling that Chamberlain must go. Admiral Hall tells me that the whole Navy are absolutely insistent upon it and that it is even worse in the Army. Walk down to the House with Barrington-Ward [Editor] of the *Times* who has come completely round and agrees with me (a) that the Germans may attack at any moment; (b) that we cannot have a prolonged Cabinet crisis; (c) that Chamberlain ought therefore to resign immediately within the next few hours.

Diary   *May 10, 1940*

Salisbury says that we must maintain our point of view, namely that Winston should be made Prime Minister during the course of the day. I am still at the Travellers when the wireless news comes telling us that the invasion of Belgium and Holland is complete, that both countries have mobilised and appealed for our assistance. Alec Dunglass[1] comes in looking rather white about the gills and we tell him that our Group will never allow Chamberlain to get away from the reconstruction [of the Cabinet] owing to this invasion. He says that the reconstruction has already been decided upon, but that the actual danger of the

---

[1] Later Alec Douglas-Home, when Prime Minister. In 1940 Parliamentary Private Secretary to Neville Chamberlain.

moment really makes it impossible for the Government to fall. The situation is really one of *videant Consules*, and that we must have a triumvirate of Chamberlain, Churchill and Halifax to carry us over these first anxious hours.

I go back to K.B.W.,[1] and on the way I see posters saying 'Brussels bombed, Paris bombed, Lyons bombed, Swiss Railways bombed.' We are all most anxious regarding the position of our Army on the Belgian frontier, since we dread it being caught in the open. What makes it worse in a way is that it is a beautiful spring day with the bluebells and primroses in flower everywhere.

I go down to Sissinghurst. Met by Vita and Gwen [St Aubyn]. It is all looking too beautiful to be believed, but a sort of film has obtruded itself between my appreciation of nature and my terror of real life. It is like a tooth ache. We dine alone together chatting about indifferent things. Just before nine we turn on the wireless and it begins to buzz as the juice comes through and then we hear the bells [of the BBC]. Then the pips sound nine and the announcer begins: 'This is the Home Service. Here is the Right Honourable Neville Chamberlain M.P. who will make a statement.' I am puzzled by this for a moment and then realise that he has resigned. He has tendered his resignation and Churchill is Prime Minister. For the moment, acting Ministers will carry on. He will agree to serve under Churchill. He ends with a fierce denunciation of the Germans for invading Holland and Belgium. It is a magnificent statement, and all the hatred that I have felt for Chamberlain subsides as if a piece of bread were dropped into a glass of champagne.

Diary   *May 13, 1940*

When Chamberlain enters the House, he gets a terrific reception, and when Churchill comes in the applause is less. Winston sits there between Chamberlain and Attlee, and it is odd to see the Labour Ministers sitting on the Government Bench. Winston makes a very short statement, but to the point [the famous 'blood, sweat and tears' speech]. Lloyd George gets up and makes a moving speech telling

---
[1] King's Bench Walk, Harold's chambers in the Temple.

Winston how fond he is of him. Winston cries slightly and mops his eyes.

Harold Macmillan told me that Brendan Bracken [P.P.S. to Churchill] had given him a vivid description of Cabinet-making. He sat up till three in the morning with David Margesson going through lists. Winston was not in the least interested once the major posts had been filled, and kept on trying to interrupt them by discussing the nature of war and the changing rules of strategy. Meanwhile they would come back to their list, and Brendan would say, 'Well what about So-and-So?' Margesson would reply, 'Strike him out. He's no good at all.' 'Why then,' Brendan would ask, 'did you appoint him?' 'Oh well,' Margesson said, 'he was useful at the time.' Macmillan had asked Brendan what was Winston's mood. 'Profound anxiety,' he replied.

Diary   *May 15, 1940*

The Dutch have capitulated and the Italians may be in by this evening. We have breakfast out of doors in brilliant sunshine with butterflies flitting in and out. I feel physically sick with anxiety. All through it the cuckoos cluck at us with their silly reiterant note. In other days this would have caused pleasure. Today it causes pain.

Harold was appointed Parliamentary Secretary to the Ministry of Information in Churchill's Government, with Duff Cooper as his Minister. After Dunkirk, he was made responsible for co-ordinating Government advice to the public in case of invasion.

Diary   *May 17, 1940*

I fear that it looks as if the Germans have broken the French line at Mezières and Sedan. This is very serious. These surely are the saddest moments of my life and I do not know how I could cope with it all were it not for Vita's serene and loving sympathy. While we are at breakfast the telephone rings. It is a message from Sibyl [Colefax]. She says 'I hear Harold is in the Government.' I have heard nothing and shall believe nothing until it is confirmed.

At 12.40 the telephone rings again and Mac [Miss Macmillan, the secretary] in an awed voice says, 'The Prime Minister's Private Secretary.' I lift the receiver and wait without hearing anything. Then after about two minutes silence a voice says, 'Mr Nicolson?' I say 'Yes.' 'Hold on please, Mr Asquith here.'[1] I tell Asquith that I was on to Downing Street and that would he mind ringing off. So on I get again and this time I hear the Private Secretary who says, 'Please hold on. The Prime Minister wishes to speak to you.' Another long pause and then Winston's voice. 'Harold! I think it would be very nice if you joined the Government and helped Duff [Cooper] at the Ministry of Information.' 'There is nothing I should like better.' 'Well, fall in tomorrow. The list will be out tonight. That all right?' 'Very much all right.' 'O.K.' says Winston and rings off. Of course I am pleased and what makes it better is that the 1 p.m. news is not as bad as we feared.

	May 19, 1940
H.N. to Vita	*Ministry of Information*

Our War Room is perfectly thrilling. It is kept going night and day, and there are maps with pins and different coloured bits of wool. The chiefs meet in conference twice a day at 10.30 and 5.30, and the Press Conference is at 12.30. I have to attend all these, and in addition I shall be given specific branches of work to take over. I have a nice sunny little room, and if bombing starts, I shall sleep here. They say the shelter under our tower is proof even against a direct hit.

Diary	*May 20, 1940*

We discuss the problem of wireless while an attack is on. If we remain on the air we definitely assist enemy bombers, but they are frightened that if we go off the air, the Germans will use our wavelength to issue false messages which will much alarm the public. A clever impersonator might imitate Winston's voice sufficiently well and give instructions that all troops are to lay down their arms. Duff will take this problem up in the Cabinet.

---

[1] Cyril Asquith, Director of the National Labour Organisation.

Diary   *May 25, 1940*

They have discovered that one of the American Ambassador's Confidential Clerks is a spy and has been furnishing Miss Wolkoff [Russian agent] with photostatic copies of all Kennedy's most confidential correspondence, including the Prime Minister's personal messages to President Roosevelt. Kennedy begs us to keep this out of the press but the American journalists have already got the scent of something of the sort.

The Germans occupy Boulogne and Calais. Our communications are almost completely severed, and it is possible that the BEF [British Expeditionary Force] may be cut off.

H.N. to Vita   *May 26, 1940*

The Government may decide to evacuate Kent and Sussex of all civilians. If, as I hope, they give orders instead of advice, then those orders will be either 'Go' or 'Stay'. If the former, then you know what to do. If the latter, we are faced with a grave predicament. I do not think that even if the Germans occupied Sissinghurst they would harm you in spite of the horrified dislike they feel for me. But to be quite sure you are not put to any humiliation I think you really ought to have a 'bare bodkin'[1] handy so that you can take your quietus when necessary. I shall have one also. I am not in the least afraid of such sudden and honourable death. What I dread is being tortured and humiliated. But how can we find a 'bodkin' which will give us our quietus quickly and which is easily portable? I shall ask my doctor friends. I think it will be a relief to feel, 'Well, if the worst comes to the worst there are always those two little pills.'

If I believe in anything surviving I believe in a love like ours surviving; it is so completely immaterial in every way.

---

[1] The 'bare bodkin' (*Hamlet, III*, i) was a lethal pill which Harold obtained from his doctor, for use in case of capture by invading Germans.

Diary   *May 28, 1940*

The Policy Committee meets rather grimly and we are told of
Reynaud's [French Prime Minister] broadcast at 8.30 this morning.
He claims that the King of the Belgians surrendered against the wishes
of his Government and army and makes it clear that this means that
the BEF is lost. He says he will reform a line on the Marne and the
Somme and fight to the death. From the purely cynical point of view,
breaking the news to the British public in this way is not a bad thing.
It will at least enable them to feel that the disaster was due to Belgian
cowardice as indeed to some extent it was.

Diary   *June 1, 1940*

We have now evacuated 220,000 men [from Dunkirk], which is
amazing when I recall how we feared we should lose 80%. But there
are few grounds for enthusiasm really, except moral grounds. We have
lost all our equipment. The French have lost 80% of their forces and
feel that we deserted them. It will constitute a real problem to recreate
good relations between the forces. Lord Gort [Commander-in-Chief
of the BEF] says that he offered to take more French off but that they
were too dead beat to move and that all those who could be galvanised
into marching a few miles further were in fact rescued. This may be
true, but the French with their tendency to attribute blame to others
will be certain to say that we thought only of rescuing the BEF and
let them down.[1]

Diary   *June 4, 1940*

The Prime Minister makes his speech about the evacuation of Flanders.
He pays warm tribute to all concerned and rejoices at the great
'deliverance' which we have been accorded. He admits, however, that

---

[1] Fifty thousand Frenchmen held the perimeter of Dunkirk while the British escaped,
which was in breach of Churchill's promise to Reynaud that they would make an
equal sacrifice. A total of 370,000 were evacuated from Dunkirk, including 110,000
Frenchmen.

we have suffered a 'colossal military disaster' and that it will take us time to replace the vast equipment which we have lost. He then passes on to the invasion and ends with a magnificent peroration on the lines that we shall fight in our fields, fight in our streets, fight in our hills, and if necessary fight alone. He ends by saying that if this country is starved into submission we shall continue the struggle from our Empire and call the New World in to rescue the Old.

Diary   *June 10, 1940*

I give my draft of the Invasion pamphlet to the Director-General, who takes it down to the meeting of the Home Defence Ministers. The War Office, to my mind, do not seem to have faced the problem that the Germans will treat as saboteurs any civilians who obstruct them. If we encourage sabotage, a tremendous responsibility will rest upon our heads and only the Cabinet can decide.

H.N. to Vita   *June 12, 1940*

What a joy it is for me to be so busy at this moment and in so central a position. I really feel that I can do some good, and I am *embattled*. I did not know that I possessed such combative instincts. Darling, why is it that I should feel so *gay*? Is it, as you said, that I am pleased at discovering in myself forces of manliness which I did not suspect? I feel such contempt for the cowards. And such joy that you and I should so naturally and without effort find ourselves on the side of the brave.

H.N. to Vita   *June 17, 1940*

We still do not know what terms the Germans intend to impose on France. If they were wise they would give good terms and treat the French population very well. This will not only enable them to exploit French resources but also increase defeatism over here. I fear that among some people defeatism is spreading. I think it is practically certain that the Americans will come in in November and if we can last till then all is well. Anyhow as a precaution I have the bare bodkin. I shall bring down your half on Sunday. It all looks very simple.

How I wish Winston would not talk on the wireless unless he is feeling in good form. He hates the microphone and when we bullied him into speaking last night he just sulked and read his House of Commons speech over again.[1] Now as delivered in the H. of C. that speech was magnificent, especially the concluding sentences. But it sounded ghastly on the wireless. All the great vigour he put into it seemed to evaporate.

Diary   *June 21, 1940*

Today the French delegates were received by Hitler in the dining coach at Compiègne in which the Armistice of 1918 was signed. Hitler gave them an allocution scolding them for having been so wicked as to win the last war.[2] Poor people, my heart bleeds for them.

Diary   *July 3, 1940*

Have a talk with Jenkins, Attlee's P.P.S.[3] Attlee is worried about the BBC retaining its class voice and personnel and would like to see a far greater infiltration of working-class speakers. He also feels that we should put before the country a definite pronouncement on Government policy for the future. The Germans are fighting a revolutionary war for very definite objectives. We are fighting a conservative war and our objectives are purely negative. We must put forward a positive and revolutionary aim admitting that the old order has collapsed and asking people to fight for the new order.

---

[1] His 'finest hour' speech.
[2] In fact, Hitler did not speak a word to the French delegates at Compiègne. He left the railway-car immediately after the Armistice terms had been read out.
[3] Arthur Jenkins, Labour MP, and father of Roy [Lord] Jenkins.

Diary   *July 4, 1940*

The news about the French fleet is not released till 3 in the morning
and therefore missed most of the morning papers.[1] This is very bad
publicity, and of course we shall be blamed. The fact is that Winston
never thinks for a moment about the publicity side. . . . We may find
ourselves actually at war with France, which would almost break my
heart. The House is at first saddened by this odious attack but is
fortified by Winston's speech. The grand finale ends in an ovation,
with Winston sitting there with the tears pouring down his cheeks.

H.N. to Vita   *July 10, 1940*

I told the Queen today [with whom he lunched] that I got homesick
and she said, 'But that is right. That is personal patriotism. That is
what keeps us going. I should die if I had to leave.' She also told me
that she is being instructed every morning how to fire a revolver. I
expressed surprise. 'Yes,' she said, 'I shall not go down like the others.'
I cannot tell you how superb she was. But I anticipated her charm.
What astonished me is how the King has changed. I always thought
him rather a foolish loutish boy. He is now like his brother [the Duke
of Windsor]. He was so gay and she was so calm. They did me all the
good in the world. How I wish you had been there. [Lord] Gort was
simple and modest. And those two resolute and sensible. WE SHALL
WIN. I know that. I have no doubts at all.

H.N. to Vita   *July 11, 1940*

I had about eleven people to see me today. I wish I were a Cabinet
Minister and could keep these people off by a barrage of private
secretaries. All this means that I do not see Duff enough. We take taxis
together and devise all sorts of dodges. But the result is that he is seeing
the Alpha Plus people all day and I am seeing the Beta Plus people

---

[1] Churchill ordered a British fleet to attack the French ships at Oran, to prevent them
falling into German hands. The British sank the battleship *Bretagne* and the battle-
cruiser *Dunkerque*, with the loss of 1,000 men.

whom he throws onto me. But that is the right system. I am there to take things off from him and to collect Parliamentary opinion. . . .

The German bombings of some of our ports are already pretty bad. God knows what they will be when they start full out. But our morale is perfect. I am cocky about the war. Cocky. All our reports show that Hitler funks invading us and yet is pledged to do so. They expect an invasion this week end. That is Hitler's last horoscope date. After that the stars are against him. I feel like a doctor watching a dangerous case of illness. But I like being a doctor. I am so busy that my beloved diary is getting to be no more than an engagement book.

Diary   *July 13, 1940*

Ben has bought a Picasso portrait of a woman entirely composed of grey cubes. It was very expensive. It is a determined portrait and it says what it thinks. But I do not like these affirmations in art. I like art to be a relief and not a challenge. But Ben, who is far more expert than I am, regrets this sentimental approach. I am sure he is right.

Diary   *July 18, 1940*

Brendan Bracken says that the moment the war is over, Winston will want to retire. He says that Winston is convinced that he has had all the fun he wants out of politics, and that when this is over he wants to paint pictures and write books. He adds that in the twenty years he has known Winston, he has never seen him as fit as he is today, and his responsibilities seem to have given him a new lease of life. He adds that he is very determined not to become a legendary figure and has the theory that the Prime Minister is nothing more than Chairman of the Cabinet.

H.N. to Vita   *July 31, 1940*

We had a Secret Session today. Mm. Hush. All that I can say is that Winston surpassed even himself. The situation is obscure. It may be that Hitler will first bomb us with gas and then try to land. At the same time, Italy and Japan will hit us as hard as they can. It will be a dreadful month. On the other hand, Hitler may feel that he cannot bring off a successful invasion and may seek to gain new, easy but sterile conquests in Africa and Asia. Were it not for this little island under a great leader, he would accomplish his desires.

Diary   *August 3, 1940*

I am feeling very depressed by this attack upon the Ministry of Information. What worries me is that the whole Press, plus certain pro-Munich conservatives, have planned and banded together to pull Duff Cooper down. He may be able to survive for a few weeks with Winston's support. But now that they have pledged themselves to his destruction, it becomes for them a matter of prestige. At present the Ministry is too decent, educated and intellectual to imitate Goebbels. If propaganda is a vital weapon as it seems, it must be entrusted to less scrupulous hands.

The Battle of Britain began on August 13 when the Luftwaffe started the air offensive on south-east England. On September 7 the Germans began to concentrate their bombing on London in an attempt to destroy civilian morale. Ten days later Hitler postponed the invasion of England.

H.N. to Vita   *August 14, 1940*

How I wonder if the invasion of England is really to begin. We do not understand what is really happening. The German attacks are more serious than mere reconnaissance, but not serious enough to justify the heavy losses they receive. They lost certainly more than 100 pilots yesterday which is more than they can afford. I cannot make it out nor can our experts.

Diary   *August 15, 1940*

Everyone is in high spirits about our air triumphs. In fact the superiority shown by our men is a miracle. Duff told me today that the only explanation is the lack of German training. Our triumph today was superb.

Diary   *August 17, 1940*

Wimbledon was bombed yesterday with 18 killed. We brought down 75 of their planes. For the moment everything is overshadowed by what seems to be the failure of the German air offensive against this island. They have done some damage here and there: they have killed and wounded many people, but they have not dealt us a really serious blow and our confidence rises.

Diary   *August 18, 1940*

A lovely day. While we are sitting outside [at Sissinghurst], the siren sounds. We remain where we are. Then comes the sound of aeroplanes and looking up we see thin streamers from the exhaust of the German planes. Another wave follows, and we see it clearly – twenty little silver fish in arrow formation. There is no sound of firing but while we are at luncheon we hear planes quite close and go out to see. There is a rattle of machine gun fire and we see two Spitfires attacking a Heinkel. The latter sways off, obviously wounded. We then go on with our luncheon. After that Ben talks to us about Roger Fry and Virginia [Woolf]. He had written to the latter saying that Fry was too detached from life and she had written a tart letter in reply. He feels that Roger Fry and his set were too ivory tower.[1]

---

[1] Virginia Woolf had just published her biography of Roger Fry, the artist and art critic. Her correspondence with Benedict Nicolson is published in *Letters of Virginia Woolf*, Vol. VI, pp. 413–22.

Diary   *August 20, 1940*

Winston says, in referring to the air force, 'never in the field of human
conflict has so much been owed by so many to so few'. It was a
moderate and well-balanced speech and he did not try to arouse
enthusiasm but only to give guidance. He made a curious reference to
Russia's possible attack on Germany and spoke about our 'being mixed
up with the United States', ending in a fine peroration about Anglo-
American cooperation rolling on like the Mississippi.

Diary   *August 26, 1940*

A lovely morning. They raided London yesterday and we raided Berlin.
I work at my broadcast talk. At noon I hear aeroplanes and shortly
afterwards the wail of the siren. People are really becoming quite used
to these interruptions. I find one practises a sort of suspension of the
imagination. I do not think that the drone in the sky means death to
many people at any moment. It seems so incredible as I sit here at my
window [at Sissinghurst] looking out on the fuchsias and the zinnias
with yellow butterflies playing round each other, that in a few seconds
above the trees I may see other butterflies circling in the air intent on
murdering each other. One lives in the present. The past is too sad a
recollection and the future too blank a despair.

Dine at the Beefsteak. An air-raid warning sounds. I wait till 10.45
and then walk back to K.B.W. It is a strange experience. London is as
dark as the stage at Vicenza after all the lights have been put out. Vague
gleamings of architecture. It is warm and stars straddle the sky like
grains of rice. Then there are bunches in the corners of searchlights,
each terminating in a swab of cotton wool which is its own mist area.
Suburban guns thump and boom. In the centre there are no guns, only
the drone of aeroplanes which may be enemy or not. A few lonely
footsteps hurry along the Strand. A little nervous man catches up with
me and starts a conversation. I embarrass him by asking him to have a
cigarette and pausing lengthily while I light it. His hand trembles.
Mine does not. I walk on to the Temple and meet no one.

When I get into my rooms, I turn the lights off and sit at the
window. There is still the drone of planes and from time to time a dull

thump in the distance. I turn on my lights and write this, but I hear more planes coming and must darken everything and listen. I have no sense of fear whatsoever. Is this fatalism or what? It is very beautiful. I wait and listen. There are more drones and then the search lights switch out and the all-clear goes. I shut my shutters, turn on my lights and finish this. The clocks of London strike midnight. I go to bed.

Diary   *September 2, 1940*

In the evening V. and I discuss the high-spots in our life. The moment when I entered a tobacconist's shop in Smyrna, the moment when we took Ebury Street, our early days at Long Barn, the night that Niggs was born so easily, the night at Kermanshah and so on.[1] Viti says that our mistake was that we remained Edwardian for too long and that if in 1916 we had got in touch with Bloomsbury we should have profited more than we did by carrying on with Mrs George Keppel, Mrs Ronald Greville and the Edwardian Relics. We are amused to confess that we had never even heard of Bloomsbury in 1916. But we agree that in fact we have had the best of both the plutocratic and the bohemian world and that we have had a lovely life.

Diary   *September 7, 1940*

At Tonbridge, where we change trains, there are two German prisoners. Tiny little boys of sixteen they are, handcuffed together, and guarded by three soldiers with fixed bayonets. They shuffle along sadly, one being without his boots, shuffling in thick grey socks. One of them looks broken-down and saturnine; the other has a superior half-smile on his face, as if thinking, 'My Führer will pay them out for this.' The people on the platform are extraordinarily decent. They just glance at them and then turn their heads away, not wishing to stare.

---

[1] The night at Kermanshah is described on pp. 45–46 of this edition. When Harold was asked in 1966 what had happened in the tobacconist's shop in Smyrna, he could not remember.

Diary   *September 19, 1940*

I get sleepy and go back to my room. I turn out the lights and listen to the bombardment. It is continuous, and the back of the museum opposite flashes with lights the whole time. There are scudding low clouds, but above them the insistent drone of the German 'planes and the occasional crump of a bomb. Night after night, night after night, the bombardment of London continues. It is like the Conciergerie, since every morning one is pleased to see one's friends appearing again. I am nerveless, and yet I am conscious that when I hear a motor in the empty streets I tauten myself lest it be a bomb screaming towards me. Underneath, the fibres of one's nerve-resistance must be sapped. There is a lull now. The guns die down towards the horizon like a thunder-storm passing to the south. But they will come back again in fifteen minutes. We are conscious all the time that this is a moment in history. But it is very like falling down a mountain. One is aware of death and fate, but thinks mainly of catching hold of some jutting piece of rock. I have a sense of strain and unhappiness; but none of fear.

  One feels so proud.

Diary   *September 24, 1940*

I detect in myself a certain area of claustrophobia. I do not mind being blown up. What I dread is being buried under huge piles of masonry and hearing the water drip slowly, smelling the gas creeping towards me and hearing the faint cries of colleagues condemned to a slow and ungainly death.

Diary   *October 8, 1940*

Go round to see Julian Huxley at the Zoo. He is in an awkward position since he is responsible for the non-escape of his animals. He assures me that the carnivores are pretty safe although a zebra got out the other day when its cage had been bombed and bolted as far as Marylebone. While we were at supper a fierce raid begins and the house shakes. The raid gets very bad and at 8.30 he offers to drive me back. It is a heavenly moon-lit night and the search-lights are swaying against a soft mackerel sky and a clear calm moon. The shells lit up their match flares in the sky. A great star shell creeps slowly down over the city under a neat parachute. We hear loud explosions all round but he gets out his car and drives me back bravely to the Ministry.

Diary   *October 17, 1940*

I go to the smoking-room with Harry Crookshank [Financial Secretary to the Treasury] and Charles Waterhouse. Winston is at the next table. He sits there sipping a glass of port and welcoming anyone who comes in. 'How are you?' he calls gaily to the most obscure Member. It is not a pose. It is just that for a few minutes he likes to get away from being Prime Minister and feel himself back in the smoking-room. His very presence gives us all gaiety and courage. People gather round his table completely unawed. They ask him questions. Robert Cary makes a long dissertation about how the public demand the unrestricted bombardment of Germany as reprisals for the raids on London. Winston takes a long sip at his port gazing over the glass at Cary. 'My dear sir,' he says, 'this is a military and not a civilian war. You and others may desire to kill women and children. We desire (and have succeeded in our desire) to destroy German military objectives. I quite appreciate your point. But my motto is "Business before Pleasure".' We all drift out of the room thinking, 'That was a man!'[1]

Diary   *October 22, 1940*

There is a Press Conference for Lord Lothian [British Ambassador in Washington]. He sits there quite placidly under the glare of arc lamps and the barrage of questions. He manages the thing with consummate ease. He says that in the early stages America had felt that this was merely a European war. They had rather despised us for our muddle in Norway. Then came the collapse of France and the sudden realisation

---

[1] In his Memoirs of this period, Churchill wrote, 'The abandonment by the Germans of all pretence of confining the war to military objectives had raised the question of retaliation. I was for it, but I encountered many conscientious scruples.'

that the British Fleet was their first line of defence. In July they were really terrified that we should go the same way as France. Then came Dunkirk, the triumph of the RAF, the abandonment of invasion and the [German] Pact with Japan. These four things swung American opinion over in six weeks. They were still averse to any European commitments, but they had come to understand that our interests and the strategic points of the Commonwealth were essential to themselves.

H.N. to Vita   *November 6, 1940*

I was so happy this morning when I heard of the Roosevelt result [elected for his third term]. I had steeled myself to pretend not to mind either way and I think it is true that three months ago it would not have mattered so much if Wee Willy Winkie [Wendell Willkie] had got in. But in the last month Roosevelt had become identified with our cause and Willkie (unfairly perhaps) with the German cause. Although the German papers have been very cautious about it all, the French papers in occupied France have not been so cautious at all. They have openly rejoiced at the apparent decline in Roosevelt's popularity and said that it shows that America has no faith in our victory. Now they all have to swallow their words.

Diary   *November 20, 1940*

We go to the Prime Minister's Room to be told of the King's Speech. We hang about in the corridor while the Chiefs of Staff creep out after a conference. Then we all troop in and there are glasses of sherry about. The P.M. reads the speech ('It is cuthtomary to thand up when the Kingth thpeech is read') and thereafter we have a sort of party. I see out of the corner of my eye that Winston is edging in my direction and I am embarrassed. He slouches up. 'I see you have been speaking in Scotland?' 'Yes.' 'Was it a good meeting?' and so on. He seems better in health than he has ever seemed. The pale and globular look about his cheeks has gone. He is more solid about the face and thinner. But there is something odd about his eyes. The lids are not in the least weary, nor are there any pouches or black lines. But the eyes themselves are glaucous, vigilant, angry, combative, visionary and tragic. In a way they are the eyes of a man who is much preoccupied and is unable to rivet his attention on minor things (such as me). But in another sense they are the eyes of a man faced by an ordeal or tragedy, and combining vision, truculence, resolution and great unhappiness.

Diary   *November 22, 1940*

Ronnie Tree says that someone complimented Winston upon his obituary oration on Neville Chamberlain [who died November 9]. 'No,' said Winston, 'that was not an insuperable task, since I admired many of Neville's great qualities. But I pray to God in his infinite mercy that I shall not have to deliver a similar oration on Baldwin. That indeed would be difficult to do.'

Diary   *December 20, 1940*

Go down to Nether Wallop [the RAF station] to lecture to the Air Force about the German character. I do not feel that the young men really like it. They are all fascists at heart and rather like the Germans. I am taken into the operations room afterwards where I watch girls moving sinister discs over a great map. It all seems very efficient. I go to bed as soon as I can and am later joined by a scientist who snores and snores.

H.N. to Vita   *December 23, 1940*

I have luck. It is not only you and the garden and the boys and the zest in life and being here at this moment, but it is also little things. For instance today people came and bothered me in Duff's absence to prevent Winston speaking tonight. What they wanted him to do was to speak on the Italian broadcast and to have the substance of his speech relayed on the Home programme. 'We have,' they said, 'read the script and it will be an absolute flop on the Home programme and in the USA. You *must* stop him.'

I said that I would do nothing of the sort. That I trusted Winston not to make that sort of mistake.

Well then, in some trepidation, I listened to his message to the Italian people. And you will agree that it was superb, not merely for Italian opinion (and we are pumping the Italian version into them without stopping for 24 hours) but also in America and here.

During the first few months of 1941 Harold was busy with the problems of civilian morale, now that the provincial cities were bearing the brunt of German air attacks, and with British relations with neutral and defeated countries. In early January he toured his Ministry's centres outside London. His own rooms in the Temple were badly shaken by a bomb.

Elvira Niggeman [secretary] to H.N.   *January 2, 1941*

I regret to say that they had either a land-mine or a heavy bomb in the Temple again last night and the windows and the window frames in no. 4 have gone, and some of the panelling is completely out. I will get some stuff to patch over the windows since you could not sit there at all to have breakfast as it is, and the shutters would be too grim and also do not go right to the top.

H.N. to Vita   *January 7, 1941*
                                    Leeds

I dined with Billy Harlech, the Regional Commissioner. He had been spending the day with the Queen visiting Sheffield. He says that when the car stops the Queen nips out into the snow and goes straight into the middle of the crowd and starts talking to them. For a moment or two they just gaze and gape in astonishment. But then they all start talking at once. 'Hi! Your Majesty, look here!!' She has that quality of making everybody feel that they and they alone are being spoken to. It is I think because she has very large eyes which she opens very wide and turns upon one. Billy Harlech says that these visits do incalculable good.

Diary   *January 20, 1941*

I lunch with General de Gaulle at the Savoy. He looks less unattractive with his hat off since it shows his young hair and the tired but not wholly benevolent look in his eyes. He has the taut manner of a man who is becoming stout and is conscious that only the exercise of continuous muscle power can keep his figure in shape. I do not like him. He accuses my Ministry of being 'Pétainiste'. '*Mais non!*' I say, '*Monsieur le Général.*' '*Enfin, Pétainisant.*' '*Nous travaillons,*' I said, '*pour la France entière.*' '*La France entière,*' he shouted, '*c'est la France Libre. C'est MOI!!!*' Well, well, I admit that he made a great Boulangist gesture. But the spectre of General Boulanger passes across my mind. He begins to abuse Pétain, saying that once again he has sold himself to Laval, saying that Weygand showed cowardice when bombed at the front. Osusky [Czech Ambassador in Paris before the fall of France] says that French opinion imagines that de Gaulle and Pétain are at heart as one. '*C'est une erreur,*' he says sharply. I am not encouraged.

To change the subject I say that I have received telegrams from unoccupied France which I was surprised had passed the censor. He said that he had received a long letter of the most de Gaullist nature, the writer of which had written on top 'I am sure the Censor will stop this.' Underneath in violet ink was written '*La censure approuve totalement.*' ...

We discuss the infinite complexity of arranging the reception of Halifax, who should arrive tomorrow at Baltimore in the *King George V.*[1] How I wish I were with him. Except that I simply could not bear to leave London or England these days. One's patriotism, which has been a vague family feeling, is now a flame in the night. I may have felt arrogant about the British Empire in past years: today I feel quite humbly proud of the British people.

---

[1] Lord Halifax was appointed Ambassador to the United States, and was succeeded as Foreign Secretary by Anthony Eden. Churchill sent him to America in our newest battleship.

Diary   *January 21, 1941*

I go to the House. We are meeting in our dear old building. We cannot go to the cloakroom which has been smashed by the Nazis. In the Members' Lobby there are steel girders and scaffolding keeping the thing together. But the rest is just the same. I sit on the bench for a bit. They are discussing man power. Winston comes in and has a long whispered conversation with the Speaker. His second chin has swollen as if a goitre: it is a real Chinese paunch. But he is as acute and gay as ever.

Diary   *January 22, 1941*

Winston refuses again to make a statement on war aims.[1] The reason given in Cabinet is that precise aims would be compromising, whereas vague principles would disappoint. Thus all those days of work have led to nothing. Winston replies to the debate on man power. He is in terrific form. Authoritative, reasonable, conciliatory and amusing. In the course of his speech he uses the phrase *primus inter pares*. The Labour people cry out, 'Translate!' Winston, without a moment's hesitation, goes on, 'Certainly I shall translate,' then he pauses and turns to his right, 'for the benefit of any old Etonians who may be present.'[2]

Diary   *February 14, 1941*

Dear London! So vast and unexpectant, so ugly and so strong! You have been bruised and battered and all your clothes are tattered and in disarray. Yet we, who never knew that we loved you (who regarded you, in fact, like some old family servant, ministering to our comforts and amenities, and yet slightly incongruous and absurd), have suddenly felt the twinge of some fibre of identity, respect and love. We know

---

[1] In collaboration with Lord Halifax, Harold had drafted such a statement, advocating a European federation.

[2] Churchill turned to his Labour colleague, Hugh Dalton, Minister of Economic Warfare, who was an Old Etonian. Churchill himself was at Harrow.

what is coming to you. And our eyes slip along your old untidy limbs, knowing that the leg may be gone tomorrow, and that tomorrow the arm may be severed. Yet through all this regret and dread pierces a slim clean note of pride. 'London can take it.' I believe that what will win us this war is the immense central-dynamo of British pride. The Germans have only assertiveness to put against it. That is transitory. Our pride is permanent, obscure and dark. It has the nature of infinity.

H.N. to Vita *February 18, 1941*

I had the dreaded meeting of the National Labour Party. Malcolm [MacDonald] was in the chair. He told us exactly what had happened about his being bumped off to Canada [as High Commissioner]. He had said to Winston, 'But you are condemning me to exile. All the lights will be on in Ottawa and I shall yearn for the dark of London.' He refused to go. He said that he would much rather join up. Winston was evidently touched by his attitude and asked him not to decide till next day. And after sleeping over it, 'I saw,' Malcolm said, 'that if Winston asked me to go to Timbuctoo I should have to accept.'

All this sounds awful bunk when one writes it down afterwards but if you had been there and heard Malcolm speak so simply and frankly you would have known that the whole thing was true, and that it reflects great credit on both the P.M. and Malcolm.

Then the leadership question came up. They wanted me to be leader [in place of MacDonald]. But I knew that they did not want it very much. So I said, 'But it is absurd that a Party which began under the leadership of Ramsay MacDonald should end under the leadership of the Parliamentary Secretary to the Minister of Information. I have neither false pride nor false modesty. But you, as sensible people, will agree that such a solution would make both the Party and myself seem ridiculous.' They agreed with that and thus we have left the leadership in suspense and only pray that there will be no Press publicity.

How silly and out of proportion it all is!

Diary   *February 26, 1941*

I am rather fussed about this diary. It is not intimate enough to give a personal picture. The really important things that I know I cannot record. And thus it gives a picture of someone on the edge of things who is so certain that he knows what is really happening that he does not dare to say so. The day to day impressions of a greengrocer in Streatham would really be more interesting. I must try henceforward to be more intimate and more illuminating. It is half that I feel that if I survive this diary will be more a record from which I can fill in remembered details. And half that I find some relief before I go to bed in putting down on paper the momentary spurts and gushes of this cataract of history.

Diary   *February 27, 1941*

I attend the Anglo-French Interparliamentary Association's lunch to de Gaulle and [Admiral] Muselier. I sit bang opposite to de Gaulle and have much talk with him. I dislike him less than I did at first. He has tired, ruminating but not unkindly eyes. He has curiously effeminate hands (not feminine hands but effeminated hands without arteries or muscles). He abuses the paper 'France' [published by the Ministry of Information] which he says is not 'avec moi'. . . .

Diary   *March 1, 1941*

The Bulgarian Ministers went to Vienna yesterday and signed a pact adhering to the Axis. At the same time German mechanised forces thundered into Sofia. This is bad for Yugoslavia and Greece and will have a depressing effect here. People do not care so much how many square miles we occupy in Eritrea so long as Germany is creeping ever closer to our jugular arteries. We know that in a few weeks we shall be exposed to a terrific ordeal.

Diary   *March 2, 1941*

Viti asks me how we are going to win this war. Hitler will shortly have the whole of Europe under his control and how are we to turn him out? It will require all our strength to resist the appalling attacks by air and submarine which are shortly coming to us. We shall be shattered and starved. Yet how are we to tell our people how they can win? The only hope is that America and Russia will come in on our side. I think we can resist the worst. But we shall be so exhausted by that resistance that Hitler may offer us an honourable peace which will be difficult to reject. I have an uneasy feeling that when things get very bad there may be a movement in this country to attribute the whole disaster to 'the war-mongers' and to replace Churchill by Sam Hoare or some appeaser. If only we could show people some glimmer of light at the end of the tunnel, we could count upon their enduring any ordeal. But the danger is that there is no light beyond the light of faith. I have that light. I know in the marrow of my bones that we shall win in the end. But I get depressed when I realise how difficult it is to convey that faith to the public, since it is not based, as far as I can see, on reason or calculation.

Diary   *March 4, 1941*

I dine with Louis Spears in his upstairs room at the Ritz. Mary Spears is there, also Ned Grigg and Monsieur and Madame Jean. The latter was diplomatic Chef de Cabinet to Reynaud with Roland de Margerie. Since then he has been in Morocco and brings back disturbing news. The Germans are gradually infiltrating into Morocco and unless we do something within the next few months he fears they will have it in their power as they have Rumania and Bulgaria.

He tells us the full story of Hélène de Portes [Reynaud's mistress]. He admits that it is *'inénarrable et inavouable'*. But after all he was there and he knew. He said that she really believed that Reynaud would become the dictator of France and she the power behind the throne. She was passionately anti-British since she felt that our democratic ideas would prevent this strange pattern of state governance. The extent of her influence and interference cannot be exaggerated. It was not so much that she dictated policy but that she surrounded Reynaud with fifth columnists and spies. For instance she and Roland de Margerie had managed at a crucial moment to convince Reynaud that he should send the fleet and what remained of the army and material to North Africa. All the plans were made. But it was Madame de Portes who made him change his mind and accept Baudouin as Foreign Minister.

We discuss how it came that this frowsty soiled woman with the dirty fur tippet managed to sway the destiny of a great nation. He said it was because Reynaud had an inferiority complex about his small stature and that she made him feel tall and grand and powerful. 'Had Reynaud been three inches taller the history of the world might have been changed.' He and Spears talk together about the final *débandade* [in June 1940]. Those hurried rushes through the night from château to château only to find that there was only one telephone in the butler's pantry and that France could not communicate with its Prime Minister. Madame de Portes was always there and keeping away from Reynaud anybody whom she felt might spur him to resistance. '*C'est moi*,' she used to scream, '*qui suis la maîtresse ici.*' And my God she was right.

Then the final scene in the two-seater car. Reynaud was driving. The luggage was piled behind. He was always a bad driver and he crashed into a tree. A suitcase hit Madame de Portes on the back of the head and killed her instantly. Reynaud was hit by the steering wheel and rendered unconscious. When he recovered in hospital they broke the news to him that Madame de Portes was dead. '*Elle était la France*,' he said. Jean thought he really felt it. *La fausse Marianne.*

H.N. to Vita   *March 5, 1941*

I hope you got my ration card. That ought to enable you to get a little more meat. But the meat ration is going to be further reduced. It seems we have got heaps of tea, sugar and oil but that meat is very short as also food stuff for cattle. It is a serious position. . . .

H.N. to Vita   *March 17, 1941*

I lunched with James [Pope-Hennessy] and he took me to see the
devastation round St Paul's. It is unbelievable. A great space as wide as
Trafalgar Square laid low. I feel that at any cost we should retain it as a
memorial to London's civilians. They deserve it, and it gives a magnificent vista of St Paul's such as Wren would have given his soul to
achieve. It is as if St Paul's stood where the National Gallery now
stands. To get that permanently cleared is worth £40 million in site-
value and should be done.

Diary   *March 29, 1941*

Rab Butler agrees with me that as the Germans have come up against
a difficult problem in their invasion of this country and in their invasion
of the Balkans, they may strike suddenly at Russia. Everybody else
regards this idea as fantastic, but I am not so sure.

Diary   *March 31, 1941*

Go to see Maisky [Russian Ambassador]. He sits there in his ugly
Victorian study like a little gnome in an arm-chair, twiddling his
thumbs, twinkling his eyes and giving the impression that his feet do
not reach the floor. He says that he takes an objective view of all this.
We shall not be beaten. Our Navy is the finest in the world and perhaps
our Air Force also. But what about our Army? Is it good for anything
but a colonial war? Shall we be able to resist the Germans in Greece
or even in Cyrenaica? We cannot afford another Norway. And how
on earth do we imagine that we shall ever defeat the Germans? Italy
we may knock out. But Germany never. I reply that I rely on my
instinct and my knowledge of the German character. They will
assuredly crash before we do. He says that this may be so: 'Time will
show,' he says, grinning mischievously. He thinks that the Labour
people here are not strong enough. They do not force the Government to come to terms with Russia. 'The Labour people are as
bad as Chamberlain.' I ask him whether he sees any prospect of a

Yugoslav-Greek-Turkish alliance. He says that Turkey is too cautious. I ask him whether he has any fear that Russia will be attacked. He says, 'Germany is too cautious.'

H.N. to Vita   *March 31, 1941*

It is always a gloomy moment for me when I unpack the *panier* which we packed together. I take out the flowers sadly and think of you picking them and putting the paper round them. But today it was worse, as I feel such a failure as a help to you. I do not know what it is, but I never seem to be able to help you when you are in trouble. I loathe your being unhappy more than I loathe anything. But I just moon about feeling wretched myself, and when I look back on my life, I see that the only times I have been really unhappy are when you have been unhappy too.

I wonder whether you would have been happier if married to a more determined and less sensitive man. On the one hand you would have hated any sense of control or management, and other men might not have understood your desire for independence. I have always respected that, and you have often mistaken it for aloofness on my part. What bothers me is whether I have given way too much to your eccentricities. Some outside person might imagine that I should have made more of my life if I had had someone like Diana De La Warr to share my career. There are moments when I think you reproach yourself for not having been more interested in my pursuits and for not having pushed against my diffidence. I never feel that myself. I have always felt that the struggle in the market-place was for me to fight alone, and that you were there as something wholly different.

But what has always worried me is your dual personality. The one tender, wise and with such a sense of responsibility. And the other rather cruel and extravagant. The former has been what I have always clung to as the essential you, but the latter has always alarmed me and I have tried to dismiss it from my mind – or, rather, I have always accepted it as the inevitable counterpart of your remarkable personality. I have felt that this side of you was beyond my understanding, and when you have got into a real mess because of it, you have been angry with me for not coping with the more violent side in yourself.

I do not think that you have ever quite realised how deeply unhappy your eccentric side has often rendered me. When I am unhappy I shut up like an oyster. I love you so much, darling. I hold my head in my hands worrying about you. I was nearly killed by a taxi today. I only missed an accident by a hair's breadth. And my first thought was, 'If I had really been taken to hospital in a mess, then Viti would have been shaken out of her muzzy moods.' I love you so much.

March 31, 1941
Vita to H.N.   *Sissinghurst*

I have just had the most awful shock: Virginia has killed herself. It is not in the papers, but I got letters from Leonard [Woolf] and also from Vanessa [Bell] telling me. It was last Friday. Leonard came home to find a note saying that she was going to commit suicide, and they think she has drowned herself, as he found her stick floating on the river. He says she had not been well for the last few weeks and was terrified of going mad again. He says, 'It was, I suppose, the strain of the war and finishing her book, and she could not rest or eat.'

I simply can't take it in. That lovely mind, that lovely spirit.

Diary   *April 9, 1941*

I go down to the House to hear Winston make his statement [on the invasion of Greece]. It had been devised as a motion congratulating the fighting services on their victories [in Africa] and I remember a few days ago how Winston promised that he would say 'Fly the flags in celebration.' These victories are now dust and ashes.

The P.M. comes in at 11.56 and is greeted with cheers. He sits between Greenwood and Attlee, scowls at the notes in his hand, pulls out a gold pencil and scribbles an addition to the last sheet. He then gets up to speak in a grim and obstinate voice. He throws out news incidentally. We have taken Massawa [chief port in Eritrea]. The Germans entered Salonika at 4 a.m. this morning. At this news there is a silent wince of pain throughout the House. He discloses that the US Government have given us their revenue cutters. His peroration implies that we are done without American help. He indulges in a few flights of oratory. He evidently feels that even graver news is ahead of us. The House is glum and sad.

Diary   *April 13, 1941*

From the propaganda point of view, all that the country really wants is some assurance of how victory is to be achieved. They are bored by talks about the righteousness of our cause and our eventual triumph. What they want are facts indicating how we are to beat the Germans. I have no idea at all how we are to give them those facts. Fundamentally (although they are unaware of the fact) the British public have lost confidence in the power of the sea. Norway was a nasty knock. 'How,' they ask, 'was Germany able to land four divisions in Libya?' There are many explanations of this feat but none of them really disposes of the question, 'But if they can land four divisions in Libya, what prevents them obtaining mastery of Africa and Asia?' I see no ostensible answer to that terrible question. I have no doubt that we shall win in the end. But we shall have to learn a new technique, the secret of mobile warfare, and only when we have learnt it will the efficacy of our sea-power be brought to bear.

H.N. to Vita   *April 16, 1941*

I dined tonight with Sibyl at the Dorchester. Dinner was all right although I question the propriety of such meals in war time. I sat between Irene Ravensdale and Mary [Mrs St John] Hutchinson. Irene is worried about Tom [Mosley] and his wife.[1] They are treated as common prisoners and not allowed to wash much or have a change of clothes. They are thus actually dirty and that shocked me. I must see what can be done about it.

I left my dinner early and stepped out into a first class blitz. There was a glow over Westminster as red as an Egyptian dawn. Of course I

---

[1] Sir Oswald Mosley and his second wife, Diana (one of the Mitford sisters), were arrested and imprisoned in May 1940 as a danger to the State, and were released on humanitarian grounds in November 1943.

could get no taxi and had to walk the whole way here [Ministry of Information]. It is really no fun. I could not put on my torch and the Messerschmitts droned overhead and the guns crashed. I did not mind over much until I fell over a brick and rolled about like a huge rabbit, breaking my glasses.

Diary   *April 21, 1941*

We are evacuating from Greece. The Americans will take this badly and there is a wave of defeatism sweeping that continent. Lindbergh has been proclaiming that we are in a desperate position. I confess that my mind goes back to my last talk with Maisky when he said, 'You cannot stand another Norway.' Another Norway is now upon us, and the news from Spain is equally bad. Hitler is evidently determined to turn us out of the Mediterranean.[1]

Diary   *April 28, 1941*

The swastika flies over the Acropolis. Not a pleasant thought. I gather that we have lost at least $\frac{3}{4}$ of our BEF from Greece but the bombing is bad and the Germans are on the Gulf of Corinth. I fear I have a cold coming on and feel pretty glum all around. . . .

H.N. to Vita   *May 13, 1941*

You will be puzzled by the Hess thing.[2] My own impression is that he was rather mad in any case but a fine fellow. He really believed in Hitler and was disgusted by the people whom Hitler had around him.

Years ago he had made friends with [Lord] Clydesdale and Nigel Douglas Hamilton. They had discussed the possibility of an alliance between Germany and Britain. The memories of these conversations

---

[1] Hitler planned to capture Gibraltar with Franco's help.

[2] Rudolf Hess, Hitler's deputy, flew to Scotland on May 11 to contact the Duke of Hamilton with the intention of persuading Churchill to make peace with Germany. His mission was unauthorised by Hitler.

came back to him. He took his aeroplane, looked out the Hamilton place on the map, and headed straight for it. His machine caught fire in the neighbourhood and he baled out. The first thing he did when the military came was to ask to see the Duke of Hamilton. The latter was much embarrassed. You can imagine what a difficult publicity problem that entails.

Diary   *May 14, 1941*

... I lunch with the Prime Minister and Mrs Churchill in the flat which has been constructed for them in the Office of Works. It is not very large, but it is well done and comfortable. Winston has brought some of his pictures in and the general effect is very gay. Winston beams there with his ugly watch-chain and his ugly ring. I try to get directives out of him about Hess, but he will go no further than to say we must not make a hero out of him. We have white wine and port and brandy and hors d'oeuvres and mutton. All rather sparse. Winston had been seeing the film *Comrade X* [about a fictional Russian spy] and simply loved it. I told him that Maisky had tried to get it suppressed. He was overjoyed that it had not been. He is in a good purring mood.

Diary   *May 17, 1941*

There are two Hess jokes about. The first says that Salisbury Plain is being cleared of troops in case Goering also wishes to land. The second is that Hess was ill and came here to consult a really good German doctor.

Diary   *May 27, 1941*

Winston comes in and rises to give the latest news. He passes on to the battle of the Denmark Straits. He does it beautifully. He builds up the whole picture from the moment we heard that the *Bismarck* and the *Prinz Eugen* were driving westwards against our convoys to the moment when we came into contact with them and the *Hood* was sunk. After paying tribute to the loss of these men, he passed on to the further pursuit. The *Prinz Eugen* had disappeared, but the *Bismarck* was followed closely and bombed. This bombing slowed down her escape. Further arrangements were made to intercept, but then the weather changed and the visibility diminished, and by a sudden change of course the *Bismarck* managed to elude our vigilance. The whole House felt at that moment that Winston was about to break it to us that the ship had escaped. There was a hush of despair. At dawn next morning (Winston continued) we again resumed contact. He told us how the Fleet Air Arm then fired torpedoes at the ship, destroying her steering gear and forcing her to go round and round in immense circles in the ocean. From all sides our fleet approached to destroy her. Such is the innate sporting feeling of the House that we all began to feel sorry for the *Bismarck*. The P.M. went on to say that our ships had established contact; that they had begun to fire; that their shells had not made any effect; and that the only hope was to fire torpedoes. 'That process,' he said, 'is in action as I speak.' He then went on to speak about con-scription in Northern Ireland and left the House with a sense of *coitus interruptus*. I saw one of the secretaries in the official gallery make a violent sign with a small folded sheet to Brendan Bracken. He took the missive and passed it up to Winston. The latter rose at once and interrupted Griffiths. 'I crave your indulgence, Mr Speaker,' he said, 'I have just received news that the *Bismarck* has been sunk.' Wild cheers, in which I do not join.

Diary   *May 29, 1941*

Here is an instance of how one suffers from bad reporting. On Tuesday I deputised for Duff at the Advertisers' luncheon. I did not give a hand-out to the Press, since I am always afraid that the P.M. may read what one says and make a fuss. Then today when I entered Church House [where the Commons were temporarily meeting], I bumped into him. There was a moment of silence as we climbed the stairs together, and then he said, 'I thee that you have thaid that I am about to propothe peathe terms.' I said, 'But what on earth makes you think that?' He said, 'I read it in the newspapers. I read that you had said that if Hitler proposed peace, nobody would believe him, but that if I

proposed peace, everyone would believe me.' 'That', I said with some
heat, 'is a false rendering of what I said.' 'I believe you,' he said. 'I was
only getting a rise out of you.' I do not really believe that Winston
thought I had said anything silly. But my word, how he scrutinises
one's speeches.

Diary   *June 10, 1941*

Duff tells us that the P.M. is under the impression that the anxiety
which exists is purely a House of Commons anxiety and is not shared
by the country as a whole. We all say that this is not true, and that the
country is deeply anxious and shocked.

The Middle East have no sense of publicity. The Admiralty is even
worse. We complain that there are no photographs of the sinking of
the *Bismarck*. Tripp [Navy spokesman] says that the official photographer was in the *Suffolk* and that the *Suffolk* was too far away. We
say, 'But why didn't one of our reconnaissance machines fly over the
ship and take photographs?' He replies: 'Well you see, you *must* see,
well upon my word, well after all, an Englishman would not like to
take snapshots of a fine vessel sinking.' Is he right? I felt abashed when
he said it. I think he is right. It reminds me of Arthur Balfour when
Brockdorff-Rantzau refused to stand when he was handed the Treaty
[at Versailles]. 'Did he remain seated?' said someone to Balfour afterwards. 'I did not notice. I do not stare at a gentleman in distress.'

*The German Army, having cleaned up the Balkans, now launched its massive
campaign against Russia, and within three weeks had advanced 450 miles and
captured Smolensk. Few considered that the total defeat of Russia could be
avoided. It was at this moment that Harold lost his ministerial job. Churchill
asked for his resignation so that the office could be given to a Labour Member.
He was deeply shocked and saddened. In partial compensation, Churchill made
him a Governor of the BBC.*

Diary   *June 22, 1941*

We have breakfast outside. Vita arrives to say that the 7 o'clock news announced that Germany has invaded Russia. Goebbels has declared that Hitler's patience was exhausted and that the frontier has been crossed in Poland and Rumania.

Most people in England will be delighted. I am not so optimistic. It will have a bad effect on America, where many influential people do not like to see themselves as the allies of Bolshevism. It will have a bad effect on Conservative and Catholic opinion here. And if, as is likely, Hitler defeats Russia in three weeks, then the road to the oil is open, as also the road to Persia and India.

At 9 Winston broadcasts. He says that he is on the side of the Russians who defend their homes. He does not conceal that Russia may be beaten quickly, but having indicated to us the approaching collapse of India and China, and, in fact, of Europe, Asia and Africa, he somehow leaves us with the impression that we are quite certain to win this war. A masterpiece.

Diary   *June 24, 1941*

Walk to the Beefsteak with Ned Grigg [Under Secretary of State for War]. He says that 80% of the War Office experts think that Russia will be knocked out in ten days. They are not at all pleased by this new war, which will give great triumphs to Hitler and leave him free to fling his whole force against us.

Diary   *July 8, 1941*

I drive down to White's Club with Duff and beg him to treat the P.R.O.s[1] this afternoon with all gentleness. They are a touchy lot. There are 21 of them, and we meet after luncheon in the Chancellor's Hall. Duff glowers at them as if they were coolies in some Cingalese copper-mine. He then tells them an angry story about how he had been brought up from Bognor on false pretences. He then scowls at

---

[1] Public Relations Officers of the various Ministries.

them and says that this is all he has to say. He then stalks out of the room. We are left ashamed and wretched and do not know which way to look. I cannot make out what happens to Duff on such occasions. He seems to lose all power over himself. I think it is a sort of shyness.

Diary   *July 18, 1941*

When I get back to the Ministry after lunch, I get a message from the Prime Minister's Private Secretary to say that he wants to see me at No. 10 at 5.30. I discuss this with Duff. He says that he is to be made Chancellor of the Duchy of Lancaster and to go to Singapore to coordinate. The P.M. had just mentioned me, and said that the Labour Party wanted a Labour man in my job. Duff thinks that if I am offered something as good, I should accept it, but if something worse, I should refuse and go back to my writing. A later message comes that the interview is cancelled and that I shall receive a communication 'in another form'.

At 5.55 it arrives in the shape of a black box from Downing Street. I get Sammy Hood to open it for me, and I find a letter inside. I think it might have been more politely worded.[1] Could I afford it I should not accept a Governorship of the BBC. But both Duff and Walter [Monckton] urge me to accept. I realise that this means the end of any political ambitions which I may ever have cherished. I am hurt and sad and sorry. The P.M.'s Secretary telephones to say that he wants a reply at once, and could I send it by taxi. Well, I send it.

Diary   *July 19, 1941*

I wake up feeling that something horrible has happened, and remember that I have been sacked from the Government. Go to the Ministry and start clearing out some of my private possessions. Then attend the Duty Room, probably for the last time.

I come back to the bench below the gangway having had my chance

---

[1] Churchill's note began: 'The changes at the Ministry of Information lead me to ask you to place your office as Parliamentary Secretary at my disposal ...', and ended, 'Yours sincerely, Winston Churchill.'

and failed to profit by it. Ever since I have been in the House I have been looked on as a might-be. Now I shall be a might-have-been. Always up till now I have been buoyed up by the hope of writing some good book or achieving a position of influence in politics. I now know that I shall never write a book better than I have written already, and that my political career is at an end. I shall merely get balder and fatter and more deaf as the years go by. This is an irritating thing. Success should come late in life in order to compensate for the loss of youth; I had youth and success together, and now I have old age and failure. Apart from all this, I mind leaving the Ministry where I did good work and had friends.

Diary   *August 13, 1941*

Dine with Camrose at the Dorchester. The guest of honour is Dorothy Thompson [the American journalist].

She talks a great deal about the difficulty of welding American opinion together up to the point where they will be prepared to enter the war on our side. She says that we must always remember that America is composed of many millions of people who left Europe because they hated it, and that there are many millions of Italians and Germans whose hearts go out to their mother countries. Although these emotions pull America apart, they feel at the same time a strong longing to remain together. What we don't fully understand in this country is the actual dread of the American soul at being split. There is always the fear that they will cease to be a nation, and this is the fear which Roosevelt understands so perfectly and which he guides with such genius.

Diary   *September 9, 1941*

The House meets. The Prime Minister makes a long and optimistic review. He stands there very stout and black, smoothing his palms down across his frame – beginning by patting his chest, then smoothing his stomach and ending down at the groin. He does not attempt any flight of oratory but he quotes Kipling's lines about the mine-sweepers, and is so moved by them that he chokes and cannot continue. His speech has a good effect, and the slight anti-Churchill tide which had begun to be noticeable was checked.

Diary   *September 12, 1941*

Dylan Thomas comes to see me. He wants a job on the BBC. He is a fat little man, puffy and pinkish, dressed in very dirty trousers and a loud checked coat. I tell him that if he is to be employed by the BBC, he must promise not to get drunk. I give him £1, as he is clearly at his wits' end for money. He does not look as if he had been cradled into poetry by wrong [Shelley]. He looks as if he will be washed out of poetry by whisky.

Diary   *October 6, 1941*

Dine with Sibyl [Colefax] in Lord North Street. The American Ambassador [John G. Winant], R.A. Butler, the Master of the Rolls, and the Kenneth Clarks. Winant is one of the most charming men that I have ever met. He has emphatic eyes and an unemphatic voice. Rab says that he was dining the other night with Winston, Eden and Beaverbrook, and that Winston spoke with deep sympathy of Baldwin. Winston has no capacity of meanness, and that is why we love him so. A great soul in a great crisis.

They bother me to write a book about the British Empire. I am tempted. Winant adds his persuasion. It was a lovely dinner, and we walked away in the mist with the moon, and felt so pleased to be in London in October 1941.

Diary   *October 9, 1941*

There is deep gloom about the Russian news. It looks as if Moscow might be taken and the Russian armies divided. Hitler will then declare that the Russian war is over and turn to the south-east. There will be great resentment in this country that we did not strike while the iron was hot, and Winston will be blamed. I have complete confidence, however, that everything strategic will be done: it is in administration and tactics that we are so weak.

Diary   *October 10, 1941*

Vita comes up in the morning, the first time she has been in London for two years. I have always tried to explain to her that the destruction of London is very bad in the places where it is bad, but not very bad in the places where it is not very bad. That sounds a dull way of putting it. She now agrees that it is absolutely right. She cannot conceive why St Paul's is still standing, or why our dear Temple should have been banged so badly about the head.

We go down to Evesham, I to inspect the BBC's Monitoring Service, and Vita to visit the garden at Hidcote.[1] The latter is devised on the right scheme of vistas running through small intimate gardens. I am much impressed by a quincux of hornbeam trees (not hedges) round a grass plot. There is also a marvellous huge lawn enclosed by yew, with elms upon a stage in the background. Vita meets me at the station with a huge sack of lilac and many cuttings from Laurie's garden. When we get home, we put our loot from Hidcote into pails and have a lovely dinner.

Diary   *October 28, 1941*

Roosevelt last night made an address in which he pledged the USA to bring supplies to British ports in their own bottoms and escorted by their own Navy. This is a tremendous advance. He said, 'We know who fired the first shot!' A great date. A very great date. Probably the turning point of the war. I walk the streets in silent elation. What a master he has been! I am cheered when I think of the aged and bewildered Mussolini (for whom I have a growing sympathy) and the

---

[1] The famous Gloucestershire garden created by the American, Laurence Johnston. It is often supposed that the design of Sissinghurst was based upon it, but this was Harold's first visit there.

neurotic genius of Berchtesgaden – and then of dear Winston and that consummate politician of Hyde Park.

Diary   *November 17, 1941*

I go to Pratt's and find Harold Macmillan there. He talks about Beaverbrook. He thinks him half mad and half genius. He says that he thinks only of his present work [Ministry of Supply], and that all his old fortune, newspapers and women are completely forgotten. But he also says that Beaverbrook gives no man his complete confidence. Thus, although there is great enthusiasm among the staff, and a feeling that they are important and useful, there is also a sort of uneasiness at not knowing what is really happening.

Diary   *November 20, 1941*

The papers and even the BBC take a very optimistic view of our Libyan offensive.[1] This distresses me, since if things go wrong (as they well may) public opinion will have a bad shock. Winston in the House today, while warning us against premature exultation and making it clear that the real fighting has not yet begun, makes the error of proclaiming that this is the first time that we have met the Germans on equal terms. I dread these forecasts. Moreover, in his Order of the Day to the troops, he said that the battle might prove the equal of Blenheim or Waterloo. The 1 o'clock news announces progress in almost hysterical terms. At the BBC Board I bring up the question of the Libyan bulletins, and we damp them down.

---

[1] After very heavy tank battles, the New Zealand Division recaptured Sidi Rezegh, but on the 25th General Cunningham, commander of the 8th Army, was relieved of his command by General Auchinleck.

Diary   *December 4, 1941*

Aneurin Bevan says an interesting thing. He says that we intellectuals
are in a difficult position. Our tastes attract us to the past, our reason
to the future. Hitherto we have been able to appease this conflict since
our tastes were still able to find their outlets, whereas our reason could
indulge in the picture of the shape of things to come. Now, however,
the future is becoming very imminent and we are faced with the fact
that our tastes can no longer be indulged. Gone are ease and income
and travel and elegance. There is a tendency therefore for the weaker
souls to escape to mysticism. Their reason tells them that the future is
right, but it is agony for them to lose the past. This is what has
happened to Aldous Huxley and Joad. I pray to God it will not happen
to me. 'I don't think it will, Harold,' says Aneurin, 'your courage is
great.'

*On December 7 the Japanese attacked the American fleet in Pearl Harbor, and
sank four of their finest battleships. 'A mad decision', Churchill later called it.
But he also reflected, 'So we had won the war after all.' He crossed the Atlantic
to confer with his ally. But the new war began badly for Britain with the loss
of their battleships* Prince of Wales *and* Repulse, *and* Hong Kong *was
captured on Christmas Day.*

Diary   *December 7, 1941*

After dinner we listen to the 9 o'clock news. The Japanese have
bombed Pearl Harbour. I do not believe it. We then turn on the
German and French news and get a little more information. Roosevelt
has ordered the mobilisation of the American Forces and instructed
the Navy to carry out their sealed orders.

I am dumbfounded by the news. After all, Roosevelt was still in
negotiation with Kurusu [the Japanese envoy], and had dispatched a
personal letter to the Mikado. While these negotiations were still in
progress, the Japanese deliver a terrific air-attack 7,000 miles away
from Japan. The whole action seems as insane as Hitler's attack on
Russia. I remain amazed.

The effect in Germany will be bad. They will not say, 'We have a new ally.' They will say (or rather they will think in the recesses of their anxious souls), 'We have outraged the most formidable enemy in the world.' Their sense of destiny will begin to hover again as a sense of doom.

Diary   *December 8, 1941*

The House has been specially summoned. Winston enters the Chamber with bowed shoulders and an expression of grim determination on his face. The House had expected jubilation at the entry of America into the war and are a trifle disconcerted. He makes a dull matter-of-fact speech. He has a great sense of occasion. The mistake he makes is to read out his message to the Siamese Prime Minister. The Siamese are bound to capitulate, and it was a mistake to expect them to do anything else.

Diary   *December 9, 1941*

Lunch with de Gaulle at the Connaught Hotel. I cannot make out whether I really like him. His arrogance and fascism annoy me. But there is something like a fine retriever dog about his eyes. He challenges me on my defence of Weygand. He says that he was a bad strategic ally. He asks what I meant by saying the French in England should 'compose their differences'. What he wanted me to say was that I had meant that they should all join de Gaulle. I am not prepared to say that as yet. I say that I was cross at having one Frenchman telling me that de Gaulle was surrounded by Jews and Freemasons, and another that he was surrounded by Jesuits and *cagoulards*. He does not like this at all, and his A.D.C. blushes. But it was not a bad thing to say.

Diary   *December 11, 1941*

The House is depressed. I have a feeling that our nerves are not as good as they were in July 1940, and that we are tired of defeat. We still

face the central issue with courage and faith, but in minor matters we
are getting touchy and irritable.

Germany and Italy have declared war on the United States. The
BBC gives us extracts from Hitler's and Mussolini's speeches in the
Reichstag and the Palazzo Venezia respectively. An admirable performance. But the main factor of this declaration (which should have
filled us with the springing hope and aroused tumults of exultation) is
ignored. We take it flatly. The loss of the *Prince of Wales* [the day before]
has numbed our nerves.

H.N. to Vita   *December 11, 1941*

Winston this morning was very grim and said we must expect 'heavy
punishment'. I like him best when he makes that sort of speech. I am
full of faith. We simply can't be beaten with America in. But how
strange it is that this great event should be recorded and welcomed
here without any jubilation. We should have gone mad with joy if it
happened a year ago.

I bet de Gaulle that Germany would declare war on the United
States. He said, '*Jamais de la vie.*' I said, 'But will you take my bet?' He
said, 'No, since you may be right.'

Not an American flag flying in the whole of London. How odd we
are!

Diary   *December 19, 1941*

Go up to Leicester. I find them all rather depressed. The sinking of
the *Prince of Wales* has made an impression out of all proportion. They
ignore the Russian victories, the Libyan advance and the entry of
America. They are faced with the fact that two of our greatest battleships have been sunk within a few minutes by the monkey men, and
that we and the Americans have between us lost command of the
Pacific. I try to cheer them up.

Diary   *December 28, 1941*

Feeling much better. I do a *Spectator* article on keeping diaries, in which I lay down the rule that one should write one's diary for one's great-grandson. I think that is a correct rule. The purely private diary becomes too self-centred and morbid. One should have a remote, but not too remote, audience.

The new year began disastrously. Japan gained almost all her objectives in the Far East. Singapore was lost, with the surrender of 60,000 British troops; the sinkings in the Atlantic neared their climax; Rommel threw the British out of Cyrenaica; and Churchill's leadership was challenged at home.

Diary   *January 1, 1942*

Mr Auren of a Stockholm newspaper comes to see me. He asks how I explain the British love of self-criticism. I say it is partly pride and partly our love of fresh air. He says it does our propaganda harm abroad. I say that it is worth it from our point of view since it keeps our public opinion healthy. We should die if we were not able to abuse our institutions and public men. Moreover in the end it is good long-term policy even from the propaganda point of view. He says that all Swedes know that they will come in in the end. I do not suggest that 'the end' means the moment when it is quite clear which side is going to win.

I then go round the House to fire-watch. I have my bread and butter and sausages and then read Rebecca West's Yugoslav book [*Black Lamb and Grey Falcon*] in the library. I am not sure it is not a masterpiece.

Diary   *January 2, 1942*

Dine at Brooks' with Jim Lees-Milne, James Pope-Hennessy and Guy Burgess. We discuss everything and mainly the question of success. James says, 'It is ridiculous of you, Harold, not to realise that it does not matter your having been a failure at the M. of I., since you have

written such good books.' This annoys me, since I was not a failure at
the M. of I. but merely politically inconvenient. I say that I would
rather be able to send 100 tons of grain to Greece than write an
immortal work. That impresses them since they agree. What does even
the *Symposium* matter compared to the death by hunger of 200 Greeks
a day?

Diary   *January 20, 1942*

Bitterly cold. Go down to the House. I arrive a bit late and do not
hear the reception given to Winston at his entry [he had just returned
from America]. Some say it was most enthusiastic; others say it had
about it a note of reserve. I ask Randolph Churchill how it struck him.
He said, 'Nothing like the reception which Chamberlain got when he
returned from Munich.' ...

Diary   *January 27, 1942*

Down to the House. Winston speaks for one hour and a half and
justifies his demand for a vote of confidence. One can actually feel the
wind of opposition dropping sentence by sentence and by the time he
finishes it is clear that there is really no opposition at all – only a certain
uneasiness. Winston does nothing to diminish that uneasiness. He says
that we shall have even worse news to face in the Far East and that the
Libyan battle is going none too well. He thrusts both his hands deep
into his trouser pockets and turns his tummy now to the right, now to
the left in evident enjoyment of his mastery of the position.

Diary   *January 29, 1942*

Third day of the Vote of Confidence Debate. Winston winds up. He
is very genial and self-confident. He does not gird at his critics, but
compliments them on the excellence of their speeches. When he
reaches his peroration he ceases to be genial and becomes emphatic. 'I
have finished,' he says, 'I have done,' and he makes a downward gesture

with his palms open as if receiving the stigmata. He then crouches over the box and strikes it. 'I offer no apologies, I offer no excuses, I make no promises. In no way have I mitigated the sense of danger and impending misfortunes that hang over us. But at the same time, I avow my confidence, never stronger than at this moment, that we shall bring this conflict to an end in a manner agreeable to the interests of our country and to the future of the world.'

Loud cheers. It takes a long time to count the votes and finally they are recorded as 464 to 1. Huge cheers. Winston gets up and we rise and cheer him. Then he joins Mrs Winston and arm-in-arm and beaming they push through the crowd in Central Hall.

As I pass the tape I find it ticking imperturbably. It tells us that the Germans claim to have entered Benghazi, and that the Japs claim to be only eighteen miles from Singapore. Grave disasters indeed. A black day for a vote of confidence.

Diary   *February 12, 1942*

What has saddened me is not merely the bad news from Singapore and Libya, but a conversation with Violet [Bonham Carter]. She had been to see Winston yesterday and for the first time in their long friendship she had found him depressed. He was querulous about criticism, unhappy at [Sir Stafford] Cripps not consenting to take office [Minister of Supply], worried about the absence of alternative Ministers whom he could invite into the Government. But underneath it all was a dreadful feeling, she felt, that our soldiers are not as good fighters as their fathers were. 'In 1915,' said Winston, 'our men fought on even when they had only one shell left and were under a fierce barrage. Now they cannot resist dive-bombers. We had so many men in Singapore – so many men – they should have done better.' It is of course the same in Libya. 'Our men cannot stand up to punishment. WE ARE NOT FIGHTING WELL. That is the sadness in my heart There is something wrong with the whole morale of our army.'

Diary *February 13, 1942*

A bad date. The *Scharnhorst* and *Gneisenau* [German battle-cruisers] nipped out of Brest yesterday in broad daylight and steamed through the Channel to Wilhelmshaven. We sent out our Air Force and lost 20 bombers without, apparently, doing any harm. Altogether we lost 42 aircraft on this venture. Singapore is still holding out and Rommel is massing for another attack in Libya.

Diary *February 15, 1942*

Winston Churchill tells us that Singapore has fallen. He is grim and not gay. Unfortunately he appeals for national unity and no criticism in a manner which recalls Neville Chamberlain. Moreover, though he is not rhetorical, he cannot speak in perfectly simple terms and cannot avoid the cadences of a phrase.

Diary *February 16, 1942*

I fear a slump in public opinion which will deprive Winston of his legend. His broadcast last night was not liked. The country is too nervous and irritable to be fobbed off with fine phrases. Yet what else could he have said? A weaker man would have kept away from the wireless and have allowed someone else to tell us the bad news.

Diary *February 27, 1942*

I do a talk on Winston for the Empire programme. I cannot bear the thought that this heroic figure should now be sniped at by tiny little men.

This Singapore surrender has been a terrific blow to all of us. It is not merely the immediate dangers which threaten the Indian Ocean and the menace to our communications with the Middle East. It is dread that we are only half-hearted in fighting the whole-hearted. It is even more than that. We intellectuals must feel that in all these years we have derided the principles of force upon which our Empire is built. We undermined confidence in our own formula. The intellectuals of 1780 did the same.

Instead of the much needed victory, Britain suffered another defeat. Tobruk fell on June 20. Churchill returned from Washington to face another Vote of Confidence at the beginning of July.

March 16, 1942

H.N. to Vita   *Farmhill, Dundrum, Co. Dublin*

I gave a lecture in Dublin in the evening. It went well. There was one man afterwards who made an impassioned speech saying that there was only one thing that should be subject to Government censorship, and that it began with the letters 'c.o.n.'. I imagined, of course, that he was attacking the cruelty of Great Britain and all the wrongs that we were still doing to Ireland. I looked down my nose. I merely said, when, panting with passion, he had resumed his seat, that I do not wish to comment on controversial matters. It was only when I was walking away with one of the Professors that I was told that what he meant was 'contraceptives'.

March 18, 1942

Diary   *Dublin*

I go to see de Valera in his office.[1] He is not what I expected. I expected a thin sallow man with huge round spectacles, a thin mouth, great lines from nose to lip-corner, and lank black Spanish hair. But he is not thin, pale rather than sallow, not a bit haggard, benevolent cold eyes behind steel-framed glasses, hair that is soft, and almost brown, no great lines in his face anywhere. An unhealthy look about the gills, and faint indications of white puffiness. A firm gentle voice with a soft

---

[1] Eamon de Valera was born in New York in 1882 of a Spanish father and an Irish mother. He had been head of the Irish Government and Minister of External Affairs since December 1937.

Irish accent. An admirable smile, not showing teeth, but lighting up
the eyes and face very quickly, like an electric bulb that does not fit
and flashes off and on. Yet not an insincere smile. A happy smile.

His conversation is uninteresting. He talks rather in a monologue. He
asks me about things at home and sympathises much with Churchill's
difficulty in having to cheer up the country and yet not give us bright
and optimistic forecasts. 'I know that difficulty – I know it all too
well.' He talks about the 'partition' [of Ireland], but in a stereotype
way and I do not feel much fire behind it. He regrets the presence of
American troops [in Northern Ireland], 'since they won't understand
our people as well as the Tommy does'. He thinks that if we in Britain
were beaten, America would not carry on an Atlantic war, but would
compromise with Germany and Japan. He is indignant with Churchill
for not supplying Ireland with arms. I say that it is due to our shortages.
He taps thick whitish fingers on the table. 'No, it is something more
than that.' I fear he is right about this. He then touches on the Press.
I tell him that he only gets the disagreeable cuttings, and that on the
whole our Press is good about Ireland.

He is a very simple man, like all great men. He does not look like
a strong man, nor are there any signs in his face of suffering and
endurance. Rather he reminds me of Lothian in his last years. Deep
spiritual certainty underneath it all, giving to his features a mask of
repose.

Diary   *March 30, 1942*

The wireless booms out the Indian agreement.[1] 'Under Article Six it
is provided that the States and Provinces . . .' I feel so enraged that the
Cabinet did not listen to Leo Amery a year ago and did not give India
Dominion status then. Now we have done it under threats from the
Japanese. Our whole Eastern Empire has gone. Australia has as good
as gone. Poor little England. But I should not have minded all this so
much if we had fought well. . . .

---

[1] The British proposal was to give India her independence after the war.

H.N. to Vita   *April 14, 1942*

I was busy yesterday. Winston in the House was not at his best. He feels deeply the loss of naval units and becomes like a surly buffalo – lowered head – eyes flaring right and left. He becomes angry and not triumphant.

Diary   *April 15, 1942*

We are addressed by Harry Hopkins [Roosevelt's personal representative] in the large Committee Room. He is very astute and makes a good impression by telling us amusing stories such as how Winston was introduced to Mrs Roosevelt in his pyjamas. The implication was that we should be mad to get rid of Winston since he is the only man who really understands Roosevelt. It was cleverly done. He talks of Anglo-American relations and tells us that there are many people in the USA who say today that we are yellow and can't fight. It is true that we have been beaten in everything we do. Somebody asks him whether America can advise us on the sort of propaganda we ought to conduct. He gets out of it well. He says, 'Well, we are the worst propagandists in the world and you are the next worst. Why not consult someone better?'

Diary   *April 22, 1942*

Malcolm [MacDonald] had been lunching today with Winston. He said that the latter had no illusions at all about the decline in his popularity. 'I am like a bomber-pilot,' he said. 'I go out night after night, and I know that one night I shall not return.' Malcolm is in fact rather appalled by the slump in Winston's popularity. A year ago he would have put his stock at 108, and today, in his opinion, it is as low as 65. He admits that a success will enable it to recover. But the old enthusiasm is dead for ever. How foul is public life and popular ingratitude!

Diary   *April 23, 1942*

Secret Session in the House. I am not allowed, even in my diary, to
give all the details of what passed, but I can at least give an outline.
Cripps, on his return from India, was received with a cheer stronger
than that accorded to Winston. The latter when he rose (and after all
the strangers had been spied and harried from the House) adopted his
stolid, obstinate, ploughman manner. He tells of Singapore, where the
conduct of our large army 'does not seem to have been in harmony
with the past or present spirit of our forces'. He tells us of our present
dangers and prospects and dwells at length upon the heavy sinkings we
are sustaining in the eastern Atlantic. It is a long and utterly remorseless
catalogue of disaster and misfortune. And as he tells us one thing after
another, gradually the feeling rises in the packed House. 'No man,'
Members begin to feel in their hearts, 'no man but he could tell us of
such disaster and increase rather than diminish confidence.' And as this
feeling rises, there rises with it a feeling of shame at having doubted
him. The House gives him a great ovation and the debate thereafter
peters out.

H.N. to Vita   *April 29, 1942*

I went to the House to hear Cripps on India. I know nothing about
India and just cut it out of my interests. He was very competent, very
clear, very straightforward, very tactful. But he is so dry and he lacks
fire; he lacks sympathy. I do hate the way philanthropists are so cold in
their affection for their fellow human beings. I do not think that Cripps
will ever make a leader. He at present enjoys a legend, but it is a false
legend. He is a perfect Lord Chancellor. . . .

Diary   *May 11, 1942*

I have a long talk with Ed Murrow[1] who has just returned after three
months in the United States. He says that the anti-British feeling is

---

[1] The European Director of CBS, and the most influential of American journalists in
London.

intense. I ask him why. He says partly the hard-core anglophobes (Irish, Italians, Germans and isolationists); partly the frustration produced by war without early victory; partly our bad behaviour at Singapore; and partly the tendency common to all countries at war to blame their allies for doing nothing. He feels moreover that we have sent the wrong type of person over there. Halifax is not popular with the people although he has gained the esteem and confidence of the administration. The problem is largely one of proper boasting. I tell him that it is profoundly repugnant for us to boast, and he replies that it is taken by the Americans either as feebleness or as arrogance. It is in fact a major element in the *superbia Britannorum*.

Diary   *May 19, 1942*

Debate on the Adjournment. Attlee opens with a long and rambling statement which is so dull and so badly delivered that the House can scarcely refrain from yawning. The only interesting thing about it was the fact that the Deputy Prime Minister, at such a crisis in our history, *could* make a dull speech. But Attlee succeeded where lesser men would have failed.

Diary   *June 11, 1942*

BBC Board. We discuss whether the clergy should use the microphone to preach forgiveness of our enemies. I say I prefer that to the clergy who seek to pretend that the bombing of Cologne was a Christian act. I wish the clergy would keep their mouths shut about the war. It is none of their business.

Diary   *June 22, 1942*

Another lovely day and I bathe before breakfast. I have not slept well as I kept on waking up with the word 'Tobruk'[1] echoing in my ears, and rolling from side to side with gigantic apprehensions.

---

[1] Tobruk had fallen to Rommel, and 33,000 British prisoners were taken.

The *Chicago Sun* ring up to ask me whether I feel the fall of Tobruk will lead to a major political crisis. I think it may but do not say so. Had Winston any alternative he might be severely shaken by this event. There must have been either serious miscalculation or else our tank and anti-tank guns are very inferior.

Diary June 23, 1942

Victor Cazalet comes to me. He says, 'Let's have a word ...' We sit on a retired bench. 'What do you feel?' he asks. I say, 'Well, Victor, there is one thing about which I am certain – we must all get together.' 'I am glad to hear you say that, Harold.' 'Yes, we have kept silent too long. We must now speak out with courage and together.' 'That is exactly my view.' 'You see,' I continue, 'you see, Victor, none of us who know what Winston did in 1939 and 1940 have really spoken out. We must now close the ranks to defend him.' Victor's jaw drops. 'You are pulling my leg again!' he says and walks away.

Diary July 2, 1942

The second day of the Vote of Censure Debate. Aneurin Bevan opens with a brilliant offensive, pointing his finger in accusation, twisting and bowing. Then comes Walter Elliot and then Hore-Belisha.

Winston sits there with a look of sullen foreboding, his face from time to time flickering into a smile. He rises stockily. His hands in his trouser pockets. He makes a long statement which really amounts to the fact that we had more men and more tanks and more guns than Rommel, and that he cannot understand why we were so badly beaten. In the end, after one hour and thirty minutes, he is quite fresh and gay. He gets his vote of confidence by 475 votes to 25, plus a great ovation afterwards. But the impression left is one of dissatisfaction and anxiety, and I do not think it will end there.

Diary   *July 4, 1942*

For the first time an American squadron joined us in a raid on occupied
France. This is the beginning of a great air offensive which will go on
and on.

Diary   *July 8, 1942*

I go to the House. A Scottish debate. I like these family affairs. What
a good Parliamentarian was lost in me!! I am too busy with other
interests to give the House that passion for trivialities, that constant
assertion of an individual point of view, which leads to power. I feel
sometimes that my failure is due entirely to myself; I have had every
opportunity and have missed them. But I am a happy, honest, loving
man and I don't care – not one hoot. When I think of Nigel I don't
care about success. When I think of Viti I do not care even about
death. Few men have achieved that certainty of love.

Diary   *August 18, 1942*

A perfect summer day. After tea, at 7 p.m., I finish my book. I call it
The Desire to Please.
    We are told on the wireless in the evening that Claude Auchinleck
has been succeeded by Alexander and that Montgomery is to have the
8th Army.

Diary   *August 28, 1942*

I go to see William Beveridge who has been charged by the Government to make a report upon social insurance.[1] We [the National
Labour Group] had put in to him a memorandum urging (a) that the
medical services should be completely taken over by the State. He
evidently doesn't think much of this. (b) that there should be an

---

[1] The Beveridge Report on the reform of the social services was published in December
of this year.

increase in old age pensions on the theory that people should be bribed to retire from industry and thus to leave more employment for the young people. He takes exactly the opposite point of view. At present one person in twelve is over 65. By 1961 one in six of the total population will be old people. Therefore we must provide for them. He hopes to create a contributory scheme which in the end will enable all old people to have a really life-giving benefit. He thinks that this self-supporting scheme will become practicable 'in my own life-time'. He foresees also a comprehensive family allowance giving people 7/6 a week for 'large families'. But when does a family become large? And if the allowance begins only for the third child, will that child not come to have a different status in the family from the others, and lose that atmosphere of sacrifice-gratitude which is the best parent-child relationship? He is optimistic about grappling with the unemployment problem after the war, and looks forward to a simplified all-in system of insurance. I come away more cheerful and encouraged than I have been for weeks.

H.N. to Vita   *September 9, 1942*

Winston was splendid yesterday. He reduced the art of understatement to a virtuosity such as I have never seen equalled. People were meaning to speak about the changes in command in Egypt, about the [Canadian] Dieppe raid, about the Second Front. But he took the wind so completely out of their sails that they tore up their notes and remained seated. The debate therefore collapsed. This would have been all right if Cripps had not profited by the occasion to give the House a rather sharp talking-to and to accuse them of preferring their luncheon to their duties. This has enraged everyone.

Diary   *September 9, 1942*

To the House. They are still enraged by Cripps having rebuked them for not attending the debate yesterday in sufficient numbers.

Guy Burgess [then attached to the Foreign Office] has heard from his friends who are in close touch with Cripps that the latter is so discontented with the conduct of the war that he proposes to resign: Guy and I agreed that Cripps' attitude was probably wholly disinterested and sincere. That he really believed that Winston was incapable of dealing with the home front and that his handling of the minor problems of production and strategy was fumbling and imprecise. We had agreed also that Cripps would find the atmosphere of Downing Street, with its late hours, casual talk, cigar smoke and endless whiskey, most unpalatable. Whereas Winston never regards with affection a man of such inhuman austerity as Cripps, and cannot work with people easily unless his sentiments as well as his respect are aroused. We also agreed that Cripps (who in his way is a man of great innocence and narrow vision) might be quite seriously unaware that his own resignation would shake Winston very severely, that around him would gather all the elements of opposition, and that in the end he would group around him an 'alternative Government' and take Winston's place. We agreed that Cripps was actually too modest a man to realise what an immensely disturbing effect his resignation would produce, and too simple a man to see how it would be exploited by evil men to their advantage. There was a hope that if Winston would show real consideration to Cripps, and give him a vital part in the direction of the war, then something might be done to avert this disaster.

Violet Bonham Carter is the only outside person I know who is on terms of intimate friendship with Winston and also has the confidence of Stafford and Lady Cripps. We told her the story. She said that she was in an awkward position as Lady Cripps had taken her into her confidence and told her much the same. She could not betray this confidence, much as she agreed with our point of view. We arranged therefore (a) that Violet should see Cripps or his wife and ask if she might say a word to Winston – a word of warning. (b) that failing this I should go and see Bracken.[1]

---

[1] Sir Stafford Cripps put his resignation in writing on 21 September. Churchill persuaded him to suspend it until after the invasion of North Africa. In November he became Minister of Aircraft Production, but left the War Cabinet.

H.N. to Vita   *September 24, 1942*

I do not think that, except for Winston, I *admire* anyone as much as I admire you.

I remember your saying (years ago) that you had never established a complete relationship with anyone. I don't think you ever could – since yours is a vertical and not horizontal nature, and two-thirds of you will always be submerged. But you have established, with your sons and me, a relationship of absolute trust and complete love. I don't think that these things would be so fundamental to the four of us were it not that each one of the four is a private person underneath.

I have often wondered what makes the perfect family. I think it is just our compound of intimacy and aloofness. Each of us has a room of his own. Each of us knows that there is a common-room where we meet on the basis of perfect understanding.

Diary   *October 21, 1942*

Duff Cooper tells me some of his experiences as head of the Cabinet Security Committee. Most of the indiscretions are due solely to an inability to make conversation or write letters. Young men having no power of invention fall back in despair upon talking shop. There have been grave cases lately: two staff-majors have been cashiered and one imprisoned for indiscretion. He told me of a letter from a young Air Force officer to his girl-friend. 'The ops,' he wrote, 'which I told you about on my last leave, has been put off because some idiot of a man wrote and gave the exact date. I cannot understand how people can be so careless after all the warnings we have had. This particular op has been put off till October 22nd.'

Diary   *October 24, 1942*

A new offensive has started at El Alamein [at 10 p.m. on the 23rd].

Diary   *October 25, 1942*

Ben and I walk round to the Temple Underground, carrying his big
fibre suitcase and his funny little handbag. We have to wait some time
for the train, but eventually it lumbers through the tunnel. We sit
beside each other for the short journey between the Temple and
Charing Cross. I cannot speak. When the train stops, I get up and go.
'Goodbye, Benzie.' 'Goodbye, Daddy.' I close the carriage doors
behind me. I stand there waiting for the train to go out. It jerks away,
taking Ben to Paddington and then to Bristol and then to Avonmouth
and then to Lagos and then to Cairo. My eyes are blinded by tears.

Diary   *November 4, 1942*

I reach K.B.W. at 11.40 p.m. and turn on the wireless. The announcer
says, 'I advise listeners to hold on as in the midnight news we are
giving the best news we have heard for years.' Then it comes. It is
Alexander's communiqué. The Germans are in retreat in Egypt.
We have captured 9,000 prisoners and are pursuing 'their disordered
columns'. It is a great victory.

*The victory at El Alamein was the turning-point in the war. It was also the
end, in the words of A.J.P. Taylor, of Britain's 'strategic independence'. On
November 8, American and British troops landed in Northern Africa, and by
the end of the month, the Russians closed behind the German 6th Army in
Stalingrad.*

*   Harold's sons left England for military service abroad, Ben in the Intelligence
Corps for Cairo and Syria, Nigel in the Grenadier Guards for Algiers and
Tunisia. Every Sunday, for the next two-and-a-half years, he wrote to them,
expanding (and censoring) his diary entries.*

Diary   *November 6, 1942*

At 1.15 I stroll across to Downing Street where I am to lunch. I waved
my blue pass and was not interrupted. The War Cabinet were breaking

up when I got there. I go downstairs to the basement where the Churchills are living, since the upper floors have been knocked about [by a bomb]. They made it very pretty with chintz and flowers and good furniture and excellent French pictures – not only the moderns, but Ingres and David.

We go into luncheon: sea-kale, jugged hare and cherry tart. Not well done. In a few minutes Winston comes in. He is dressed in his romper suit of Air Force blue and carries a letter in his hand. It is a long letter from the King written in his own handwriting, and saying how much he and the Queen have been thinking·of Winston these glorious days. Winston is evidently pleased. 'Every word,' he mutters, 'in his own hand.'

He gazes round the table with his curious eyes. They are glaucous and look dead. When he gazes at people like that, there is no light either of interest or intelligence in his eyes. There is a faint expression of surprise, as if he were asking, 'What the hell is this man doing here?' There is a faint expression of angered indignation, as if he were saying, 'What damned cheek coming to luncheon here!' There is a mask of boredom and another mask or film of obstinacy, as if he were saying, 'These people bore me and I shall refuse to be polite.' And with it all, there are films of stubbornness, perhaps even a film of deep inner thought. It is very disconcerting. Then suddenly he will cease thinking of something else, and the film will part and the sun comes out. His eyes then pucker with amusement or flash with anger. At moments they have a tragic look. Yet these passing moods and phases do not flash across each other: they move slowly and opaquely like newts in a rather dim glass tank.

He turns to me and thanks me for my article [in the *Spectator*] on his oratory. I say I hope that I was right in saying that he was not a born orator. 'You are perfectly right,' he mumbles. 'Not born in the very least – just hard, hard work.' He then talks to us about the battle. He begins with the first two battles of Alamein [in July 1942]. 'I refuse,' he says, 'to call it El Alamein. Like those asses who talk about Le Havre. *Havre* [to rhyme with carver] the place is to any decent man. Now this third battle must not be called Alamein. It must be called "The Battle of Egypt". Harold, see to that at once. Tell your people henceforward to call it the Battle of Egypt.' He tells us at length how he decided to remove Auchinleck and how he broke the news to him.

'It was a terrible thing to have to do. He took it like a gentleman. But it was a terrible thing. It is difficult to remove a bad General at the height of a campaign: it is atrocious to remove a good General.' He admits that he wanted Gott for the 8th Army. 'I made my decision. I telegraphed to the Cabinet. I then took off all my clothes and rolled in the surf. Never have I had such bathing. And when I got to Cairo, I heard at the Embassy that night that Gott was dead [shot down over the desert]. I sent for Montgomery.'

Brendan Bracken comes in and Winston tells him to arrange for all the bells in England to be tolled on Sunday. Some hesitation is expressed by all of us. 'Not at all,' says Winston, 'not at all. We are not celebrating final victory. The war will still be long. When we have beaten Germany, it will take us two more years to beat Japan. Nor is that a bad thing. It will keep America and ourselves together while we are making peace in Europe. If I am still alive, I shall fling all we have into the Pacific.'

H.N. to Vita   *November 9, 1942*

My first intimation that the American invasion of North Africa was imminent came from Fred Kuh, the United Press correspondent. I never imagined, however, that it would be on so large or far-flung a scale. I got up yesterday morning and turned on the wireless. When I heard that they had landed at Algiers, I held my breath. That means, eventually, Tunis, and brings us within eighty miles of Sicily and closes the Western Mediterranean. The Italians must be in a grave state of alarm. Nor can they be feeling very pleased with their allies. Six Italian Divisions (the whole Italian Army in fact) have been cut off [at Alamein] and will have to surrender. There has been no such military disaster since Sedan.

Diary   *December 9, 1942*

We have a Committee meeting at which several representative Jews tell us of the extermination of their fellows by the Nazis. They have ringed off the Warsaw ghetto and transported two-thirds of the inhabitants in cattle-trucks to die in Russia. It is horrible that we are so saturated with horrors that this Black Hole on a gigantic scale scarcely concerns us. They put lime and chloride in the cattle-trucks and bury the corpses next morning. They are particularly vindictive against children. I have a sense that my fellow-Members feel not so much 'What can we do for such people?' as 'What can we do *with* such people after the war?'

Diary   *December 10, 1942*

To the House where there is a Secret Session on North Africa and Darlan.[1] It is opened by Winston who speaks for an hour and I have never heard him more forceful, informative or convincing. He convinces us that (a) we were never consulted about the Darlan move; (b) when it happened he himself realised at once what trouble would be caused and warned Roosevelt accordingly; (c) it is purely temporary. I cannot say more than that.

I see that it illustrates the difficulty of all Secret Sessions. Winston could not have convinced us as he did convince us unless he had been able to quote telegrams and documents which it would have been wholly impossible to quote in public. But some public statement can be made, and must be made.

H.N. to his sons   *January 7, 1943*

I had an appointment to conduct some American doughboys round the Palace of Westminster. In they slouched, chewing gum, conscious of their inferiority in training, equipment, breeding, culture, experience and history, determined in no circumstances to be either interested or impressed. In the Chamber we bumped into another party, of Dominion heroes this time, being shown round by no less a person than the Lord Chancellor of England. I have never cared for John Simon, but I must confess that on this occasion he displayed energy and even charm. Embarrassing he was, to be true. For having stood at

---

[1] Admiral Darlan, the leading Vichy advocate of French collaboration with Hitler, was in Algiers when the invasion began. He then supported the Allies, but it was considered disgraceful to uphold him as political head of French North Africa.

the Prime Minister's place and lifted up the dust-cloths from the box
and table, he asked me to go opposite to show them the relations
between the Government and Opposition benches. Fifty blank faces,
their jaws working at the gum, turned in languid interest in my
direction. 'Now Harold . . .' But I was firm. 'No,' I said, 'I am no good
at amateur theatricals.' So then we went into the House of Lords [then
sitting in the Robing Room] and Simon sat on the Woolsack and
showed them how the Lord Chancellor behaves. 'The Amendment
standing in the name of the noble Marquess . . .' Jaws chewed unflinch-
ingly in silence. 'Now,' he said briskly, 'come to my room, boys – or
should I call you doughboys? – and I will show you the Great Seal.'
Through the corridors they slouched apathetically, expecting to be
shown a large wet animal such as they had seen so often at the
Aquarium in San Francisco. But not at all. All they were shown were
two cylinders of steel with a pattern inside. And then a man fetched
the mace for them to see. 'I must now ask you, my friends, to leave
me to my labours. Even a Lord Chancellor sometimes has work to do.'
Harold, perhaps you will conduct our friends to the exit?' Harold did.
We slouched along to Central Hall. To my surprise and pleasure one
of the doughboys suddenly ceased chewing, flung his wad of Wrigley
into his cheek with a deft movement of his tongue, and said 'Say, Sur,
who was that guy?'

H.N. to Vita   *January 20, 1943*

I went to the House. We had a tribute to Lloyd George [who was
celebrating his eightieth birthday] and the poor old man was much
moved. He stood there, very pale and white, unable to find his words.
What is tragic is that he retains all his old manner of impressive
oratorical pronouncements. But nothing comes. It is like an old Rolls
Royce back-firing and spluttering. We then had a Secret Session.
Merely to give us a piece of information. And then Attlee got up to
make his war statement.[1] He is so dull and puny that if he had told us
about the fall of Bizerta, we should have been bored. Everybody filed
out.

---

[1] Churchill was away, conferring at Casablanca with Roosevelt, Eisenhower and
Alexander.

Diary   *January 23, 1943*

On the 1 o'clock news we hear that our troops [the 8th Army] entered
Tripoli at dawn today after having pursued Rommel for 1,400 miles.
Lord Haw Haw at 10.30 says, 'May I quote the picturesque if slightly
vulgar phrase used by General Montgomery? He said his object was
"to put Rommel in the bag". In fact his aim was not to take Tripoli,
but to take Rommel. He has failed.'

Diary   *January 29, 1943*

Kingsley Martin[1] and Aneurin Bevan start a hare by saying that Ll.G.
was a finer man than Churchill. Churchill is 'adolescent', which is
suitable in times of emotional strain. Ll.G. is the wise statesman. I say
that Ll.G., if he had not been so gaga, would have been our Pétain.
They agree to this, but still say he is a great man. We also agree that
the main quality demanded of a politician is not that he should be
gifted or honest or wise – but 'formidable'. But to be formidable
implies the capacity to bring votes into the lobby.

Diary   *February 2, 1943*

The whole country is under floods. On the midnight news we hear
that the last of the Germans at Stalingrad, including Field Marshal
Paulus, have surrendered.

Diary   *February 18, 1943*

We have the Division [on the Beveridge Report]. 338 to 121. This
means that if one deducts the Cabinet Ministers, Parliamentary Secretaries and the P.P.S.s, practically all the Labour Party have voted
against. They may now ask their Ministers to retire from the Government. A major political crisis would then arise.
    I met Beveridge in the lobby, looking like the witch of Endor. I

---

[1] Editor of the *New Statesman and Nation*.

said, 'Well, are you enjoying this?' He said, 'I am having the fun of my life.' 'Upsetting Governments and wrecking constitutions?' He said, 'My two previous reports[1] led to the fall of two Ministers; this one may bring down a Government.' He is a vain man.

Diary   *February 22, 1943*

In the evening I dine with our Monday Evening Club, which is a group of British and Americans. We dine at the Connaught. I have to address them afterwards. I say that a difficult diplomatic situation may arise between us and Russia and the USA. The Russians will demand a gigantic reward which may entail the suppression of the independence of ten smaller powers. America's missionary spirit will resent this, and her isolationist spirit will do nothing to help us resist it. Anti-British opinion will concentrate on the theme that America was again ensnared by British propaganda and that so far from making the world safe for democracy, we have made it safe for Jo Stalin. It would have been better to take Germany's side. Ed Murrow refers to my 'soul-satisfying pessimism' and agrees with what I say.

H.N. to his sons   *March 18, 1943*

We had a debate on the reform of the Foreign Service. The main idea is to fuse the Diplomatic with the Consular and Commercial Services. I have been in favour of this for thirty years. But the debate went wrong as usual. The women Members felt that their rights were being trampled on, and staged a full-dress attack on the exclusion of women from the Service. Nancy Astor, as the senior woman Member, insisted on voicing their complaint. She has one of those minds that works from association to association, and therefore spreads sideways with extreme rapidity. Further and further did she diverge from the point while Mrs Tate beside her kept on saying, 'Get back to the point, Nancy. You were talking about the 1934 Committee.' 'Well, I come from Virginia,' said Lady Astor, 'and that reminds me, when I was in Washington ...' I was annoyed by this, as I knew I was to be called

---

[1] On the coal industry in 1925 and unemployment insurance in 1936.

after her. It was like playing squash with a dish of scrambled eggs. Anyhow I made my speech and it went well enough. Lady Astor had said that women had never been given any chance to show their capacity in foreign politics. I said that they might not have been *given* chances, but from the days of Helen of Argos to the days of the Noble Lady the Member for the Sutton Division of Plymouth they had *taken* chances, and that the results had been disastrous. 'You mean mistresses,' shouted Lady Astor. I said No, I was thinking of women's virtues and not their frailties. Intuition and sympathy were the two main feminine virtues, and each of these was of little value in diplomacy.

Diary   *April 14, 1943*

I go to the Aeolian Hall for the poetry reading organised by Osbert and Edith Sitwell for the benefit of the Free French. The Queen arrives accompanied by the two Princesses. The poets file in – Masefield, T.S. Eliot, Gordon Bottomley, Arthur Waley, Edmund Blunden, and Vita. Masefield pays a tribute to Laurence Binyon [who died on March 10], and then the readings start. I cannot hear most of them as I am in the gallery and they are impeded by a lectern which Osbert found in the Caledonian Market and which impedes voice and sight. I am impressed by Eliot's reading and rather moved by the Poet Laureate [Masefield]. Then there is an interval during which the Poets are received by the Queen in an ante-room. Then the second series begins and Vita reads her piece. She stands there looking magnificent and modest and recites *The Land* quite perfectly. I hear a low murmur of delight passing through the audience. She was by streets the best of the lot and I am so proud of her. She is as serene as a swan.

H.N. to Vita   *April 20, 1943*

I was talking in the Smoking Room to Duff [Cooper], when I saw an odd expression of embarrassment in his eyes and at the same time I felt an arm on my shoulder. 'May I join you?' said a voice. It was Winston. OH MY GOD what a man he is!!!! Two of his incidental remarks picked out from the whole sea of delight. I told him of Niggs's hope that the Americans would cut Rommel off. He grunted deeply. 'Yes,' he said, 'tell your boy that it will now be scrunch and punch.' I also asked him what was happening and would happen to the Bey of Tunis. ' "Obey" is what his name is now.'

Diary   *May 4, 1943*

I go down in the evening to Denham to dine and sleep with the Vansittarts.[1] I find Van well enough, but getting deaf. We have a lovely pre-war dinner with trout, lamb, fruit and a bottle of Pomeroy '98. It is a lovely house with stately rooms and a stately butler.

Van feels that he is an aggrieved man. When I consider that he was head of his profession, received every honour, was given a peerage, married a rich and lovely wife and is now a national figure, I cannot understand this. There is in Van a deep underneath of real conceit. I like him enormously, but I fear that it is wounded conceit that makes him so bitter.

H.N. to his sons   *May 8, 1943*

I was suddenly awakened five minutes after midnight by Mummy standing at the door. She had been listening to the midnight news. 'Tunis,' she said, not without a touch of drama, 'and Bizerta are ours.' That is how the news came to Sissinghurst. A gale blowing outside and my open windows straining at their catches; my door open against the light on my staircase; and Mummy standing there in her pyjamas enunciating these great truths.

I dined last Monday with Rob Bernays. He says that the mistake I make in the House is not to be formidable. 'But, my dear Rob, I was not designed by nature to be formidable.' 'Well, take it from me, unless you become formidable, you will be overlooked.' 'But nobody can become formidable when he has been unformidable for 55 years.' 'You take it from me, Harold . . .' So I suppose something has got to be done.

---

[1] Sir Robert Vansittart had been created Lord Vansittart in 1941, when he retired as Chief Diplomatic Adviser to the Foreign Secretary.

H.N. to his sons   *May 11, 1943*

We had a short Secret Session, and then Attlee as Deputy Prime
Minister made a statement about the Tunisian position. I cannot
convey to you the absurdity of that small man. As someone remarked
afterwards, 'It is difficult to make a defeat sound like a victory; but to
make such a victory sound like a defeat is a masterpiece in human
ingenuity.' Attlee stood there like a little snipe pecking at a wooden
cage. The House likes and respects him, but had he gone on five
minutes more, we should have burst into a *fou rire*. And what was so
strange was that he did not give us the latest news. Already the word
was circulating that the 6th Armoured Division had cut through
Hammam Lif. Already we knew they were at Grombalia, and even on
the outskirts of Hammamet. But Attlee just pecked and pecked as if
nothing had happened.[1]

*The summer months saw the invasion of Sicily, the fall of Mussolini and the
capitulation of Italy. The armistice was signed on the very day, September 3,
when British troops landed in the toe of Italy, our first re-entry onto the
mainland of Europe. The war which won the war was meanwhile being waged
in Russia, where the Germans were retreating fast. Harold was deeply involved
in the disputes of the Free French in London, seeing as much of de Gaulle as
of his opponents.*

Diary   *May 13, 1943*

The Italians had announced that an important statement was to be
made on their wireless at 9 p.m. It was made by General Vittorio
Ambrosio, Chief of the General Staff. It was a perfunctory and formal
explanation of defeat. But, according to the tape which we read at
Brooks' at 11.15 he ended up 'Viva il Re! Viva Italia!' Now the

---

[1] The German Afrika Korps surrendered next day. Two hundred and fifty thousand
prisoners were taken by the converging First and Eighth Armies. Harold knew that
Nigel was serving in the 6th Armoured Division at the breakthrough at Hammam
Lif.

omission of Mussolini's name and the appeal to the House of Savoy is deeply significant.

Diary   *May 17, 1943*

Dine with Sibyl at Lord North Street. The Devonshires, Camroses, Rothermeres, D'Arcy Osborne [British Minister to the Holy See] and Desmond Morton [Personal Assistant to the P.M.] are there. Morton tells me that Monsignor Spellman [Archbishop of New York] had cast a spell over Churchill. He had told him exactly what he intended to say to de Valera. Churchill said, 'I would not say that, Monsignor; you will give the poor man a fit.' 'Far be it from me,' replied the Archbishop, 'to cause the death of any man, but if Almighty God should wish that de Valera lose his life on hearing the truth, I shall say many Masses for his soul.' Osborne does not share this enthusiasm for Spellman who is much affected by the desire to please and who apparently gave the Vatican the impression that he was bitterly anti-British. We discuss the future of Italy and Osborne is convinced that there will be a great universal desire to get out of the war coupled with the realisation that Italy in her present condition must lose her Empire and will only exchange one form of occupation for another.

The latest idea is that we should give Libya to the Maltese.

Diary   *June 1, 1943*

Go to Chips' [Channon] house to meet Field-Marshal Wavell.[1] A stocky man with one blind eye. I am reminded of the day when I was waiting in the ante-room of the Quai d'Orsay and there entered a square little man clasping an enormous portfolio. I thought, 'That must be a sergeant in the Ordnance Department come with statistics for his chief.' Then I thought, 'What a remarkable face for a sergeant!' I then thought, 'My God, it's Foch!' Wavell is rather restless and embarrassed. He talked to me about his book on Allenby in which he corrects or contradicts a statement I made in *Curzon*. I say I do not

---

[1] Commander-in-Chief, India, and later Viceroy of India.

mind. What worries him, I think, is that Chips has also invited some of the wives of his staff. They do not fuse very well.

That is what makes Wavell anxious and ill at ease.

H.N. to his sons June 9, 1943

I had to go to a *conversazione* given by the Authors' Society. I arrived late and H.G. Wells was already talking nonsense in front of a microphone and a plate of biscuits. Gilbert Murray also spoke. Thereafter I mingled with my fellow authors. There was Rose Macaulay and G.M. Trevelyan and Elizabeth Bowen and Lady Astor and Lindsay Drummond [publisher] and Arthur Koestler. The latter talked to me about Richard Hillary.[1] He is editing a book about him or a collection of correspondence. This is always a guilty spot in me. I do not like heroes. I feel mean about all this, but I do not like the T.E. Lawrence brood. Koestler is intelligent on the subject. He thinks that Hillary would have become a great writer. He says that he was marred first by his amazing good looks, secondly, after his skin-graft, by his horrifying ugliness. But surely, surely, the man was a cad at heart, even as T.E.L. was a cad at heart. The literary temperament is only tolerable so long as it remains cowardly. Once it becomes courageous it is an unpleasant thing to meet.

Diary July 14, 1943

People are terribly optimistic. They say that the German offensive in the Kursk area has collapsed; that our troops in Sicily are meeting with no resistance and we shall be in Catania in three days, and Messina within a fortnight. They say we have beaten them in the air and over and under the sea; that they have no hope at all; that collapse will come. I admit that were I a German I should be feeling pretty glum. But I distrust optimism in any case.

---

[1] Author of *The Last Enemy* about his experiences as a fighter-pilot in the Battle of Britain. His face was terribly disfigured when he was shot down.

H.N. to Vita   *July 14, 1943*

I went down to the House for the Colonial Debate and felt that I should say something about African education. But somehow I felt that I could not do it. I have never before suddenly lost confidence in myself to that extent. I do feel it strange that a person of my experience is so much ignored nowadays. I suppose that the fact that I got into the Government (and in a post where I *ought* to have made good) and was thereafter discarded has created the impression that I am a dud. What I mind is that it has damaged my self-confidence. I don't want to drift into being an old buffer.

Vita to H.N.   *July 15, 1943*

I am so glad you have written as you have, because for a long time I have suspected that something of that sort was going on in that curly-box [head]. It seems to me that your mind has never been more vigorous or more capable of canalisation, but that you are allowing it to run into many little rills, each of them clear and useful, but in the aggregate detracting from the power of the main stream. Let me tabulate your activities into two separate categories:

(1) *Marginal Comments* [*Spectator*]. Altogether admirable. BBC. Financially essential.
    Free French. Yes. Important. Specially well-qualified.
    Your own books. You know what I feel about these.
    House of Commons. Well, obviously you must keep that on.
(2) *Endless committees and odd speeches and odd articles*, mostly undertaken because you cannot say NO.

To be constructive, I should like to see you scrap as much of No. (2) as you can, and to devote yourself to *one* thing in their place. Personally I should like you to take up the re-building of England, both urban and rural. I think you have very special gifts in this direction, but I believe you have an idea that it is not sufficiently 'public life'.

Diary   *July 21, 1943*

I have breakfast at the Dorchester with Lord Baldwin. We sit at opposite
ends of a tiny table, with a kipper in front of each of us. He is lame
and slightly deaf, but I see no diminution either in his curiosity or his
memory. He talks of Kipling [his cousin], and is trying to find out
whether he ever refused the laureateship. Salisbury offered it to him;
so did Asquith; did MacDonald also? He then talks of Ramsay and
describes his last visit to him when he left in the funereal boat [Mac-
Donald died at sea in 1937]. Ramsay was talking of all the books he
meant to write and all the journeys he hoped to make. Baldwin knew
all the time that he was a shattered man. He talks of human ambition
and endeavour, and says that in his long life he has found always that
in the end men and women are as good as one thinks them.

He then passes on to Winston. The latter had asked him to luncheon
and given him three hours, telling him about all that was happening.
'I went out into Downing Street,' said Baldwin, 'a happy man. Of
course it was partly because an old buffer like me enjoys feeling that
he is not quite out of things. But it was also pure patriotic joy that my
country at such a time should have found such a leader. The furnace
of the war has smelted out all base metals from him.' He lives in a sort
of pool or ambient water of forgiveness. He said that the only man he
could never forgive was Beaverbrook.

I did not notice much change in old Baldwin. His nose has got
more square and bulbous and now really looks like what Low [the
cartoonist] made it look like years ago. His face is still that strange
colour as if lightly dusted by ginger powder.

Diary   *July 25, 1943*

I had written my diary and gone to bed, leaving Viti as I hoped and
believed recovering from her disease ['flu] in the North Cottage. But
scarcely had I laid my head upon the pillow when I heard a strange
sound below followed by Martha's [dog] familiar padding on the stairs.
The door opened and there stood Viti dressed in her brown overcoat
and an old Etonian sweater of Ben's. I was horrified, thinking for a
moment that she had had delirium and was wandering in her mania.

'Go back to bed at once,' I said. But she said, 'Mussolini has resigned.'

She had been listening to Reginald King at the piano with his quintet when suddenly at 11.4 the programme was interrupted and a voice said 'We interrupt this programme to say that the Rome wireless has announced the resignation of Mussolini.'

Diary   *August 2, 1943*

We go to the village fête at Sissinghurst Place. All the village children dress up and there is one little boy who impersonates Montgomery riding in a tank. There are many side-shows. One of them is a dart contest in which people are invited to throw darts at large cartoon drawings of Hitler, Tojo and Mussolini. The Mussolini target does no business at all. Hitler and Tojo attract great crowds but people do not want to throw darts at Mussolini as they say he is 'down and out'. Really the English are an amazing race.

H.N. to Lady Violet Bonham Carter   *August 28, 1943*

On my long journey to Edinburgh yesterday, I thought over the sad episode of the [William] Haley controversy [he was a candidate for the Deputy Director-Generalship of the BBC]. Throughout my life (at Balliol, in diplomacy, in literature and even in politics) I have been dealing with people who, if they did not share my opinions, did share, or at least understand, my values. We may have differed as to the relative values of such virtues as truth, beauty, tolerance, fairness, generosity, courage, faithfulness and taste. But the assumption has always been that these were desirable virtues possessing a certain absolute validity. We took it for granted that to these ethical values certain intellectual values should be added – intelligence, wit, humour, knowledge – and the importance of these great things formed the 'language' in which we discoursed. They were even more than that. They were the accepted currency with which we interchanged ideas. Suddenly I have found myself faced with a group of people who not only do not understand, but actually do not know, these weights and measures. It is as if for such current phrases of measurement as '$2\frac{1}{2}$ feet', 'forty-two minutes', 'eleven stone', '4/-', one used Siamese expressions indicating *yens* or *tickals* or whatever it may be. I feel in dealing with these men the same gap in communication as I do when I hear people talking about batting averages or football pools or racing form. I believe that they are honestly quite unaware of the standards which to us seem the axioms of life.

Thus even when we have reached agreement on some point, we have not really reached agreement. It is as if, having agreed with someone to meet him at the Travellers Club at 7.30, he supposed that one had fixed a meeting at Lyons Corner House at 11.45. I do not accuse them of dishonesty; only an honest lack of comprehension.

It is the absence of any sense of corporate function which renders the [BBC] Board so contemptible a body. We are about to enter an age when all the old values will be called into question and many of the most precious of them discarded, not because they lack validity, but merely because they are old. We cannot hope that the Press as a whole will swim against the tide of vulgarisation which will sweep in from the west. Only the BBC can teach the public to think correctly, to feel nobly, to enjoy themselves intelligently, to have some conception of what is meant by the good life. Our responsibility is tremendous. I do not want to shirk that responsibility. And yet in seeking to convey it to my colleagues, I have to introduce words and concepts of which they have no understanding at all. They remain completely unaware of what we mean when we talk of the BBC's unerring instinct for the second-rate.

Diary   *September 8, 1943*

To Aldford House for our Greek Committee. The Greek Ambassador had telephoned to say that he would be late as he had been sent for by Anthony Eden. He arrives about 6.30 with his eyes shining like two stars. I go off and he accompanies me into the corridor. 'It's all over,' he says. 'The Italians have surrendered unconditionally. Eden has just told me.' 'Is it to be published?' I ask. 'Not till they are certain that Badoglio will broadcast to his people telling them to oppose the Germans.'

What a day for the Germans! Stalino has fallen; they have lost nearly all the Donetz basin; and on top of it comes this dastardly stab in the back from Italy.

Diary   *November 10, 1943*

BBC Board. I am warmly welcomed. We finish early and I walk with Violet [Bonham Carter]. She tells me the details of Mark's [her son] escape.[1] When the Germans arrived at Modena they divided the prisoners into eleven categories. Mark foresaw that they would move them in numerical order and thus got himself into the eleventh category, which would be the last. He thought at first of hiding in the sewer but it was really physically impossible. Then a man who had tunnelled a hole under the floor of his hut and covered it with boards said, 'You can have my hole. I cannot manage to remain there more than two hours at a time.' So Mark, with a Major in the Grenadiers, climbed down into the hole and remained there for 36 hours. The lack of air was agonising, and he felt his heart would burst. They were stung by mosquitoes and Mark said, 'If a mosquito can live in this, so can I.' After three days in the hole they thought it might be safe to come up. The camp was basking in sunlight and not a soul was to be seen. They climbed the wall and jumped over. Some little Italian boys rushed at them whispering – 'I Tedeschi I Tedeschi' – and surely enough the prison wall was being patrolled by German sentries. They mingled with the children and walked very slowly away. Mark had dyed his khaki trousers by pouring ink on them. They then started on their fifteen day trek, keeping to the hills and avoiding bridges and roads. They begged food from the peasants and were always given it. The only map they had was one torn out of Trevelyan's book on Garibaldi. As they came nearer to the front the peasants would tell them where the Germans were. On one occasion they were about to knock at the door of a cottage when they saw a field telephone wire in the grass. They knew that it was a German post. As they got closer to the line, they descended to the valleys foreseeing that the German gun-positions would be on the hills. The Germans whom they met

---

[1] Mark Bonham Carter was a subaltern in the Grenadier Guards, when they attacked an outpost of the Mareth Line in southern Tunisia. He was taken by the Germans as a prisoner to northern Italy.

took them for peasants. Then suddenly one afternoon they emerged from a wood straight upon an English gun-crew. They shouted in English. 'By God! I thought you blighters were Jerries,' said the corporal. 'Then why,' said Mark – his officer status returning to him – 'Then why the hell did you not fire at us?'

Diary   *November 19, 1943*

I dictate letters in the morning and then go to the Dominions Office to meet Paul Evans and Bobbety Cranborne by appointment. They had said they had wanted to see me urgently. I had a suspicion what it was. My suspicion was correct. For after a long desultory conversation about my visit to Sweden,[1] Bobbety says, 'Would you undertake another trip?' 'Where to?' I ask. 'Australia.' At first I said No – pointing out that I am a civilian of the old liberal school and that this might not go down. 'You need have no feelings of inferiority,' says Bobbety, 'with the Australians about not fighting.' 'But seriously,' he adds, 'I really want you to go.' 'Well, if it's like that,' I say, 'I have only one answer. But Vita will never forgive you.'

Anyhow that is that.

I lunch with Raymond [Mortimer]. I ask him as my dearest friend whether I should be cowardly in not defending Oswald Mosley [released from prison the day before] if he is attacked in the House. He says I should leave it to Morrison [Home Secretary] to defend his action and that I should be quixotic to rush into the breach over Mosley. I loathe feeling that I funk any moral obligation. But he says, 'My dear Harold – nobody thinks you disloyal or cowardly – keep your powder for better causes.' But there is something in me (my enemies call it 'lack of judgement') which forces me to espouse hopeless causes.

I go to Pratt's [Club]. I walk back feeling miserable about Australia. If the Government think I am any good why do they not give me a real job and not these potty little lecture tours?

---

[1] Harold had been flown by the RAF to Stockholm, where he lectured on behalf of the Ministry of Information. He was away from October 19 to November 4.

Diary   *November 23, 1943*

Down to the House. We are prorogued. When I get there I find a
procession of workers with banners protesting against the release of
Mosley. Herbert Morrison makes a statement which I find admirable.
He takes full responsibility for the release and says that he is not going
to allow a man to die in detention. The House is really with him. But
the *Daily Worker* has been stoking up the communists and there are
demonstrations all over London.

I go to the Beefsteak with Rob [Bernays]. I tell him about Australia.
He says (a) that I am mad to absent myself from Parliament at this
moment; (b) that I shall be a ghastly failure in Australia. They will see
in me all that they most dislike about the British.

Diary   *December 30, 1943*

I go to Pratt's and I meet Bobbety Cranborne. He says to me, 'Halloa
Harold! I gather I am seeing you tomorrow.' I had heard nothing of
this. He says that after full investigation they find that they cannot send
me out [to Australia] except by sea, and cannot guarantee that they
can get me back by air. This means that my CONDITION that I
should be back by April cannot be fulfilled. Therefore he thinks I had
better chuck the whole Australian idea.

When he indicated 'NO' I felt a rush of relief and delight. So I
never wanted to go at all. Or is it that my rush of delight was simply
my relief about Vita's anxiety? I do not know. All I know is that I felt
a definite pleasure thrill and not a disappointment sink.

*The main military operations of the early months of 1944 were in Italy, where
the Allies attempted to turn the German flank by landing a large force at
Anzio. The Germans reacted quickly, and the manoeuvre temporarily failed.
There was stalemate in Russia for the rest of the winter. In London, German
air attacks were renewed in retaliation for Allied attacks on German towns.*

Diary   *January 4, 1944*

I get a letter today from John Masefield, as President of the Incorporated Society of Authors etc. asking me why the BBC have 'banned' P.G. Wodehouse.[1] If anybody we do not want to employ is regarded as 'banned' then the BBC will lose all freedom of selection. Moreover, there is no doubt that Wodehouse allowed himself, for a 'consideration', to be used for broadcasts which were in the interest of the enemy. As such he is a traitor and should not be used. I do not want to see Wodehouse shot on Tower Hill. But I resent the theory that 'poor P.G. is so innocent that he is not responsible'. A man who has shown such ingenuity and resource in evading British and American income tax cannot be classed as unpractical.

H.N. to his sons   *January 11, 1944*

I go to the Foreign Office as one of a deputation to see Anthony Eden. It was a fine deputation. Lords Horder, Perth and Lytton from the Lords, and Eleanor Rathbone, Quintin Hogg and myself from the Commons. I sat there gazing round at that ugly and once familiar room. The room in which I had seen Edward Grey pacing the carpet, gnawing at his underlip; the room in which I stood by Curzon while he munched hot toast and raspberry jam; the room in which I had seen Ramsay MacDonald actually twisting in agony over the Dodecanese question; the room in which we had first discussed with Austen Chamberlain the basis of Locarno. It is true, of course, that Anthony is apt to hide behind his own charm. One goes away thinking how reasonable, how agreeable and how helpful he has been, and then discovers that in fact he has promised nothing at all.

---

[1] Wodehouse had been interned by the Germans at the start of the war, and unwisely broadcast from Berlin a series of talks in English which acknowledged that the enemy had treated him very well.

Diary   *January 18, 1944*

The House opens after the Xmas Recess. During questions there is a
sudden gasp of astonishment and then the whole House begins to yell
and cheer and wave their order papers. Winston strolled in.[1] He flushes
slightly, beams at the House, and then sits down. A tear trickles on to
his flushed cheek which he wipes off. He answers questions afterwards.
His voice is not as strong as it was.

He then comes into the smoking-room. I do not think he is looking
really well. He tells how, on being flown from Tunis to Marrakesh, he
finds that there is cloud cover and that the pilot is flying very low.
'Can't we go higher?' he asks, 'we shall bump into the Atlas at this
height.' 'That is what I was afraid of, sir,' replied the pilot, 'but I have
strict orders not to take you more than 2,000 feet.' 'Go up to 15,000
at once,' said Winston.

Dine at the Dorchester with Sibyl. There are 30 people there. The
cloud of the evening is Archie Clark Kerr [British Ambassador in
Moscow]. I had found the House this morning very fussed and bothered about (a) the Russian reply to Poland which suggests that they
will not listen to any reason at all; (b) the *Pravda* report that we have
been in secret conference with Ribbentrop. They fear that this means
or indicates some desire to break with us and make a separate peace
with Germany. It is thus of great value to talk to Archie whose good
sense and sincerity I trust absolutely. He says (a) that the Russians will
not make a separate peace. 'I shall eat my hat' if they did. 'No, no,
Harold, that is not a thing to worry about.' (b) That they very much
want to 'belong to the Club' and that we can have influence with
them by playing that card. (c) That the Polish thing is just bloodiness
and the Ribbentrop canard just oriental silliness.

Diary   *January 29, 1944*

Our wireless has gone wrong and when (during a raid) Viti and I start
fiddling with it there is a swish in the air and then two explosions
which shake the cottage. Poor Martha [dog] gets in a terrible state and

---

[1] For three weeks Churchill had been absent in North Africa, where he endured a
severe attack of pneumonia and from which he barely recovered.

starts panting. We lift the curtain and see a white incandescent light outside which shortly turns to red. We go out into the rose garden and see a great blaze of fire at what seems to be the Hammer Brook bridge. As we watch, the fire engine with its bells clanging dashes along the road. Mrs Staples [cook] comes to tell us that it was a bomber which crashed in flames, only missing the tower by a few yards.

Diary   *February 7, 1944*

I fear that Winston has become a liability now rather than an asset. This makes me sick with human nature. Once the open sea is reached we forget how we clung to the pilot in the storm. Poor Winston who is so sensitive although so pugnacious will feel all this. In the station lavatory at Blackheath last week I found scrawled up 'Winston Churchill is a Bastard'. I pointed it out to the Wing Commander who was with me: 'Yes,' he said, 'the tide has turned. We find it everywhere.' 'But how foul,' I said. 'How bloody foul!' 'Well you see, if I may say so, the men hate politicians.' Winston a politician! Good God!!!

Diary   *February 9, 1944*

I dine with Emerald Cunard. I recite my few Persian poems and would have gone on to Italian had it not been for the arrival of others. We go back to talking about poetry and the subject of Tennyson is raised. 'But Harold dear,' says Emerald, 'pull yourself together; stop writing about French poets and diplomatists and give us a book on Tennyson.' 'Well, Emerald, I have done my best in that direction [in 1923].' She is absurdly embarrassed by this. I promise to send her a copy. Kenneth Clark rescues the situation by saying that my Tennyson book changed the attitude of his Oxford generation.

I come back by Underground. As usual it is crowded by American soldiers and each one has his girl. Now where the hell do these women come from? I suppose the East End. They are horrible to look at and I should imagine dissolute and diseased. But what will the Americans think of our womanhood when they get back? I am all for a little promiscuity. But nymphomania among East End Jewesses and for such large sums of money makes me sick.

Kenneth [Clark] told me this evening that when at a Brains Trust recently he was asked whether the Russians had any good painters. He replied that it was a curious circumstance that although they had such gifted writers and choreographers and composers, they never produced a painter of the first class. He had many letters afterwards accusing him of being an enemy of the Soviet. Has the whole world gone mad?

Diary   *February 10, 1944*

I lunch with [Lord] Camrose at the *Daily Telegraph*. Among the other guests is Sir Alan Brooke [Chief of the General Staff]. Brooke had been in Italy. He says that the terrain defies description. It is like the North-West Frontier; a single destroyed culvert can hold up an army for a day. He then went on to talk about the Germans. He says they are fighting magnificently. But that their strategy must be dictated by Hitler as it is all wrong. The Russian offensives indicate that he is short of immediate mobile reserves; the fact that he has had to reinforce Italy from the Balkans and Southern France indicates that he has not many reserves in Germany itself. He cannot hope to run four fronts – Russia, the Balkans, Italy and France. It does not look as yet as if the Germans are short of material. Our hopes that they would run out of oil have been disappointed. The morale of their troops is still admirable and only a slight change can be seen in the quality of the prisoners captured.

Diary   *February 16, 1944*

Go to supper with Rothermere. A discussion starts as to whether we should sacrifice lives in order to spare works of art. I say that we do not realise at all that works of art are irreplaceable whereas no lives are irreplaceable. If the war could be shortened by destroying Perugia then I might agree to do so.[1] But I am not satisfied that the strategic value

---

[1] But in the *Spectator* on February 25 he wrote, 'I would not hesitate for a moment to save St Mark's even if I were aware that by so doing I should bring death to my sons.' When this declaration reached Italy, where both his sons were serving, it caused more amusement than consternation.

of fighting up through Italy justifies the enormous loss to civilisation which it entails.

Diary   *February 18, 1944*

Miss Niggeman comes up to say that Vita is very upset about the bombing of Knole and broke down completely. It seems that it was a blaster bomb and that it crept round the house and broke windows in every part including that of her old bedroom. She minds terribly and the whole incident opens a sad wound.

Diary   *February 21, 1944*

Stuart [Preston, a young American art historian] pulled slyly out of his pocket a review by Edmund Wilson in the *New Yorker*. He said, 'Harold, are you one of those people who are hurt by criticism?' 'Depends who it is by.' 'Well, you better have this,' and he handed me a copy. It was, seemingly, a review of *The Desire to Please*, but was in fact a review of all my work. It said that my work was 'unsatisfactory' and disappointing and that I had only written one good book – *Some People*. That I feel to be true. I mean that there is no inner divination in my books and sometimes a lack of muscle in my mind. But the reason he gives is not quite true. He thinks I am class-bound and inhibited. I think I am family-bound and should not wish, while Mummy [Lady Carnock] still lives, to write things which would cause her pain. But that is all I think. To suggest that I was 'shocked' by Verlaine and Byron is to suggest something which simply is not true. But Wilson is a fine critic and I feel flattered that he should have devoted so much time to my books.

Diary   *February 22, 1944*

I go down to the House early. It is packed. Winston gets up soon after noon. He is looking well again, but he has a slight cough. He begins quite abruptly with the words, 'This is not a time for sorrow or

rejoicing. It is a time for preparation, effort and resolve.' He goes on
to state our own contribution to the war-effort. He disclosed that we
have lost 38,300 pilots and aircrew and over 10,000 machines since the
beginning of the war. He forecasts reprisals by the Germans which
have hitherto been 'modest', but which will increase. He refers to the
secret weapon [the V-1 and the V-2]. In describing how our air
superiority is gradually asserting itself, he ends with the words, 'There
is a strange, stern justice in the long . . .' and then he sways his hands
below the level of his waist '. . . long swing of events.' He admits that
the Anzio landing has proved a disappointment and was not carried
out according to plan. He then refers to the new commands. The
names of Eisenhower and of Alexander are warmly greeted; on the
mention of Montgomery there is one isolated 'Hear! Hear!'

Diary   *March 1, 1944*

. . . I pick up Vita and go to Buckingham Palace for a tea party. It takes
place in the hall and we do not go upstairs. The company is divided
into two groups each side of the Propylaea, and the King and Queen
stand in the middle. There are many foreign diplomatists whom they
greet. I am taken to talk to the Princesses. Princess Elizabeth is a clear
nice girl, with a most lovely skin. I talk to her about the Grenadiers.
She is very keen about them [she was their Colonel-in-Chief]. . . .

I dine with James [Pope-Hennessy] at Rules and we go on to Pratt's.
James cannot understand how it comes that I am so interested in
politics. Pratt's is a political kitchen. During the raid last Wednesday
there was a committee meeting on. Suddenly there was a crash, all the
lights went out, and the building rocked. Then the lights went on.
'Well, gentlemen,' said Eddy [Duke of] Devonshire, 'I am not quite
clear whether we elected that bugger or not.'

It is sad on my return to see so many people sleeping on the tube
platforms.

Diary   *March 10, 1944*

The Russians, this week, have launched three separate offensives in the Ukraine. They have, in one sector alone captured 500 tanks intact. It looks as if they managed to cope with the thaw while the Germans have been caught by it. Their ardour and skill are truly miraculous. When one considers that the Americans during the same week have made three devastating day raids on Berlin, one almost sympathises with the Germans.

The miners' strike here continues and is creating much ill feeling. Public opinion at the moment is not good. They are exhausted by five years of war and do not stand things as well as they used to. The recent raids have created far more fear than the great blitz of 1940–1941. People dread another winter of war. But let us hope that the second front, when it comes, will again galvanise our energies.

H.N. to his sons   *March 19, 1944*

I went up to Leicester for my annual general meeting. I had to tell them what I would do if there were a General Election. I said that National Labour is over; that I would not go either Conservative or Labour; and that if they wanted to choose another candidate, they must let me know in time; otherwise I should stand as Independent with their support. So if they refuse to support me, I shall not fight the seat but stand somewhere else.

Diary   *March 27, 1944*

People seem to think that Winston's broadcast last night was that of a worn and petulant old man. I am sickened by the absence of gratitude. The fact is that the country is terribly war weary and that the ill-success of Anzio and Cassino is for them a sad augury of what will happen when the second front begins. The upper classes feel also that all this sacrifice and suffering will only mean that the proletariat will deprive them of all their comforts and influence and then proceed to render the country and the Empire a third-class State.

On April 20, Harold flew to Algiers for a speaking tour of North Africa.

Diary   *April 21, 1944*

I am warmly greeted [at Algiers] by Duff Cooper, who is I think
delighted to see me. I am given luncheon – lobster and cold viands
and vin rosé.

We dine with de Gaulle. It is getting dark, and as we enter the villa
the white turbans of the Guard of Honour twinkle under the trees.
Duff salutes gravely. We are received at the door by de Gaulle's a.d.c.
The house is in the Moorish style, but is brilliantly lit by what is
evidently an elaborate electric system just installed. We go in. De
Gaulle greets me with what for him is almost warmth. Then I am
greeted by André Gide, looking old and ill but as gay as a *perroquet*.
Then Massigli [Commissioner for Foreign Affairs], and Bonnet (the
Minister of Information) and Gaston Palewski [Chef du Cabinet]. The
only other guests are [Albert] Marquet the painter and his wife. We go
into dinner. Caviar eggs and sole and meringues. A good white wine.
Very simple.

Massigli is enraged by the ban on diplomatic correspondence.[1] He
points out that it is all right for the other Allies, as they have their
Governments in London. I have a long talk with de Gaulle. He is
bitter about things, especially the ban. We go off early. I go to bed
happy – not knowing whether today is yesterday or tomorrow.

                                                                April 24, 1944
Diary   *Algiers*

I am woken by one of the batmen (who are in fact Mrs Ronald
Greville's footmen heavily disguised in battle dress) bringing with him
a huge glass of iced orange juice. I read an account of my lecture in
the newspaper. Considering that they only print one sheet, they do
me proud indeed. I then walk a bit in the garden. The roses are thick
everywhere.

---

[1] On that very day the British Government had vetoed coded correspondence between
de Gaulle in Algiers and his Ambassador in London, on the grounds of security.

Duff comes back from his office and we drive in the smart ambassadorial car with flag flying to General Catroux's villa. He is Governor-General of Algeria and also one of the National Committee. He is most courteous. The ribbons on his tunic extend to four rows interrupted by many rosettes like the buttons on my wireless set. Duff and I had been somewhat apprehensive of this luncheon since the wireless this morning from Vichy had announced that Catroux's family had been arrested and would be held as hostages for any further Pucheu incidents.[1] But Catroux shows no signs of anxiety or distress.

He complains in a gentle way about the lack of discipline among the American troops. There are many 'incidents'. Our people, it seems, are better behaved. '*Vos Tommies aiment les enfants et les animaux. Ça nous touche.*' I do my usual stunt of sticking up for the Yanks. But it is evident that the French here really hate them and dread their ignorant and amateurish interference in French affairs.

I go down to the University. The theatre is packed to the ceiling, but it is not a large theatre and the audience is nothing like as huge as it was yesterday. I lecture on 'Proust and England'. It was a lecture that I gave in 1936 in Paris when it proved a great success. But I can feel at once that they don't like it here. They do not like my making fun of their insularity; they do not really care about Proust.

April 26, 1944
Diary   *Algiers*

I go to see Harold Macmillan [Minister of State in Algiers], who arrived today from Naples. Harold greeted me with outstretched arms as if I had been his oldest and most intimate friend, which is not a fact. He showed me his reports on Giraud and de Gaulle. They are brilliantly written, but really brilliantly written, in the style of Macaulay. He describes how Giraud had every card in his hand and threw them away one by one. His only fault was lack of strength and his successive abandonment of his friends destroyed even his moral authority. His brain is nil. Of de Gaulle he wrote that he was conscious always that a Sieur de Gaulle had been one of Jeanne d'Arc's knights. This gave him

---

[1] Vichy Minister of the Interior who had been executed on de Gaulle's orders.

that visionary and ecstatic attitude. Moreover he was deeply conscious of descending from a puritan and provincial milieu and this made him sensitive to ridicule.

Diary

May 1, 1944
Algiers–Oran

We are to start at 7.30 a.m. and as I stand at the door with my luggage ready, a van arrives with two peacocks for Diana [Cooper]. They are carried off screaming loudly in the arms of two Italians.

Then we started off [from Algiers to Oran]. Our objective was Rélizane near Oran where I was to lunch and address the First Division *Blindée* of the French Army. We had arranged to be there by 12.30. But as we were skimming along the road at 11.0 there was a sudden sigh and our tyre went flat. We had no spare wheel and nothing to mend it with. We took off the tyre and examined the damage. The inner tube had a large rent. So there we sat. But eventually an American lorry came along. We thumbed them. They stopped and jumped off and with many jokes mended our tyre for us. They also gave us their rations. Nothing could have been more obliging or more gay than they were. But all this made us two hours late. Instead of arriving at 12.30 we arrived at 2.40. General de Vigier, who commands the Division, had made elaborate preparations. A banquet had been pre- pared in a tent erected over a swimming pool. And for my address a site had been prepared among the pine-trees. We were given a hurried and delicious luncheon. We then walked to the place where I was to speak. It was on the side of the pine-wood and some 800 officers and men had been drawn up in a semicircle.

I spoke to them [in French] without notes for some 45 minutes and they listened with extreme attention. Afterwards they crowded round me and asked questions. 'Did I really think France would be treated as an equal after the war?' and so on. Pathetic and deeply moving it was to see those young clean faces and to note their anxiety. I spoke to them at length again and the General was delighted for me to do so. Then I was introduced to all the officers (including one of Giraud's sons) and we were given a drink before leaving. Of all the speeches I have ever made, that is the one which I shall never forget.

H.N. to his sons   *May 24, 1944*

I went to the House feeling rather hollow inside. Winston spoke for
exactly one hour and a half. He went round the map of Europe and
with amazing frankness told us of our relations with each of the Powers
he named. To our surprise he went miles out of his way to shower
roses and lilies upon Franco. To our regret he spoke of France, correctly,
but in a cold, cold voice. He was as lucid as ever. There were here and
there some of the old striking phrases. His humour and charm were
unabated. But his voice was not thunderous and three times Members
called out to him, 'Speak up!' Then finally he sat down, and, as
foreseen, 300 Members left for luncheon.

I bobbed up and my name was called. The first three minutes was a
confusion of moving figures, and then the crowd cleared and I was left
with about 100 Members on the benches. Winston sat there to my
left, cocking his head forward, popping eyes up at me, as if to say,
'What is the fellow going to say, poor chap?' But I managed all right
and reproved him for his ill-treatment of small Powers and the snubs
he gave to France.[1] That was the theme set for criticism, and thereafter
members of all Parties echoed my remarks. The French, of course,
were delighted. Well, I bear many crosses, and the *Croix de la Libération*
is not the least desirable.

*On May 11, the day when H.N. returned from North Africa, General
Alexander opened his offensive on the Italian front, which led to the capture
of Rome on June 4. Two days later, the Allies landed in great strength on the
coast of Normandy, and on June 20 the Russians attacked in the East. Soon
the Germans were in full retreat to Poland and Rumania. Harold was lecturing
to the Navy in its northern bases when he heard the news from Italy.*

---

[1] In the course of his speech, with Churchill listening, Harold said: 'It seems to me and
many Frenchmen that the United States Government, with His Majesty's Government
in their train, instead of helping the French and welcoming them, lose no opportunity
of administering any snub which ingenuity can devise and ill-manners perpetrate. I
hope that the Foreign Secretary will go further than the negative and ever ungracious
statement made on this subject by the Prime Minister.'

June 5, 1944
Diary   *Scapa Flow*

I come down to breakfast and find Colonel Simpson there. He looked up at me and said in his Caithness accent, 'Heard the news? We entered Rome at 11 p.m. last night.' Well, I never.

Diary   *June 6, 1944*

I turned on the 9.0 a.m. news in the General Forces Programme – and heard to my excitement the following announcement: 'The German Overseas News has just put out the following flash. "Early this morning the expected Anglo–American invasion began when airborne forces were landed in the Seine estuary . . ." ' I then wait till a later flash which says 'The combined landing operations comprised the whole area between Havre and Cherbourg, the main centre of attack being the Caen area.'

I go down to the House, arriving there at about ten to twelve. When I enter the Chamber, I find a buzz of conversation going on. Questions had ended unexpectedly early and people were just sitting there chatting, waiting for Winston. It was an unusual scene. He entered the Chamber at three minutes to twelve. He looked as white as a sheet. The House noticed this at once, and we feared that he was about to announce some terrible disaster. He is called immediately, and places two separate files of typescript on the table. He begins with the first, which is about Rome. Alexander gets a really tremendous cheer. He ends with the words, 'This great and timely operation,' stressing the word 'timely' with a rise of the voice and that familiar bending of the two knees. He then picks up his other file of notes and begins, 'I have also to announce to the House that during the night and early hours of this morning, the first of a series of landings in force upon the Continent of Europe has taken place. . . .' The House listens in hushed awe. He speaks for only seven minutes.

H.N. to his sons   *June 11, 1944*

You will want to know the general atmosphere during invasion week. First, at Sissinghurst. It is literally dominated by aeroplanes. All night they howl and rage above us. Then in daytime there is also much activity: great fleets of bombers floating slowly above us in the empyrean, their drone being a throb all round us. Otherwise the trains run on time, the papers come the same, everything is the same. We listen intently to the wireless at all hours.

In London it is different. There are people who ring up under the illusion (a) that I have inside knowledge, and (b) that if I had it, I should repeat it over the telephone. There is a continual crowd around the ticker-tape in the House of Commons corridor. There are all sorts of rumours buzzing through the smoking-room. And there is the hourly expectation that Winston may make another statement. Newspapers are snatched up the moment they appear on the streets. People are relieved that it has begun. They scan the weather a little more acutely than usual, and notice the direction of the wind. But on the whole they are all amazingly calm.

Diary   *June 14, 1944*

There certainly have been mysterious rocket-planes [the V-1] falling in Kent. The thing is very hush at the moment.

H.N. to Vita   *June 15, 1944*

Poor de Gaulle. He must have hated his longed-for visit to French soil. It was very rough and he had a bad crossing. Then to find the population dazed and bewildered and the little villages in flames cannot have been much fun for him.

Diary   *June 19, 1944*

The German propaganda is making a great deal of its secret weapon
[V-1] and putting out stories of the evacuation of London, of panic,
of vast explosions and of a pall hanging over the city which does
not enable the Luftwaffe to take photographs. I see no signs of all
this. My train arrives on time, there are buses running as usual, and
I can see no difference in the streets. One of the robot planes fell
near the Law Courts and smashed many windows. Another fell in
Tottenham Court Road. Another fell yesterday full on the Guards
Chapel while there was a service. The worst effect is that it deprives
people of sleep.

Diary   *June 25, 1944*

In the 9 o'clock news we hear that the Germans put out at 7.30
that Cherbourg had fallen. Nothing official. But reporters say that
the Americans have entered the town. The doodle-bugs begin just
before 9 and we hear five explosions all round us. The sixth seems
to get away. The Spitfires on patrol circle around us all the time. I
do not feel they are factors of protection: I feel they are elements
of danger.

Diary   *July 5, 1944*

Anthony [Eden] tells me about his bitter battles on behalf of de Gaulle.
The Prime Minister had invited de Gaulle to come over here for the
big battle of France. On June 4 Winston and he had gone down in a
special train to near Portsmouth where they waited. De Gaulle and his
party came there by car and Anthony went to meet them. They then
lunched in the train and Winston produced champagne and drank to
the health of France. Roosevelt had said that de Gaulle was not to be
told the plan of operations but Winston ignored that, told him everything, took him across to see Eisenhower and forced the latter to show
him the maps. Not one word of thanks from de Gaulle. Winston,

feeling rather hurt, said to him, 'I thought it only fitting that you should be present with us today.' 'I see,' said de Gaulle glumly, 'I was invited as a symbol.' Viénot and Béthouart were in despair. Anthony was almost beside himself, feeling that Winston was deeply moved emotionally by the thought of the occasion, and that de Gaulle's ungraciousness would make him dislike the man all the more. Finally Winston asked de Gaulle to dine with him. 'Thank you – I should prefer to dine alone with my staff.' 'I feel chilled,' Winston said to Anthony.

Anthony went on to say that his great difficulty throughout has been that Winston is half American and that he regards Roosevelt with almost religious awe. Anthony does not share these feelings; he regards Roosevelt as an astute politician and a man of great personal vanity and obstinacy. Thus over this de Gaulle business Winston and Anthony have had terrible rows.

Anthony says that he cannot understand why the Germans have brought so many troops to the West. I say it is because they do not believe that the Russians will go outside what they consider their own borders. 'But even the Germans can't think that,' he said. 'They must know more or less that the whole zones of occupation were settled in Teheran.' He also thinks the war will be over soon. 'Luckily,' he said, 'we have now reached full agreement regarding the armistice terms. They are ready to be delivered at any moment.'

H.N. to his sons *July 9, 1944*

I dined with James [Pope-Hennessy]. Philip Toynbee was there, distinguished and polite. I can't make out why I ever disliked him. We are joined by Cyril Connolly. He admits to being frightened by the V-1s. I said that he ought to think of his dear ones at the front who are in far greater danger than he is. 'That wouldn't work with me at all, Harold. In the first place I have no dear ones at the front. And in the second place, I have observed that with me perfect fear casteth out love.'

Diary   *July 19, 1944*

I go to Pratt's with Charles Peake. He is now working at Shaef.[1] He
tells me that we have now got a thousand tanks and over a million men
in Normandy. The battle there is not really as successful as Montgomery
pretends. It had been intended to take Falaise on the first day and we
are no further than Cagny. Shaef criticised Montgomery for being
over-cautious and they regret that he told his commanders to 'take no
risks'. They are also irritated by his informing the Press yesterday that
it was 'a good day' and that he is 'satisfied'. They do not regard it as a
good day and they are not satisfied. Winston is going to go over to
Normandy for four days today and so is Eisenhower. It may still be,
however, that the crossing of the Orne means a great victory in a day
or two. Meanwhile the Poles have captured Ancona and the Americans
Leghorn.

Diary   *July 21, 1944*

Hitler broadcast to Germany at 1 a.m. this morning to the effect that
a bomb had been placed in his room by Colonel Graf von Stauffenberg,
and that although one of his staff had been killed and others injured,
he himself was unhurt. He adds, 'What fate would have been in store
for Germany had this attempt on my life succeeded is too horrible to
think of.'

Diary   *July 24, 1944*

At 4.45 this morning I am suddenly awakened by the sound of a
flying bomb zooming over my head. As I hear it (a few seconds
only) it cuts out and I know that it is about to descend. I bury my
head in my pillow and then comes quite a small crash and no sense
of blast through the room. But a second later I hear things falling
and splintering in my sitting-room and I get up to look. The shutters

---

[1] Supreme Headquarters, Allied Expeditionary Force. This was Eisenhower's headquarters in London. Meanwhile, Montgomery was in command of all the Allied
troops in Normandy, including the Americans.

have been thrown open and the iron bars smashed out. Only one pane is broken. All of my pictures have come down and two of them are broken. My lovely apothecary pot with lilies in it is also destroyed. I put on my great coat and go out into the court. They tell me that it has fallen in Essex Street. I notice a thick soup-like haze in the air and all today my eyes have been red and smarting. I go back to bed and sleep.

Diary   *August 15, 1944*

I turn on the 1 o'clock news and hear the bald announcement that we have landed in the South of France between Nice and Marseilles. The announcement is followed by the strains of the *Marseillaise*.

                                                    August 23, 1944
Diary   *Sissinghurst*

I am working at my notes on the Congress of Vienna and have just reached the point where the Allies enter Paris. I look up and see it is already 1 p.m. and I dash up to Viti's bedroom to listen to the news. It takes some time before the juice gets through so I come into the middle of the first sentence: '... fifty thousand armed men with the assistance of many thousands of the unarmed population. By noon yesterday all the official buildings were in the hands of the FFI [the Resistance]. Paris is free.' I am so excited that I scarcely notice that we have taken Grenoble.

Viti rushes across to share the excitement. I have a hurried bathe and am back in the dining room in time to hear the French 1.30 news. They give it quite moderately. Miss Niggeman, who is down for the day, manufactured a French flag and stuck it upon the green-gages. Mrs Staples [the cook] said, 'How glad I am they did it them-selves,' which is characteristic of our deep spirit of generosity. All of us (including Mrs Staples) have a glass of gin and toast the future of France.

August 27, 1944
H.N. to his sons   *Sissinghurst*

This evening the bee-man came. He looks like the Apostle James-the-less and he puts on a big black veil and talks through it about the mystery of the Pyramids and the lost tribe of Israel. Little Jo[1] joined me as I watched him dowsing the bees. 'Why does he wear that funny hat, Mr Nicolson?' 'So that the bees won't sting his eyes, Jo.' 'But why should the bees sting his eyes, Mr Nicolson?' 'Because they might be angry when he opened their hive.' 'But why should they be angry when he opens their hive?' 'Because they know that he means to take their honey away from them.' 'But how do they know that he means to take their honey away from them?' 'The bee,' I answered, 'although you would not call it an intelligent insect, is a creature of amazing instinct.' 'But why do you call it an intelligent instinct, Mr Nicolson? And why doesn't Mrs Nicolson come?' I explained that she was allergic to bees. 'Allergic,' she muttered to herself in the intoxicating way that children have when they find a new and lovely word.

Diary   *September 17, 1944*

At 1 o'clock we hear that we have landed a huge airborne army in Holland behind the German lines [at Arnhem]. It is the largest force ever sent by air.

Diary   *September 27, 1944*

Rob Bernays says, 'I hope what I've heard is not true?' 'What have you heard?' He says, 'That you are thinking of going to the Lords.' Now if he had heard this from Oliver Stanley or someone of that sort I should be quite prepared to believe that this was a tentative suggestion from on high. But I suspect that it is one of Sibyl's little plans. Anyhow I said, 'I should love to go to the Lords but I see little prospect of it.'

---

[1] Josephine Hayter, Mrs Staples' daughter by her second marriage. She was then aged six.

He said, 'But you never realise that you are a national figure' (pause) 'of the s-s-s-s-s-second d-d-d-d-d-degree.'

Diary   *September 28, 1944*

I go to the House to hear Winston. On my way there I consider how, were I in his place, I would treat the Arnhem surrender. On the one hand it was necessary to represent it as an episode of relative unimportance in proportion to the wide sweep of the war. On the other hand it was necessary not to suggest to anxious parents that it had all been no more than an incident. Winston solved this difficulty with mastery. He spoke of the men of the 1st Parachute Division with great emotion. ' "Not in vain" is the boast of those who returned to us. "Not in vain" is the epitaph of those who fell.' He then passes on to the war as a whole. He tells us that since the Battle of Normandy we have taken nearly half-a-million prisoners, and thereby he puts the thing implicitly in its right proportion.

Diary   *September 29, 1944*

I cancel my engagements in the morning and concentrate upon what I am to say this afternoon. Winston had said that we would not recognise the Provisional Government [in France] until they were responsible to a 'Legislative' Assembly. That taken literally means that only after a general election shall we accord recognition and that means two years from now. What he ought to have said is 'Representative' assembly. I then go to the House. The Speaker (who is amazingly kind and useful – unlike old grouchy Fitzroy who kept one in uncertainty on purpose) tells me that he will call me after luncheon. I make a fairly good speech. But the value is that Anthony [Eden], in his reply, takes up two of my points and gives definite assurances. (1) Bulgaria will not be given Greek or Yugoslav territory; (2) The French Provisional Government will be recognised as soon as the Consultative Assembly has been turned into a Representative Assembly; (3) France will become an 'equal and potent' partner in the reconstruction of Europe. These are important assurances. I am very pleased.

Diary   *October 4, 1944*

To the House. I find that people are really horrified at the collapse of
the resisters at Warsaw and feel that Russia has behaved abominably.
Moreover the idea is gaining ground that Russia is seeking to establish
herself in the Balkans and has given up all idea of fighting the Germans
in East Prussia. Anthony does not share this pessimism. But nonetheless
distrust of the Russians is universal.

Dine with Tilea [leader of the Free Rumanian Movement]. He does
a 'told you so' about Russia. He does not wish to return to Rumania.
He asks me about the marvellous secret weapon which we shall have
ready in six months and which will change the face of the war.[1] Armed
with this weapon we could afford to go to war with Russia. I discourage
him from such fantasies, which are worthy of Goebbels.

H.N. to his sons   *October 9, 1944*

At 5 p.m. Attlee rose to make a statement. He announced that he was
glad to inform the House that Winston and Anthony had arrived safe
and sound in Moscow. Now, such a statement, a year ago, would have
provoked a burst of cheering especially from the Labour benches. But
there was a hush and a mutter instead. I thought at first that this was
due to the fact that Holy Russia is momentarily in disgrace for her
conduct of the Warsaw business. But it wasn't that. It was merely that
people are worried about Winston's health. It is difficult to conceive
the personal affection which Winston enjoys among all Members of
the House.

H.N. to his sons   *October 19, 1944*

I went to St Paul's for the service to commemorate the liberation of
Athens. It was a service conducted jointly by the Church of England
and the Greek Orthodox. For the Church of England there was the

---

[1] This is the first reference in the Diary to the atomic bomb, but Harold did not know
what Tilea was talking about.

Bishop of London arrayed in a terrific cope, surrounded by the Dean
and Chapter in purple and gold and accompanied by an orderly dressed
in scarlet who carried his crozier. For the Orthodox Church there was
my little friend the Archbishop of Thyateira, whom I know so well as
a member of my Greek Relief Committee. On these occasions, when
we meet under the chairmanship of Irene Ravensdale, it is a small
round mousy prelate who sits there saying, 'Yes, Madame German: no,
Madame German.' But in St Paul's I was faced by the semblance of
God the Father in all his majesty. Arrayed in gold, surmounted by a
huge black head-dress, grasping a crozier in the shape of those walking-
sticks we bought at Olympia, he sailed along majestically, his chin
thrust out in vigour, the great amethyst cross on his bosom catching
countless reflections from the lights, and his train carried by an elderly
gentleman in a frayed white dressing-gown and pince-nez, who did
not look like a Byzantine deacon or archimandrite, but like a shipping-
clerk from Nauplia.

There we all were – the King of Greece, the Duchess of Kent, the
Ambassadors and Generals and the Greek choir from Bayswater who
were hidden behind a screen. The Bishop of London said, 'Brethren,
we are met today to return thanks to God . . .' and so on, all in a very
Church of England voice. Then we knelt down and were told to give
thanks unto the Lord our God, to which we replied in a general
murmur, 'It is meet and right so to do.' I was becoming bored at this
stage, and was startled from my day-dream by a loud ululation which
echoed through the dome and sent the pigeons outside scurrying in
panic. My little Archbishop of Thyateira had reached the microphone
and let forth a loud Greek cry. A second time he yelled aloud through
the microphone, and then from behind the screen the Greek choir
began intoning *Kyrie eleison! Kyrie eleison!* to which the British choir
responded, 'Lord, have mercy upon us', after which the Bishop of
London took off his cope, handed it to his orderly, climbed the
pulpit arrayed in lawn sleeves and delivered an address which was so
inadequate as to be almost unbearable.

As I walked out, I felt my arm gripped from behind. It was the Lord
Chancellor. 'You and I, my dear Harold, could have devised that
a trifle better, I think. A passage from Simonides, perhaps, or even a
few words from the funeral oration?' God, what a toad and a worm
Simon is!

Diary   *October 20, 1944*

Go up to Leicester. I am taken out to the suburbs where a course is
established for officers going to Germany on a Control Commission.
I lecture to them on the 'German Way of Life'. I dine in the Mess
afterwards and then listen to the 9 p.m. news. The Brigadier was called
out but on his return he says, 'Well, any news?' 'No, Sir, nothing of
importance.' 'Steady on!' I say, 'we heard of the capture of Belgrade,
Aachen, Dubrovnik and the American landing in the Philippines.' It
wasn't liked. But I am always astounded at the ignorance of serving
officers about anything not within their immediate orbit.

H.N. to his sons   *October 23, 1944*

It was the anniversary of Alamein, and we had on the wireless a message
from Montgomery. He introduced few sporting images, but he did
end with Kipling's 'If'. My distaste for that General passes all reasonable
definition. It is childish to be deterred from admiration by a few quirks
of language and intonation which recall the least pleasant of masters at
a private school. He must be a *grand stratège* – that I am prepared to
believe. But he remains distasteful. But then none of us at the time
would have cared for Nelson. I had all my feathers smoothed down by
hearing that the three Governments have at long last recognised de
Gaulle's Government. So that is settled after months of fuss and
estrangement.

Diary   *November 8, 1944*

The American election results come in all day and at 11 a.m. it is
clear that Roosevelt has won. Tommy [Lascelles, the King's Private
Secretary] tells me that the King was so delighted that he wished
to send him a telegram. But Tommy suggested that it would be
unconstitutional.

Diary   *November 14, 1944*

Anthony makes a statement in the House regarding his visit to Paris. Winston only gets back later in the day having been to visit the Vosges front in a dreadful snow storm. I have a talk with Anthony in the Lobby afterwards. He tells me that when they drove up to the Arc de Triomphe, the crowd did not recognise Winston in his Air Force uniform and that it was only when he came back and they saw him walking with de Gaulle that they realised who he was. I asked him whether de Gaulle was better as a host than as a guest and he replied 'Yes, I *think* he was, but anyhow he was a very stiff host.' He added that not for one minute did Winston stop crying and that he could have filled buckets by the time he received the Freedom of Paris. He said it was really amazing the way crowds sprang up wherever they went and the way they really yelled for Churchill as he has never heard any crowd yell before.

Diary   *December 21, 1944*

I am writing this diary when the telephone rings. A young man says that Ben was knocked down by a lorry on December 15 and injured his head. He is in hospital and they think he will be there for four weeks. No permanent injury reported.

Diary   *December 28, 1944*

It is the coldest Christmas we have had for 54 years. But it is bright and clear and bombers stream over on their way to Belgium.

The news is better. Winston has left Athens [he arrived on Christmas Day], having been shot at by a sniper and used the expression 'Cheek!' In the Ardennes and Belgium we seem to have held Rundstedt some seven miles from the Meuse and to have relieved Bastogne. The Germans are beginning to blame 'the unprecedently fine weather' for their failure to achieve a complete break-through.

Diary   *December 31, 1944*

The end of 1944. A wonderful year marked by the most successful military operation we have ever undertaken. But a year in which internal dissension and distrust have much increased. A year saddened towards its end by Viti's arthritis, which I fear will become a permanent affliction. And by Ben's accident.

1945 began with some disappointments. Germany's offensive in the Ardennes, though eventually unsuccessful, created disharmony in the Allied command. Russia began to control the countries which she was overrunning in Eastern Europe, especially Poland. And there remained the question of Japan.

Diary   *January 1, 1945*

Viti and I hear the new year in crouching over the fire in the dining-room. I turn on Berlin, the *Deutschlandsender*, and then Hamburg – and we get Hitler's horrible but quite unmistakable voice. The reception is not good and he gabbles off his piece so fast that I may have missed something. But it seemed to consist entirely about reflections upon Germany's fate if she loses her moral staunchness, about the fate of the satellites who have dropped out, about the strength of the Führung, on the need for unanimity, on the *sein oder nicht sein* theme.

Diary   *January 12, 1945*

To Leicester. A trail of visitors. A man who wants me to get his boy to study dentistry, a man who wants my advice as to whether he should settle in the Bahamas, a man who wants me to allow Jehovah's Witnesses to import their newspapers from the USA, a man who is worried about the effect of Beveridge on friendly societies, and then three boys from Burma who are worried about their leave. They say that the Japs are brave but incompetent; in the jungle they are so frightened at night that they give away their position by calling out to each other. Rather exhausted by all this.

Diary   *January 18, 1945*

There is a big debate opened by Winston on the war situation. He
begins by warning us that he has a cold but in fact he is in as
good form as I have ever seen him. In dealing with the question
of unconditional surrender he indicates that this will not mean the
extermination of the German people. At this he takes off his glasses
and swings round to the House, hitting his chest with his hand like an
orang-outang. 'We remain bound,' he shouts, 'by our own customs
and our own nature.'

Diary   *January 26, 1945*

Lunch at the Beefsteak with Christopher Sykes. He has been back to
the area of the Ardennes to identify the bodies of his fellow paratroopers
who were murdered in the woods by the Germans. It was a horrible
business. He says the French peasants really love us mainly because
they hate the Americans so much. I then go to Hatchards and send
some art books to Ben.
    Coming away I buy a copy of the *Evening Standard* and read that
Rob Bernays is missing in a 'plane over Italy.[1] This knocks me silly. I
go on to the House where I find gloom and apprehension. I gather
from Anthony [Eden] that there is mighty little hope. I feel crushed
by this. I go to bed feeling sore and sad about Rob. All my best House
of Commons friends are now dead – Rob, Ronnie Cartland, and Jack
Macnamara.

H.N. to Vita   *February 7, 1945*

There has been another 'plane accident. This time it occurred to one
of the machines bringing the F.O. and War Cabinet staff to the Three
Power Conference [at Yalta in the Crimea]. They lost their way and

---

[1] Robert Bernays, Harold's most intimate friend in the House of Commons, was a
member of a delegation visiting British troops in Italy. He had spent a night with
Nigel's Brigade in the northern Apennines, and two days later flew towards Athens.
The plane was never heard of again, presumed crashed in the Adriatic.

crashed near Lampedusa. About a third of them were rescued, but two-thirds were drowned. Moreover all the papers and maps are now at the bottom of the Mediterranean and it will cast a gloom over the Conference. It will do more than that. It will raise a stink in the House about War Transport. They say, of course, that in ordinary circumstances no airman would have taken the risk of flying in such weather, and that it was only the urgency of the thing that forced them to act dangerously. But all the same, if we cannot secure the safety of these key people, then nobody will travel after the war by British airlines. Already it is said that people prefer American pilots.

Diary   *February 21, 1945*

Lunch at the Beefsteak. Gladwyn Jebb is there having returned from the Crimea Conference. Gladwyn says that at Yalta he and the staff were put in a sort of Convalescent Home which was crawling with bugs, and that Lord Moran [Churchill's doctor] came down with disinfectants in the hope of saving them from typhus. He says that President Roosevelt was an utterly changed man since he had last seen him. Not only did he look 20 years older, but that he was scarcely able to speak and that he reminded him of Ramsay MacDonald in the last year of his life. Gladwyn naturally defends the decisions of the Conference but disclaims all responsibility for what happened later in Cairo. It looks as if Winston had repudiated all our pledges both to the French and to the Jews.[1]

Diary   *February 27, 1945*

I put on my new brown suit. Go down to the House fairly early. It is more crowded than I have ever seen it. Winston opens punctually at 12 and we adjourn for an hour at luncheon and he continues afterwards. He goes on to talk about the San Francisco Conference [which drafted the UN Charter] and the general problems of the control of Germany. He then talks about Poland. He makes an extremely good case for arguing that Poland, in her new frontiers, will enjoy an independent

---

[1] The rumours mentioned in this last sentence proved to be unfounded.

and prosperous existence. But in his closing words before luncheon he rather destroys all this by saying that we will offer British citizenship to those Polish soldiers who are too frightened to return. The extreme Tories rush about getting signatures for an amendment expressing regret at the Polish provisions.

Buck De la Warr is there and I take him out for a drink. We are joined by Winston who, for once in his life, does not seem to be in the least bit of a hurry. 'Collins,' he says, 'you will give me a large brandy. I deserve it.' He then shakes himself contentedly and begins talking. He is really very sensible. He says that he does not see what else he could possibly do. 'Not only are they [the Russians] very powerful, but they are on the spot; even the massed majesty of the British Empire would not avail to turn them off that spot.' Moreover, he said, it seemed to him a mistake to assume that the Russians were going to behave badly. Ever since he had been in close relations with Stalin, the latter had kept his word with the utmost loyalty. During the three weeks of the Greek crisis for instance, a single article in *Pravda* would have tipped the whole balance, but Stalin kept an obstinate silence which was of immense value to us. At the mention of Greece his whole face lit up, and he put his hand on my arm. 'I have had great moments in my life,' he said, 'but never such a moment as when faced with that half-million crowd in Constitution Square [on February 14]. You will understand that.' ... As he goes, he says, with his funny schoolboy grin, 'I hope in your speech tomorrow you will not attack me very bitterly. I count you among my firmest friends.'

Winston is as amused as I am that the warmongers of the Munich period have now become the appeasers, while the appeasers have become the warmongers. He seemed in wonderful form during his speech, but he confessed afterwards that he felt 'tired all through'.

H.N. to Vita   *February 28, 1945*

I telephoned to you this evening to say that I had made my speech. I was fussed about it. I was not quite clear where my conscience was. Emotionally I feel for the Poles very deeply. As you know, I think the Russians imperialistic and unscrupulous. But on the other hand I really do believe that Winston and Anthony did save Poland from a fate far

Harold Nicolson in 1945

more terrible than might otherwise have been hers. I was absolutely
sure in my own inner heart and mind that the Yalta decisions were
not expedient only, but ultimately to the benefit of the Poles and
mankind. So I supported these decisions with complete ease of mind
and conscience.

I was called late in the debate on purpose and for that reason my
speech will not *read* very well as it was replying to all manner of cross-
currents which had been ebbing and flowing. Moreover my throat was
very hoarse (too many cigarettes) and I spoke inaudibly. But apart from
that, it was, I think, the most effective speech I have made. Afterwards
in the smoking-room Winston took his glass up from where he was
sitting and crossed the room to sit beside me. He said, 'Harold, you
made a powerful speech. A most powerful speech. You swung votes. I
thank you. I congratulate you. I give you' (and here he made a sort of
offering gesture) 'my congratulations. I only wish that I could also
have given you one of my throat lozenges. Excellent they are. That
horrible man, Lord Moran, who bullies the life out of me, prescribed
them.'

Darling, you don't think I am being boastful and silly do you? It is
simply that when one is successful one feels warm inside, and you are
the only person in the world to whom I can say these things without
seeming silly or caring even if I do.

Diary   *March 1, 1945*

As we [Anthony Eden and Harold] were walking to our seats through
the tangle of the smoking-room we passed the *Evening News* spread
out over the back of an arm chair. It bore the headlines 'Tanks mass
for Cologne'. Anthony tapped it as he passed with the back of his
fingers. 'I think it is almost over, Harold.' 'What – the offensive?'
'No – my dear – the WAR.'

H.N. to his sons   *March 11, 1945*

On 2nd March, after the debate, I went to Paris. As I stepped ashore
from the steamer at Dieppe, I bent down and touched the soil of

France with a sacerdotal gesture. '*Monsieur a laissé tomber quelque chose?*' asked my porter. '*Non*,' I replied, '*j'ai retrouvé quelque chose.*' I told this story to Jean Marin next day, and he relayed it on the *Radiodiffusion Française*. I am not quite sure that I was pleased by this.

Diary   *March 19, 1945*

It has turned cold again. In the afternoon Viti and I tidy up Ben's room and then go to meet him. He comes by the 4.34. Mr Harvey [the station–master], hearing that a wounded soldier is to arrive, mobilises all the porters. They rush to his carriage and his tall thin figure emerges wrapped in dirty bandages. His plaster is right over his chin and up his back [he had broken two dorsal vertebrae]. He has a tremendous heavy dragoon moustache. But he seems to suffer no pain. He says that the last two and a half years have been among the happiest in his life. So that is a comfort.

Diary   *March 28, 1945*

We have funeral orations for Lloyd George [who died two days before]. I meet Winston in the smoking-room and ask him whether the news is as good as it seems. 'We have nothing in front of us,' he says. But owing to the blackout on troop movements we do not know where people have got to and there are fantastic reports flying round. What we all dread is that the Führer will gather all his followers and S.S. and S.A. into the Bavarian highlands and surround them with all our prisoners of war. He will then say 'Come on and do your damnedest.' If Patton could only get to Nüremberg in time he might prevent this plan.

I am elected Chairman of the Anglo-French Interparliamentary Committee.

H.N. to Nigel *April 1, 1945*

Ben and I came down here by the afternoon train. Like a wounded camel Ben stalked down the platform at Charing Cross. The train was crowded with people leaving for their Easter holidays. We found a carriage in which all the corner-seats were occupied, but in which two middle seats were vacant. Ben, with a wince of suffering nobly borne, lowered himself into the seat opposite me. Beside him was a Major-General covered in decorations. He gazed at Ben in a comradely way, as one soldier to another. Observing the pangs of agony which from time to time would pass over Ben's face, he addressed him politely. 'Let us exchange places,' he said. 'I feel you might be more comfortable in a corner-seat.' 'I am sure I should,' said Ben contentedly, and took his place. Not a word about thank you or 'Sir' or anything like that. Just a stricken warrior relapsing with relief into the comfortable seat vacated by an unstricken warrior. Ben closed his eyes for a moment, indicating gratitude and a momentary release from pain. The train started and at Tonbridge we got out. It was a disgraceful proceeding, since in fact Ben suffers nothing at all except an occasional itch.

H.N. to Vita *April 13, 1945*

I woke up to hear the Composer of the Week, then Lift up Your Hearts and then the awful news about Roosevelt [who died from a stroke on April 12]. It is really a disaster. I feel deeply for Winston and this afternoon it was evident from his manner that he had had a real body-blow. Under that bloody American Constitution they have now to put up with the Vice President [Truman] who was actually chosen because he was a colourless and harmless man. He may, as Coolidge did [in 1923], turn out to be a person of character. But I have not heard any man say one good word in his favour. AND when one thinks of the problems ahead it is a misery that this has happened.

Diary   *April 27, 1945*

I dine at the Grand [Hotel, Leicester] and listen to the news afterwards.
It is pretty startling. The American and Russian forces linked up on
Wednesday [April 25] afternoon at Torgau on the Elbe. Messages are
relayed from Churchill, Truman and Stalin. It is odd to hear the latter's
voice echoing through the lounge of the Grand Hotel. The Russians
have completely encircled Berlin and taken Spandau and Potsdam.
They are in the Tiergarten. The Germans insist that Hitler and Goebbels are still in the capital and it may in fact be true that they wish to
do their final suicide act in Berlin. Thus the capture of Berlin means
the end.

Diary   *April 30, 1945*

It has snowed again very hard during the night and the lilac is weighted
with great puffs of snow looking very odd. It is very evident that we
shall accept an offer of surrender from Himmler and that it may
come at any moment. Meanwhile the news of Mussolini's murder is
confirmed. He was caught near Como and murdered.

H.N. to Nigel   *May 1, 1945*

We had really dreadful photographs of his [Mussolini's] corpse and that
of his mistress hanging upside down and side by side. They looked like
turkeys hanging outside a poulterer's: the slim legs of the mistress and
the huge stomach of Mussolini could both be detected. It was a most
unpleasant picture and caused a grave reaction in his favour. It was
truly ignominious – but Mrs Groves [Harold's housekeeper] said that
he deserved it thoroughly, 'a married man like that driving about in a
car with his mistress'.

I dined at Pratt's. Lionel Berry was there (the son of Lord Kemsley)
who told us that the German wireless had been putting out *Achtungs*
about an *ernste wichtige Meldung*, and playing dirges in between. So we
tried and failed to get the German wireless stations with the horrible
little set which is all that Pratt's can produce. Having failed to do this,

we asked Lionel to go upstairs to telephone to one of his numerous newspapers, and he came running down again (it was 10.40) to say that Hitler was dead and Doenitz had been appointed his successor. Then Ben and I returned to King's Bench Walk and listened to the German midnight news. It was all too true. '*Unser Führer, Adolf Hitler, ist ...*' – and then a long digression about heroism and the ruin of Berlin – '*... gefallen.*' So that was Mussolini and Hitler within two days. Not a bad bag as bags go.

Diary   *May 2, 1945*

I dine with Mrs George Keppel at the Ritz. I sit between Lady Moncrieff and Ava Anderson. I lean across to Cartier [de Marchienne, Belgian Ambassador in London] and say, 'Well, Mr Ambassador, I saw you in the House this afternoon, expecting a statement by the Prime Minister which never came.' 'But it came tonight,' said Ava. 'What came?' And then she told me that Churchill had come in at 7.30 and told the House that the whole German and Italian forces in Italy and the Tyrol had surrendered unconditionally to Alexander. I get [Sir] John Anderson to repeat it carefully. I feel quite ecstatic. It is almost incredible.

Diary   *May 7, 1945*

3 p.m. and the news. It says that an hour ago Schwerin von Krosigk [Doenitz's Foreign Minister] had spoken on the wireless from Flensburg [on the Danish border]. He has said that Germany was obliged to surrender unconditionally, crushed by the overwhelming might of her enemies. Ben and I dash off to tell Vita who is in the courtyard. The three of us climb the turret stairs, tie the flag on to the ropes and hoist it in the soft south-west breeze. It looks very proud and gay after five years of confinement.

Diary *May 8, 1945*

V.E. day. Lunch at the Beefsteak. Up till then everything had been normal, but I then find the streets very crowded and people wearing all manner of foolish paper caps and cheering slightly. When I leave the club at 2.15, I find the roads packed. Trafalgar Square is a seething mass of people with figures draped all over the lions. Whitehall is overflowing, but a few buses try to push their way through. After the Cenotaph it is just a jam. I squeeze in behind a car and manage to reach the House about 5 to three. I pause to recover myself in Palace Yard and regret to observe that I have torn a hole in my new suit. The crowds are packed against the railing and the mounted police have difficulty in clearing a path for the Government cars. Then came the great strokes of Big Ben and thereafter an immense hush. From the loudspeakers in Parliament Square Winston's voice booms out to all those thousands. It echoes on the Palace behind me so that I hear it doubly. He tells of the signature of surrender and its impending ratification in Berlin. He is short and effective. The crowd cheer when he finishes and when *God Save the King* has been broadcast. But it is not frantic cheering.

I then enter the House. The place is packed and I sit on the step below the cross bench. I see a stir at the door and Winston comes in – a little shy – a little flushed – but smiling boyishly. The House jumps to its feet, and there is one long roar of applause. He bows and smiles in acknowledgement. I glance up at the Gallery where Clemmie [Churchill] should be. There is Mrs Neville Chamberlain there instead. And thereupon Winston begins. He repeats the short statement he had just made on the wireless ending up with 'Advance Britannia' and then he lays his manuscript aside and with more gesture and emphasis than is customary to him, he thanks the House for its support through-out these years. He then proposes that we adjourn to the Church of St Margaret's Westminster. The Speaker then leaves his seat and the mace is fetched before him. He is in Court Robes with gold facings to his gown and his Chaplain and the Sergeant-at-Arms are also in full dress.

We file out by the St Stephen's entrance and the police have kept a lane through the crowd. The crowd are friendly, recognising some of the Members. I am with Nancy Astor who is, I feel, a trifle hurt that she does not get more cheering. We then have a service – and very memorable it is. The supreme moment is when the Chaplain reads out the names of those Members of Parliament who have lost their lives. It is a sad thing to hear. My eyes fill with tears. I hope that Nancy does not notice. 'Men are so emotional,' she says.

We all go to the smoking-room. Winston comes with us. Passing through Central Hall he is given an ovation by the crowd. They clap their hands. A tiny little boy, greatly daring, dashes up to him and asks for an autograph. Winston solemnly takes out his glasses and signs. He then pats the delighted little boy on the head and grins his grin.

I have difficulty in getting to the Travellers afterwards as all the roads are closed. I eventually get there by going round by Berkeley Square. In the downstairs room we listen to the King's speech at 9. The words are excellent and he does not stammer too badly. Then I go to a party at Chips Channon's after calling in at Pratt's. I wish I had not gone to that party. The Amalienburg room is lit by candles and all the Nürembergers and Munichois were there. I sit with Sibyl and Ivor Novello and get away fairly soon. I walk all the way back to K.B.W. The search-lights have been turned on and make a cone of light above my head. The streets are absolutely packed with happy people; but there is not much drunkenness.

Diary   *May 16, 1945*

The newspapers, I regret to say, are starting an agitation against war-criminals. The fact that our military authorities are obliged to employ ex-Nazi civil servants as administrators tempts them to suggest that we are 'trying to get in with the old Nazi gang'. Memories of Badoglio and Darlan are revived. This is dishonest and inconvenient propaganda. It has been encouraged by the interviews which journalists were allowed to have with Goering and by a photograph of Kesselring lunching luxuriously with American generals in some Berchtesgaden hotel. Eisenhower has rightly stopped this form of fraternisation. But meanwhile there is a growing agitation to bring these criminals to trial. I foresee an unpleasant period during which a few guilty men will be shot and many comparatively innocent men handed over to the Russians. It is not by such means that we can re-educate Germany or restore sanity to a nerve-shattered world. We are the only Power which possesses sufficient moral authority, prestige and good sense to impose reason upon all this witch-hunting.

Now that the war in Europe had been won, the Labour Party pressed for a General Election. Harold found himself in an awkward position. The National Labour Party had ceased to exist. And while his admiration for Churchill was great, he refused to stand as a Conservative, although the West Leicester Conservatives backed him. He therefore stood, somewhat ambiguously, as the 'National Candidate' in full support of Churchill. He knew from the outset of his campaign that his chances of winning were slim. Polling Day was on July 5, and he was defeated.

H.N. to Nigel   *May 27, 1945*

I am frankly dreading the General Election. I dislike the falsity, the noise, the misrepresentation, the exhaustion and the strain of the whole thing. I dislike being abused and heckled. I have not the combative instincts which lead some people actually to enjoy the conflict. And, above all, I have no prospect of success. In normal times, if things were quiet, I might possibly reap some reward from the long and conscientious work I have put in at Leicester. But times are not normal. People feel, in a vague and muddled way, that all the sacrifices to which they have been exposed and their separation from family life during four or five years, are all the fault of 'them' – namely the authority of the Government. By a totally illogical process of reasoning, they believe 'they' mean the upper classes, or the Conservatives. Class feeling and class resentment are very strong. I should be surprised, therefore, if there were not a marked swing to the left.

I have loved my ten years at Westminster, and have found there that the combination of genial surroundings with useful activity is the basis of all human happiness. If I learn on July 26th that my political career is over (perhaps for ever), I shall accept it with philosophic resignation and devote such years as may remain to me [he was then fifty-eight] to serious literary work.

Darling Niggs, whatever disasters may happen to you, there is always

a sure haven for you in the love that Mummy and I bear towards you,
and although neither of us will ever intrude upon your private life,
you know that all your pleasures are our delight and all your pains our
sorrow. It is something even in the worst thunderstorms, even when
the rain pours down in sheets, to know that outside the monsoon there
is always one spot on earth where you will always be loved and
cherished, and where your interests and adventures are welcomed and
shared.

Diary   *June 15, 1945*

To the House at 11. We have prayers, and then just sit chatting till
11.20 when Black Rod knocks on the door. We all crowd into the
House of Lords, but the entrance is too narrow to see anything and
we stand and chatter outside. We then stroll back to the House. Finally
the Speaker returns without the mace. He sits down at the Clerks'
table and we file past him and shake hands. I then sadly leave the
building. The police are very affectionate. My special friend who calls
me taxis bids me fond farewell: 'Good luck, Sir, and by God, you will
need all of it in Leicester!' I shake his hand and leave the House,
perhaps for ever.

   I then take the train for Leicester.

H.N. to Vita   *June 19, 1945*
                                              Grand Hotel, Leicester

The campaign opened yesterday. The first meeting was inauspicious.
It was in a slum quarter and the Communists were there. It was not
that they made a row exactly, and in fact they listened quite politely.
But then the questions began: 'I wish to ask the Candidate why on
April 12, 1938 he voted against the proposal of the Labour Party?' I
naturally say, 'What was that proposal about?' 'Oh, I see you have
forgotten it.' Then it turns out that it was something to do with the
Catering Bill. But I was rather amused when they said I had no right
to support Churchill since I had slavishly supported Chamberlain when
he was in power. I must say this led to some protests among the

audience. One man got up and said that they didn't want a chap who always talked about Czechoslovakia rather than the wages of the poor. I was able to reply to this that if they had listened to me about Czechoslovakia the war might have been prevented. But all this is saddening in that it shows such a complete distortion of the facts and an utter ignorance of motives and realities. One ought to grow another skin and not mind. But I am one of those people who are depressed and made miserable by ignorance.

Diary   *June 21, 1945*

Small despair. I gather that Barnett Janner [Labour Candidate] has been attacking me for living in a Castle. Poor Sissinghurst! I do not like that dignified ruin to be dragged into my election.

H.N. to Vita   *June 22, 1945*

The usual election day yesterday. Catholic deputation in the morning. Then the small shopkeepers. Then the Farmers' Union. The Catholic woman, who is one of my voters, and who is a dim earnest little thing, says she is speaking for Janner and although she has always voted Tory she will now vote Labour as she is a friend of the poor. That is what I fear will decide the election. Everybody agrees, more or less, that I am a better Member than Mr Janner would be. But they want to 'give Labour a chance'.

Diary   *June 26, 1945*

Vita arrives looking so lovely and graceful and gentle. We go on to a woman's meeting and V. makes a little speech. The women are enraptured.

The UN Charter is signed at San Francisco.

Diary   *July 5, 1945*

Polling Day. A beautiful hot day and a cloudless sky. This is supposed to help me on the ground that Labour people turn out whatever the weather, whereas non-Labour people won't budge if it is overcast. I hear the Town Hall clock strike nine and know that the Election is over. About 9.30 we see policemen carrying away the boxes in which the votes will be stored until July 26.[1]

July 18, 1945
Diary   *Sissinghurst*

Start on Chapter XIII [of *The Congress of Vienna*]. I have done some 68,000 words so far. Weed in my life's work [the lime walk].

At 4 we go to the station and Niggs arrives. He is looking thin and brown and far more handsome. It is a delight to have him back. We talk all evening and at dinner we open the bottle of champagne we have kept. What he seems to have minded most was handing over the Russian collaborationists to the Russian forces and the Chetniks to Tito. He loathed that.[2]

Diary   *July 24, 1945*

I leave [Pratt's] about 10.30 and am astonished to find a completely different London. For years I have crept out with my torch. Last night I emerged into a London coruscating with lights like Stockholm. My old way along the Embankment from the Temple Station, which I have traversed such countless times feeling my way between surface shelters and trees, was lit by a thousand arc lights. All these were turned up on July 15 when double-summer-time ended. I had not realised

---

[1] The delay between polling day and the Election result was to give time for the Service votes, cast abroad in the different theatres of operations, to be collected and counted.
[2] Nigel had returned to London from Austria via Naples on the previous day. As Intelligence Officer to 1st Guards Brigade, he had been involved in surrendering to Tito the anti-Tito Yugoslavs to whom we had granted asylum in Austria. All were murdered. This betrayal was the subject of the famous Aldington–Tolstoy libel action in 1989, at which Nigel was Tolstoy's chief witness.

what a transfiguration had been created. And meanwhile all the sticky stuff has been taken from the windows of the buses and the Underground and we shall no longer remember how we used to peep out through a little diamond slit in the texture to read the names of stations as they flashed by. One forgets these things at once.

Diary

July 26, 1945
Leicester

We [Vita, Nigel and Ben] breakfast and then I pay the bill. In the hall an old gentleman in uniform mutters to me, 'Bad luck: you are out – well out.' I do not know who he is but imagine he must be some assistant to the Returning Officer.

It is thus with a heavy heart that I go to de Montfort Hall. All the tables are set out and the counting has begun. I watch the piles being collected and it is evident that I am badly out. My own workers are sad but resigned as the counting continues.

At 11.15 the piles have been passed on to the platform and the Mayor, Alderman Minto, knocks on the rostrum and there is a sudden hush. He begins with the East [Leicester] vote. He then takes up another sheet of paper and announces Leicester West. I am standing in the body of the hall, and Viti is sitting at one of the tables to my right. He reads out: 'Janner, 20,563; Nicolson, 13,348; Kirby, 4,639.' There is slight cheering. Janner and I then go on to the platform. Janner makes his speech. He is not bad. He compliments me on the 'decency and distinction' with which I have conducted my campaign. I second in a few words, saying that there is no bitterness in my sadness since I was indeed fortunate to have on so slight a majority represented West Leicester for ten years in the most historic of Parliaments. There is applause at this in which Janner's supporters join. I then come off the platform and am greeted by my disheartened supporters and also by many Labour people who say, 'I only wish it had not been you.'

The train is late and we only reach London at 6. On our arrival we are greeted by Elvira Niggeman and the 6 p.m. results. Churchill is out and Attlee has a clear majority! Nobody foresaw this at all. We have a drink and then motor down home. We get there just in time for the 9 p.m. news. Winston drove to Buckingham Palace at 7 and handed in his resignation. Attlee followed at 7.30 and was entrusted with the new Government. Winston has issued a statement expressing his gratitude for the support given him by the people of Great Britain in the dark years.

I go to bed with two aspirins – a rare performance on my part. I feel as if I had been run over by a tram, but mainly owing to physical exhaustion and nervous strain. I had never expected to win myself. But I feel sad at closing what has been a very happy chapter in my life and bidding farewell to Leicester and my beloved House of Commons.

Diary   *July 29, 1945*

Last Wednesday [July 26] was indeed an unfortunate day, more so than I imagined. On that day the Temple treasurer gave me notice that I must evacuate No. 4 King's Bench Walk by Christmas as they cannot afford, owing to the loss of premises during the war, to retain residential chambers for non-practising barristers. This is such a terrible blow that Viti has wisely kept it from me until I should have recovered slightly from my Leicester disaster.

Diary   *August 1, 1945*

Robin Maugham rings me up. He had been round to No. 10 on July 26. Winston was in magnificent form and took his defeat with humour. He confessed that it was distressing after all these years to abandon 'the reins of power'. Someone said, 'But at least, Sir, while you held the reins, you managed to win the race.' 'Yes,' said Winston, 'I won the race – and now they have warned me off the turf.'

Somebody mentioned that I had lost my seat at West Leicester. Robin remembered the actual words Winston used and memorised them. 'The House,' he said, 'will be a sadder place without him' – and then he paused – 'and smaller.' I believe that Winston really said that. And it pleases me more than anything.

PART IV

VALEDICTION
1945–1964

The Labour Government had come to power under Clement Attlee, and Harold had lost his seat in Parliament, never to gain another. He was now fifty-eight. He was greatly depressed by his defeat, although it was not unexpected, and returned to literature and journalism. During and after the period when the atom-bomb was dropped and Japan surrendered, he continued to write The Congress of Vienna *and his weekly article for the* Spectator. *He was still a Governor of the BBC.*

Diary   *August 6, 1945*

The 9 o'clock news announces that we have split the atom. A long statement is read, drafted by Winston, explaining how the discovery was made. It cost £500,000,000 and took four years. They have used it today on a Japanese town [Hiroshima]. They cannot tell exactly what damage was done. They estimate that one atomic bomb equals 2,000 ten-ton bombs. It is to be used, eventually, for domestic purposes. Viti is thrilled by the atomic bomb. She thinks, and rightly, that it means a whole new era.

Diary   *August 8, 1945*

I have a talk with Tommy Lascelles.[1] He says that the King does not like the way the BBC treats his constitutional position. Instead of saying 'Mr Bevin was sworn in as Privy Councillor,' they should say 'The King held a council etc. . . .' He tells me that when Truman came to Plymouth [on his way back from the Potsdam Conference], all went very well indeed. Truman is short, square, simple, and looks one straight in the face. [James] Byrnes, the Secretary of State, is a chatterbox. At luncheon in the *Renown* Byrnes began discussing in front of the waiters the impending release of the atomic bomb. As this is

---

[1] Sir Alan Lascelles, Private Secretary to King George VI.

Security Silence No. 1 the King was horrified. 'I think,' he said, 'Mr President, that we should discuss this interesting subject over our coffee on deck.'

Raymond [Mortimer] gives me a terrible talking to about my writing. He says I am too impatient. That I work with facility but do not distinguish between authorship and journalism. That I have never written a book, except that on my father, which is worthy of my gifts. He begs me to go through the [Vienna] Congress book in the mood of Flaubert, not allowing a single meaningless word, or a single unbalanced paragraph, to pass.

Diary   *August 9, 1945*

The 8 a.m. news announced: (a) that the Russians have declared war on Japan; (b) that the Americans have dropped another atomic bomb, this time on Nagasaki.

Diary   *August 10, 1945*

I bump into Harold Macmillan who is without a coat or hat. He says, 'What a pity that we could not keep on the old House and the Coalition until today. Then we could have had a final celebration.' 'Is there any news? I have heard nothing,' I say to him, feeling foolish. 'Yes,' he answers, 'the Japs have surrendered.'

Well that is very odd. I have no feeling of elation at all. It seems remote. There is no sign of jubilation and I observe that the newsvendors have stacks of evening papers unsold and unasked for. I meet a small procession of American soldiers carrying Old Glory and followed by a very few urchins. It is not inspiring at all. . . .

I dine at the Travellers with Robin Maugham. He tells me in great detail how he visited Number 10 on the night of July 26th. Clemmie [Churchill] had retired to her room with the migraine. He and Mary [Churchill] were alone until Winston and Brendan [Bracken] came in. Winston said, 'The new Government will have terrible tasks. Terrible tasks. We must do all we can to help them.' He said, as if to himself, 'It will be strange tomorrow not to be consulted upon the great affairs of State. I shall return to my artistic pursuits. Mary, get the picture I did the other day in France.' The picture was brought. He was pleased with it. Not one word of bitterness; not a single complaint of having been treated with ingratitude; calm, stoical resignation – coupled with a shaft of amusement that fate could play so dramatic a trick, and a faint admiration for the electorate's show of independence.

H.N. to Nigel   *August 30, 1945*

If you examine my political career, you will admit that I muddled the logistics of the thing. It is true that I managed to acquire a certain reputation and influence, that I made some good speeches, and that I was almost always right. It is true that I became on terms of intimacy and confidence with most of the leading figures of all parties. But as a career the thing was mucked. I never became a Cabinet Minister, and my presence on the front bench was only temporary and never effective. The reason was (apart from personal defects, such as lack of push and daring) that I was not part of a powerful organisation. When I look back, I see that I made two fatal errors. The first was when I attached myself to Mosley; the second was when I joined National Labour. Now why did I make those errors? People would say that it was due to 'lack of political experience and judgement'. It was due rather to the fact that I allowed myself to be influenced by personal affections and associations for Mosley and Ramsay MacDonald – without thinking how these would operate at a later date.

H.N. to Vita   *September 26, 1945*

I saw William Jowitt [the Lord Chancellor] at luncheon yesterday and he told me that he had written me a long letter about my going to the Upper House. I must say that his letter is as sympathetic and tactful as it could be. Now that the matter has passed from the stage of a Sissinghurst joke to the stage where it is being seriously dealt with I think we should be very discreet about it. I don't want it to get about either that I have asked for a Peerage and been refused, or that they offered me a Peerage and I refused. Therefore if asked about it I shall

merely say that I don't feel free, owing to my previous attitude, to join
any of the two main Parties.

Diary   *September 30, 1945*

In the evening the boys abuse me for my literary style. They say that I
am so afraid of the obvious that I deliberately take refuge in the
recondite; they say that I so love extraordinary words that I introduce
them without the slightest knowledge of their meaning. It is a very
agreeable conversation, and I love them dearly.

Diary   *October 2, 1945*

Lunch at Beefsteak. Sit between the Belgian Ambassador and Esher.
Old Cartier [de Marchienne] is miserable because the cuisine in
Belgium is declining; this cuisine, which was the finest in the world,
and superior (as I agree!) to the finest French cooking, was based upon
the lavish use of butter. Now they have to use margarine. The tone in
which the old boy used the word 'margarine' was replete with all the
loathing of the nineteenth for the twentieth century. It was a crowded
day at the Beefsteak, and William Jowitt, coming in late, had to find a
seat at the little side table which serves in extreme cases as an overflow.
'Observe that,' said Cartier, 'in what other country in the world would
a club like this allow the Lord Chancellor to take a seat away from the
table: in what other country would that happen quite naturally, without
any of us regarding the occurrence as unusual?' 'In the United States,'
I say. 'Certainly not,' he answers. 'If the Chief Justice came into a club
in Washington a place would be found for him at the head and not at
the bottom of the table.'

*Harold Nicolson failed to obtain the peerage for which he had hoped, and was
employed on various literary and speaking projects. In October he gave two
lectures in Athens (on Byron and British democracy) for the British Council,
and in May 1946 attended the trial of the Nazi war-leaders at Nuremberg.*

October 27, 1945
H.N. to Vita   *Athens*

After luncheon Rex Leeper [British Ambassador to Greece] drove me out to Pentelicon. There are Mediterranean pines and little Byzantine chapels and slim autumn croci in the pine-needles. And a view such as only Attica can give. The great sweep of the Attic plain and then the mountains of the Peloponnesus and the islands. And Athens bathing in a clear light. My God! I am not surprised that from this wonderful air and setting should have come the greatest lucidity of mind.

October 31, 1945
Diary   *Athens*

... At 10.55 I go to see the Regent [Archbishop Damaskinos] at his office. I find him sitting enormous, with his back to shuttered windows. We have coffee and cigarettes. After compliments of a very high order, the Regent tells me that the Royalists and the Liberals are meeting this afternoon to agree upon a joint programme. I say that the economic situation is far more urgent than the political situation; he makes a helpless gesture indicating, 'What would you?' He then embarks on a long disquisition about the political and economic claims of Greece. He says that the communists are not worthy of being regarded as Greek citizens since they take their orders from abroad. It is not a really satisfactory discussion.

Diary   *November 20, 1945*

I have an odd experience. I go at 10.30 to lecture to the young men who have just got into the Foreign Service under the new examination. What amuses me is that the lecture takes place in the former German Embassy [in Carlton House Terrace] which the F.O. have taken over. . . . I talk to them about the qualities required of a member of the Foreign Service. I define the main quality as 'reliability' and analyse its five components as truthfulness, precision, loyalty, modesty, and a sense of proportion. I have good questions afterwards. One young man asks me what one ought to do if a foreign official asks one whether some important fact is true. I say that if one doesn't know, one should say 'I have no idea at all.' But if one does know one should say, 'You ought not to have asked me that question.' The session lasts for more than two hours and I think it was a success.

I dine at Sibyl's. Harold Macmillan, T.S. Eliot, Cyril Connolly, the Kenneth Clarks, the Julian Huxleys, [Sir Pierson] Dixon of the F.O. Harold says that we shall only with the greatest difficulty convince the work-people of this country that they have got to work. They have no conception of the realities of national wealth and have been taught that it is merely the profits of the rich. They think they can now be idle and that the Government will provide. He says, and I agree with him, that France will become a prosperous power long before we do.

Diary   *December 3, 1945*

Guy Burgess comes in and I go across with him to the Reform. He tells me (on what authority I know not, but I suspect Hector McNeil [of the F.O., for whom Burgess was Private Secretary]) that Bevin has turned me down for the post of Chairman of the British Council and that in some way my peerage was involved in that appointment and that this also has disappeared. I am not sure how reliable this is.

Diary   *December 19, 1945*

We drive to the French Embassy. Vita looks quite beautiful in diamonds and emeralds. The party consists of the John Andersons, the Kenneth Clarks, Lady Cholmondeley, the Oliver Lytteltons, a young man called Giles[1] who was Bevin's secretary, and Winston Churchill, Clemmie and Mary. The Churchills were the last to arrive and I was surprised to notice that when they enter, the whole room stands up as if they were reigning sovereigns.

Winston pays me lavish compliments on my speeches in the House, and deplores my absence from it. He had, he said, been reading the

---

[1] Frank Giles left the Foreign Office to become *The Times* correspondent in Rome and then in Paris. Later he became Editor of *The Sunday Times*.

speeches of Pitt and was amazed that any House could have stood such long, involved, empty and repetitive orations. 'It would not do today. The essence of our debates is the choice of prejudicial points of attack.' He said that he had made friends with de Gaulle at last, whom he had found 'much mellowed'. He said that he had liked the Russians. 'The disadvantage of them is', he said, 'that one is not sure of their reactions. One strokes the nose of the alligator and the ensuing gurgle may be a purr of affection, a grunt of stimulated appetite, or a snarl of enraged animosity. One cannot tell.'

He is lively, happy, young. I have never seen him in better form. It was not so three days ago when the Conservative MPs gave him a dinner. They put him beside some of their younger Members, and it had not been a success at all. Winston sat there scowling and silent. Afterwards he said to Malcolm Bullock, 'They are no more than a set of pink pansies.' His passion for the combative renders him insensitive to the gentle gradations of the human mind.

Diary   *December 31, 1945*

What a year it has been! For me (in spite of my defeat at the General Election and my failure to acquire a peerage) a happy year. The worst blow has been leaving K.B.W.[1] But all this fades into a greater surge of thankfulness that we have Nigel safe with us and Ben safe (I hope, but there is a fog) up in London. Never have I felt so acutely as in the last few days what a loving and united family we are. There is an underlying sense of harmony and love. It is perhaps the best thing that life can give.

I thus embark with thankfulness and faith upon my 60th year.

                                                    January 9, 1946
H.N. to Vita   *10, Neville Terrace, S.W.7*

James [Pope-Hennessy] came in last night to see me. He found me sitting over my gas fire correcting my proofs [of *The Congress of Vienna*]. He said that the house was like a boarding house which had been

---

[1] He had moved, with his sons, to 10 Neville Terrace, South Kensington.

turned into a reception centre for bombed-out people. No, not even that. Bombed out Indian students. At any moment he expected to see a sleek black head looking over the banisters.

Diary   *January 9, 1946*

Ivone [Kirkpatrick, Deputy Commissioner of the Control Commission, Germany] tells me about his early experiences in Germany in June and July last. . . . There were two concentration camps for the Nazis, known respectively as the 'Ash Can' and the 'Dust Bin'. He had visited them both. At the former all the Nazi leaders were interned. On his arrival he found it to be a large hotel surrounded with barbed wire with sentries at look-out posts. All the Nazis were out on the terrace sitting in basket chairs. They had been told to stand at attention when he and Murphy [American diplomat] arrived and they did so obediently. Then after inspecting the kitchens and other accommodation, he sent for Goering who entered under the escort of a G.I. and stood sharply to attention. Ivone did not greet him by name. 'You may sit down,' he said. Goering was so bored that he was delighted to talk. He sat there for an hour. He was absolutely frank. Ivone asked him whether he thought the date chosen for the declaration of war was a good one. He said that although he had felt personally that Germany could get all she wanted without forcing us into war, yet given that Hitler was determined on a general war, the date of September 1939 was the correct date. Anything later or earlier would have been wrong. Ivone asked him what was the greatest mistake that Germany made. He answered in a flash, 'Not invading Spain. If we had seized Gibraltar we should have won the war.' He also said that it was our bombing of the centres of communication which brought on the final collapse.

Thereafter Ribbentrop was brought in. He was not frank at all. He denied everything. . . .

Diary   *January 28, 1946*

I dine with the Camroses. Senator Vandenberg and his wife are there.
The Senator tells me that he had visited Roosevelt a week before he
died, and that 'the shadow of death was already on him'. The Senator
asked him whether, in view of his known anti-Russian attitude, it
would be better if some less controversial figure went to San Francisco
[the United Nations Conference]. Roosevelt had replied, 'No – I want
you to go and for that very reason. At Conference after Conference I
have been forced to agree to things which I do not agree with in fear
lest Russia should make a separate peace. She will now blackmail us
again by threatening to withdraw from our League.' Prophetic words!

Diary   *March 11, 1946*

I lunch at the Beefsteak and sit next to Barrington-Ward [Editor of
The Times]. His view is that our working people will not work, not
because they are temperamentally lazy, not because they dislike income
tax, but because they have nothing to buy with what they earn. Once
there are things in the shops then they will work well enough. I do
not believe this. I believe that our lower classes are for some curious
reason congenitally indolent; and that only the pressure of gain or
destitution makes them work. When their profits are taken for income
tax and they are insured against destitution their natural indolence
comes to the surface.

Diary   *April 8, 1946*

I lunch at the French Embassy to meet Gafencu [former Foreign
Minister of Rumania]. He says he has derived much relief and refresh-
ment from his visit to London. There is such exhaustion and defeatism
in other countries that it is an amazing discovery to find a country
which seems self-confident, active and calm. He says that we are faced
with a very grave Russian danger and that it is no use pretending it is
not a danger. Russia is determined to create a unitary system in Europe.
She is assisted in this by the fact that although her theories appeal

only to a minority in every country, it is a very active, ruthless and unscrupulous minority. In Germany our great difficulty is that Russia can claim that her system would not be worse than any other, and that it is only under communism that Germany can attain her unity. Thus the sense of national unity (which is strong in Germany) is identified with communism; social democracy implied the division into zones. To combat this we must provide an alternative ideal; the only possible ideal is a federal Germany in a federal Europe.

Diary   *April 16, 1946*

I lunch at the Beefsteak with Desmond MacCarthy. I go to the flower show and buy many little things. In fact I am rather extravagant. I then go to the London Library and analyse *Punch* jokes from 1860 onwards [for his *English Sense of Humour*]. I see a man opposite me looking on with disapproval. I can see that he is thinking, 'How strange that a man, obviously a man of education and even refinement, can spend a lovely afternoon like this sitting in the reading room and poring over old volumes of *Punch*!'

I have a talk with William Jowitt. I say, 'You remember that there was some suggestion that I should go to the House of Lords as an Independent? You remember you told me that Lord Addison did not like this idea and said that all Labour peers must be Labour peers? Well, I have thought it over and I would gladly accept the Whip.' He said he thought that a wise thing to do. I said that I was heart and soul with the Government in its foreign policy and that I also agreed with its domestic policy. What worried me were the left-wing elements who seemed to me too revolutionary. 'They are what worry all of us,' he said. I did not feel that all my difficulties would be solved by my joining the Labour Party – nor did William. But anyhow I have taken the plunge and am rid (at some cost to my pride) of the incubus of being an independent. But no evasions will obscure the facts (a) that I have ASKED for a peerage; (b) that when I found I could not get one as an independent I then changed my party coat.

H.N. to Vita   *April 25, 1946*

It is now confirmed that I fly with [Sir] George Clerk [former British Ambassador in Paris] to Nuremberg next week. I do dread it so. I know I am squeamish about this sort of thing, but I hate the idea of sitting all comfy in a box and staring at men who are certain to be hanged by the neck and who are in any case caught like rats in a trap. You know as well as I do that my feelings for Ribbentrop have always been cold feelings. But I do not want to see the man humiliated. And Schacht [Hitler's Finance Minister] was a friend of mine. I do not want to see him like a prisoner in the dock. Nor really do I want to see Germany in its present state. But I should never forgive myself if I shirked this opportunity.

                                       April 30, 1946
Diary   *Nuremberg*

The colouring of the courtroom is dark brown relieved by heavy green marble surrounds to the several doors. The room is lit by slit-lights from above but there are alternative reflectors in position for illumination when photographs are taken. The room is far smaller than I expected; the dominant note is silence. The proceedings are carried out almost in a hush.

My gaze then turns to the dock. The defendants sit in the following order: Front row: Goering, Hess, Ribbentrop, Keitel, Kaltenbrunner, Rosenberg, Frank, Frick, Streicher, Funk, Schacht. Second row: Doenitz, Raeder, Baldur von Schirach, Sauckel, Jodl, Papen, Seyss-Inquart, Speer, Neurath, Fritzsche.

They look drab, depressing, ill; they have the appearance of people who have travelled in a third-class railway carriage for three successive nights. It seems incredible that such a dim set of men should or could have done such huge and dreadful things. When one looks more closely one observes differences between them. Goering is the dominant figure. Clad in a loose light uniform without badges of rank, he leans his pasty face upon a fat pasty hand, and at times he will place the fist against his chin in the attitude of Rodin's *Penseur*. For so vast a man, although he is now shrunken, his movements are alert, rapid,

nervous, impulsive. Beside him sits Hess – bearing a strong resemblance
to the Duke of Rutland – apparently not attending much, opening a
book occasionally which he holds on his knees, but not reading it with
any attention, just glancing down as if it were something he happened
to be holding in his hand.

Ribbentrop is much changed; his face is grey and thin; his soft collar
flops; he closes his eyes and adopts a mask; he seems inarticulate, utterly
broken.

Dr Dix, the leader of the Berlin bar, is making a long, rambling and
to my mind ineffective speech in Schacht's defence. Schacht sits in the
witness box opposite him. He is flanked by two young Americans in
white helmets. Every hour, two other snowdrops appear from behind
and silently take from their comrades the white batons of office,
stepping into their place. At 3.15 there is a short recess. The German
counsel rise from their seats and talk to their clients in the dock. They
are carefully watched by the snowdrops as they do so.

When we begin again Schacht is asked questions by his counsel. He
answers in a loud clear voice. He is completely master of himself and
of his dates and facts. 'Did you adhere to the Nazi *Weltanschauung*?' 'I
reject every philosophy which is not based upon true religion.' 'What
was your true opinion of Hitler?' 'A man of *diabolische Genialität*
[diabolical genius] . . . a man who may at the start have had fine ideas
but who in the end became infected by the poisons which he instilled
in the masses.'

At 5.0 the Court rises. We drive back to [Sir Norman] Birkett's
[one of the British judges] villa. He is carefully guarded. He has military
policemen in his car and is followed by a jeep containing other red-
caps armed with Tommy guns. Only gradually does he begin to talk
about the trial. He says that the Nazi leaders would never have allowed
themselves to be taken alive had they known that we should find such
utterly damning documents.

Diary

May 1, 1946
Nuremberg

We go into the court room. This time we are in the Visitors' Gallery
above the Press Gallery where we were yesterday. When we enter,

Schacht is again being examined. He sits there, benign, confident, a complete master of his own defence. He remarks that Ribbentrop was one of the most incompetent men he has ever known. The latter drops his strained mask for a second and shakes his weary head.

At 11.15 there is an adjournment and we gather in Birkett's room. Colonel Andrus, who is Commandant of the prison, comes to fetch us. We start going round the prison under Colonel Andrus' guidance. The courts are connected with the adjoining prison by a long covered wooden passage, which twists and turns, and which has a duck-board floor. Our feet resound upon this floor as if it were a xylophone. The defendants as they walk to the court must hear either their own feet or those of their guards echoing upon this duck-board. For those whose lives are spared, that sound will echo till they die. Two-thirds of the way down this wooden corridor there is a gate leading to an exercise yard. There are lilac bushes in flower and the grass is worn by miserable feet.

We enter a prison gallery, identical with those I have seen at Brixton and Wormwood Scrubs. The only difference is that the prison smell is absent; it is replaced by the smell of beans cooking in tomato. The cells run along each side, and the names of the prisoners are attached outside. Andrus takes us into Sauckel's cell, and then to Ribbentrop's. They are made to clean the cells themselves and to fold their blankets. They have a bunk, a chair and a table. They have books and papers, and on their tables are pasted the photographs of their wives and children. In Ribbentrop's cell it was sad to see, not the accustomed prisoners' photographs taken at Margate, but Bond Street photographs of charming boys.

We saw the food, which was good. 'Ah yes,' said Colonel Andrus, 'no mother has ever cherished her children as I cherish these men. I must keep them fresh for the last day.' But he is not a gloating man; he is a nice, clever man, and humane.

He takes us to see the depository where the prisoners' luggage is kept. It is pitiable luggage. A fat suitcase of imitation leather belongs to Goering. It contained his particular drug. 'We have suppressed that parcel,' says Andrus, 'and friend Goering has never been so healthy in his life.' In a way, these waiting suitcases, gathered together as in a cloakroom at Victoria, were more expressive than anything else.

The court rises at 5. We have some tea in Birkett's room, and then drive with him to the *Heldenfeld*, or stadium, now called 'The Soldiers' Field'. I visit this scene of the great Nazi rallies with awe. It is a fine and tremendous erection, being a tremendous affirmation of the drama and power of the whole system. The huge eagle and swastika by which it was surmounted have been taken down, showing brick scars upon the stone plinth. We mingle with the crowd. The people glance at us, realise we are the conquerors, and look aside as if we were not there. If I were a Nuremberger I should feel nothing but undying hatred for those who have destroyed my lovely city. We see no scowls; merely a pretence of ignoring us.

Diary
May 2, 1946
Nuremberg

Sir Geoffrey and Lady Lawrence [President of the Tribunal and his wife] come to dinner. Lady Lawrence tells me that the most dramatic moment in the trial was when they turned on a film showing the trial by Nazi justice of some wretched young man who had been involved in an attempt on Hitler's life. The judge yelled at him, pointing accusing fingers, shouting, 'You beast! You brute! You traitor!' The sound of his objurgations echoed through the court room, rising in the end almost to a scream. Then the film stopped, the lights went up, and the gentle voice of Lord Lawrence intervened: 'Please continue your examination, Dr Dix.' The contrast between violence and calm was such that even the defendants moved uneasily upon their hard and narrow bench.

Diary
June 4, 1946

I lunch with the Walter Elliots. The other guests are Peter Thorneycroft and Jan Christian Smuts. Smuts is in terrific form. He is more genial than I remember, and immensely friendly. He chatters all the time. He is less subtle (or should I say less sly?) than I remember him, and conveys the impression of a philosopher-king – very old, very wise, very convinced that in the end it is conduct and principle which

decides events, not ingenuity. His eyes are as bright blue as ever with
a dancing light in them.

He talks about England. 'You are not an old country,' he says.
'Believe me, my own country and certainly Canada and the United
States are older than you. There is no touch of age about England.
And why? Because you allow new ideas to enter your blood-stream.
Your arteries remain elastic. Never in your history have you had so
many young men of energy and intelligence. Never! I have seen them.
They are superb. The Conservative Party will again come to power.
But it must find a faith and a policy. And to do that it must rid itself
of its older men, perhaps even some of its older leaders, perhaps even
of the greatest leader himself.'

They all feel that. They all feel that Winston must go. This saddens
me. But he is not elastic in domestic affairs. He cramps their thought,
and renders it pugnacious when it should be conciliatory.

Diary   *July 14, 1946*

In the evening we discuss the rumour that I am to succeed Duff
[Cooper] as Ambassador in Paris. Viti says that any such idea would
be quite intolerable. Ben says it would be convenient to stay at the
Embassy. Niggs is all in favour of it. He says that he does not want me
to end my life on a flat note; that I should be good at the job; that I
should be mad to refuse. I am amused by all this, especially as the issue
will never arise.

*Harold went to Paris to report for the BBC on the Peace Conference, which
was to draw up the draft texts of the peace treaties with Italy, Hungary,
Rumania, Finland, and Bulgaria. The problems of Germany and Austria
were not considered. The Conference met in an atmosphere of increasing
antagonism between the United States and Russia: 'Instead of open covenants
openly arrived at,' Harold commented in one of his broadcasts from Paris, 'we
have open insults openly hurled.'*

July 26, 1946
Diary   *Ritz Hotel, Paris*

I believe that if we are very industrious and united we can make the
BBC reports from Paris as useful and influential as our reports during
the war. The newspapers after the first days will become bored with
the Conference which will drop out of the front page. It will be our
business to keep public interest alive. I see no reason why, if the thing
is carefully done, we should not teach the British Public that foreign
affairs can be as interesting and as comprehensive as a test match. I am
slightly startled by the size of my audience. I shall be speaking probably
to 20,000,000 [people].

July 29, 1946
Diary   *Paris*

I walk across to the Luxembourg [for the opening of the Conference].
The roads are barred by gendarmes but we have passes. I am shown to
a place bang in the centre of the front-row [of the gallery] from where
I can see everything. The great theatre of the Senate is lit, partly by
sunlight, and partly by spotlights. The delegations sit in the red plush
stalls with little black book-rests in front of them; the presidential desk
is on the stage, a vast Empire affair, and the interpreters sit in the
orchestra. It is all like a first night at Her Majesty's or Covent Garden
except for the absence of women in the stalls. People stroll in and take
their places which are marked with the names of their countries on
large placards. The minor delegates and experts enter first, making
polite handshakes and bows. Then at 4 p.m. precisely the main delegates
emerge from the back of the stage and walk across it, down the
steps to the proscenium and then up among the stalls. Molotov and
Vyshinsky stride across the stage with all the consciousness of power;
Byrnes and his [American] delegation walk slowly and sedately with
all the consciousness of great virtue; and then in trips little Attlee,
hesitates on finding himself on the stage, tries to dart back again into
the door through which he has come, and is then rescued by an official
who leads him across the stage with a hand on his elbow. A lamentable
entry. In fact our Delegation does not look impressive. How insig-

nificant they look there in their red plush stalls! How different from Lloyd George and Balfour – how terribly different from Winston.

They all take their seats and the hum subsides. The *huissier* then shouts 'Monsieur le Président', and Bidault [Prime Minister and Foreign Minister] walks in with neat little feet and takes his seat. Any dignity which the meeting might have had is completely marred by the photographers and cinema-men. They are everywhere. All the time American photographers creep about, now on the stage, now off the stage, flashing with their cameras. It might be Hollywood itself. In a somewhat rasping voice, Bidault opens the proceedings, making a short but conventional speech.

August 4, 1946
Diary   *Paris*

An unexpected and most undesired fame has descended upon me. I am Rip Van Winkle, the veteran of 1919, the only man in Paris who remembers the last Conference. It would seem in fact that, except for a dotard on the Brazilian delegation whose memory is unreliable, I am the only survivor of the former Peacemaking. The *New York Times* correspondent asks me to tell him differences ... etc. etc. 'Of course,' he says, 'there is a difference in personalities – they were giants in those days.' 'Balls,' I say, 'don't you believe it. Mr Byrnes, to my mind, is more effective than President Wilson; Bevin is certainly a stronger and finer character than Lloyd George; and old Orlando cannot be compared for force and capacity to Molotov; and in the circumstances Bidault is a far more suitable person than Clemenceau could ever have been.' He is distressed by this remark.

August 11, 1946
Diary   *Paris*

To the [Hôtel] Scribe for my 6.15 talk. I then go into the recording room in order to hear Viti [who was broadcasting an appeal from Wales for the National Trust]. We arrive just in time to hear Vita announced as Miss VICTORIA S–W. I expect a row, but she does her piece with

swan-like calm. Only at the end when she has to give her address does
she fling into the initial 'V' all the loathing which she has of her full
name or of my name or of any name except V.S-W.

Diary

September 6, 1946
Paris

I go to see [Ernest] Bevin in the morning. I find him installed at a
Louis XV table in an ivory-coloured room at the George V. He is
most welcoming and genial.

He begins by saying polite things about my broadcasts. I say that it
is difficult for me to put the Russian problem in its right perspective.
He says that he has only just begun to understand how little we know
of the Russians and how much our gaps in interpretation are due to
the actual misemployment of words. For instance, when he first met
Molotov, he once said to him, 'Let us assume that as a basis of
discussion.' It was only later that he discovered that Molotov had
interpreted the word 'basis' as implying a fundamental agreement.

Unfortunately, however, Mr Byrnes (being a victim of his Press) has
insisted on full publicity. That means that one can never think aloud
without being overheard. That means that all real negotiation is impossible. I say, 'But what about the Big Four meetings?' He chuckles at
that. He says that the first one went splendidly, since he had prepared
it in advance. But the second one was an absolute flop. 'I have my
instructions,' began Vyshinsky. 'Well,' Bevin answered, 'I have no
instructions other than those which I give myself. Clearly therefore
we are not discussing on the same level and I had better turn you over
to my deputy.' Vyshinsky blinked at that but he could go no further.
Therefore the meeting broke up pending Molotov's return.

He thinks that the Russians are bitterly enraged with the Americans
for having forced a show-down over Yugoslavia. He thinks that their
insane proposal to transfer the UNO to Paris or Geneva was just a
lunge back at the United States. He agrees with me that all this scoring
points is lamentable.

None the less Bevin feels that we are getting on.

September 10, 1946
Diary
Paris

In the evening at 5.30 we motor out to Versailles for the reception given by Georges Bidault as President of the Provisional Government. The big courtyard is lined by mounted Gardes Républicains and by Goums and Spahis in their scarlet cloaks. On the staircase there are men dressed in liveries of the eighteenth century with wigs. Bidault receives us in the antichambre du roi and we pass through the Oeil de Boeuf into the Galerie des Glaces. It is a lovely evening and the sun is pouring in. An absolutely superb Savonnerie carpet is on the floor and there are two vast buffets. I have short talks with many old friends. I stand in the window where I stood twenty-seven years ago after the signing of the Treaty of Versailles and look out on the ponds and canal turning green and purple in the sunset. In the Salon de la Paix there is a small orchestra playing Lully's minuets. When they stop playing one can hear the fountain splashing. When the darkness falls they turn on the flood-lighting. It is a scene of amazing magnificence and beauty. But the people look foul.

September 28, 1946
Diary
Paris

I have to hurry a bit as I promised to receive Smuts at 12 p.m. at the Luxembourg. We go upstairs to the *studio des personalités* – a title which is typical of French protocol verbiage. I take the Field Marshal into the studio. I leave him. He has to record his BBC talk for tomorrow. When he is gone, Venables [of the BBC] again mops his brow. I ask him whether anything went wrong. 'Yes,' he says, 'you know that white statue of a completely naked boy which stands in the *studio des personalités*? When the Marshal had finished speaking, he said in a loud voice to me, "That young man does not seem to mind very much exposing his person." I think and pray that this remark did not go out all over South Africa. But I am quite sure it was heard by all the engineers, officers, directors and typists in Broadcasting House. I shall have to give an explanation this evening.'

October 1, 1946
Diary   *Paris*

We put on the records [of the Nuremberg verdicts] at once. Eventually
we could hear [Lord Justice] Lawrence say, 'Can you hear me now?'
'Yes,' said Goering. Then Lawrence said, 'The defendant, Hermann
Goering, having been found guilty on all indictments, is condemned
by the International Military Tribunal to death by hanging.' Then
comes Hess who gets life imprisonment. Then Ribbentrop – 'The
defendant [hesitation on Lawrence's part] Joachim von Ribbentrop
etc. is condemned to death by hanging.' I cannot bear it. To sit there
in that familiar room at the Scribe and to hear those men being bumped
off one by one. I take off my earphones and rise to go. I see the
glistening surface of the disk revolving pitilessly ticking off the lives of
other men.

October 11, 1946
Diary   *Paris*

Molotov walks slowly to the platform. He speaks in a quiet voice with
small gestures of his little hands: very feline it all is. He has a slight
stutter, but masters it. From time to time he will emphasise a point by
jabbing downwards with a short finger. His speech is really dreadful.
He said that our desire to enter the Danube basin was a hidden desire
to encompass the economic servitude of Europe. He said that America
had made money out of the war and now wanted to make even more
money by penetrating into the Danube basin, but Russia would protect
those countries against enslavement and the wiles of dollar diplomacy.
Not a single argument of any sense at all: just the old utterly meaningless
slogans trotted out again. It is very depressing.

October 22, 1946
Diary   *London*

I go to see Rab Butler who is to lead for the Opposition in the Foreign
Affairs debate this afternoon. He has obtained from Bevin the text of

the opening speech. We go through it together. He is dreading what Winston will say tomorrow. He says that Winston is a 'magnificent animal' who has really no spiritual side at all. He fears he is going to trot out the bolshevik bogey and do much harm. They all wish that he was not their leader. Rab says that my talks from Paris have had 'an immense effect'. He thinks that for the first time they have induced the ordinary public to take an interest in foreign affairs.

Diary　　　　　　　　　　　　　　　　　　　　*November 21, 1946*

I reach the age of sixty. Until about five years ago I detected no decline at all in physical vigour and felt as young as I did at thirty. In the last five years, however, I am conscious that my physical powers are on the decline. I am getting slightly deaf and the passions of the flesh are spent. Intellectually, I observe no decline in vigour; I can write with the same facility, which is perhaps a fault. But I do not notice that my curiosity, my interest or my powers of enjoyment and amusement have declined at all. What is sad about becoming sixty is that one loses all sense of adventure. I am well aware, moreover, that I have not achieved either in the literary or political world that status which my talents and the hard work I have done and do might seem to justify.

Now how much do I mind all this? I have no desire for office or power in any sense. I know quite honestly that if I were offered the Embassy in Paris or Rome, I would hesitate to accept, not only because Vita would hate it, but because I have no wish to be prominent or grand. But of course I am disappointed by my literary ill-success. Nor do I quite relish the idea that my reputation rests not so much upon my political or literary work, as upon my journalistic and broadcasting work. I regret all this quite faintly. I see, on the other hand, a long life behind me, dashed with sunshine and gay with every colour. And to have three people in my life such as Vita, Ben and Nigel is something greater than all material success. For if in fact happiness is the aim of life, I have had forty years of happiness from the day when as a little boy I walked down to the station at Wellington College with a surge of freedom in my heart.

Diary   *December 6, 1946*

My book on *The English Sense of Humour* arrives from the Dropmore Press. It is very excellently produced. Ben remarks with some astringency that the exterior is superior to the interior.

I return to Neville Terrace, do some dictation and then await my lecture [on the Lawrence portraits of the Congress of Vienna]. Elvira [Niggeman, his secretary] realises that I am nervous. 'I have never seen you nervous before,' she says. She is quite right. The reason is (a) that I do not like lecturing about subjects on which I am not an expert; (b) that I dread letting Ben down in front of his colleagues; (c) that I am uneasy at the presence of Queen Mary. Anyhow, V. and I drive to Burlington House. Queen Mary arrives on the tick accompanied by the Princess Royal. I give my lecture and it goes very well. I finish and step down from the platform. Queen Mary says, 'Your lecture was too short.' (It was 55 minutes.) 'No lecture,' I reply, 'can be too short.' 'Yours was,' she says. The Queen says she wants to see the pictures again and compare them to what I had said. We go from picture to picture and the Queen nods her head. She is specially interested in Lawrence's treatment of Alexander I's red face. She had not known about that before.

Diary   *December 9, 1946*

[Monday] Since I came down on Friday night I have (a) finished my article for *Contact*; (b) done my Marginal Comment; (c) done my talk for the Overseas Service; (d) done an article for the BBC Yearbook; (e) done another talk for the European Service; (f) done my article for the *Figaro*; (g) done two reviews. I have also read two books. The bad weather has some advantages.

Diary   *December 10, 1946*

Ben tells me that the Palace have agreed to his becoming Editor of the *Burlington*.[1]

Diary   *December 29, 1946*

In the afternoon I moon about with Vita trying to convince her that planning is an element in gardening. She wishes just to jab in the things which she has left over. The tragedy of the romantic temperament is that it dislikes form so much that it ignores the effect of colour. She wants to put in stuff which 'will give a lovely red colour in the autumn'. I wish to put in stuff which will furnish shape to the perspective. In the end we part, not as friends.

What a lovely Christmas holiday I have had! So quiet, so busy, so useful. Ben and Niggs take an amused view of our domestic affections, but are, I think, grateful for a comfortable home, admiring parents, and an opportunity to work without interruption. Vita and I are equally amused by them, and so fond.

It has not been a very special year. I enjoyed Paris. But I shall not be really happy until I get back into Parliament.

The winter of 1947 was one of the severest on record, and the nation suffered acutely. Harold, for once, was writing no new book, and occupied himself mainly with weekly journalism. In February he joined the Labour Party, hoping to begin a new political career in the Commons or the Lords.

Diary   *January 5, 1947*

It is horribly cold. Raymond [Mortimer] reads my essay on [English] humour and lays it down without a word and picks up another book. When pressed, he says it is very bad and sham philosophy and that I

---

[1] The leading scholarly journal of the fine arts. Ben remained Editor until his death in 1978. Hitherto he had been Deputy Surveyor of the King's pictures under Kenneth Clark and Anthony Blunt.

ought not to try my hand at that sort of thing. I like that about Raymond. He never for one moment says what he does not think merely out of affection or a desire to please.

Diary   *January 9, 1947*

I dine with General Jacob [Assistant Secretary to the War Cabinet, 1939–46]. He is full of talk and I enjoy my dinner. We begin by discussing the present and future international situation. I say that in five years from now we may find that France, Spain, Italy, Germany and Greece have all gone communist. That the smaller Western Powers are like rabbits in the python's cage. That the whole of India is under communist direction and that we will have troubles in all our colonies and dependencies. At the same time there will have occurred in this country a split between the present Labour leaders (who take a patriotic or nationalistic point of view), and their left wing (who take an international or Red Flag point of view). The latter will, owing to the acute poverty of the country, gain ground among the working classes. Thus if a conflict comes between the USA and the USSR we shall have a very active fifth column in this country. The great bourgeois mass, terrified as they will be by the prospect of atomic war, will wish only to please Russia. The minority who see that we must side with America will be called 'war mongers'. And we shall thus lose our independence and our Commonwealth. I say that this is what will *probably* happen. To ignore this probability is to be both cowardly and blind. To be frightened of it is to deny one's own soul. Because nothing really happens which is as bad as the imagination forecasts. Time brings unexpected alterations. The danger may pass.

Diary   *February 12, 1947*

I go to the Historic Buildings Committee of the National Trust. There is no heat at all and we crouch round the table in fur coats and gloves. The electricity is cut off between 9 and 12 and 2 and 4. The black out is to be imposed. My God! What the poor people of this country have had to suffer in the last seven years!

Diary   *February 13, 1947*

The coal crisis is really disastrous. Our industry is at a standstill and it
will take us months and months to recover from this disaster. There is
a demand for vigorous leadership and of course all sorts of rumours.
The most prevalent is that Attlee is going to retire in Bevin's favour.
But I fear that Bevin is seriously ill – angina. He goes to Moscow with
a doctor and a nurse. There was a leading article in the *Times* today
which reached bottom for sheer pessimism.

Diary   *February 28, 1947*

I write a letter [applying for membership of the Labour Party] to the
local Labour office. I am glad I have taken this difficult decision after
all these months of worry and uncertainty. It will lead to a row at
home. But this is the best moment, when the Labour Party are being
banged on the head, to make my act of faith. It is NOT an impulsive
act.

     This decision will expose me to much obloquy, misinterpretation,
ridicule and attribution of false motive. People will say I did this
because I wanted to get a peerage. If I scrape my conscience I must
admit that there is some truth in that accusation. I hate being out of
Parliament. I do not want to fight an election. I should be at ease in
the Upper House and able to do some good. If there were no prospect
of my getting a peerage would I have done this? No. And if I do not
get a peerage within a reasonable time will I fight an election as a
Socialist? I might. What I will not do is abuse my former friends. I
cannot get up and speak ill of Winston or Eden. Anyhow one thing is
certain. I could never have become a Tory. It would be madness to
become a Liberal. Therefore, becoming Labour is the only alternative
to dropping out. That is not a noble motive. But what people will not
know is that I am convinced that the only angle from which to fight
communism is the Labour angle. The only thing that worries me is
that my integrity is my most valued possession. Will this make people
doubt my integrity? I do not think so. Because God knows my integrity
is a solid thing with me; I am unambitious and devoted – I really am.

     When I read the above again I say to myself, 'You are making

excuses, and very lame excuses, for yourself. That means that you are
not spiritually at ease.' No, not exactly that. It is the rows I dread; how
it will hurt Vita and Mummy [Lady Carnock, aged eighty-six]; the
publicity that will follow. I wish I were more tough.

H.N. to Vita   *March 6, 1947*

I must break the fact to you that I have joined the Labour Party. I have
done this because in the end it was inevitable and I had better do it
when the night of misery is on them rather than when they are basking
in the sun of popular acclaim. I did it quite quietly by joining the local
branch [Kensington]. They registered me as 'H. Nicolson' and it is
probable that there will be no publicity. I told Elvira, who emitted a
short sharp scream. I told the boys, who received the news in horrified
silence. I shall get a real scolding when I come down on Saturday. But
I know I was right. This is NOT (repeat NOT) an impulsive gesture.
I have been worrying over it for months.

Diary   *March 13, 1947*

I go to see Mummy. She takes my having joined the Labour Party as a
cruel blow. 'I never thought,' she said, 'that I should see the day when
one of my own sons betrayed his country.' Freddy [Harold's brother]
is equally indignant. 'I suppose,' he says, 'you will now resign from all
your clubs.' They live such a sheltered life, poor people, that they see
things out of proportion. But I hate hurting Mummy.

H.N. to Vita   *April 2, 1947*

I meet Emerald [Cunard] who told me that last night she had been
abusing me for joining the Labour Party ('There's that horrid Harold
...'), when Anthony Eden jumped on her. 'No,' he said, 'he was quite
right. He is a person apart and has every right to his own decisions.
He will do a world of good to the Labour Party.' Emerald, who in her
funny way, is a loyal soul, was much impressed by this.

Diary   *April 28, 1947*

... I have got to make a speech to the Westminster Labour Party on
Wednesday. I do not know what to say. My socialist convictions are
purely academic and even negative. I hope by socialism to preserve
our essential personal liberties. But I feel that I am being dragged in
to the wake of the future; not that I am in the van. The awful thought
gnaws like a rat at my conscience that I should have accepted being
out of public life and done nothing at all. I feel a decline in energy
and faith. I am in a bad mood.

I read Charles du Bos on [Benjamin] Constant.[1] When he was
young he suffered, or thought he suffered, tortures of unhappiness and
self-dispraisal. Now I when young was as happy and irresponsible as a
lark. It is in my late age that happiness has become clouded. But if
unhappiness comes to the young it gives them depth; coming at my
age it confirms my superficiality. I am haunted by mental decay such
as I saw creeping over Ramsay MacDonald. A gradual dimming of the
lights.

Diary   *May 28, 1947*

I go to Sibyl's. I come into the room to find Osbert Lancaster there
and a young man with his back to the window. He says, 'Not recognise
an old friend?' It is the Duke of Windsor. He is thin but more healthy-
looking than when I last saw him. He has lost that fried-egg look
around the eyes. He is very affable and chatty. I notice that he has
dropped calling his wife 'Her Royal Highness'; he calls her 'the
Duchess'. I notice also that people do not bow as they used to and
treat him less as a royalty than they did when he had recently been
King. He takes all this quite for granted. I have an impression that he
is happier.

The Duchess of Windsor then comes in. She also has much
improved. That taut, predatory look has gone; she has softened. I have
a talk with her alone. She says that they do not know where to live.
They would like to live in England, but that is difficult. He retains his

---

[1] The French politician and thinker, whose biography Harold was writing.

old love for Fort Belvedere. 'We are tired of wandering,' she says. 'We are not as young as we were. We want to settle down and grow our own trees. He likes gardening. But it is no fun gardening in other people's gardens.' Where can they live? They are sick of islands, otherwise they might go to the Channel Islands. They are sick of France. He likes America, but that can never be a home. He wants a job to do. 'You see,' she says, 'he was born to be a salesman. He would be an admirable representative of Rolls Royce. But an ex-King cannot start selling motor cars.' I feel really sorry for them. She was simple and sincere for the first time I have talked with her.

Diary   *June 10, 1947*

The Chinese Ambassador comes up to me and says nice things about my books. He asks me whether we in England were surprised by the long resistance put up by China. I say we were, as we had always supposed that the Chinese regarded war as an uncivilised practice, and soldiers as among the most despicable of mankind. He said that this was true, but they were fighting for their lives. 'We have,' he said, 'a problem – I mean a proverb – in our country which says, "Better to be a tile intact than a broken piece of jade."' 'That is a very good proverb,' I say. 'I shall take a note of it,' and I write it down in my notebook. 'I wonder,' I say, 'whether your Excellency could repeat that proverb in Chinese?' He then screws up his face and begins with closed eyes. Then he stops. 'No,' he says, 'I was mistaken in the problem. It is as follows: "Better to be a broken piece of jade than a tile intact."'

Diary   *July 8, 1947*

To my dentist. I then lunch at the French Embassy, where Cyril Connolly and I are invested with the Legion of Honour. We come in as usual, and the guests arrive. We hang about a bit and then [Ambassador] Massigli asks us to stand in a row. He then stands opposite us and makes an allocution. He does it very well, but I am overwhelmed by embarrassment. I feel angry with myself getting so shy about so simple an occasion. Then he motions to his staff and they advance with little medals on a tray. He then pins those on to us and gives the accolade – cheek against cheek. I hate it. Then champagne is produced and we have a *vin d'honneur* and then we lunch. I am annoyed at myself for having felt so clumsy and self-conscious.

Diary   *August 6, 1947*

We go to Ramsbury.[1] We drive in quite boldly and draw up in front of the house. Jim [Lees-Milne] had warned us that the owner, Sir Francis Burdett, was an old, fashionable gentleman who did not like tourists staring at his front door. While we are thus engaged, the door opens and out comes a stout old man with huge moustaches and a blue coat with brass buttons. Our first idea is to bolt, and in fact we do retreat a yard or two when the old man starts to run after us. We then stop, and he asks us angrily what we are doing. Vita says, 'We have made a mistake. We want to go to Littlecote.' It is quite clear that he does not believe us. An embarrassment occurs. Off we go at last, feeling uneasy and cross. The incident combined four things that I most dislike: intruding upon the privacy of others; telling lies; being scolded; being made to look foolish. Silently we drive on to Avebury.

Diary   *October 2, 1947*

To the offices of *Time*. They had, as I had asked them, consulted Winston about my doing the introductory article for his book.[2] I had told them that I would not consent to doing it unless he raised no objection. When my name was mentioned, he apparently went into a dirge about my having joined the Socialists. But he had no objection

---

[1] For ten days Harold, Vita and James Lees-Milne, the historian of architecture and Secretary of the National Trust, went on a motor-tour of southern England as far west as Cornwall. Ramsbury, not a National Trust house, was in Wiltshire, and was built for the Earl of Pembroke in the 1660s. Sir Francis Burdett was then seventy-eight.
[2] In *Life* magazine, where Churchill's history of World War Two was about to be serialised.

to my doing the article. 'Tell him,' he said, 'that I shall sue him in every court for any libel.'

Diary   *November 9, 1947*

Read [Sir] Arthur Bryant on Pepys. It is odd how the English love a man who is not a humbug like themselves. To my mind Pepys is a mean little man. Salacious in a grubby way; even in his peculations there was no magnificence. But he did stick to his office during the Plague which is more than most men did. It is some relief to reflect that to be a good diarist one must have a little snouty, sneaky mind.

Diary   *November 10, 1947*

I discussed with Vita today the problem of my allocation of time. Now that I have dropped out of public life, I do nothing of any real importance. I do my 'Marginal Comment' once a week; my *Daily Telegraph* reviews once a week; my *Figaro* once every other week; and my many broadcasts. I also have a succession of Boards and Committees.[1] I find that I seem to have less time for my own work than when I was a Member of Parliament. These small diverse occupations interfere with my timetable. I should not engage in them, of course, were it not that they are my means of living. Why, being so hard-working, have I so little free time?

When Vita says that I am cheapening myself by all these stickleback activities, I feel she is right. But I have dropped out of the main stream, and all I can do is paddle in the backwaters. I have not the strength of will, the *os*, to pull or push myself back into the stream. I knew at one moment the tide in the affairs of men, but I did not take it at the flow − I took it at the ebb. This does not mean bitterness or disappointment or even self-reproach. God knows that I am interested and happy enough. It just means a small degree of perplexity why I should not be wanted, and why, not being wanted, I have so little time

---

[1] Among others, the National Trust (of which he became Vice-Chairman), the London Library (Chairman), the National Portrait Gallery, War Memorials and the Royal Literary Fund.

for Benjamin Constant. I am not in the least ready to depart – not for one moment. But I know that I am dropping out.

Diary   *November 11, 1947*

Come back and change and then go with Viti to the Royal College of Physicians where I lecture on 'The Health of Authors'. Niggs is also there. Lord Moran takes the chair. I ask him how Winston is. He says he is not well at all and that it was madness for him with such a bad cold, to go down to the House today. 'Nothing will persuade him to take care of his health. Anyhow, I told him that in his present condition he would make the worst speech of his life.' That evening I see a chap from the Commons who tells me that Winston has made one of the most brilliant and powerful speeches he has ever made – about the House of Lords. What vitality that blessed man has got!

Diary   *December 3, 1947*

We drive in a lovely hired Daimler to Buckingham Palace. There is a party there for the Foreign Ministers Conference. . . . I am taken under the arm by Bevin [Foreign Secretary] and dragged to a seat. He is tired, having had to stand up for two long hours. He has a drink. He tells me that yesterday he had had a real heart-to-heart with Molotov in his (Bevin's) flat. He spoke as follows: 'Now, Mr Molotov, what is it that you want? What are you after? Do you want to get Austria behind your Iron Curtain? You can't do that. Do you want Turkey and the Straits? You can't have them. Do you want Korea? You can't have that. You are putting your neck out too far, and one day you will have it chopped off. We know much more about you than you imagine. We know you cannot stand a war. But you are behaving in such a way that one day there will be a showdown. And you will have to give way in the end and lose your credit with your own people. You cannot look on me as an enemy of Russia. Why, when our Government was trying to stamp out your Revolution, who was it that stopped it? It was I, Ernest Bevin. I called out the transport workers and they refused to load the ships. I wanted you to have your Revolution in your own way and without interference. Now again I am speaking as a friend. You are playing a very dangerous game. And I can't make out why. You don't really believe that any American wants to go to war with you – or, at least, no responsible American. We most certainly do not want to. But you are playing with fire, Mr Molotov, and one day you will be badly burnt. And I don't see the object of it all. If war comes between you and America in the East, then we may be able to remain neutral. But if war comes between you and America in the West, then we shall be on America's side. Make no mistake about that. That would be the end of Russia and your Revolution. So please stop sticking out your neck in this way and tell me what you are after. What do you want?'

'I want a unified Germany,' said Molotov.

'Why do you want that? Do you really believe that a unified Germany would go communist? They might pretend to. They would say all the right things and repeat all the correct formulas. But in their hearts they would be longing for the day when they could revenge their defeat at Stalingrad. You know that as well as I do.'

'Yes,' said Molotov, 'I know that. But I want a unified Germany.'

And that is all that he could get out of him.

Diary   *December 5, 1947*

Viti shows me a letter from the Prime Minister saying that she has got the CH.[1] I am overjoyed, but she takes it quite calmly. Benzie, when he arrives, has never heard of the CH and thinks it all ridiculous. Viti says it is my Civil Service mind which attaches importance to these things. But somewhere inside herself she is pleased, I think.

Harold was now invited to stand as Labour candidate in the by-election which was impending at North Croydon. He accepted, with misgivings. The seat had been held by the Conservatives with a majority of only 607. They were as determined to retain the seat as the Labour Party was to capture it. Harold hated the electioneering process, but campaigned conscientiously. He

---

[1] The Companion of Honour, the second highest decoration, after the Order of Merit, for the arts. Clement Attlee was an admirer of Vita's poem, *The Land*.

was defeated, but not ignominiously. Vita played no part in the Election. She was lecturing in North Africa.

Diary   *December 9, 1947*

Williams [Assistant National Agent of the Labour Party] rings me up from Transport House and asks whether I would take on the by-election at North Croydon. I say I must have time to think it over.

Diary   *December 11, 1947*

I am really perplexed to know what to do about this North Croydon business. I gathered from Frank Pakenham [later Earl of Longford] that he had expected my name to be on the list of those to be given a peerage in the New Year's Honours. Evidently I had been taken off the list at the last moment. Why? Is it because of Viti's CH? Or is it because Transport House said I was the chap to fight Croydon for them?

My perplexity takes two forms. One practical. If I refuse to fight this seat, then they will feel that I am not a good member of the party and I shall not be rewarded. If I fight the seat and lose honourably then all will be well. If I fight and win (which seems impossible) then it will be a tremendous triumph. But if I fight and lose badly, then I shall have missed both the lower and upper House. But my main perplexity is a moral one. If I refuse to do what they ask, I shall make it clear to my own conscience that I joined the Labour Party in order to get a peerage; and this will cause me such remorse that if offered a peerage I shall decline to accept it. I absolutely loathe fighting a by-election in circumstances of great publicity. I may make a muck of the whole thing. But the horror with which the prospect fills me is in itself an indication that I should undertake this horrible task.

[Later] But the crucial piece [of news] was at 3.15 when I went to see Williams at Transport House. I say that I will consent to meet the Local Committee on Thursday. I practically commit myself to fighting the seat if the local Committee adopt me which, I gather from Williams, they are certain to do.

Diary   *December 14, 1947*

Lord Baldwin has died. Poor old Baldwin. He was a man of little imagination and less vision, but he certainly had a gift for dealing with awkward situations as they arose. Generally his method was to evade them. But when he was forced to tackle them, as at the Abdication crisis, he did it very well. He was an agreeable, companionable man. He was really far more simple than he seemed. Or rather his simplicity appeared so naïve that many thought it was put on for effect: I do not think so. He enjoyed life and had certain excellent principles.

Diary   *December 17, 1947*

In the evening I go down to Croydon. On the platform at Victoria I meet Williams of Transport House and Frank Shepherd, their Southern Regional Organiser. They are evidently old cronies, but they have to be polite to me. The contrast between the ease and intimacy of their own relations and their joint uneasiness with me increases the sense of unreality. I feel like a cow being led garlanded to the altar, and they probably regard me as a very doubtful old horse.

We go to Cypress Road, South Norwood Hill. It is a small villa belonging to the Secretary of the local Labour Party. Mr Nicols, the Chairman, arrives. A silent man. Others drop in and sit stiffly on chairs round the room. Then a blind woman, led by a dog, enters. The dog crouches under her chair and whimpers slightly. When ten people have come in, the meeting starts. Williams explains briskly that a by-election is not like a General Election. In the latter event organisations can choose their own candidates. In by-elections Transport House has a right to recommend. He does it quite tactfully, but a woman objects. She says that they were promised that they would be given a list of candidates, and that they could choose the one they wanted. Now there is only one candidate. The Chairman ignores this interruption and calls on me to speak.

I make a short statement outlining all my disadvantages – Tom Mosley, National Labour, Churchill, my Election Address of 1945, my inability to be violent or denunciatory, my belonging to the upper class, Vita, Nigel.[1] I have the impression that they regard these things as very grave disadvantages, but are too frightened to say so. But there is one young man who has the courage to speak up. He says I am not the type they want. I am too right-wing. Would I swallow the whole of the Socialist programme? Would I agree to the nationalisation of land? I say that I would in such matters do what Cripps and Attlee decided on. If they felt it was wise to go as far as that, I would accept their decision. But I would not take an independent line and urge it against them or upon them. A vote is then taken. The woman who was angry with the Chairman, and the young man, vote against me. The others vote in favour. Result: 8 to 2. We then break up and walk back to the station.

I have a feeling that Williams and Shepherd feel that it did not go too well. The differences between me and them were all too apparent. The similarities between us were not very wide or deep or strong. We come back by train. They get out at London Bridge. I say goodnight to them with forced geniality. I do not feel that I have been a comrade.

                                                                February 25, 1948
H.N. to Vita   *Croydon*

Yesterday I had a horrible day. I had to go round with the *Daily Herald* photographer for feature pictures. Well, the first thing they wanted me to do was to visit an old Trades Unionist of 89 years of age. We drove up to his horrid little house. The old man was very ill in bed. He insisted upon getting up. He sat on the bed while the photographer dressed him. He panted terribly and I thought he was going to die. Then we sat him down in his armchair and I posed beside him. Suddenly he remembered that he had not brushed his hair and up he struggled again and poured a little oil into a tin and then dabbed the brush in it. Thereafter the photograph was taken.

Then I was dragged into a grocer's shop. A woman customer was dragged in to give more life to the group. I told her who I was. 'Oh

---

[1] Vita would play no part in the Election, or after it, if Harold won. Nigel was adopted as Conservative candidate for West Leicester, his father's old seat. In his 1945 Election address Harold had written, 'Your choice is now between a Government led by Winston Churchill and Eden, and a Government led by Attlee. I prefer Churchill.'

yes, I have often listened to you on the wireless. I should have voted for you had it not been for the Air Vice-Marshal [Bennett, Liberal candidate]. Such a raw deal that man has had – and a hero too!' So you see, I was right. Off I went again to a housing estate. The photographer in the excitement of the chase made me climb up a ladder of an unfinished house and interview the workmen doing the roof. I had to make explanatory gestures to them. Not my sort of thing at all.

	February 26, 1948
H.N. to Vita	*Croydon*

After a meeting last night a man came and entered into conversation. 'By the way,' he said, 'do your family object to your standing Labour?' 'Well, my mother said I had betrayed my country.' He was a Press Association man and all the papers this morning have been ringing Mummy up. Oh my God!

	February 29, 1948
H.N. to Vita (in Fez, Morocco)	*Croydon*

I actually enjoy canvassing, and it does good. That is one of the advantages of being Labour. I have no hesitation about penetrating into working–class homes, and they are so grateful and loyal. It really moves me. I am so glad that I belong to the Party now. I really feel much more comfortable as a Labour man than I ever did as a hybrid. There is a quality of mutual confidence which is moving and rare. It was a lovely warm day at last, and the whole thing seemed brighter and happier.

	March 4, 1948
H.N. to Vita (in Tunis)	*Croydon*

You know, this election will have done me a lot of good. It has given me self-confidence as a platform speaker and a queller of hecklers. It has improved my health, as it has forced me to give up smoking cigarettes. And, above all, it has brought me into intimate relations with the Labour movement, and made me feel at ease with them. That sense of wearing a new stiff jacket has quite gone. It is now as comfortable as an old tweed coat. They are such nice, decent people, they really are. It is a joy for me to be on their side.

March 9, 1948
H.N. to Vita   *Croydon*

This time tomorrow I shall have had my last meeting and deliver my last speech. Probably in actual fact the last election speech I shall ever, thank God, deliver. I long for that hour with sick longing. I have not really enjoyed one moment of this election. The first few days were true hell, partly because it was cold, partly because I felt ill at ease with my staff, partly because I had not discovered Ovaltine, but mainly because the election seemed to stretch in front of me as a long grey regiment of days. But now it is over and will shortly be an unpleasant memory.

H.N. to Vita [telegram to Tunis]   *March 12, 1948*

Beaten by twelve thousand. Oh my.[1]

March 12, 1948
Diary   *Croydon*

I get to bed at 4.30 a.m. and am roused by the nice maid at 7.45 a.m. I get up and go down to breakfast. The old buffers are evidently delighted. One of them who came down later said rubbing his hands, 'Well, what a result! What a triumph! Harris [the Conservative

---

[1] The result was: Harris (Conservative)   36,200
                    Nicolson (Labour)   24,536
                    Bennett (Liberal)   6,321
                    Conservative majority   11,664

candidate] has socked that cad Nicolson on the jaw!' 'Shhh!' they
answer, indicating me.

*Harold never received the peerage he had hoped for, possibly because he wrote
for the* Spectator *an article ('I was certainly not intended by nature or by
training for one of the central figures in a harlequinade') which affronted his
supporters. His consolation was that he was invited to write the official biography
of King George V, which was to remain the central occupation of his life until
its publication in 1952.*

Diary   *May 28, 1948*

I had been expecting to be offered in the Birthday Honours the
peerage which I nearly got in the New Year. But I have not had a
word from Attlee and this means, either they are giving no peerages
this birthday, or that my name is not among them. I am rather relieved
really as I have *Benjamin Constant* to finish in the latter part of this year,
and if they reform the House of Lords they are certain to make me a
life-peer. I should prefer that in many ways. But I am amused to find
in myself a fat grub of snobbishness. I have always hated the name
'Nicolson' as being a common plebeian name. I don't mind it for
myself, since 'Harold Nicolson' is familiar and all right. But I hate it
for Viti. Thus if I were made a real peer, I could change it to Cranfield.
But if a life-peer, I could not change my name and 'Lord Nicolson',
and even more so, 'Lady Nicolson' would sound absurd. Now really
at my age I ought not to mind such things. And yet I am conscious of
that grub or slug inside me. How little one knows oneself, even when
one probes and pokes and is amused.

H.N. to Vita   *June 8, 1948*

This letter is about the 'proposition' made to me yesterday by Tommy
[Sir Alan] Lascelles [the King's Private Secretary]. I walked across the
park to Buckingham Palace and entered by the side-door. I was at
once taken to Tommy's room. He said the King had often spoken to

him during the war about the need for an official life of George V. They had put it off from year to year. Then a few months ago the King had returned to the subject and said how important it was that this life should be written before Tommy and Owen Morshed [the Librarian at Windsor Castle] died. Tommy had therefore taken the opinion of five distinguished figures, and three of these five suggested me. He therefore told the King and the King said, 'What do you feel yourself, Tommy?' And Tommy of course said that he would not have wished to put forward the name of an old personal friend, but that he agreed with the three elder statesmen. Then the Queen also agreed and Tommy was delegated to approach me.

At that stage I asked whether Queen Mary had given her assent. He said she had not been consulted. I said I could not even consider the proposal unless she gave her consent. He said, 'Very well, we shall ask her. If she objects, then we shall have to persuade her.'

I then said that in principle I did not like writing biographies when I could not tell the whole truth. Tommy said – well I thought – 'But it is not meant to be an ordinary biography. It is something quite different. You will be writing a book on the subject of a myth and will have to be mythological.' He said that I should not be expected to say one word that was not true. I should not be expected to praise or exaggerate. All that I should be expected to do was to omit things and incidents which were discreditable. I could say as much in the preface if it eased my mind.

The idea was that I should be shown every scrap of paper that existed. I should have a table of my own in the library at Windsor and go down there three days a week. I should stay in Tommy's house if I wished to spend the night. Owen Morshead would help me. There was no hurry about the book – I could take four years if I liked.

I asked what about finance? He said that the King would not pay me anything at all, and that I should receive nothing from him even to meet secretarial expenses. All the King would do was to give me a table to work at, a cupboard to keep my papers in, and a free run of his archives. It was for me to make such arrangements as I could with my publishers.

Now what do you think? I see the balance-sheet as follows: *Advantages*: A definite task taking me three years at least and bringing a large financial reward. Access to papers of deep interest and importance.

Close collaboration with charming people such as Morshead and Tommy. The opportunity of writing the history of my own times. Added to all of which I suppose is the compliment at having been chosen. *Disadvantages*: To have to write an 'official' biography. The lack of charm in the King with whom I am dealing. My inability (and indeed my unwillingness) to poke fun at the monarchy. My not being allowed to mention discreditable or foolish things. My having to be mythological.

I told Elvira as she knew I had got an appointment with Tommy. She was delighted and as usual most intelligent. She said, 'But it is just what you need — an anchor. It will keep you busy for three years and prevent you doing silly things like Croydon. People say that young men need anchors. That may be true — but people of later middle-age need anchors far more than the young.' All of which, in a way, is true.

H.N. to Vita   *June 9, 1948*

I write to Tommy and say 'Yes'. I shall not regret it.

Diary   *June 12, 1948*

Niggs says that my highbrow friends will think it wrong of me to write a book on a subject when I have to indulge in suppressions of the truth. What will interest people is to know exactly how far the King exercised his authority. If I hedge over that, the book will be valueless. If I tell what may be the truth, then what I say will be used against the monarchy by left-wing agitators. In fact, I get discouragement from my family all round. What a beautiful rose-scented day it is, all the same!

Diary   *July 16, 1948*

Two distressing things have happened. The Americans are sending squadrons of Flying Fortresses to land in East Anglia. And the Russians

have stated that they will be carrying out the training of their fighter
aeroplanes across our corridors to Berlin. This is very dangerous, since
it increases the prestige battle and may lead to accidents.[1] The City is
getting panicky. Yet I cannot seriously believe that war is possible. It is
so different from previous wars and rumours of wars. It seems to be
the final conflict for the mastery of the world. The prizes are so
enormous; the losses so terrible. It is so easy to criticise; to blame
Winston and Roosevelt for Yalta; to blame Bevin for having allowed
this untenable Berlin position to consolidate itself. But, as always, these
things are governed, not by mistakes or intentions, but by the dreadful
chain of circumstance.

The Barbarians are at the gate.

Diary   *July 22, 1948*

I go to Buckingham Palace for the Garden Party. I have a talk with
Anthony Eden. He tells me that in his long experience he has never
known such enthusiasm as he had during his visit to Berlin [at the start
of the blockade]. There were crowds when he came out of the lecture
hall, and they yelled and cheered. He was embarrassed, first because
he does not like Germans, and secondly because he realised that it was
an anti-Russian demonstration.

Nancy Astor is there and comes up to me in a crowd and says loudly,
'The man who sold his soul.' I ask why? She says because I joined the
Labour Party in order to get the Embassy in Paris. I say (a) I hate
Embassies and left the service in order to avoid one; (b) that Vita would
never have enjoyed an Embassy and that this in itself would have made
it impossible. She says, 'Yes, you are right. I never thought of that.'
Then the other side of her comes out and she is charming. I really
love that woman and admire her – but what enemies she must make
among people who only see her silly sallies.

---

[1] Following a dispute over currency reform, the Russians blockaded the western sectors
of Berlin, cutting off Germans and Allies alike from supplies of food, light and fuel.
The Allies thereupon undertook to supply West Berlin entirely by air, and did so
until May 1949.

H.N. to Vita   *September 9, 1948*

Poor Benjamin [Constant] was finished off today and this afternoon
he goes to Constable. I feel quite sorry to say goodbye to him and to
replace that gay companionship by such an old Thames pilot man. It
will be fun being 'In search of George' – but it will be hell writing the
thing. I quite see that the Royal Family feel their myth is a piece of
gossamer and must not be blown upon. So George VI will cut out all
the jokes about George V.

*On September 25 Harold flew to Berlin to deliver four lectures at the request
of the Foreign Office. It was a gesture of British solidarity with the Berliners
during the Russian blockade.*

                                                        September 26, 1948
H.N. to Vita   *Savoy Hotel, Berlin*

Well this is tormentingly interesting but more horrible than anything
you can conceive. A deep unhappy helplessness seems to brood over
these ruins. My main impression so far is one of utter bewilderment.
I have never felt quite so *stupid* in my life. Everything contributes to
this. My cold (which is pursuing a normal course), the fact that I have
forgotten my German, the fact that Hitler changed the monuments
from one place to another, so that my sense of direction is completely
misled, the fact that every now and then I recognise things for a second
and that they then fade away into oblivion.

They picked me up for dinner and drove me out to a large villa in
the Grünewald where there is a Press Club. They made me an honorary
Member. It is pretty bleak I assure you. Only one bulb in the chandelier
allowed to be on and of course no heating. The food was all British
rations – not badly cooked. But there is a sense of living in a dugout.

It is far far worse than I expected. But it may be the shock of first
impressions. It is like a moon landscape across which figures flit.
Everything is almost unrecognisable. But what a deeply unsettling
experience and how glad I am I came.

H.N. to Vita   *October 26, 1948*

How cold and lovely it was this morning. I walked about the platform of Staplehurst Station (since my train was late owing to coastal fog) and watched the leaves turning and thought how much nature had meant to me in life. Sissinghurst has a quality of mellowness, of retirement, of unflaunting dignity which is just what we wanted to achieve and in some ways have achieved by chance. I think it is mainly due to the succession of privacies: the forecourt, the first arch, the main court, the tower arch, the lawn, the orchard. A series of escapes from the world giving a progression of cumulative escape.

Diary   *November 29, 1948*

Vita and I discuss after dinner whether Bertie Russell was right in stating that we should make war on Russia while we have the atomic bomb and they have not. It is a difficult problem. I think it is probably true that Russia is preparing for the final battle for world mastery and that once she has enough bombs she will destroy Western Europe, occupy Asia and have a final death struggle with the Americas. If that happens and we are wiped out over here, the survivors in New Zealand may say that we were mad not to have prevented this while there was still time. Yet, if the decision rested with me, I think I should argue as follows: 'It may be true that we shall be wiped out, and that we could prevent this by provoking a war with Russia at this stage. It may be true that such a war would be successful and that we should then establish some centuries of Pax Americana – an admirable thing to establish. But there remains a doubt about all this. There is a chance that the danger may pass and peace can be secured by peace. I admit it is a frail chance – not one in ninety. To make war in defiance of that one chance is to commit a crime. Better to be wiped out by the crime of others than to preserve ourselves by committing a deliberate crime of our own. A preventive war is always evil. Let us rather die'. And the New Zealander would say, 'The man was mad – or cowardly, or stupid, or just weak.'

Diary   *December 1, 1948*

V. and I come up in the fog. Our train is more than two hours late. I lunch with Willy Maugham at the Dorchester. We discuss, among other things, how it is that Cyril Connolly has managed to impose his personality upon his contemporaries. With scarcely any work at all he has managed to render himself an important literary figure. Willy says it is by sheer self-assurance. I say that Cyril is the natural parasite – he prospers on the labours of others.

Diary   *December 31, 1948*

For me it has in some ways been a bad year. My Croydon venture was a misfortune. It shocked my Tory friends and it left upon the Labour people the impression that my heart was not in it. The peerage which I so nearly got last year has now, it seems, eluded me. Nor am I feeling any younger. My deafness has increased slightly. My political career (which was never very brilliant in any case) is now closed forever. That is one of the worst things about getting old. One ceases to believe the miraculous can ever happen.

But it is now evident that I have not been a successful man but a failure; and this owing to lack of courage.

H.N. to Vita   *January 7, 1949*

My visit there [to Windsor] was a great success. I met Owen Morshead who first showed me the [King's] diaries. They are really little more than engagement books and not at all revealing. But they are invaluable for checking dates, etc. There are also those extracts from Queen Victoria's diary which Princess Beatrice preserved. She burnt all the rest. Wicked old woman. Morshead tells me he does not think the King or the Queen or even Queen Mary will be difficult so long as I do not attack the principle of monarchy. (Which I assuredly have no intention of doing.) But he fears that all the old aunts will descend upon them and bully them. He says that the difficult thing to treat will be his handling of his children. 'The House of Hanover, like ducks, produce bad parents – they trample on their young.'

Diary   *January 20, 1949*

Nigel has got his friend [Jim] Rose of the *Observer* to offer me a weekly article of 800 words on one book chosen by myself. This would mean leaving the *Telegraph* and I should gain having to read only one and not two books a week. Moreover it is quite evident that the *Daily Telegraph* public is not one worth writing literary articles for.

Diary   *March 15, 1949*

. . . I go to the [Army & Navy] Stores to get them to make into a suit the tweed that Nigel gave me. I say I want it double-breasted. The man is deeply shocked. 'Surely not, sir; not in the country.' I say I don't care a hoot and it must be double-breasted. 'It will give you a Continental look, sir.' 'That is what I require. I have always wanted to be mistaken for an Austrian count.'

Diary   *March 21, 1949*

I go to see Queen Mary at Marlborough House. She seems smaller than I expected, has her back to the light, and I first took her for a lady-in-waiting. But I quickly recovered myself and we sat side by side. She asked me whether I wished to put any questions to her. I said that in the course of my reading there would evidently be many things that puzzled me, but that for the moment there were very few things about which I was uncertain. For one thing, I found I had taken likes and dislikes as always happened when one steeped oneself in the life of an individual. I had acquired a great liking for Queen Olga of Greece [the King's aunt]. 'Quite right too,' she said. 'The Queen was a second mother to him.' Similarly I had taken a great dislike to Canon Dalton [tutor to Prince George in 1871]. She was surprised by this at first.

'The King was very fond of him,' she said ruminatively. I said that I did not like the way he had written letters complaining of the naval officers and not allowed the Princes to consort with their fellow-midshipmen. She had never heard of his sneaking about the naval officers, which was wrong. The segregation of the Princes was even more wrong. But what she had against Dalton was that he never tried really to educate the Princes. It was disgraceful that 'the King' had not been taught more. I asked her whether he could speak French really well. She did not quite like that question. 'No,' she said rather stiffly.

The King was by nature an immensely loyal man. He loved his old friends and servants. He was also extraordinarily truthful in that he never liked 'going round and round', and at this she made a circular movement with her fingers.

She then turned to the question of his relations with his sons. She said that the real difficulty had been with the Duke of Windsor and never with 'the present King', who always got on well with his father. I said that I had heard that he was good to the children when they were young; and good to them once they married; but that when they were young bachelors he was so terrified that they might fall into bad company that he nagged at them. She said this was true.

She added that 'the present King' had been appalled when he succeeded. 'He was devoted to his brother and the whole abdication crisis made him miserable. He sobbed on my shoulder for a whole hour – there, upon that sofa. But he had made good. Even his stammer had been corrected. And now he is so ill, poor boy, so ill.' This in such a sad voice.

Diary   *April 17, 1949*

After tea, a great event happens. I actually begin writing *George V.* I am starting on the chapter dealing with the 1931 crisis as I want to have that chapter checked by people while still in the possession of their faculties. I do not get very far, but at least I have made a start.

After sunset I climb up the tower to pull down the flag. There is a great red glow in the west and the whole of Kent lies below me bathed in golden light. The garden looks so rich from the eminence; masses of blossom and daffodils among the dark of the yews. It truly is a most beautiful garden – so varied, so calm, so enclosed. It is a garden I should envy much if it belonged to someone else.

Diary   *April 27, 1949*

The Prime Ministers of the Dominions plus Attlee plus Nehru go to see the King this afternoon and inform him that India wishes to be both a Republic and a member of the Commonwealth. They have drawn up a formula in which, with a smile of bland self-satisfaction, they make a wholly illogical, meaningless, self-contradictory but admirable statement. India refuses to recognise the King in so far as India is concerned, but does recognise him as Head of the Commonwealth and 'symbol of the free association of its independent member States'. Of course all this makes utter nonsense and will make the French smile. Of course it will arouse in the British that particularly irritating form of self-applause: 'Only we could be quite so illogical as that.' But in fact it is a fine piece of good sense and will enhance Attlee's already growing prestige. People are ceasing to think of him as 'a dear little man'. They realise that he has vision and courage and integrity so compelling that it is a force in itself.

Diary   *June 10, 1949*

National Trust all day. We are getting more and more evidence that the present Government (or rather their supporters) do not like the Trust because it is managed by aristocrats working on a 'voluntary' basis. One of the things I do not like about Socialists is their distrust of gratuitous public service. A man like [Lord] Esher, for instance, devotes his whole life to the furtherance and protection of the arts. But as he gives his services free, he is regarded with some suspicion by the doctrinaires.

Diary   *July 17, 1949*

I start writing the first chapter of my book on George V. I begin 'Prince George was born at Marlborough House, London, at 1.30 a.m. on the morning of June 3, 1865.' I gaze at the sentence in wonder, realising what a long journey I have to go before I reach his death. It is like starting in a taxi on the way to Vladivostok.

H.N. to Vita   *August 17, 1949*

I fear I am getting rather down on George V just now. He is all right as a gay young midshipman. He may be all right as a wise old King. But the intervening period when he was Duke of York, just shooting at Sandringham, is hard to manage or swallow. For seventeen years in fact he did nothing at all but kill animals and stick in stamps.

Diary   *September 7, 1949*

T.S. Eliot is so modest and charming. He is off to lecture in Germany. He asked me whether they would expect a 'message'. I said the only thing to do was to treat them as ordinary members of a cultured society, much as one would treat a dipsomaniac. 'Thank you,' he says. 'I shall do that.'

I go to the British Museum, where they had ready for me the novel *Wrong on Both Sides* [by Vin Vincent, 1885] which made King George cry so frequently. It has no literary merit whatever, being written in the *Little Lord Fauntleroy* style. The theme is that of a proud and harsh old Earl who snubs and bullies the beautiful young Viscount, his son, but loves him deeply underneath. Interesting psychologically.

I dine with the Hamish Hamiltons to meet Judge Learned Hand [of the United States Circuit Court]. The Judge, who is a dear, denies that there are any absolutes in life. I say that untruthfulness and cruelty are always wrong anywhere and in any circumstances. He shakes his fine head.

Diary   *September 24, 1949*

We are all feeling depressed about the Russian atomic bomb. We were
told they would not have one for five years and they had got it in four.
Does this really make so much difference? It may encourage the
satellites to be more overweening, but it may also encourage Russia to
be a little less nervous.

Diary   *October 4, 1949*

I spend the morning visiting York Cottage, the nest, the dairy, the
gardens and the big house [at Sandringham]. There is nothing to
differentiate the cottage from any of the villas at Surbiton. How right
the Duke of Windsor was to say to me, 'Until you have seen York
Cottage you will never understand my father.' It is almost incredible
that this heir to so vast a heritage lived in this horrible little house for
33 years. It is now partly estate office and partly flats. But it is still
untenanted in the upper floors and we went all over it. The King and
Queen's baths had lids that shut down so that when not in use they
could be used as tables. His study was a monstrous little cold room
with a north window shrouded by shrubberies, and the walls are
covered in red cloth which he had been given while on a visit to Paris.
It is the cloth from which the trousers of the French private soldiers
used to be made. On the walls he had some reproductions of Royal
Academy pictures. The servants' rooms are mere attics with skylights.
There is no garden.

Diary   *December 31, 1949*

Just before midnight I go out and walk in the spring garden. There is
a bright moon. I hear the clock strike midnight and say 'rabbits'
between the sixth and seventh stroke. When it is finished there is a
hush over the world, and only a light in my own sitting-room. Then
the bells of Frittenden ring out over the moon-drenched land. I walk
in again. I close the door and go to bed. That is the end of 1949.
    I am conscious that during this year I have become much older

[sixty-three]. I do not think that my deafness has seriously increased, nor are my limbs much less supple than they were in 1948. But I have put on weight and lost many teeth and much hair, and perhaps vigour. I am not really conscious of a decline in my mental energy. But I have intimations that my thoughts move in the old grooves and do not push into new grooves, and that my ways of expression are becoming stereotyped. It is not a good period of history in which to grow old. Money difficulties arise. I have to go on slogging away at articles and broadcasts in order to maintain my income. I cannot save; and when my mind decays, how will I live? How? How? How? I do not want to become an *achthos aroures* [Homer's *Iliad*: 'A burden on the earth']. Or a burden upon my sons. Nor am I temperamentally suited to old age. I have no liking for dignity, sobriety, repute and authority. I do not want to be reverenced. I suffer from the sad defects of every epicurean. But I have at least the honesty to remain convinced that the epicurean is the only philosophy, if rightly understood as the art of life. Which implies a certain degree of virtue.

Anyhow, goodbye to 1949, and thank you for not having been worse.

Diary   *January 17, 1950*

Down to Windsor. I lunch with Owen Morshead. I suggested that there might come a moment when my conscience as a biographer became strained. What would happen if I found something which was really damaging to the King – for instance, a threat to abdicate if the Home Rule Bill were passed? My duty to the student would be to publish this; but if they asked me to cut it out? Could I resign my task? Owen said rather primly, 'Your first duty will always be to the Monarchy.' At which all the contrariness in me surged up in a wave of sudden Republicanism. I fear I have no mystic feeling about the Monarchy; I regard it merely as a useful institution.

H.N. to Vita *January 25, 1950*

I dined with Guy Burgess.[1] Oh my dear, what a sad, sad thing this constant drinking is! Guy used to have one of the most rapid and acute minds I knew. Now he is just an imitation (and a pretty bad one) of what he once was. Not that he was actually drunk yesterday. He was just soaked and silly. I felt angry about it.

Diary *February 2, 1950*

If I say the King has no power at all he may be hurt and say he is a mere cypher. But if I indicate that in any circumstances he can dissent from the advice of Ministers, then assuredly the radical Press would claim that the Crown was too powerful.

H.N. to Vita *March 9, 1950*

I got into my huge Daimler and drove to the Travellers where I picked up Raymond [Mortimer] and Clive [Bell] and James [Pope-Hennessy]. In high spirits we went on to the French Embassy [for a reception for M. Vincent Auriol, President of the French Republic]. James and I went to the buffet and had foie gras sandwiches and champagne. There were masses of people there and James and I and Clive stood at the back and watched while the King and Queen came round and did *cercle*. It was amusing to see how some people edged themselves into the front row. Then the King and Queen retired to their own supper-room and we all started talking to friends. While thus engaged a *maître de cérémonie* came to me and said the President wanted to talk to me. *Grand ami de la France*. So I was dragged through the two crowded salons into the ultimate Royal (so Royal) supper-room and presented to Auriol. He is a sweet and speaks with a strong accent – not exactly méridional but regional. He said how sorry he was that I no longer wrote for the *Figaro*. But I evaded that subject as I do not really want

---

[1] He was then working in the Far Eastern Department of the Foreign Office, and was to join the staff of the Washington Embassy later in the year. He was recalled from Washington because he behaved badly, and defected to Russia in May 1951.

to start writing for it again. Well, after an exchange of civilities, I shook hands and was about to join the common herd when I heard a voice say, 'Just the man I want to see.' It was the King. He talked to me for about 20 minutes about the book. From time to time [René] Massigli came up to interrupt, but the King ignored him. In the end he said, 'I seem to be neglecting my duties. I should like to talk for hours about this. You must come and stay at Windsor.' I had been so interested in our conversation, that I had not noticed that there were only about twelve people in the room – the Kings and Queens and Presidents and so on. So I bowed my bow and then talked to the Queen and to Princess Elizabeth, and then rejoined the proletariat.

But no – I was seized by the arm and this was Winston. 'So you did not stand for your party – cowardice or conversion?' I said that I had not stood because Niggs was standing. 'Oh yes,' he said, 'Birmingham, wasn't it?' I said, 'Leicester.' He said, 'Well, I knew it was a hopeless seat – beastly place, Leicester.'[1] He then asked what the King had been talking to me about for all that time. I said it was the book. He said, 'Oh yes, I remember. I want to talk to you about that. I have much information, very much information. Clemmie, remember to ask Harold for lunch one day.' At that moment Attlee passed. 'Well, Attlee,' Winston said, 'if we have many more parties like this, we shall be in a coalition together without noticing it at all.' Then I went away. But doesn't it sound like something one has made up in one's bath. Anyhow, you must get an evening dress. Even off the peg.[2]

Diary   *June 15, 1950*

I am horrified by the Labour Manifesto [refusing to join the European Community]. It will do immense harm abroad and shake any authority which we have left. It is a truly deplorable document. It means that Dalton, who sponsored it, cannot possibly succeed Bevin. I am deeply distressed by it. How I wish I had not been such an impulsive fool as to join the Labour Party. It was certainly the cardinal error of my life. But I cannot redeem it now.

---

[1] Churchill stood unsuccessfully for Leicester in 1923.
[2] Vita's last evening dress was bought in 1927. She had been invited to this party but refused, with the excuse that she had nothing suitable to wear.

H.N. to Vita *July 25, 1950*

I know you are right in thinking that I should make my book less documentary and more alive. I shall certainly try at later stages to introduce more vivid pictures of people and places. It may be that I have been so preoccupied with rendering the style and tone of the book of an equable surface (like linen) that I have refrained too austerely from any brocade. But I am sure that in a book of that length it would be a mistake to try and be 'bright'. One has just got to be intelligent.

Diary *July 28, 1950*

The state of public opinion after Winston's grim speech regarding the armed might of Russia is one of paralysed shock. The dreadful thing is that we can do nothing and that we know nothing. Nobody has any idea what is in the heads of those twelve men in the Kremlin. We are in a condition of blind and dumb dread.

September 23, 1950
Diary *Florence*

A glorious hot day. At 4.30 we are picked up by the Berensons' chauffeur and driven all the way up to Vallombrosa where we stay the night. We are received by Nicky [Mariano, Berenson's secretary] and walk out to see the sunset where we find B.B. and Luisa [Vertova, Berenson's assistant librarian, who later married Ben Nicolson]. They tell us they have received a telegram saying that Sibyl [Colefax] died in her sleep yesterday at 6.30 in the morning. We are shocked. At dinner B.B. is the gracious host. He talks well. He tells us about Rilke. 'He must have been a very small man,' said Vita. 'Small?' said B.B. 'Not in the least. He was my size. But I suppose you would call me small.' He is neat and tidy but only about 5ft 3. B.B. does not care for the moderns. He deplores Ben wasting his energies on the *Burlington*. He says that all the pioneer work of art criticism has been done long ago and that only finicky subjects remain. He says that there are so few English art historians that Ben is obliged to fall back upon foreigners, whose style is heavy and dull. He has a great belief in Ben. 'There is,' he says, 'something very important at the bottom of that well.'

Diary   *December 11, 1950*

At 11.45 a.m. Jim Lees-Milne picks me up with Jack Rathbone [Secretary of the National Trust] and we go down to Hertfordshire to see Bernard Shaw's house which he left to the Trust. We first go into the garden. A sloping lawn and rough grass intersected with a few rose-beds. A bank, with a statue of St Joan. A hut in which he worked. Everything as he left it. Postcards, envelopes, a calendar marking the day of his death [November 2, 1950], curiously enough a Bible and prayer book and Crockford's Directory, a pair of mittens. The grass path and the bed around the statue of St Joan are still strewn with his ashes and those of Mrs Shaw [who died in 1943]. The Trustees and the doctor got both urns and put them on the dining-room table. They then emptied the one into the other and stirred them with a kitchen spoon. They then went out into the garden and emptied spoonfuls of the mixture on to the flower-beds and paths. All this some fifteen days ago, but the remains are still there. Just like the stuff Viti puts down for slugs.

The house is dreadful and not really lettable. It will, moreover, be difficult to show to tourists as it is so small. It will be essential to keep the furniture exactly as it is and we shall have to send down a photographer. All his hats and coats and nailbrushes etc. are there. His long woollen stockings and his thick underclothes. The pictures, apart from one of Samuel Butler and two of Stalin and one of Gandhi, are exclusively of himself. Even the door-knocker is an image of himself.

Diary   *December 13, 1950*

Historic Buildings. We decide that we must accept Shaw's house morally and leave the discussion of finances to the Finance Committee on Friday. I am not happy about it. I do not think Shaw will be a great literary figure in 2000 AD. He is an amazingly brilliant contemporary; not in the Hardy class.

Diary   *December 31, 1950*

So ends a horrible year with worse to come. I fear that the discomfiture of UNO in Korea is a bad portent. It indicates that although these international organisations can cope with small opposition, they become hesitant when the opposition is serious. We are all oppressed by a terrible sense of weakness and foreboding. We cannot count for one moment on France, Italy or Germany, and even the United States is afflicted with cold feet, taking the form of Hoover isolationism. The year closes in a mist of anxiety. We shall be lucky if we get through 1951 without a war.

How futile all my heavy work on George V seems in comparison to these gigantic ordeals and menaces! More and more do I cling, in almost desperate affection, to Viti, Ben, Nigel and my work and garden.

It is sad to become old amid such darkness.

Diary   *January 24, 1951*

I dine at Broadcasting House with Bertrand Russell and Lord Samuel, and afterwards we have a discussion upon 'Why defend liberty?' Russell makes some good points. He says that the reason why communists are so zealous in pursuit of their own ideal is because they are a minority and because they are not quite positive it is true. Russell himself came to the conclusion that Marx's theory of values was bunk as early as 1895. He cannot conceive how any intelligent young man can be taken in by it. As for zeal – nobody has any zeal about arithmetic. It is not the vaccinationists but the anti-vaccinationists who generate zeal. Zeal is a bad mark for a cause.

H.N. to Vita   *January 25, 1951*

I sent to Tommy Lascelles the piece I had done on the relations between King George and his children. I had put in everything I wanted to say, and expected him to cut something out. I did not want to submit to Queen Mary and the present King anything that would

Harold Nicolson broadcasting with Bertrand Russell (left) and Lord Samuel
in 1951

certainly be rejected, and thought that Tommy with his knowledge of
the Royal mind could tell me what to modify and what would cause
pain. But he telephoned to say there was nothing that he thought I
ought to alter. They may be stung by it, but then that was just too bad.
He also said that he had had a talk at Sandringham with Queen Mary
and that she had spoken very highly of my book. 'You may be sure,'
he said, 'that you have her solidly on your side.' Good.

Diary   *February 8, 1951*

Tommy Lascelles says that the present King never tells him actually
what happened at interviews. The late King always sent for Stamfordham after he had seen a Minister and told him exactly what
happened. Stamfordham then went off and wrote it down and sent his
memorandum to the King to approve. The present King just says to

Tommy, 'Oh, he was optimistic as usual' or 'He was worried about the coal situation' and never goes into detail. Therefore if George VI's life is ever written there will be no material at all.

Diary   *March 12, 1951*

I go round to see Mummy. She is half-conscious, but only recognises me when I shout at her, 'I am Harold.' She smiles so affectionately and murmurs, 'My darling, darling Harold.'

Diary   *March 23, 1951*

Good Friday. Gwen telephones at 7.50 a.m. to say the nurse says Mummy is dying and we better get round there soon. We have a hurried breakfast and walk to Tedworth Square. When we get there we are told she is just dead. She died at 8.10.[1]

Diary   *May 4, 1951*

I go to Waterloo and meet Viti. We then enter the South Bank Exhibition [the central feature of the Festival of Britain]. We are entranced from the first moment. It is rather a bore as we keep getting caught by the King and Queen, but nonetheless we enjoy it uproariously. It is the most intelligent exhibition I have ever visited. I have never seen people so cheered up or so amused, in spite of a fine drizzle of rain and a Scotch mist.

Diary   *June 7, 1951*

Owen Morshead tells me the story of George III's ghost. The King had been shut up in the bachelor flat at Windsor which is now the library. The only thing of which he was conscious (except Handel) was the stamp of the guard on the terrace. He would always toddle to

---

[1] Lady Carnock was ninety.

the window, salute, and the ensign in charge of the guard would cry, 'Eyes right!' A week after his death, there the King still was. The ensign hesitated what to do, and then called 'Eyes right!' The spectre saluted. Owen Morshead asked George V whether this was correct. 'Perfectly,' the King answered, 'I was told of it by the ensign in question.' Now, this is not impossible. Supposing the ensign was born in 1800, the episode took place in 1820, and the ensign could have told the King in about 1884.

I come back to Neville Terrace and am horrified to read headlines in the evening papers that Donald Maclean [head of the American department in the Foreign Office] and Guy Burgess [of the Far Eastern department] have absconded. If I thought that Guy was a brave man, I should imagine that he had gone to join the Communists. As I know him to be a coward, I suppose that he was suspected of passing things on to the Bolshies, and realising his guilt, did a bunk. During my dreams, his absurd face stares at me with drunken, unseeing eyes.

| | *July 3, 1951* |
| *H.N. to Vita* | *10 Neville Terrace, S.W. 7* |

It was not at all nice leaving our garden on so lovely a day, and when it is blazing in all its calm beauty. I agree with you that we have certainly created something of great loveliness, and that all the trouble you have taken has had its reward. We must go on and on. The garden today is a thing of exceptional merit; but we must make it one of the loveliest in all England. The bones are there and much of the flesh. Now we must attach rare cosmetics, lovely clothes and unusual jewellery. I never have any fear that you will commit an error of taste. I believe that you will be ruthless enough to remove anything that does not look well or do well (Paulownia? Catalpa?). In any case, it is a great work upon which we are engaged, and a solace for our senility.

| *Diary* | *August 29, 1951* |

A busy and useful day. In the morning I go to the BBC and go through King George's broadcasts. His voice is so like the present King's. Very virile, rather bronchial, very emphatic. I notice the closed 'o' as in 'those'; it is what the BBC call 'off white' meaning thereby slightly cockney. I then go to the London Library and look up the actual texts of what I have just heard. I then go, after a quick luncheon, to St James' Theatre where I meet Viti and we see Olivier and Vivien Leigh in *Antony and Cleopatra*. The minor parts are very poorly played; the production excellent; Larry and Vivien good – she beautiful to look at, but not grand enough for so superb a part.

Diary   *September 19, 1951*

This morning at 1.20 p.m. I finish the last word of Chapter XXX and thus my life of King George V. I was first asked to do the book on June 7, 1948, but at that time I was finishing *Benjamin Constant* and did not get down to it till September. It has thus taken me roughly three years. I have enjoyed it immensely. It has been a most congenial task.

After tea I start on my 'Author's Note'. There are the genealogical trees to do, and the index and the illustrations and the proof revisions. But the main battle is over. I am satisfied. It was hard, hard work, but I think the result is pretty solid. I have a Gibbon feel.

Diary   *October 25, 1951*

We have a meeting of the sub-committee of the London Library to consider who is to be President. We decide to separate the posts of President and Chairman and to choose for the latter, not a man of eminence, but a man who will attend meetings. They therefore choose me.

Diary   *November 15, 1951*

In the evening I take the chair at a BBC Forum on the theme 'Are cliques necessary?' I have Bob Boothby and Kingsley Martin, and we have a good discussion. I speak about the Souls, Kingsley about

Bloomsbury and Bob about Cliveden and Sibyl. We say that the disappearance of Society means that young men have no opportunity of meeting great men of their age.

Bob had been to see Winston this afternoon. He says he is getting 'very, very old; tragically old'. Winston wants him to lead the British Delegation to the discussions on United Europe. If he does well at this, he may get a job. 'I would have you know', said Winston, 'what a deep concern I take in your career.' Bob was pleased but not convinced.

H.N. to Vita   *December 5, 1951*

I went to a party for [Konrad] Adenauer [the German Chancellor]. He is looking well and young. He said that I had given him *viele freudige Stunden* [many happy hours] by *Public Faces*. It is always a matter of sadness to me that the books I take long to write never seem to attract anyone, whereas the ones I write in ten days or so seem to acquire fame immortal.

H.N. to Vita   *December 11, 1951*

Do you know how much *Life* offer me for my article on Alexander the Great? They offer me 2,000 dollars which amounts to over £600. Now that is more than I shall probably make over *George V.* Three years' work compared to a fortnight's work. But I know it is not a logical point of view. I mean it is rather like Whistler when asked whether he felt justified in charging 100 guineas for a sketch that had taken him two hours to make replied, 'Not two hours – a lifetime.' Which is true in a way.

Diary   *December 29, 1951*

I have my bath at 7.30 and am out of it by 7.50. Then I hear Viti running up the stairs and banging on the door. 'Nigel has been adopted!' she shouts. I open the door and she is all excited. He had just telephoned. How miraculous![1]

Diary   *January 2, 1952*

Horrible income tax demands and letters from my bank about overdraft. I am going to get into debt and have nothing to fall back on. I simply cannot work any harder than I do and it means that I shall have to cut down all my expenses. My financial position has always been precarious, mainly because I have no responsibilities other than for myself.

Diary   *January 11, 1952*

I get a letter from Tommy saying the King has no comments to make on Part IV so the thing goes off today to Constable's. FINISHED.

                                                             February 6, 1952
Diary   *Bournemouth*

[By-election day] It is about 11.20 in the morning. We draw up at the Central Committee Room to find Cowley [Tory agent] waiting on the pavement with an expression of solemn anxiety. 'Something terrible has happened,' he says. 'The King is dead.' We are stunned, but almost at once we relate this national misfortune to the question of Polling Day at Bournemouth on this sixth of February 1952. Will the Conservative voters be too shocked to indulge in anything so mundane as voting? Will they jump to the conclusion that the Election is cancelled? How are we to let them know? Obviously all loudspeakers must be withdrawn from the streets. But the Labour people will have their voters gathered together in the workshops and they will vote in strength. Supposing no Tory voters come at all? Then Labour will win. In the shock of the moment these nightmares loom as large as

---

[1] Nigel was chosen as Conservative candidate for the by-election at Bournemouth East and Christchurch.

the huge photographs of Nigel [on the hoardings]. He himself gets a little white. Viti suggests aptly that we should get on to the BBC and persuade them to put out on the 1 o'clock news that the poll is still on.

I have to go back by the 12.40 train. Viti remains behind. At 7 I go to the Travellers. By that time I am convinced that Nigel will lose the seat. I pace the corridors of the Travellers up and down, waiting for a telephone call. It comes at 7.30. Niggs' voice. 'It's not as bad as we feared. They started voting again after 3. About 60% of those who voted last time.' I am much relieved.

Princess Elizabeth is flying back from Kenya. She became Queen while in a perch in a tree in Africa, watching the rhinoceros come down to the pool to drink.

Diary   *February 19, 1952*

Tommy says that there will be no Coronation this year. 'Can't have Coronations,' said Winston [once again Prime Minister], 'with the bailiffs in the house.' I get back about 11 p.m. and Niggs comes in at 11.30. He had enjoyed this the first of I hope thousands of days in the House of Commons. I go on working at my proofs till 1.30 a.m. and finish them. Bed at 2.

Diary   *April 24, 1952*

In the afternoon I have a discussion on the wireless with Simenon.[1] His wife came with him. She is like a Madonna in middle age and he clearly adores her. She manages all his business. He is a nervous excitable man, striding about the room puffing at his pipe. He does not speak English very well, but just well enough to get across to the Third Programme people. He tells me that he has written 300 books in his life, 148 of which are in his own name. He says he has decided to write one Maigret book a year and then leave time for more straight fictional works. He says his method is to soak himself in the atmosphere

---

[1] Georges Simenon, the Belgian-French writer of detective fiction and the creator of Maigret.

of a place for three days; then to soak himself in his main character; thereafter the plot and the minor characters form themselves. His identification with his main character is so intense that if the man is old, he himself for three days adopts the movements of a dotard. If the main character is a drunkard, he himself will start drinking hard. Then he writes in a fever for ten days and the book is finished. He says that the necessity of soaking himself in atmosphere and then writing about it is why he always moves from place to place. He is now writing a novel about American life. He will one day, when he knows us better, write about London. He says his son, aged 13, has never read a single book he has written. I rather like both him and his wife.

Diary   *May 22, 1952*

Rab [Butler] drives me to the Albany. He is, as usual, very outspoken. He says that the difficulty is that Anthony [Eden] is assumed to be the heir apparent. He says that in any case Anthony has more appeal than he has, because Anthony has charm. I say I hope he will not seek to mimic charm, but remain reliable. He agrees. He says that Winston is so brave in war and so cowardly in peace; the Tory Government convey the impression of a wobble.

At the Albany I walk for the first time to C.1 [his London home until 1965].

Diary   *May 31, 1952*

Viti wakes me at 7 a.m. to say that Freddy [Harold's brother, 2nd Lord Carnock] is dead. I come up [to London]. I am met by a car at the station and drive straight to Sister Agnes' Home for Officers. I then go up to see Freddy lying there. He died in his sleep at 6.15 and without any pain or struggle. Poor old boy, it is such a wasted, lonely end.

I take the 4.38 home. It has rained today after a long drought, and the garden is fresh and beautiful. The roses are on the verge of being at their best. I walk with Viti in the garden after dinner when all the half-light plays on the flowers. It is peace unutterable, and in my heart there is great sorrow for Freddy. There ought to be relief, I suppose, that he is eased of all his loneliness and self-contempt, and that he died without suffering. But there is just sorrow at the thought of so wasted a life. I feel aching pity for him, and wish I were one of those who felt that he had been united with Mummy in some happy state. The mere fact that I want at this moment to find that sort of comfort convinces me more than ever that the belief in life-after-death is a human illusion.

Diary   *July 29, 1952*

Constable send round three copies of the revised and improved *George V.* It is excellently produced. I send a copy to the Queen and to the Queen Mother. After luncheon I go round to Marlborough House and am received by Queen Mary. She is getting older and toddles on her feet. But her mind is as clear as ever. She said two things which touched me. I was speaking of the King's forthrightness, 'Yes,' she said, 'he was sometimes too outspoken. We in our position have often to avoid answering indiscreet questions. I remember that I once had a Lady-in-Waiting who was a fool and used to ask indiscreet questions of my husband in the motor-car. He always answered exactly what he thought. I had to get rid of the woman.' Then she said, when looking closely at the picture of Prince George as a young man, 'How like he was to my poor silly son!' She stroked the book affectionately, and kept on murmuring, 'Very well done. Very dignified.'

Diary   *August 17, 1952*

There is an excellent review of *George V* by Kingsley Martin in the *New Statesman*. Also a really good one by [Lord] Samuel in the *Sunday Times*. A rather cross one by Walter Elliot in the *Observer*. But the whole effect is one of wide and lengthy adulation. How much of this is due to the very real respect that people have for King George? Never have I witnessed such a chorus of praise. I suppose I ought to feel elated. But somehow I am rather indifferent and do not experience any inner feelings of self-satisfaction.

H.N. to Sir Alan Lascelles   *August 31, 1952*

I have received two letters from you which I must now answer.

In the first, that of August 21, you were so good as to convey to me the congratulations of Her Majesty upon the excellent reception of my life of King George V. I am humbly grateful to the Queen for the interest she has taken in the book and for the appreciation which she has been gracious to express.

In the second – a private letter of August 22 – you envisage the possibility of my being offered the KCVO and you ask me whether my previous disinclination remains obdurate. I do not think that literary people should be accorded knighthoods, although, if you ask me to state rational grounds for this objection, I should be unable to do so. For snobbish considerations also, I do not want to change the shape of my own name or that of Vita. On the other hand, I quite see that, after the reception the book has received, the conferment of the CVO would suggest to people that my biography had not been accorded full royal approval. To maintain my objections might be considered churlish and embarrassing.

I have discussed the matter with Vita, who is always so wise in such matters, and I now write to say that I should be honoured to accept a KCVO if it were offered.

Diary   *November 4, 1952*

Gerry [Wellington] told me how struck he was by the Queen's astonishing radiance at the opening of Parliament this morning – her lovely teeth, hair and eyes, and that amazing quality of skin. Then add the wonderful voice and the romance, and you have a deeply moving effect.

Sir Harold Nicolson (as he was about to become) started his new book, Good Behaviour, *in October 1952. He was living during the week in London, and spent weekends at Sissinghurst. He gave up his articles for the* Spectator *but reviewed a book a week for the* Observer, *and broadcast regularly on foreign affairs for the BBC overseas service. His younger son, Nigel, was married in July 1953, and Ben two years later.*

Diary   *November 5, 1952*

I turn on the wireless at 8 a.m. to hear Eisenhower's voice. It comes through the atmospherics of the Atlantic and the wild yells of his supporters. He is President-Elect. No details yet. Anyhow, thank God all is over and that the US can now become comparatively normal again.

We have a dinner at the House of Commons for the Brains Trust people. We discuss Eisenhower as President. Professor Goodhart [Master of University College, Oxford] says he will be good for NATO which is the rock to which we cling now that the UN is dead and done for. But what can he do in Korea? The electors will expect him to end the war, but he cannot do that without either abandoning the prisoners or bringing in new divisions from Formosa. In fact he is out on a limb. Goodhart says that he hopes Foster Dulles does not become Secretary of State, as he is deeply anti-British.

Diary   *December 30, 1952*

Up to London. Many letters, including a charming one from [Sir William] Haley, expressing regret at my abandoning Marginal Comment.[1] Of course, now that I have decided to do so, all sorts of ideas come into my head, and I regret being unable to express them.

Diary   *January 1, 1953*

My KCVO is published in the New Year's Honours and I get masses of telegrams. One that pleases me from Balliol. It is all very embarrassing and I feel ridiculous and rather angry. How few people will realise how far far rather I should have received nothing at all!

---

[1] The last of his 670 articles for the *Spectator* was published on December 26.

Diary   *January 3, 1953*

Why is it that I hate so much being congratulated on my KCVO? Partly natural shyness. Partly because it is embarrassing to express pleasure about something one loathes. And partly a conceited feeling that after all the work I have done in life, a knighthood is a pitiful business, putting me in the third eleven. I know that the KCVO is not supposed to be an assessment of my contribution to life, but rather a present from the Queen for a service rendered to the Monarchy. But other people do not realise that, and I feel as if I had got a fourth prize in scripture when I should have liked the Newcastle [Senior Classics Prize at Eton]. So one is really much more snobbish and vain than one imagined.

James [Pope-Hennessy] says that my diary is too boring for words and that there is no use going on with it. But it has become a habit, and is useful for reference. He thinks that no diary is of any value unless it expresses personal opinions, feelings and gossip, and recounts all that is said. I must try and render it less of an engagement book, as otherwise I agree that it is not worth the trouble entailed. So henceforward my diary will be an expression of deep internal thoughts and emotions. But no gossip. I do not think it right to record day by day all the turpitude or sexual aberrations of my friends. I love them too dearly for that.

Diary   *February 26, 1953*

I go to Buckingham Palace for an audience and investiture. I am introduced as Mr Nicolson. The Queen is standing by the fireplace and I advance and bow. She says not one word, but motions me to a faldstool that is ostentatiously standing in the corner of the room. Beside it there is a table with a scabbard and a sword. I kneel down and the Queen lays the sword, gently but quite firmly, first on my left and then on my right shoulder. I then rise and she gives me her hand to kiss. She then gives me the box containing the star, and says with a pleasant smile, 'This is a personal present.' Then she motions me to a chair and we sit down.

I am now Sir Harold, damn, damn, damn, damn.

Diary   *March 4, 1953*

Niggs comes back holding out the *Evening Standard* with banner headlines, 'Stalin has had a stroke and is dying'. My God, what danger that means!

Diary   *March 24, 1953*

Queen Mary dies at 10.20, and Winston announces it in sobs at 10.45.

H.N. to Philippa Tennyson-d'Eyncourt   *April 1, 1953*
(Nigel's fiancée)

I am glad you are coming to Sissinghurst on Saturday, as it will give us time to get to know you and to break through the awful embarrassment inseparable from such introductions. You will find us shy, eccentric, untidy, but most benevolent. You will find Sissinghurst the strangest conglomeration of shapeless buildings that you ever saw, but it is an affectionate house and very mellow and English.

Viti says that she asked you to call her 'Vita', and you must call me 'Harold'. That is far simpler. I always called my own beloved father-in-law 'Lionel', and it seemed quite natural after the first ten years or so.

Diary   *April 16, 1953*

I ask [Sir] Malcolm Sargent[1] whether the musical profession is as mean and jealous as the acting profession. He says it is far worse. I really think that writers are the only people who do not wish to devour their competitors.

---

[1] The chief conductor of the BBC Symphony Orchestra.

Diary   *April 30, 1953*

The Royal Academy Banquet. Coming up on the train, I think out my speech, or rather I learn it by heart, as I had already written it out. It had poured with rain all day, and when I enter the yard of Burlington House, it is all umbrellas. There is a Guard of Honour for Winston formed by the Artists Rifles. They look more like rifles than artists.

I am placed at the top table between the French and Portuguese Ambassadors. I eat no dinner and sip no drink. I get Alan Herbert to come out with me before the speeches and we are caught in the lavatory when the band plays *God Save* for the Royal Toast. I creep back into my seat. Winston speaks first. Then [Field Marshal] Alexander, and then me. I repeat my piece all right, but it is *not* liked. Alan Herbert is far, far better, and the impression I give is one of nervous pomposity. Afterwards we disperse into the rooms and I meet many old friends. They do not congratulate me with either warmth or conviction. I return miserable and humiliated to Albany.

Diary   *May 6, 1953*

I lunch at the Austrian Embassy to meet the Queen of Spain.[1] She is unlike other royalties since she really is interested in the past. She began by saying that Queen Mary had given her a copy of my book and had said to her, 'It is not only a true book, as you will see, Ena, but it is also beautiful.' She tells me that at the age of five she had acted as bridesmaid to George V. She remembers it perfectly, mainly because she got into trouble. She had been told that she must keep quite silent, since nobody ever spoke in church. Then, when she heard the Archbishop beginning to read the prayers, she piped up, 'But, Mummy, *that* man is talking.' Queen Victoria told her afterwards that she had been 'very pert'. She also remembers that after the service there was a buffet at St James's Palace and that the children were in the corridor. An old gentleman with an odd collar and fur said, 'I want to see the royal children play.' They did not know what he meant and hung back shyly, but Princess Patricia said, 'He wants us to dance.' So they danced

---

[1] The daughter of Princess Beatrice (youngest daughter of Queen Victoria) and wife of King Alfonso XIII of Spain. In 1953 she was aged sixty-six.

in front of him up and down the corridor and he beamed at them. She now realises that it was Mr Gladstone.

She said that Queen Victoria never understood children and asked them so many questions that they became confused. She had a horrible bag of gold and coral out of which she would take sovereigns and give them to them. When it was too snowy at Balmoral to go out to Crathie church, she would give them Bible talks in her room. That was a great ordeal, as she always lost her temper with their stupidity. She can still recall her lovely girlish voice and that silver laugh. But no liberties were permitted. The Battenberg children, being resident family, were always given dull nursery meals – beef, mutton and milk-puddings – but visiting children were allowed éclairs and ices. Once, Princess Ena, in indignation at this, said as her grace, 'Thank God for my dull dinner.' Queen Victoria was enraged at this and punished her.

I enjoyed my conversation and returned to Albany meaning to record it. Elvira said, 'Honours heap upon you.' There was a letter from the Master of Balliol saying that I am to be elected an Honorary Fellow. Only Niggs, and perhaps Viti, know that of all honours this earth can give, this is the one I most desire.

Diary   *June 2, 1953*

Coronation Day. We are called at 6 and walk round to the Travellers. There is television in the dining-room and we see the whole service quite beautifully. I am much moved. Then we have an excellent luncheon and go to our places on the stand. After a short wait the troops appear. There is a long pause while the Guardsmen wait in front of us and the rain pours down on their bearskins. This is due to the horse-artillery being unable to get their guns up the slippery slope of St James's Street. But off they move again and eventually comes Winston in his Garter robes waving his plumed hat and making the V sign, the Queen of Tonga immense and in an open carriage getting drenched, the Queen Mother and Princess Margaret, and finally the vast gold coach. The procession characteristically is ended by an ambulance for any horses that might get hurt.

Diary June 21, 1953

Ben today made a strange remark while we were discussing what an effect a private school had on little boys, and how they separated their home from their school life. 'It is an effect,' says Ben, 'which lasts all one's life. To this day I have a horror of rendering myself conspicuous or of seeming different from other people.' Considering that his hair is like that of a gollywog and his clothes noticeable the other end of Trafalgar Square, this is an odd assertion. Yet it was made in absolute sincerity, and with that naiveté which is part of his compelling charm.

Diary July 16, 1953

At the Beefsteak there is an American called Colonel Matthews. I beg him that when he returns to New York he will not encourage the idea that England is deluged under a flood of anti-American hatred. It isn't that. It is that we are frightened that the destinies of the world should be in the hands of a giant with the limbs of an undergraduate, the emotions of a spinster and brain of a pea-hen. He says, 'The difference is that we are a democracy and you are not.' What he really means is that they idolise the common man or woman and we only pay attention to the uncommon man. He is utterly unable to explain how [Senator Joseph] McCarthy's witch-hunting and book-burning can be reconciled with democratic principles. In fact he is a foolish man who thinks only in terms of small-town politics. I return distressed.

Diary July 30, 1953

[Nigel's wedding-day.] We go in a car to St Margaret's. There is an awning and a large crowd. The church is already packed when we get there. All goes perfectly and we come out and walk down the aisle to Mendelssohn's silly tune. We drive off to Fishmongers' Hall. Everything there is magnificent and V. and I stand beside the Tennyson-d'Eyncourts shaking hands with troops of people. Ben makes a sweet little speech and we drink their health, and Niggs makes a speech in which he refers to our (his parents) happy married life. This brings a lump to my throat and tears to V.'s eyes. Then off they go in their little car to Sissinghurst.

I feel crushed and exhausted and sad. I really believe that one can love a person so deeply that their happiness becomes far more important than one's own. I shall miss Niggs dreadfully.

Diary   *September 28, 1953*

The Americans, after three years of negotiation, have come to an agreement with Franco whereby they obtain bases in Spain. They are also obliging the Greeks to get rid of our naval mission and to have an American one instead. Gradually they are ousting us out of all world authority. I mind this as I feel it is humiliating and insidious. But I also mind it since it gives grounds for anti-American feeling, which is I am sure a dangerous and quite useless state of mind. They are decent folk in every way, but they tread on traditions in a way that hurts.

Diary   *November 1, 1953*

I read Virginia Woolf['s Diary]. She rightly says that to a diary one entrusts what is a mood rather than the expression of a continuous personality. There is nothing of her distinction, charm, and occasional affection and kindness in this diary. She seems neurotic, vain and envious. But it is fascinating nonetheless.

I know well the mood that is entrusted to this diary. It is the timetable mood.

Diary   *November 19, 1953*

I go to hear T.S. Eliot speak on 'The Three Voices of Poetry'. The lecture takes place in Central Hall and I have never seen such a crowd for any literary lecture. They told me there were more than 2,500 people there and they remained silent throughout. I am on the platform and Norman Birkett takes the chair. Tom talks about his Three Voices – the voice of the poet talking to himself or nobody, the voice of a poet addressing an audience, the voice of a poet speaking through a dramatic character. He has much that is new to say. He says that for him inspiration is like matter that must be expelled in the form of a poem.

H.N. to Vita   *March 9, 1954*

Did you feel very old when you got up this morning [her 62nd birthday]? It is horrible this business about Time's Winged Chariot. It simply does not give us a chance at all. And I do want to get m.l.w. [my life's work – the spring-border] really perfect before I die, and I want to write five more books, and I want to see Jemima and Jasper [imaginary names for his unborn grandchildren] grow up, and, oh dear, what a lot of things I want!

Diary   *June 27, 1954*

I am depressed by my Manners book and wish I had never embarked upon it. In fact I am feeling old, deaf, stupid, with no new ideas. Nothing agreeable can happen in the future and the disagreeable things are large and numerous. This is just a mood.

H.N. to Juliet Nicolson [Nigel's daughter, aged seven weeks] July 31, 1954

Now that you have been admitted into the Church [she was christened the day before] and had a paragraph all to yourself in the *Daily Telegraph*, you should be able, if not to read, then at least take in, private letters.

I thought it noble of you to remain quiescent while your godfather and godmother promised such glum things on your behalf. But I did not think it noble of you to sneak when I gave you a silver spoon and you went and bashed your own eye and forehead with it. It is foolish, in any case, to bash oneself with spoons. But it is evil for a girl about to be blessed by a bishop to sneak about her grandfather. You did not see the look your mother gave me. You did not realise the deep suspicion with which your nurse thereafter regarded me. (What an ass that woman was, flattering you like that; and how weak of you to respond with a grin to her blandishments.)

Will you tell your father that were I a Conservative, I should blush at the way they have behaved over Cyprus. 'We cannot allow self-determination for Cyprus since it is a vital strategic base. We could not have remained in the Canal Zone, since, because it is a vital stragegic base, it would have been bombed out of existence.' Nothing shows up the Tories so badly as situations which they know to be false. It emphasises the falsity both of the situations and of the 1922 Committee.

And will you tell your mother that I really believe that you will have large eyes as lovely as she has and a character as sweet as hers, and that I really will not spoil you when you reach the age of 2, since I detest spoiled children. And even if I do spoil you, I shall do so surreptitiously in order to avoid a look from her like the spoon-look.

Diary   *August 19, 1954*

We go to see the Château de Montaigne.[1] One enters it by a short avenue of conifers. There is a vast modern castle built by some wealthy merchant of Bordeaux on the *emplacement* and according to the design of the original, which was burnt. But Montaigne himself lived in a little tower, no larger than an oast-house, detached from the main building. There is a chapel on the ground floor with a hole cut in the roof, by which he could hear prayers in his bedroom above without going down. The bedroom is small and low, with the remains of Italian painted decoration. There is a privy outside it, with a shoot down to the ground. Some of the steps of the stone staircase are worn by the little man's feet. Then comes his study. The beams in the roof are inscribed with mottoes in Greek and Latin, all of them bearing on the theme that worldly activity is the vanity of vanities, and the only possible life is one of seclusion and study. There are extracts from his writings referring to the room, 'where I can get away from the company of others and be King of my own'. It looks as if the poor man, only just five foot in height and bowed at that, was bullied by his wife and family and enjoyed this distant refuge 'looking down on my garden and woods'. It is extremely moving, and V. and I are entranced.

---

[1] The château near Bordeaux where Michel de Montaigne, the essayist (1533–92), was born and died.

H.N. to Vita   *September 16, 1954*

I took Richard Ward to Albemarle Street to see the Byron relics. Jock
Murray, as always, was an angel and took so much trouble. He opened
a drawer, saying to Richard, 'It's Portugal, isn't it, that you go to next
week?' 'Yes, Lisbon.' 'Well, this may interest you . . .', and at that he
flung a huge tress of hair at Richard with a label on it in Byron's
writing, 'Lisbon – March 12, 1811'. It is still quite fresh and brown.
But what passes my understanding is how any woman could have
allowed the English lord to take such a vast fid of hair away with him.
It must have left the wench almost bald.

Diary   *September 22, 1954*

We go to see Edith Evans in Christopher Fry's *The Dark is Light
Enough*. I can scarcely hear a word, which shows me how deaf I
am becoming. But it seems a silly pretentious play to me, redeemed
only by the excellence of Edith's acting. We come back and have
supper with pink champagne. Edith joins us and is charming. She,
like all the other lot, regrets that young people are not trained sufficiently. She says her own training was rigorous and at times almost
unendurable. Unlike most actresses, she says nothing unkind about
other actresses, speaking with real warmth of admiration about Peggy
Ashcroft.

H.N. to Vita   *September 30, 1954*

Tomorrow is a fiesta day [their wedding anniversary]. How little did I
or you realise when we said 'Till death do us part' on that October
day [1913] at Knole that it would be so absolutely true. But what
should I do without you? What should I do? I should be as lonely as a
mouse in Santa Sophia. Just vastness and emptiness all around me. But
I think one is wise not to brood on such disasters, and to live day by
day grateful for each evening when it arrives without misfortune,
accumulating a store of happiness on which to feed during the darkness
and the cold. My sweet, what a store we have!

Diary   *October 12, 1954*

Up to London. Masses of boring letters. I lunch at the Travellers with
dear old Clive Bell. He has aged. He is writing a book about Virginia
[Woolf, and others, entitled *Old Friends*] to undo the harsh impression
left by Leonard [Woolf]'s edition of the diary.

I take the chair at the Press Conference given by Chatham House
in celebration of the completion of Arnold Toynbee's *A Study of
History*, the last two volumes of which come out on Thursday. I make
a speech in which I welcome 'our more slender but no less weighty
Gibbon'. Not a smile does this quip evoke. I am hopeless at making
an amusing speech, since my jokes never seem to the British public to
be jokes at all. The only thing I am at all good at is making funeral
orations. Anyhow, Toynbee made a speech and then they asked questions to which he replied with consummate charm and brilliance. One
journalist asked him what purpose had impelled him to devote
thirty-five years of his life to this single great work. Toynbee rose
politely in his seat and replied with one word, 'Curiosity'. I like that
sort of thing.

Vita's Diary   *November 29, 1954*

H. said that Nigel had sounded him on whether I would ever consider
giving Sissinghurst to the National Trust. I said, Never, never, never!
Au grand jamais, jamais. Never, never, never! Not that hard little metal
plate at my door! Nigel can do what he likes when I am dead, but so
long as I live, no National Trust or any other foreign body shall have
my darling. It is bad enough to have lost my Knole, but they shan't
take Sissinghurst from me. That at least is my own.

Diary   *December 1, 1954*

[Sir] Arthur Bryant tells me a nice story. His old tutor at Harrow, a Mr
Mayo, told him that as a young master he had had to cope with a most
unruly class. In despair he exclaimed, 'I don't know what to do with
you boys!', and a voice had answered him, 'Teach us, Sir!' The voice

came from a chubby imp with carrot hair – Winston Churchill. Mayo
never forgot it.

Diary   *December 16, 1954*

Viti and I go to the Royal Literary Society where she reads her poems
to an appreciative audience. Cecil Day Lewis is in the chair and is
charming. Viti is asked for an encore and, rather bewildered, begins
with the opening of *The Land*. Then she suddenly realises that the
word 'Boeotian' is approaching, which she always forgets how to
pronounce. So when she reaches it, she pauses and exclaims, 'Harold!'
in agony. So I say in a loud voice, 'Boeotian!' The audience were much
amused, but some of them thought it must be a put-up job.

Diary   *February 6, 1955*

I work at my Duff [Cooper] article [for the *Dictionary of National
Biography*] and find it absurdly difficult. It is not my gift to compress
into tiny spaces. In fact it is more trouble to me than five articles. It is
like writing a chapter of Ezekiel on a sixpence.

Diary   *February 18, 1955*

There is heavy snow and Viti is late. I pick her up at her hairdresser
and then go to Buckingham Palace. In come Winston and Clemmie,
looking grand. Then the Iranian Ambassador. Then the Queen
Mother. Then the Queen and the Duke. And finally the Shah and
his wife. Then we pass into luncheon. Viti sits between [Sir Ivone]
Kirkpatrick and Winston. The latter is in his best mood and talks gaily
to her about history. On his other side is Madame Soheily [the Iranian
Ambassadress] and he recites Omar Khayyam to her. He tells Viti that
he is astonished to discover that we never had central heating in this
country from the day the Romans left until the day the American
heiresses arrived. After luncheon we stand around in groups and
Winston is very nice to me. He says, 'It was sad you leaving the House.

You were developing into a good debater.' He looks far, far better than when I last saw him. The children then come in and are very well-behaved and natural. Prince Charles [aged six] crams his mouth with coffee-sugar; Princess Anne [aged four] picks at it delicately.

H.N. to Vita   *February 24, 1955*

I lunched with Nigel and Philippa. We were discussing the ethics of suicide and I said that if you died, I think I should kill myself. At which, with wide-open eyes, Philippa said, 'But you can't do that. You have Juliet to think of, and both of us!' It was so spontaneous and simple that it wrung my heart. And it is true in a way. But I should not remain at Sissinghurst, but go and live in a little house in Putney.

Vita's Diary   *March 11, 1955*

Oh dear, this has been a dreadful day, or, rather, evening. H. got up at 7.30 p.m. to have a bath while I made his bed, and came back saying he had lost all power in his left hand and that his arm felt numb. I looked at him and saw that his poor mouth was all twisted, also his speech was so thick that I could only just understand what he said. I feared that he had had a stroke, and rang up Dr Parish who confirmed it. He was perfectly clear in his mind and insisted on going on with the proofs of his Manners [*Good Behaviour*] book, which he had been doing all day. But he soon gave it up and said he would go to sleep.

I spent much of the night wondering how I could most tidily dispose of myself if he died, as I should not care to go on living without him.

Diary   *April 5, 1955*

I listen to the 6 p.m. news which tells me that at 4.30 Winston handed his resignation to the Queen, who was graciously pleased to accept it. I suppose the Queen will send for Anthony [Eden] tomorrow.

Ben is engaged on a book on a Flemish 17th century artist [Hendrick Terbrugghen] whose name is unknown to me. That is why he is off on this trip [to Holland]. But how very odd that he should never have mentioned it to V. or me! It is actually rude to be so reserved and uncommunicative and I feel annoyed with him. It is as if, taking no interest at all in our doings, he is determined to exclude us from taking any interest in his.

Diary   *April 13, 1955*

I am dictating to Elvira when the telephone rings and it is Vita. She had got a letter from Ben telling her that he is engaged to Luisa [Vertova]. Well I'm blowed! I telegraph to Ben and to Luisa. I pray that it will work out all right; I think it will. Anyhow, I am delighted.

Diary   *May 15, 1955*

I have a second small stroke. I had a good breakfast, came over to my room, and got up to take a book out of the shelf. I noticed that my fingers in the right hand were too numb to type, so I started rubbing them. I then thought I would go out for a breath of air and found my right leg was wonky. It felt as if my foot or shoe were cased in lead. I got out to my garden chair and could do no more. I staggered up to my bedroom and rang my bell for Mrs Staples [the cook] and she came. She summoned Viti who arrived looking rather white, bless her, and sent for Dr Parish. Parish took all the tests and said that it was probably an 'arterial spasm' since it passed off so quickly. But he warned me that arterial spasms, if repeated, lead to clots, and clots to real apoplectic strokes. I must in future take things more easily. I realise that all this means I become a semi-invalid.

Diary   *May 22, 1955*

I decide that my next book will be on Sainte-Beuve. It is just what I want — a long spell of leisurely reading and not much travel or research, to which I am no longer up. So I get Ben to help me take down all *Les Causeries du Lundi* from a top shelf. I know that in all probability I shall not live to write such a book. But I hate not having a book on the stocks, and it cheers Vita up to see me have such confidence in my future. I don't think she was quite taken in, but she was touched by the experiment.

H.N. to Vita	*June 16, 1955*
	C.1 Albany, W.1

This is a business letter. I have heard from the Income Tax people who want to know 'what proposals I can make for paying what I owe them in arrears' on *King George V.* I had put aside £1,500 for this, but they want £1,800 more. Now, can you lend me £1,000 from your capital? I would pay you 4 per cent interest. Oh dear, George V may have brought me fame, but he has also brought me ruin and that beastly KCVO.

Diary   *June 19, 1955*

I wish to God I were well and able to have confidence in my own health. The bore of this apoplectic condition is that one never knows how bad one is. One feels perfectly well and then the fear of a stroke comes down on one for no reason. I do not notice that my mental or physical powers are in any way affected. I mean, I seem to read and write as well as I did, but that may be an illusion. But the fact remains that at any moment I may pass out and become paralytic.

	August 8, 1955
Diary	*Florence*

[Ben's wedding-day.] We drive to the Palazzo Vecchio. We stand under the statue of David with his enormous hands and buttocks. Signora Vertova and Luisa arrive. We go up to the Sala de Matrimonio. It is a high room with early 18th century tapestries. Red gilt and damask chairs, rather faded. Ben and Luisa sit in two larger chairs in front, and Viti and Signora Vertova and the immediate relations in a row behind.

There are some twenty close relations and friends present. The Councillor comes in by a side door. An old gentleman with a tumbly beard,
dressed in evening tails with a black tie, and round his middle a huge
écharpe of the national colours. They sign registers and then the old
boy starts an oration which goes on for 45 minutes. In the end they
have to pull his coat to get him to stop. I cannot hear a word he says,
but Viti hears him and is amused. He makes *punchinello* gestures. He
evidently much enjoys making such a speech. Viti tells me afterwards
that he warns Ben not to behave either like Hamlet or Othello, and
that Italians are more *espansivi* than the English, and that he must kiss
Luisa when he leaves the house and again on his return. The audience
titter slightly at his jokes. He begins by calling Ben 'Benedict', but it
soon becomes 'Benedetto'. To me, who hears nothing, it is not
impressive, but farcical. Then he presents Luisa with a bouquet on
behalf of the Commune and Ben with a book by Mazzini entitled *The
Duty of Man*. Everybody seems to have forgotten about the ring, and
Ben just shoves it on as an afterthought.

Diary   *November 9, 1955*

I dine with Baba [Metcalfe] to meet the Duke of Windsor. The Duke
is looking far fitter than he seemed when I saw him last time. He
chatters and chatters. He pretends to be very busy and happy, but I
feel this is false and that he is unoccupied and miserable. Poor man, he
is as nervous as ever. He has a vast cigar which he chews and wets but
does not even light and then lays aside. Although he must have talked
to me for three-quarters of an hour without stopping, there was
nothing of any interest at all that he had to say. But his memory is
acute.

H.N. to Vita   *December 1, 1955*

I am discouraged about Sainte-Beuve. I find *Port Royal* really dreadfully
dull, being uninterested in sin and redemption, and not caring at all
for the doctrine of Jansenism or la Mère Angélique. I have a naturally
pagan soul – *anima naturaliter pagana*. It is not that I am wholly material

444 *Harold Nicolson Diaries and Letters* DECEMBER 1955

or despise spiritual things. It is that I hate the idea that God enjoys people mortifying the flesh and being inelegant. And they were all such BORES. I always said it was a mistake to embark on the biography of a man whom one does not respect or like, but I thought the amusing side of S-B would carry me along. But *Port Royal* has got me bogged. I don't want to publish a bad book at the end of my life, and I may chuck the whole thing.

H.N. to Vita
December 14, 1955
C.1 Albany, W.1

I went with Baba, the Douglas Fairbankses and the Walter Moncktons to the first night of Olivier's *Richard III*. The Queen was there, radiant in pink and diamonds. Oh, I did love the film so! They took John Gielgud by the heels and pushed him head forward into a butt of Malvoisie; they cut off Hastings' head on a block; they strangled the young princes; and in the end off they went to Bosworth Field which, for film purposes, was situated in the vicinity of Madrid with a distant line of Castilian mountains – not one bit like Shropshire. But Olivier was superb, really superb, and in the end he is cut to pieces and thrown over the back of a packhorse and carried away a bleeding corpse quite dead. The crown is found under a bush and placed on the head of Henry Tudor. Oh my word, what a film! Then off we all went to supper with Douglas Fairbanks. Twenty-one people, including the Oliviers. I got back at 2 a.m. to find John [Sparrow] sitting up for me all anxious, thinking that I was dead too.

Diary
December 29, 1955

The *Sunday Express* telephoned to ask me what was my main wish for 1956. 'Not,' I said, 'to be telephoned to by the *Sunday Express* when I am busy.'

H.N. to Vita   *January 25, 1956*

I have had an odd proposition made to me. Would I stand as candidate for the Professorship of Poetry at Oxford? It wasn't John [Sparrow]'s idea – it emanated from some other quarter. It seems now, Cecil Day Lewis having completed his term of office, Enid Starkie [Fellow of Somerville College] has put up W.H. Auden as candidate. This has enraged the older members, as Auden shirked the war and went to America. Thus they ask me to stand as his opponent. Now, of course, my first instinct was to say 'NO'. Partly because I am not a poet; partly because I do not like opposing Wystan Auden; and partly because of my health. But I am always carried away by the mention of Oxford even on a pot of marmalade, and it would be a great and glamorous honour. As for health, it means only one lecture a term, and that would not be a strain for me. The appointment lasts for five years and is purely honorific, although expenses are paid. So I said 'YES', and now you will be cross with me. Anyhow, I expect they will choose Auden in the end and I rather hope they do. But, oh dear! I should like to be Professor of Poetry at Oxford!!!!!!!!

Diary   *January 29, 1956*

There is a nasty paragraph in the *Sunday Times* about the Oxford Chair of Poetry. It says that Auden is the best poet of the last 25 years, and that the post needs a poet and not 'the urbane H.N.'. I wish to God I hadn't agreed to stand, as I hate this sort of controversy and rather agree that Auden would be better. It all comes, not exactly from my impulsiveness, but rather from a hatred of giving way to my old age and invalidism.

H.N. to Vita   *February 1, 1956*

I had a nice dinner with Baba. The Oliviers were there and the [Douglas] Fairbanks. Vivien Leigh says that one of the things we don't realise about Shakespeare is how wonderful he is to act. 'Shaw is like a train. One just speaks the words and sits in one's place. But

Shakespeare is like bathing in the sea – one swims where one wants.'
I thought that a good metaphor.

February 8, 1956
H.N. to Vita   *C.1 Albany, W.1*

Oh I had such fun just now! A woman telephoned asking whether I
was Fergus & Fergus, and would I have her fiancé's kilt ready by the
first of March without fail? I said that we were an old Scotch firm,
perhaps a wee bit old-fashioned, but that we did not think that a young
woman should mention her fiancé's kilt. She gasped in astonishment.
I said 'I am afraid that I cannot answer so delicate a question, and you
must get your fiancé to write to us himself.' 'But he is in the Cam-
eroons!' she wailed. 'Oh!' I answered, 'I thought you said he was in
the Black Watch.' By then she was getting suspicious, so I replaced the
receiver.

Diary   *February 9, 1956*

John Sparrow telephones from Oxford to give me the result of the
election. The final figures are: Auden, 216; myself, 192; [Professor]
Wilson Knight, 91. John says that all the women dons and most of the
scientists voted against me. There was some excitement, and slogans
'Vote Auden' were chalked up on the walls of New College. I am
delighted by this result. What I feared and dreaded was that either
Wystan Auden would be beaten by me by a tiny majority, thus enraging
the undergraduates, or else I should be beaten by a vast majority. As it
is, my vote was most honourable and there is no humiliating defeat,
and youth gets what it wanted. There is some disgust at Miss Starkie's
violent propaganda. I am glad we did no campaigning on our side and
that it was never mentioned that Auden had run away to America.
This imputation would in fact have been wholly irrelevant.

H.N. to Vita   *March 1, 1956*

It is unfortunate that Nigel always seems to espouse causes which are
unpopular [with his Party and constituency] – Israel, abolition of the
death penalty, Cyprus, and so on. He is too honest and progressive for
those old Bournemouth tabby–cats. I hate that type of person. He has
had many letters referring him to the Old Testament about 'eye for
eye and tooth for tooth'. He can reply by referring them to the Sermon
on the Mount. I wish the Archbishops would make a statement. I
mean, they are glib enough to give their views about disarmament or
the UN or Mr Dulles, but here, where there is a direct moral issue on
which Christians seek for guidance, they remain dumb.[1]

H.N. to Vita   *April 25, 1956*

My Labour friends told me that the dinner given by the Labour
Executive to Bulganin and Khrushchev was a ghastly failure. Khrushchev made a speech saying that it was Russia alone who defeated
Germany. George Brown, a Labour front-bench hearty, exclaimed,
'May God forgive you!' Khrushchev broke off and asked the interpreter
what he had said. It was translated. Khrushchev then banged the table
and said, 'What I say is true!' George Brown is not the mild type of
Socialist. He replied, 'We lost almost half a million men while you
were Hitler's allies!' *Silence pénible.* And at the Speaker's luncheon
yesterday George Brown went up with an outstretched hand to apolo-
gise, but Khrushchev put his hand behind his back and said sharply,
'NIET'. My friend told me that in a long experience of unsuccessful
banquets, that will live in his memory as the most acid failure that
he has ever witnessed. Apparently the Russians are furious at the
undergraduates ragging them at Oxford and have told *Pravda* to say
that it was a demonstration organised by fascist elements. Poor silly
boys. I think they were rude in a way, but fascist, NO!

---

[1] The House of Commons, on a free vote, had voted 293 to 262 in favour of abolishing
the death penalty for murder.

H.N. to Vita   *July 12, 1956*

Eric [3rd Lord Carnock] came up to vote [yesterday] in favour of the
abolition of hanging Bill. Charlie [Lord Sackville] and Sam [Lord St
Levan] voted against. 'Three uncles,' Nigel snorted, 'left the backwoods
to vote, and only one of them voted the right way.' But he was pleased
that all the bishops but one were on his side.

H.N. to Vita   *July 26, 1956*

I went to a party yesterday given by Bob Boothby. Nye Bevan was
there, and talked to me about the 'decay' of the present government.
He attributes it entirely to Eden,[1] who, he says, is much disliked,
weak and vacillating, and in fact, hopeless. He was not talking as an
Opposition leader, but as a student of politics. He said that in his
experience the character of a government was determined by the
character of the Prime Minister. To choose Eden had been a mistake,
since he was not a strong man. He interfered with his colleagues and
did not control them, and gave the impression to the House that he
did not know his own mind. Now when I hear a man abused like that,
I immediately wish to take his side. But I fear that it is all too true.

Diary   *July 27, 1956*

The Egyptians under Nasser have nationalised the Suez Canal. That is
a pretty resounding slap in our face.

*The crisis which stemmed from Nasser's action, and ended in the abortive
attempt by Britain and France to regain control of the Suez Canal by force,
profoundly affected the Nicolsons. Harold's first reaction was that Nasser should
not be allowed to escape unpunished for his behaviour. But as Anthony Eden's
intention to resort to force became evident, he feared the consequences which in
fact occurred.*

---

[1] Anthony Eden had succeeded Winston Churchill as Prime Minister in April 1955.

Diary   *July 31, 1956*

Nigel says that most of the Tories are breathing fire and slaughter
against Egypt, but that he expects that in the end 'wiser counsels' will
prevail. That means that under American pressure we shall enable
Nasser to get away with it. I wish sometimes that we were less
encumbered and more powerful.

   Dulles is flying over to take part in Suez Canal discussions. It looks
as if he were coming to urge us to pipe down.

Diary   *August 2, 1956*

Talks continue all day between Pineau [the French Foreign Minister],
Dulles and Eden. It looks as if Dulles agrees with an international
conference but disagrees with the use of force. The difficulty is that
Nasser has not, so far as I can see, violated any International Treaty.
What the treaties provide is that the Canal should be open in time of
peace and war, not who should own the Canal. It is highly inconvenient
that a man like Nasser should have control of the Canal and be able to
blackmail us by threats. It is also most unpleasant that his seizure may
encourage other Arab countries to do the same. But we cannot
persuade the Americans that the situation justifies the use of force, and
I am not absolutely sure myself whether we should use it or threaten
it. In fact the Government have shown their accustomed irresolution
and confusion of purpose.

Diary   *September 12, 1956*

I dine at the Beefsteak where I find many peers back from the House
of Lords debate. They are a little shaken by the fact that Lord McNair
[President of the International Court of Justice, 1952–5] stated that we
were breaking the Charter of the United Nations by moving troops in
such a way as to constitute a threat of force. Shortly after I have got
home, Nigel appears. He had returned from Oslo this morning and
went straight to the House from the station. He was in time to hear
the P.M.'s statement and Gaitskell's reply. Eden had brought out his

Users' Association proposal [which called for co-operation between Egypt and the main users of the Canal on pilotage, signalling, etc.], and had indicated that if Egypt refused to co-operate, we and France, with the tacit approval of America, would use force. This led to an outburst in the House, the Tories cheering wildly and the Labour people shouting 'Resign!' and 'Warmonger!'. I think Niggs is himself rather alarmed by this bellicose attitude, which he regards as bluff. No government could drag the country into war over the Suez Canal with the Opposition against them.

Diary   *September 15, 1956*

I go on with *Sainte-Beuve* and finish him at 12.20 this morning. I do not feel the usual feeling of elation, since I regard the book as bad, and as clear and overt evidence of my waning powers.

Nasser, as was expected, has refused the plan for a Users' Association. He describes the proposal as an act of war. The Russians have issued a threatening communiqué saying that they cannot remain indifferent to war in the Middle East.

Diary   *October 30, 1956*

At 6 p.m. I turn on the news. Eden and Mollet [French Prime Minister] have addressed to Cairo and Tel Aviv an ultimatum summoning them to withdraw their forces ten miles from the Canal. This ultimatum expires in twelve hours, after which we shall take our own measures to enforce the decision and to occupy Port Said, Ismailia and Suez. The House had received this announcement at 4 p.m. and Labour had protested that such action independent of the USA and UNO was a terrible gamble.

                                                       October 31, 1956
H.N. to Vita   *C.1 Albany, W.1*

I lunched yesterday with the Rothschild firm in their City premises. They were crushed and saddened by the woes of Israel and they sat down and wept, hanging up their harps in the counting house. Oliver Franks [British Ambassador in Washington, 1948–52, and Chairman of Lloyds Bank, 1954–62] was there. He is a wise man and he was deeply worried by the situation. He would have been even more worried had he known that the Government had addressed an ultimatum to Egypt and Israel. That news only broke at 4 p.m. How they can have done such a thing with the whole world opinion against us passes my comprehension. We shall now be accused of exploiting the crime of the Jews in invading Sinai in order to resume control of the Canal. To do this we have sacrificed our principles and practically destroyed UNO and the Charter. We are in danger of being denounced as aggressors. Of course, if the occupation of Port Said, Ismailia and Suez proceeds without a hitch or much loss of life, and if we can maintain ourselves on the Canal against the united armies of Arabia, then the Tories will acclaim it as an act of great resolution and courage. But to risk a war with more than half the country against you, with America and UNO opposed, and even the Dominions voting against us, is an act of insane recklessness and an example of lack of all principle.

Niggs, who has just appeared, is also in despair, and thinks of resigning from the Party and of chucking up his whole Parliamentary career. I am allowing him to simmer down and am lunching with him. I shall preach discretion and silence. But he says rightly that if he does not speak out now, it will be thought later that he waited to see how things turned out. He says that the mood of his Party is like that at the outbreak of the Crimean or Boer wars.

Diary   *November 2, 1956*

There was such an uproar in the House last night that the Speaker had to suspend the sitting. The United Nations Assembly has voted with but five exceptions [Britain, France, Australia, New Zealand and Israel] ordering a cease-fire. Eden refused to tell Gaitskell what we would do [next]. There is a suggestion put forward by Canada that UNO should police the area, but it will take a long time before the police-force can be assembled, and meanwhile we and France will go ahead. The whole Egyptian bluff has been called good and proper. But that makes no difference. Success does not render a dirty trick any less dirty.

Diary   *November 4, 1956*

Anthony Nutting [Minister of State for Foreign Affairs] has resigned.
This is extremely important since it deprives backbench Members
of the excuse, 'The Government must know best.' Nutting knew
everything, and has yet decided that it is evil. The central fact remains
that Eden has deliberately ignored the recommendation passed by the
overwhelming majority of the United Nations Assembly. This is a
breach of law. I am not surprised that the House, at their special
meeting yesterday, should have burst into disorder.

I telephoned to Nigel at 9.15 this morning. He says that he can
scarcely, feeling as he does, vote for the Government. He was disgusted
by the hypocrisy of Eden's broadcast. He says that he thinks some
twenty Tories will abstain, although this may mean the fall of the
Government.

The Russians have sent seven divisions into Hungary and are closing
in on Budapest with 1,000 tanks. But we have no right to speak a
word of criticism.

H.N. to Vita   *November 8, 1956*

At the club, Bobbety [Salisbury] sought to defend the policy of the
Government, but Halifax, Waverley, Oliver Franks and other eminent
men said that our action had been iniquitous from the start and a
failure in the end. I agree, of course. Our smash-and-grab raid got
stuck at the smash.

Nigel heard yesterday afternoon that there was a meeting in Bournemouth of the United Nations Association. He jumped into the train
and went down there, taking Philippa with him. He spoke strongly
against the policy of the Government, and said that he intended to
abstain in the vote of confidence. Philippa said that there were murmurs
of 'Traitor!' and 'Renegade!' Of course, he was terribly unwise. But
there are times when wisdom becomes akin to caution, caution to
expediency, and expediency to subordinating one's conscience to one's
interests. I am entirely behind him in what he has done, and feel that
he has timed things beautifully. Poor Philippa sat there with wide
anxious eyes.

Diary   *November 10, 1956*

The analogy with the Munich crisis is curiously close. Even as people
then said, 'Chamberlain has saved us from war,' now people say, 'Eden
has saved us from war,' forgetting that we have been humiliated in the
face of the world and broken our word. The sad thing is that whereas
at the time of Munich, we who opposed Chamberlain were proved
right in six months, it will never become utterly apparent how bad
Eden's action was.

I read the Lytton–Virginia letters [*The Letters of Virginia Woolf
and Lytton Strachey*] and am appalled by their silliness, dirtiness, and
cattishness.

H.N. to Vita   *November 15, 1956*

Nigel's Executive met last night and reprimanded him for his speech
but did not ask him to resign. There will be a full meeting of the
Association in three weeks' time which he will address. For the
moment, all Tory opinion, bemused though it be, is in favour of Eden.
Simple minds work simply. The ladies of Bournemouth do not like
the Russians, the Americans or Nasser: Eden has dealt a blow to these
three enemies: therefore Eden must be right. It is as simple as that.
Nigel and I have always believed that there was some collusion between
the French and the Israelis to which we were a consenting party. If the
story gets out, I do not see how the Government can survive. It is an
utterly disgraceful tale.

H.N. to Vita   *November 21, 1956*

It is no good pretending that I like being 70, because I loathe it. I had
a gay breakfast with heaps of telegrams and presents. Then the bell
rang and the knocker knocked and a lovely girl appeared with an
envelope which contained a cheque for £1,370 and a list of some 200
names. Really, I was overwhelmed. I am such an odd person. I scarcely
dare look at the list for fear it may contain names of people whom I
have long ceased to know. I simply loathe people being asked to give

me presents when they don't want to. This is not ingratitude, but a sort of disordered and diseased pride.

Diary   *November 27, 1956*

I dine at the 200th Dinner of the 63 Club which is held in the Royal College of Physicians. The health of the guests is proposed by Sir Russell Brain [President of the Royal College of Physicians] and replied to by Douglas Woodruff [the author, Editor of *The Tablet*]. The latter says that my real claim to immortality will not be my books so much as my Diary. Poor chap! If he only realised what a pitiable little engagement book it is.

Diary   *December 3, 1956*

In the House today Selwyn Lloyd announced that we are clearing out of the Canal forthwith. He claims that our action stopped a war and brought in UNO. I suppose some people will believe him.

Diary   *December 15, 1956*

Looking back at the Suez crisis, it seems strange to me that I should at the age of seventy have been so passionately moved by the whole business. Of course there was a personal interest in its effect on Nigel. But apart from that, the moral issues affected me as much as anything since Munich. My admiration of the Hungarians and my realisation of the immense importance of Russia suppressing by force a movement which was a patently working-class movement, were nothing like so intense as the shame and sorrow of the Suez incident. It meant much to me that a Prime Minister who had made his reputation by [his] moral courage should out of exasperation have violated his principles and told his country a series of shameful lies. It was a disappointment also to realise that my countrymen, in whose political good sense I had firmly believed, could prove as gullible and emotional as the Germans.

On January 15, Harold and Vita went to the Far East, the first of six
successive winter voyages. Later he revised his diary of this trip and published
it under the title, Journey to Java.

Diary   _January 9, 1957_

I dine at the Beefsteak, and as I drive there my taxi-man says, 'Here's
a pretty mess, the Prime Minister resigning like that.' It seems that
Horace Evans had made a thorough examination, and decreed that
Eden could not live if he carried on. My only feeling is one of profound
compassion.

Diary   _January 10, 1957_

I go to the BBC, and the woman who works the lift says, 'Well,
Macmillan is our new Prime Minister.' The Queen had seen Winston
and Bobbety [Salisbury], and come to this decision. It is sad for the
left wing of the Tory Party, since Butler was the leader of young
conservatism, but I daresay that in the circumstances it is right.

                                                       February 21, 1957
                                                       _MV_ Willem Ruys
H.N. _to Nigel_   _Sumatra–Colombo_

I got your letter of February 9 at Singapore, and had only time to dash
off an acknowledgement, since Vita's frightful Chinese friend had
been observed waving frantically from the dockside, and thereafter
clambering up the gangway with an expression of happy expectation
on her face. We had believed her safely absent in Hong Kong. Vita is
a fly-paper for bores. Not only does she attract the homely flies of
Kent, but the bumble-bees of Sussex and the dragon-flies of Surrey,
but exotic insects wend their way towards the fly-paper from distant
Borneo and Cathay. Chop–Suey (as I call her) is the worst of all bores,
since she does not really understand or speak the English language.
She insisted on taking us in the steaming heat of a Singapore afternoon

to what she called 'a dear little Chinese restaurant'. Vita loves native taverns, and her eyes brightened. But when we got there, it was on the top floor of a modern apartment house. The lift was made of pink plastic, and when we reached the restaurant, it was like that of the Carlton Hotel in Bournemouth, with endless napkins tastefully displayed, air-conditioning and enamel walls and chromium plate. Vita's face fell, but brightened again when she found beside her plate a tissue-paper envelope containing chop-sticks of ivory or bone. I firmly asked for a fork and spoon.

We drank beer, and were given food that was so disgusting that I felt ill. The conversation was equally sticky. 'Tell me,' Vita began brightly, 'is there a canteen at the University where you teach?' 'Beautiful flowers,' replied Chop-Suey, 'beautiful flowers.' 'Do you teach your pupils English?' I enquired with malice. 'I know one shop near Raffles Place,' she answered, 'which has many of them.' 'Has your husband joined you,' asked Vita at dictation-speed, 'or is he still in Formosa?' 'Most beautiful flowers,' she answered, 'all green and blue and – how do you say – ponk.' 'Pink', said Vita, and the conversation languished.

Diary   *March 17, 1957*

Slowly we tie up. At 9.40 a.m. we leave the *Willem Ruys* and step on the shore of our native land through the same covered and illumined gangway that we traversed on January 15. Since then we have travelled more than 25,650 miles. V. has written 40,000 words of *La Grande Mademoiselle* and I 60,000 of this diary with its inserts.

Diary   *April 2, 1957*

We motor to Buckingham Palace at 8 p.m. and pause for a while in the Mall as we are too early, and then enter at 8.20 punctually. We are met and escorted to the drawing-room upstairs; then lined up; then the Queen and Prince enter; then dinner. I talk to Hugh Gaitskell. He says that his Party is split over the atom-bomb question. He must not commit them to any definite rejection since he may soon be responsible for the decision himself. It is the difficulty of the Leader of the Opposition that his Party wish to oppose always and do not realise that the leader has always to consider what policy he would himself adopt if he were to become Prime Minister tomorrow. He is charming about Nigel, saying that it is so maddening that local associations have no idea of a man's true value in the House. I am pleased by this.

Diary   *May 1, 1957*

I attend the Royal Academy banquet. When Winston arrives, the crowd in the courtyard cheer loudly. Winston is given a little chair at the entrance to the main rooms where he sits looking rather childish. On the wall in one of the rooms is a monstrous caricature of him by Ruskin Spear R.A. which makes him look like a village dotard from the Auvergne. I cannot think how the Committee allowed it to be hung. The dinner is far better than the last time, having been done by Fortnum and Mason. There is unstinted champagne, port and brandy. Winston sits there looking very old, and there is a hint of dribble about his lips.

H.N. to Vita   *June 13, 1957*

The BBC Overseas people want me to take part in a broadcast justifying the West. I agreed to do so. The whole of modern civilisation, including the hydrogen bomb, derives from the Mediterranean basin, and the East is no good at all except at poetry and art. I despise everything east of Suez (including Suez itself), with the exception of the Chinese, for whom I have deep respect. My word, some of their carvings I saw at Spinks yesterday were magnificent!!!

Diary   *September 12, 1957*

I get up. I shave and wash and dress. I enter the sitting-room, and help myself to a sausage and pour out a cup of coffee. The telephone rings. 'Yes?' I answer. A very young voice reaches me from the distance saying, 'Harold, I have got a brother [Adam].' Then Niggs' voice intervenes, and explains that Philippa had a boy at 6.30 this morning. My delight at this news shows me how really worried I had been. I am so happy that I find myself singing.

Diary   *October 5, 1957*

I am woken up by V. bringing her portable wireless into my room, and saying that I must listen to the 8 o'clock news. It was announced before midnight that the Russians have released a satellite which is now circling the earth at tremendous speed giving out signals. The BBC had managed to record the signals, and play them over to us – just ping, ping, ping, ping. I am annoyed that the Russians should have been the first to get away with this, since it will increase their scientific prestige. Damn them.

Diary   *November 3, 1957*

The Russians have launched a bigger and better satellite with a dog inside it. The British public will mind more about the dog than the satellite. There is a suggestion that Our Dumb Friends League should stand outside the Soviet Embassy and celebrate a two-minutes' silence.

                                                           December 24, 1957
H.N. to Nigel   *SS* Reina del Mar, *near Venezuela*

This is a marvellous ship – really exactly like a luxury hotel. Vita has most meals in her cabin as she has, until a few day ago, this recurrent fever and feels too limp to dress. She was up all yesterday without ill effects. She has been wonderfully patient and uncomplaining. Were it not for the constant anxiety I have been through, and for my loneliness, I have myself got much out of the journey – doing steady reading, taking notes for my book on the eighteenth century [*The Age of Reason*], bathing in the delicious swimming pool, gazing at the mountains of Jamaica and Cuba, and talking to Lady Magnus-Allcroft, who is

married to Philip Magnus – a clever Oxonian and an excellent writer
[of biographies]. She is a real person – obstinate and kind – and has
been a friend to me during these dark days. I shall always be grateful
to her.

Diary   *March 19, 1958*

I write an article for the *Spectator* on the subject of Urbanity. In a
Beaverbrook periodical called *Books and Art* a young man writing
under the name of Humphrey Clinker has accused me in two
successive articles of being cultured, snobbish and urbane. I rather
like having the chance to answer him, although I do not really understand what his real grievance is. He says that 'virtuosi' such as Cyril
Connolly and myself live in ivory towers and do not possess the
common touch or understand the dust and roar of life. We should treat
literature as a smart columnist treats life and should not discuss general
ideas but concentrate on personalities and be more newsy. I say in
my article that I am writing for an educated public and not for an
uneducated public and that it would be absurd for me to put on a
proletarian tone.

H.N. to Vita   *May 14, 1958*

What a world we live in. The sense of authority has decayed and the
young revolt against the old and the irresponsible against the responsible. I suppose something of the same sort occurred after the French
Revolution, but people were then mainly uneducated and could not
be driven to violence by propaganda. But here, simultaneously, we
have the Lebanon on the verge of rebellion, the French Algerians
setting up a separate Government worse than anything that happened
in Ulster, and the Venezuelans spitting at Mrs Nixon. The Americans
are so deeply hurt when they discover that they are not loved, and in
truth I feel that the students of Lima and Caracas have behaved rudely
and wildly. It is all, I suppose, due to the fact that the use of force is
now prohibited and that agitators like Nasser and his myrmidons can
lash any crowd into rage and excitement.

H.N. to Vita   *September 10, 1958*

I said [to James Pope-Hennessy] that you and I might differ in political
opinions but that we saw as one about VULGARITY which we
regard as 'the enemy'. Rich vulgarity like that of Mrs Simpson is worse
than poor vulgarity. In fact, when the latter descends to hop-picker
level, it is not vulgarity at all. I said that what had shocked us was
that he had half-admired the luxury of the Windsor mill. He said that
we had 'feudal' conceptions and were class-conscious, whereas he
had no class-consciousness at all. I said it was not snobbishness but
fastidiousness. I think he was slightly impressed as he listens to what
we say.

H.N. to Vita   *October 16, 1958*

At noon I took a taxi to the German Embassy. I was waiting for the
driver to give me change, when the portals of the house were flung
open and out rushed a neat secretary who bowed low to me. The
taximan must have been impressed. Then up I went to the Ambassador's private flat and the secretary bowed me in and left me alone. I
started making amicable conversation, but the Ambassador said that he
must first make an allocution and present me with my citation or
Verleihungsurkunde. Then he made a set speech while I stood sufficiently
stiffly to attune with my *visage de circonstance* but not exactly at attention,
which might have seemed too military a pose. He then handed me a
box containing *Das Grosse Verdienstkreuz mit Stern*. The Order consists
of an enamelled dingle-dangle and a brass star. The *Verdienstkreuz* is
awarded to distinguished men who have rendered services to Germany.
I then went away clasping my *Verleihungsurkunde* and my blue box with
the star against my chest, thinking how you would have turned on the
gramophone record about, 'I can't understand how you can possibly
accept Orders from those horrible people who tried to destroy us.'
But I was pleased.

Diary   *November 4, 1958*

I look at the enthronement of Pope John XXIII on the television. He
looks like a head-waiter at a Soho Italian restaurant. The ceremony is
badly rehearsed and conducted. Acolytes rush about making signs to
other acolytes or whispering in the ear of the Vicar of God what he is
expected to do next. It is a great technical achievement to be able to
send this living photograph from St Peter's to Sissinghurst, but I
get into the train feeling all my anti-Catholic and anti-priesthood
sentiments very active.

Diary   *November 11, 1958*

Nigel and I lunch together. He is worried about what to do in
the debate on the Wolfenden Report [which proposed to legalise
homosexuality]. The mere fact that if he supports it he will seal his
fate at Bournemouth makes him all the more eager to express his views
openly and defy the consequences. All this is noble but inexpedient.
Unfortunately [Professor] Freddy Ayer joins us, and Nigel asks him
whether he thinks that the Government should lead or follow public
opinion. Ayer is very positive – Government and Parliament must
always be in advance of public opinion. That means a gulf fixed
between the Member for Bournemouth East and his electors.

Diary   *December 4, 1958*

I lunch in a private room at the Connaught at a luncheon given by
David Astor [Editor of the *Observer*] for Igor Stravinsky. Stravinsky is
a fan of mine and greeted me warmly. I sit next to him and he tells me
how much he enjoyed *Some People*, and what a delight *Journey to Java*
has been to him and his wife. I groan inwardly. 'But of course,' he
adds, putting his hand on my shoulder, 'your best book is your life of
your father.' I was overjoyed at that. He said that as a composer he
admired technique, and that he felt my technique was superb. I swelled
with pride. He said how much he envied us writers, who had finished
our work when the book was published and bound. It was so different

for a composer. His composition, when played at Buenos Aires or Melbourne, was entirely different from anything that he composed or intended.

H.N. to George Weidenfeld   *December 30, 1958*

I am writing to you about *Lolita* which Vita and I have just read.[1] We do not feel that its literary merits justify in any way the obscenity which underlies the whole book. Only one person in a million will feel that the book is really a moral or cautionary tale, or that it is anything but 'corrupting' in the sense of the Obscene Publications Report. To the great mass of the public it will seem a salacious treatment of the very worst sort of perversion, a vice in which an extreme form of lechery confronts the extremest innocence. It will be universally condemned, and will give your firm the reputation, not of a courageous and 'advanced' firm of publishers, but as a firm which specialises in obscene books. You may regard this as old-fashioned and puritan on the part of the public, but the vast mass of the public is puritan in these respects and there is no form of perversion which fills them with greater horror than that described with such relish in *Lolita*.

Diary   *January 5, 1959*
                                                               Paris

As we leave Boulogne I wave at it, and Vita says, 'Who are you waving at?' I reply, 'I am greeting Sainte-Beuve.' The waiter is pleased at this and smiles delightedly. What English waiter would understand an analogous greeting to Wordsworth? We reach the Gare du Nord an hour late and then dawdle round the ceinture. It is pelting with rain and when we get sudden vistas of the boulevards they are glistening under lights. The train slides past the lighted windows of tenement houses and we see brass chandeliers for a flash with red shades and the

---

[1] The novel by Vladimir Nabokov had already become a matter of acute controversy in Britain and other countries. The main theme is the seduction of a girl of twelve by a middle-aged man. In Britain it was published by Weidenfeld & Nicolson in 1959, and there was no prosecution of the book.

evening meal below them. Unknown lives. We dine and then go to
bed.

January 8, 1959
Diary   SS Cambodge *[sailing to Japan]*

A happy day at sea, and I start on Chapter I of my book on the
eighteenth century, doing Saint-Simon, Louis XIV and the beginning
of the War of the Spanish Succession. At 4 we pass Gavdos, the island
off Crete. It has the peculiar look of crinkled tissue-paper.

February 6, 1959
Diary   *Tokyo, Japan*

We take the train from Kobe to Kyoto. It is like the Underground and
we have to stand as far as Osaka. The countryside is hideous beyond
belief – pylons, factories constructed in dirty grey cement, endless
electrical cables and telegraph poles, shanties, dumps – worse than
anything I have seen. The Japanese, for all their exquisite social eti-
quette, are bad-mannered corporately. There are lots of young men
sitting down, but not one of them offers Vita a seat. What an ugly,
loathsome race! At Kyoto we go round the temples and the shrine
garden. Nothing seems to date here. A 1200 AD temple is exactly the
same as an 800 AD temple or an 1867 temple. Ugly Etruscan red
columns and shabby pine-trees. The garden is large and very Japanese.
Cherries trained carefully over bamboo baskets like wisteria, and masses
of azalea which must be a blaze of ill-matching colour when in flower.
Get back to the ship and go to bed early, having found Kyoto a terrible
disappointment.

February 25, 1959
Diary   SS Cambodge, *Colombo*

The happiness of the day is clouded by a distressing episode. On
entering the ship a Cingalese newspaper-man, whom I had just spoken

to that morning before going ashore, rushes up to me. 'Oh Sir Harold,' he said, 'I have been waiting for you four hours. I have a cable to discuss with you.' I took him to my cabin and he undid his telegram. It ran something as follows: 'Our Moscow correspondent reports that at Press Conference Guy Burgess stated that he asked Prime Minister for a safe conduct to England and back to Russia to see his mother who is seriously ill. Macmillan, when asked, said it was not for him to intervene: the Law must take its course. In subsequent conversation Burgess said that the only one of his former friends who had kept in touch with him was Harold Nicolson, who had written regularly. Please get in touch with Nicolson, passenger *Cambodge* arriving Colombo February 25, and ask him to confirm.' I replied that certainly I had written to Guy since I felt sorry for him, as he had acted on impulse, and that my principle was not to desert friends in distress. But that I had written not one word which could not be published in any paper. I made him repeat this since I do not trust the accuracy of Cingalese reporters when faced with a scoop. God knows what he will say.

February 26, 1959
London

Nigel to H.N. (cable to SS Cambodge)

Votes for me 3671. Against 3762. Lost by 91.[1]

February 27, 1959
H.N. to Nigel   SS Cambodge, *approaching Bombay*

Our first reaction was emotional. We were enraged that you should have lost. Although you had repeatedly warned us to anticipate defeat, and although we had never really expected victory, the emotional shock when it came was distressing. Then blessed reason came to our aid. In the first place, the figures were nothing like a moral defeat and justified the whole battle. In the second place, if you had got a *majority* of only 91, it would have been difficult for you to carry on. You would have felt that almost half your constituents were bitterly opposed. In

---

[1] A ballot was held in his constituency to determine whether Nigel should remain its MP.

the third place, such disappointments are very transient, provided that one has done nothing either dishonourable or foolish.

H.N. to Vita   *April 14, 1959*

I had a charming luncheon at No. 10. Delicious food and wine. We discussed what books had first influenced us. Debré [Prime Minister of France, for whom the luncheon was given] (who is a nice *Ecole Normale* type) said it had been *Le Livre de la Jungle* by Kipling. Nye Bevan said it had been *Le Rouge et le Noir*. So that was a fine interchange of Anglo-French compliments. I like the way we invite the Opposition leaders on such occasions. Both Gaitskell and Nye were there.

Diary   *June 24, 1959*

I go to Transport House and do the enclosed flash for the Labour Party. [It reads:] 'Why should I, who have had a luxury education and lived a luxury life, vote Labour? Because I believe that they will do more than any other Party to secure equality of opportunity and to solve without violence the African problem, which may become the central problem of the next fifty years.'

Diary   *August 7, 1959*

Lunch at the Garrick and am told that it is announced the Queen is to have a baby in January or February. What a sentimental hold the monarchy has over the middle classes! All the solicitors, actors and publishers at the Garrick were beaming as if they had acquired some personal benefit.

                                      September 14, 1959
H.N. to Vita   *C.1 Albany, W.1*

I hate the lunik for having bumped into the radiant moon.[1] 'With how

---

[1] This was the first Soviet moon-rocket.

sad steps, O Moon, thou clim'st the skies!' [Sir Philip Sidney] – and then bump, crash, comes a metal projectile from Russia. I should like to feel that Selene would respond by killing Khrushchev and his scientists. Nothing remains inviolate, and no longer shall we enjoy the illusion that the great shining globe represents the unattainable. They will hit Hesperus next – 'Hesperus, thou dear jewel of the dark blue night', as Simonides wrote, never foreseeing that one day it would be bumped by Soviet bombs. Moreover, I think it ostentatious for Khrushchev to have achieved this feat on the eve of his visit to the USA. It is as if one were about to visit the Bishop of Peterborough and sent down a French chef in advance. I call it bad manners.

H.N. to Vita   *November 3, 1959*

Niggs tells me that Nabokov told him that all his life he had been fighting against being influenced by *Some People*. 'The style of that book,' he said, 'is like a drug.' Well, I can assure him that *Lolita* is not likely to influence me. Niggs has taken a liking to Nabokov and above all to Mme Nabokov.

H.N. to Vita   *November 18, 1959*

I lunched with the Swiss Ambassador at the Dorchester. The Cultural Attaché, who had arranged the luncheon, talked to me about the great conductors of the world and how the Philharmonia was about the best orchestra in the world and the Festival Hall without doubt the best theatre. I said I never went to a concert. He looked actually startled, as if he could not believe his ears and as if I had said, 'It's no use your talking to me about books. I haven't read a book in fifteen years.' I suppose my dislike of music must strike the cultured foreigner as an astonishing lack of taste or education.

Diary   *December 26, 1959*

In the afternoon vans arrive bearing Mr Maclure of the Columbia
Broadcasting System, two French electricians and three others,
together with vast trunks and suitcases. They establish their apparatus
in the kitchen and dining-room and store-cupboard. I am sat down in
a chair by the fire and the lights are turned on and adjusted. It takes
from 5 p.m. to 7 p.m. Viti is enraged. I talk to Ed Murrow in St Moritz
[for one of his *Small World* hook-ups], to Mrs Luce in, I think, Los
Angeles, and to Chip Bohlen [American Ambassador to the USSR,
1953–7] in New York. I do not see their faces (since the television
pictures are put together later) but I do hear their voices, and we have
a three-cornered discussion of the function of diplomacy. It seems to
me to go rather well, but Viti is so angry that she gets bored. The
lights, I admit, *are* rather a strain and the thing goes on far too long.
But in the end they take a final shot of me, pack their many trunks,
and sloop off into the night, where the wind howls across the fields
and woods. I am not too exhausted but glad to get to bed. Viti feels I
have been exploited, put-upon, taken advantage of, and maybe made
a fool of.

                                                  January 24, 1960
H.N. to Nigel   SS Europa, *Port Elizabeth*

I cannot describe to you the horrors of Apartheid. I asked an Englishman how one pronounced the word and he said 'Apart' and then
'hate', and my God! Hate it is. It is far worse than anything that I had
supposed. I was shocked when first landing at Durban to observe that
all the seats along the esplanade (*all* of them, literally) were marked
'For whites only'. I was shocked, as I told you, when I found that in
the vast Post Office at Cape Town there were counters for the whites
and separate counters for the niggers. In fury at this, I queued up
behind three niggers, but when my turn came the clerk said to me,
'Sorry, Sir, you are at the wrong desk.' So I had to pass on to the
guichet marked 'Whites only'.

     The Press came to see us as usual, and on this occasion it consisted
of two women and a man who represented a liberal evening paper.

What they told us was startling. Their letters are opened, their visitors noted, their telephones tapped and microphones concealed in their office. The girl was arrested for talking to a coloured fellow-student, and she would not be able to go abroad since they would refuse her a passport. They are anxious to see what the Prime Minister [Harold Macmillan] will say when he addresses the Legislature in Cape Town [on February 3; the famous 'Wind of Change' speech]. He is bound to offend somebody, even by his omissions. They want him to say, 'Well, leave the Commonwealth if you want to! You are a moral liability to us. But realise that if you do, you become a foreign country and will lose all the benefits of Empire preference.'

You know how I hate niggers and how Tory Vita is. But I do hate injustice more than I hate niggers, and Vita screams with rage. She says it is like Hitler all over again and that these nice newspaper people who came to see us last night will end their days in a concentration camp. Fists of execration are raised on high. But truly, you have no conception how shocking it all is. The pure police state. How happy we are with our freedom and our Parliamentary questions! I could not live in this Nazi country in constant fear of the Gestapo.

February 4, 1960
Diary   SS Europa, *Somaliland*

The radio news says that Macmillan made it absolutely clear [at Cape Town] that we disapproved of their racial policy. This was a courageous thing to do and I am delighted.

March 17, 1960
H.N. to Vita   C.1 Albany, *W1*

I had some American television men in during the morning and they interviewed me for a feature they are doing on Piccadilly. They asked me whether I did not feel embarrassed by the fact that the porters here wore 'livery' and top-hats. I said I should feel much more embarrassed if they didn't and if people mistook me for a porter on my way out. I could see they thought me very snobbish and old-fashioned. They asked me whether the Albany was not a 'privileged sanctuary'. I said yes it was. I added that highly developed civilisations specialised in variety, whereas lower civilisations imposed uniformity. That was not a welcome remark.

Diary   *March 21, 1960*

I dine at the American Embassy. A small but select company – the Queen Mother, the Prime Minister and Lady Dorothy [Macmillan], the Chancellor of the Exchequer [Derick Heathcoat Amory], the Profumos [John Profumo, Army Minister] and Jeremy Tree. I sit between Mrs Whitney [the Ambassadress] and Mrs Profumo, and as the P.M. is on Mrs Whitney's other side, we talk across. He was delighted at having won the Oxford Election as Chancellor. He thinks the *Times* leader recommending [Oliver] Franks did the trick. He said that he regretted the Summit Conference being called 'the' and not 'a'. He quoted me as having said that the greatest diplomatic asset was the passage of time – and that a regular series of Summit Conferences held, say, every four years, would prevent a breach and allow time to flow. He foresaw that in thirty years, if there was no war, Russia would become more bourgeois and the gap would narrow. He said that he hoped Khrushchev would remain in power as he was personally pledged to peace. He said that he had found de Gaulle much mellowed and very sensible. I thought him in wonderful form – wise and gay. I have seldom enjoyed a dinner more.

I talked to Lady Dorothy about her visit to Rambouillet. She said it was evident that Mme de Gaulle was a poor *maîtresse de maison*. There were about forty men servants with silver chains, superb food, but no soap in their bedrooms, no paper-baskets and no writing material. It was so cold that she had to go to bed in a woolly. She asked Mme de Gaulle whether there was anything special she wished to do when she came on her State Visit to London, and she replied that she wished to visit Gorringes and Mrs Leo Amery, who is bed-ridden. She said that making conversation with Mme de Gaulle is like digging at clay with a trowel.

May 19, 1960
H.N. to Vita   *C.1 Albany, W.1*

Jim [Lees-Milne] and I sat in Albany listening to Khrushchev howling
in the Palais Chaillot.[1] I heard the boos with pleasure. He sounded a
little mad, I thought, and Miss Macmillan [Harold's housekeeper] says
he was 'like a schoolboy searching for rude words', which was true.
But truly the Ukrainian moujik surprised himself, and as an old
diplomatist I became confirmed in my view that the exchange of
insults is not the best method of conducting negotiations between
sovereign states. I find great sympathy and affection expressed here for
Ike Eisenhower. I confess that I am shocked that so old and dignified
a man should be held up to ridicule and abuse.

Diary   *May 20, 1960*

I was worried last night about my budget. At breakfast I told Niggs
that I must get a job as a hack-writer who wrote the history of City
companies, and that I should have to ask a fee of £5,000, otherwise I
should have to give up living in the Albany. He said, 'Well, I must see
what can be done about it.' He then goes off to his office and returns
in an hour to put a proposal to me from [George] Weidenfeld. It is
that I write the text of a vast album he is doing about Royalty – pomp
and grandeur. I may take two years at it, do only 70,000 words, they
will do the fuss about the illustrations, and I am to get £1,500 on
signature of contract, £1,500 next year, and £2,000 on delivery of
ms – £5,000 in all. Thus my dread of having to leave the Albany and
alter my whole way of life is removed in 1½ hours. I go out at once
and get a book on Monarchy out of the London Library.

---

[1] The Summit Conference in Paris, between Macmillan, Eisenhower and Khrushchev,
had ended before it had properly begun, on the Russian pretext that America's U2
'spy-planes' over Soviet territory had rendered negotiation between them futile.

Diary   *October 29, 1960*

In the evening we listen to Vita on the Home Service doing a piece on the mistakes that past critics have made. She is furious as they refer to her as 'V. Sackville-West, the well-known authoress'. She had managed to persuade them not to call her 'Lady Nicolson' or 'Miss Sackville-West' or 'Miss Victoria Sackville-West', but had omitted to warn them not to put 'author' in the feminine. Imagine her rage, therefore, when she gets a letter from the Sevenoaks Urban Council asking whether they may christen one of their new roads 'Nicolson Road'. That is well enough in Stornoway or at Edinburgh, but not in Sevenoaks.

H.N. to Vita   *November 1, 1960*

I did like your book [*No Signposts in the Sea*] so much. It seemed to me of such lovely texture and so moving. It was such a *decent* book and all the three characters were ennobling and not degrading characters. This will make the reviewers think it old-fashioned and upper-class. But you and I prefer the upper-class to the middle-class even as we prefer distinction to vulgarity. There is so much distinction in your book that it is like a lovely room or garden. Not one ugly thing in it.

H.N. to Vita   *December 8, 1960*

In the evening came the ceremony of unveiling the tablet to Duff [Cooper]. We went down to the crypt [of St Paul's] and there were many old friends. I should say about 100. I unveiled the thing and it didn't stick as I feared. Then turning to the audience, I started, 'I have been asked to say a few words . . .' But it was at the wrong state of the proceedings, and the Dean tugged at my coat whispering, 'I come first.' So I stopped and returned, foolish-looking, to my seat. Then the Dean did his stunt and I returned to the tablet and again faced the congregation. 'I have been asked,' I said again, 'to say a few words.' And this time my words remained uninterrupted. My speech went well enough. Diana [Cooper] remained unmoved but trembling. 'Duff would so have hated it,' she said to me afterwards, 'if I had blubbed in public.'

Diary   *December 29, 1960*

I lunch at the Beefsteak with Tommy [Lascelles]. He agrees with me that to broadcast the Queen's Christmas message on television is a great error. It destroys the mystique of monarchy. He says that when he was Private Secretary he tried to stop even the sound broadcast. We walk back together and Tommy gives me a sharp scolding for not being more traffic conscious. He says my conduct in crossing Piccadilly is unfair to bus drivers and motorists.

                                                             January 29, 1961
H.N. to Nigel   SS Augustus, *Rio de Janeiro*

There is an Argentinian girl on board, aged about twelve, to whom Vita and I have taken a fierce dislike and whose antics we watch with horror. She comes into the saloon doing the act, 'Little girl in pink dress enters saloon of luxury liner.' She then sits down and does the act, 'Little girl, with finger on her chin, listens attentively to her mother.' That passes into the act, 'Little girl listens to the band with attentive appreciation.' Then comes, 'Little girl claps to show appreciation, nodding her head gracefully in the direction of the band-leader.' Then we play Bingo, and there are several acts displaying little girl in expectation, little girl in disappointment, little girl in ecstasy of triumph, little girl, cheated of victory, indicates indifference to the triumphs of this world. Vita and I watch revolted.

                                                             February 4, 1961
Diary   SS Augustus, *Mid-Atlantic*

Vita finds this long Atlantic trip monotonous. She would like to pass islands all the time. I rather enjoy the great emptiness of space and time. I get a cable from the *New York Times* asking me to do 2,500 words

on public-speaking with special reference to Kennedy's speeches. But
how can I do this without having the speeches in front of me? I send
them a negative reply.

March 9, 1961
H.N. to Vita   *London*

I had Kenneth Harris, my interviewer, yesterday. He is an excellent
interrogator, and makes one think about oneself. Why am I a Member
of the Labour Party? Why indeed? I told him that I am a 'liberal
socialist' and that is true. I am sure that the vast outlay on the Health
Service would not have been accomplished except under state socialism. But then I also believe in individualism. I fear my Labour side is
due all too much to hatred of Tories, and this hatred has had bottles of
real venom poured into it by the Bournemouth episode.

Diary   *March 16, 1961*

Kenneth Harris comes for his last instalment of interviews. We discuss
the nature and purposes of culture. I lunch at the Greek Embassy. I get
there too early and walk into the new American Embassy. The interior
is superior to the exterior. The eagle on top hasn't got a beak, but the
snout of a porpoise. I then go to luncheon. It is a luncheon of
intellectuals to meet the King and Queen of Greece. After luncheon
we go to the drawing-room. The Queen installs herself on the sofa
and we are made to group our chairs in a semi-circle around her. She
then delivers an hour's lecture on metaphysics, most of which I cannot
hear, catching only such words as 'electrons', 'brotherhood of man',
'objective and subjective', 'materialism' and 'atom-bomb'. Freddy
Ayer, with his exquisite manner, tries to intervene from time to time,
but she sweeps him aside with a queenly gesture. I dare not catch
anybody else's eye, since I fear giggles. But she does not cease until
4.15 and then says goodbye with a kind word for each of her exhausted
audience.

Henry Moore tells me that Ben has not only saved the *Burlington*,
but much increased its prestige internationally. I liked that.

H.N. to Vita   *March 22, 1961*

Raymond [Mortimer] defends the [New English] Bible. He says that
nobody knows what the original was really like, that it was written in
Aramaic, and that we do not have Christ's actual words. He says that
the present version, in that it avoids all poetry and mystery, gives us a
clearer view of the original and conveys to us better than before how
arrogant and obstinate Christ sometimes appears, if we accept every
statement in the Gospels, however inconsistent with his usual teaching.
I can't agree with Raymond's passion for precision. I was quite ruffled
by his defence of this *Hansard* type of Bible. I think we should be
allowed to keep our legends and illusions. Nothing will make me
believe that Christ possessed a harsh character and it is beastly to make
him out as a sort of Lumumba agitator.

H.N. to Vita   *June 1, 1961*

I had a really interesting dinner with Harold Caccia [British Ambassador in Washington, 1956–61]. He says that the great white soul of
America is still blushing scarlet over Cuba [the failed Bay of Pigs
invasion was on April 17]. He says that he has great confidence in
Dean Rusk, but that Kennedy must 'run himself in' before he can
inspire confidence. He says it is not true to say that Kennedy
'inherited' the Cuban situation. He wanted from the outset to show
that he was a strong man determined to defend the Monroe Doctrine,
and plunged into the Cuban adventure on false information. He
says the Americans do not blame Kennedy, who is still their red-
headed boy, but that they put it all down to the 'diplomatists', meaning
thereby their information services. 'Why can't we put a foot right?'
they wail.

H.N. to Vita   *August 9, 1961*

I went to the London Library and got a translation of the Koran. It
passes my comprehension how so diffuse, repetitive and superficial a
book can be compared to the Bible. It is because of the thinness of the

teaching of Mohammed that I deride Moslem thought and despise Christians (and they are few) who become converts to Islam.

Diary *September 21, 1961*

A letter from Nigel says that I must recast my Monarchy book since the foreign subscribers refuse to take it in its present form, in that it omits so much of importance and varies between commentary and history. What is really meant is that I am getting gaga and cannot really do such sort of books at my age. Poor Niggs! It must have been an unpleasant letter for him to write. It made me feel quite giddy at the prospect of the work of revision entailed.

Diary *September 22, 1961*

I am still feeling distressed by the obvious waning of my powers. I have not, I fear, been the same since I had my two strokes, and I am living on the fat of my former reputation. Vita consoles me, as always. She is not in the least annoyed with Nigel for ticking me off, and agrees that he is perfectly right.

Diary *December 29, 1961*

The revise of *Monarchy* is now finished, and I shall do a final revise over the weekend and never think of the book again. No book has ever given me so much distress or trouble. It is due to my waning powers rather than to any lack of interest.

H.N. to Vita *January 3, 1962*

Now they have robbed us of the thaw I was waiting for. The streets of London are edged with brown slush. But the pavements are scraped clean and are now as dry as in July. Oliver Esher creeps with a stick saying he knows he is destined to break his hip and become bed-ridden. I said, 'When you were young you would have said "leg" not "hip". Your grandchildren will say "femur" rather than "hip". Such is the progress and advance of science.' 'Yes,' he said, 'you and I are interested in the same things such as changes in vocabulary.'

On January 19 Harold, Vita and her friend Edith Lamont boarded the SS Antilles for a cruise to the West Indies. In the train from Waterloo to Southampton, Vita suffered a haemorrhage, the first indication of abdominal cancer. For over a month she concealed the fact from Harold. She told him that her tiredness and fluctuating temperature during the voyage were due to lumbago and bronchitis.

Diary   *January 19, 1962*

Called at 6.45. We leave the Albany and drive to Waterloo through dark, empty streets. The train leaves at 8.5 and we get to Southampton Docks at 10.40. Pass through passport and Customs easily. Go aboard the *Antilles*. I unpack and have a nap. Viti also has a nap.

Vita's Diary   *January 19, 1962*

Leave Albany at 7.15 and get the 8.5 at Waterloo, Edie meets us there. *Disastrous* journey. I am very worried and confide in E.

Diary   *January 20, 1962*

We are off to Bordeaux. It is already warmer. Viti sleeps or lies in her bunk most of the day because of her lumbago.

Diary
January 27, 1962
SS Antilles, *Martinique*

Viti says she is better, but still has a slight temperature and stays in bed. I stay on board. In the evening her temperature goes up to over 100. I am, as always, sick with worry.

Diary
January 28, 1962
SS Antilles, *Barbados*

Vita's temperature is down to normal, and the ship's doctor says that she can go ashore. I could not have believed it. When we get back, Vita is exhausted and her temperature is up to 101. I am worried again, but the doctor tells me to keep calm. '*Ne vous inquiétez pas, Monsieur.*'

Diary
February 1, 1962
SS Antilles, *near Jamaica*

Vita's temperature is down and her bronchitis is clearing up, but she is terribly weak and ill with all these injections they are giving her. She gets up for luncheon, but goes to bed almost immediately afterwards.

Vita's Diary
February 15, 1962

Thankful to be home. I feel really ill, and try to hide it from Hadji. The sooner I see the doctor the better.

Diary
February 18, 1962

I think Viti is better, but she never lets me know.

H.N. to Vita   *February 20, 1962*

I am anxious to hear the result of the blood–test and I trust you to tell me the truth.

Diary   *February 23, 1962*

When I reach home, Viti tells me to prepare myself for a blow. She has had a haemorrhage and went up to London yesterday to consult a gynaecologist, who said she must go into hospital and be examined. I can see that Viti thinks it is cancer, and faces it with her usual courage. She is really heroic. The haemorrhage occurred in the train from Waterloo to Southampton on January 19. She did tell Edie, but she never told me, as she knew it would worry me. Her unselfishness is phenomenal.

The shock has a strange effect on me. It seems to sunder my life in two – the past being radiant with sunshine, and the present and future dark as night. Familiar objects (my pipe, my sponge, the book I have been reading) all seem like voices from the past. 'Last time I handled you, all was sunlit.'

Diary   *February 28, 1962*

Viti leaves home by the morning train. A car takes her from London Bridge to the Royal Free Hospital in Liverpool Road, Canonbury. Edie comes with her. The surgeon comes in while I am there. She says that until she opens things up, she cannot be sure whether it will be a 'minor' or a 'major' operation. If it is a major operation, Viti's life will be in danger for forty-eight hours. She is so gay and calm, seeking to ease my dread.

Diary   *March 1, 1962*

Dies irae. At 1.30 they telephone to say that Vita is 'still in the theatre', and this fills me with horror. Then at 2.45 the surgeon telephones.

'Lady Nicolson is now back in her bed and having a blood-transfusion. She stood the operation fairly well.' 'Did you do the major operation?' 'Yes.' 'Did you find cancer?' 'Yes.' I feel like fainting, but drink some sherry.

During the afternoon there is a loud rap on the door. When Elvira opens it, she is confronted by a Grenadier in full uniform who hands her a letter. It is from Michael Adeane sending me a message of 'sympathy and encouragement' from the Queen. This makes me feel better. At 6.30 I go to the hospital. V. had felt some pain, and they had given her dope and she was fast asleep. I go away with the picture of the oxygen and blood-transfusion apparatus hanging like gallows in my mind.

Diary   *March 20, 1962*

It is odd. Two weeks ago I loathed going to the hospital, as it was a *via dolorosa* and horrible to see her so weak and ill. But now every day she seems a little better, and it is a visit I look forward to. But she is still unable to read or eat or sleep.

Diary   *April 6, 1962*

Viti leaves the hospital at 10 and has a lovely drive in the Daimler ambulance down home. She is met by Edie, Dr Julian Tower, Ursula [Codrington, secretary] and the household. She is not tired.

Diary   *April 23, 1962*

Easter Sunday. Philippa and Nigel appear unexpectedly with the children. He says that I sounded so miserable on the telephone when he rang last night, that they decided to come down. Juliet and Adam see Vita, and dance the twist in front of her. That amuses her. Then we go round the garden and Juliet dances about picking daffodils. Altogether a successful day, and for the first time since March 1, I feel almost happy.

May 17, 1962
H.N. to Vita   C.1 Albany, W.1

I had a young man from Oxford [Martin Gilbert] to see me about the
Munich crisis and let him have my diary for 1938. He is writing a
book about it, and wanted all the material he could get. I do not think
my diary will be of much use to him, but he is welcome to read it. I
seem to have played a greater part in affairs that year than I did
subsequently. There is no good reason why I should have retired to a
second place in the struggle, nor was I aware of it at the time. But I
did. Modesty, I suppose, but I am not sure. I certainly could have
played a more leading role in the crisis had I desired to do so. But I
regret nothing.

Diary   *May 29, 1962*

Dr Tower comes to see Vita. He is worried about the slowness of her
recovery, and feels that she really must undergo deep-ray treatment at
Pembury. It will make her feel low and miserable, but it must be done.
I am miserable and worried again. What a cursed year this is! Vita is
depressed in the evening, and so, by God, am I!

Diary   *May 31, 1962*

Viti goes off in an ambulance to Pembury. She is there for a long time
and emerges exhausted. She returns about lunch-time, but refuses
everything but a bowl of soup. She sleeps soundly after luncheon, but
she is miserable, and so am I. It is a lovely day, which makes it all the
more intolerable.

Diary   *June 1, 1962*

Viti is so weak this morning that she is not strong enough to go to
Pembury. Julian Tower comes after breakfast. He says that I must face
the fact that there is little hope. He does not think she will suffer

much. I return to my room in a haze of fear. Niggs comes down late at night.

Diary *June 2, 1962*

It is a lovely morning. I get up early and walk round the garden. V. is asleep, and I do not disturb her. Glen [the Labrador] dances on the lawn with his brother, Brandy. I breakfast with Niggs, and then I force myself to do my review of the composite book *Companion to Homer*. I finish it about 12.30, and start reading the newspaper. Ursula is with Vita. At about 1.5 she observes that Vita is breathing heavily, and then suddenly is silent. She dies without fear or self-reproach at 1.15. Ursula comes to tell me. I pick some of her favourite flowers and lay them on the bed.

The funeral was three days later at Sissinghurst village church. Her ashes were placed in the Sackville crypt at Withyham.

Diary *January 1, 1963*

More snow during the night. Horribly cold. Horribly unhappy. I think drink is the only end for me. But Vita would not have liked that cowardly escape. I must just go doggedly on and fortunately I have such a dear family, so many friends, and such ardent tastes. But I am very old and groggy.

Diary *January 12, 1963* *SS* Queen Mary, *sailing to New York*

At 8.10 a.m. the Daimler comes and we drive to the station. I have a pullman, and painful memories of the last time I was there. Have breakfast in the train and get to Southampton in two hours. It is very painful seeing those escalators and green sofas again.

January 19, 1963
Diary   New York

I walk to Alan Pryce-Jones' flat in East 55 Street. There are lots of
people including Brian Urquhart, Mrs Doubleday, Marianne Moore,
Wystan Auden and others. Mrs Doubleday asks me whether Viti is
writing a new novel and when I tell her she is no more than a handful
of dust, she is most embarrassed. She kisses me as a compensation. A
nice woman. I dine alone at a provencal restaurant and get to bed early.
The heating has gone wrong in my room and it is terribly cold. I seem
to be losing my memory and cannot remember the names of people I
lunched with on that very day. I ought not to have ventured alone on
this expedition. I still cry when I wake up. Viti! My Viti!

January 31, 1963
Diary   New York

I lunch with [Leon] Edel at the Century Club and he shows me the
portrait of the young [Henry] James. He is distressed how, in this
third volume [of his biography of James], he will deal with James'
homosexuality. He was a late-flowering bugger and the Boston puritanism retarded him until it was too late to get full satisfaction from
it. Edel is an honest writer and is perplexed how to handle this problem.
I advise him to treat it as a matter of course, making no apologies or
evasions.

February 1, 1963
Diary   New York

I go down to the UNO building to lunch with Brian Urquhart.[1] U
Thant [Secretary General] unfortunately is in bed with flu and I do
not see him. Brian is more than charming. He takes me up to his room
at the top which gives on to the sky-scrapers of Manhattan. He takes
me into U Thant's room which looks straight down on the frozen

---

[1] He was a British member in the office of the Under Secretary-General for Special
Political Affairs and UN Representative in Katanga, Congo, 1961–2.

river along which little tugs pass up and down hooting. We then go down in the lift, shooting like falling stars thirty-six floors down and stopping with a soft sigh. He shows me that really beautiful Roman mosaic and the somewhat horrible French and Belgian tapestries in which thistles are depicted as intertwined with the fat limbs of Olympian champions. He shows me the English room which we presented, close panelling with little symbols of rabbits and hollyhocks. He tells me that it is the favourite room for conferences as it is so subdued. Then we go to other conference rooms and finally to the Assembly hall which is vast and empty. Then a sort of chapel of all religions with no symbols but just a lit slab. Rather effective in its way if one longs for quiet reflection. I am tremendously impressed by the space and grandeur of it all. The United Nations must feel that they are really united by all this dignified space. Brian himself is off early next week to Katanga. I trust he will not be murdered. He was beaten up last time he went. He is a remarkable man and I was glad indeed to meet him. Frail yet spiritually of steel. We lunch together in the vast canteen room surrounded by niggers. Brian says one loses all sense of any colour bar in such an atmosphere. It was a most rewarding visit and I much admired him. He spoke in high praise of Nigel [then Chairman of UN Association of Great Britain]. My visit to UNO today has made the whole trip worth while.

Diary   *March 1, 1963*

In the evening I go to see [Dr] Hunt. He says that once I recover from Viti's death I shall find my general health improve. At present I am still suffering from shock.

Diary   *April 10, 1963*

Niggs tells me that Philippa had a daughter at 2.15 this morning. Both are well. Baby weighs $7\frac{1}{4}$ lbs. I am so pleased that I forget to complete my shaving, but just sponge off the soap. As a result I have a bristle chin by luncheon. The baby is to be called Rebecca after my dog. How delighted Vita would have been.

Diary   *July 7, 1963*

It is surprisingly fine and sunny and I spend the day reading Greek on the lawn. I much enjoy going back and reading my old things. I am getting older every hour and feel rotten. It is curious that my consciousness seems perfectly alert, only I cannot express it and limp over a conversation.

Harold now found little interest in keeping his diary. The entries became very brief, scarcely more than a note of where he spent each day. The last entry was on October 4, 1964: 'Pick flowers for tomorrow [to take to London]. Otherwise do nothing but sit about. It is wonderfully fine weather.'

He died at Sissinghurst on May 1, 1968, aged eighty-one.

INDEX

Page numbers in *italic* indicate letters from HN to correspondents

Titles and ranks are generally those at latest time of mention

Works by Harold Nicolson (HN) appear directly under title; works by others under author's name

Christmas message televised, 472; sends message of sympathy on Vita's operation, 479

Elizabeth, Queen of George VI (*earlier* Duchess of York, *later* Queen Mother): in Berlin, 70–1, 70n; HN fails to recognise, 156; entertains at Buckingham Palace, 174, 324; and George VI's accession, 174; HN meets in war, 252; wartime tours, 262–3; attends poetry reading, 307; and HN's biography of George V, 401, 406, 427; at French Embassy, 413–14; at Festival of Britain, 419; at Buckingham Palace reception, 439; at US Embassy, 469

Elliot, Walter, 145, 195, 239, 295, 376, 426

Emrys-Evans, Paul Vychan, 202

Ena, Queen of Spain *see* Victoria Eugénie, Queen of Spain

Englewood, New Jersey, 133–9, 142

English Sense of Humour, The (HN), 372, 384

Entebbe, Uganda, 171–2

Eritrea, 266, 271

Esher, Oliver Brett, 3rd Viscount, 366, 409, 475–6

Evans, Dame Edith, 437

Evans, Horace, 455

Evans, Paul, 182, 232, 317

Evening Standard: HN joins staff, 72, 79, 81, 85–7, 89; HN's prospective editorship of, 91; HN leaves, 94, 97

Fairbanks, Douglas, Jr, 444, 445

Ferdinand, King of Bulgaria, 20

Festival of Britain (1951), 419

Figaro (French newspaper), 384, 413–14

Finland: winter war with Soviet Union (1939–40), 231–3, 235, 237

Fisher, H.A.L., 122

Fitzroy, Edward Algernon, 337

Fleming, Peter, 238

Florence, 15, 415, 442–3

Foch, Marshal Ferdinand, 310

Foreign Office: HN joins, 5–6

Förster (Nazi Gauleiter of Danzig), 218

Fort Belvedere, 167

France: non-intervention in Spanish Civil War, 176; and Czech crisis (1938), 194, 200; guarantees to Poland, Greece and Rumania, 205, 209, 216; HN lectures in (1940), 236–7; defeat and surrender (1940), 246–9; and Dunkirk evacuation, 249 & n; German terms (1940), 250–1; fleet attacked by British (1940), 252 & n; anti-Roosevelt sentiments in, 260; post-war position, 328–9, 329n; de Gaulle returns to after Allied invasion, 331; Allied landings in south (August 1944), 335; Provisional Government (1944), 337, 341; Macmillan forecasts economic prosperity for, 368; and Suez crisis, 449, 453

Franco, General Francisco, 176, 205, 273n, 329, 434

Frank, Hans, 373

Franks, Oliver, 451, 452, 469

Frederika, Queen of Greece, 473

Free French: disputes, 309

Frick, Wilhelm, 373

Fritzsche, Hans, 373

Fry, Christopher: *The Dark is Light Enough*, 437

Fry, Roger, 255

Funk, Walther, 373

Gaer (of *San Francisco Forum*), 116

Gafencu, Gregore, 211, 371

Gaitskell, Hugh, 449, 451, 456–7, 465

Gallipoli: war graves, 35

Galsworthy, John, 239

Garroni, Marchese, 32–3, 33n, 36

Garvin, James, 110

reads HN's book on English
humour, 385–6; defends New
English Bible, 474
Morton, Desmond, 310
Mosley, Lady Cynthia ('Cimmie'), 42,
88, 97, 121
Mosley, Diana, Lady, 272
Mosley, Sir Oswald, *88*; HN joins New
Party, xii, 86–7, 365; fascist
tendencies, 93, 95–8, 104, 106;
defeated in 1931 election, 96; effect
on HN, 97–8; in Paris, 98; in Italy,
99–100; and organisation of New
Party, 99–100; HN leaves New
Party, 103; political ambitions, 104,
106; Lloyd George on, 107–8; HN
visits, 121; imprisoned in war, 272;
released from prison (1943), 317
Mr Peabody see *Public Faces*
Müller, Dr Hermann, 26, 64n
Munich, 124, 127
Munich agreement (1938), 192–3,
207, 453, 480
Murray, Gilbert, 311
Murray, John ('Jock'), 437
Murrow, Ed, 293–4, 306, 467
Muselier, Admiral Emile, 266
Mussolini, Benito: occupies Corfu,
37n; Ramsay MacDonald criticises,
39; Mosley meets, 100; invades
Abyssinia, 146; Chamberlain
proposes negotiating with, 179, 210;
avoids Schuschnigg's appeal for
help, 180; and Czech crisis, 200;
invades Albania, 209; as threat,
209–10; character, 217, 281;
Chamberlain's friendly reference to,
219; and Italian entry into war, 242;
declares war on USA, 285; resigns,
310, 314; killed, 350; *see also* Italy

Nabokov, Vladimir: on HN's *Some
People*, 466; *Lolita*, 462, 466
Nagasaki, 364
Narvik, 240
Nasser, Gamal Abdel, 448–50, 453

National Government: formed (1931),
94–5; wins 1935 election, 150
National Labour Party, 146, 151,
154–5, 179, 181, 265, 325, 354, 365
National Portrait Gallery: HN serves
on board, 392n
National Trust: HN's Deputy
Chairmanship of, 392n, 409, 416;
Vita refuses to give Sissinghurst to,
438
Nazism: HN on, 101
Nehru, Jawaharlal (Pandit), 409
Neurath, Baron Konstantin von, 373
Neville Terrace, South Kensington,
369n, 384, 420
New Party: HN joins, xii, 86–9, 91–2;
prospects, 91–2; resignations from,
92–3; failure in 1931 election, 96;
HN's disenchantment with, 96–7;
transformed into British Union of
Fascists, 98; HN leaves, 103
New Statesman (journal), 107, 109
New York, 109–11, 481–3
New York Times, 379, 472–3
Nicolson, Adam (Nigel/Philippa's
son); birth, 458; visits convalescent
grandmother, 479
Nicolson, Benedict (HN's son; Ben),
*303, 306, 308, 309, 311, 319, 325,
329, 331, 333, 336, 338, 340, 347*;
birth, 13; childhood, 42; and parents'
absence in Teheran, 46; wins Eton
scholarship, 67; at age fifteen, 79;
leaves Eton, 109; grandmother tells
of Vita's liaisons, 119; accompanies
HN to USA (1935), 143; flies with
Lindbergh, 143; and HN's diary,
192; and war threat, 205–6, 239;
buys Picasso portrait, 253; criticises
Roger Fry, 255; leaves for Cairo,
300; knocked down by lorry, 341;
returns from war, 349–51; criticises
HN's literary style, 366; lives with
HN in South Kensington, 369 & n;
and HN's hopes of Paris Embassy,
377; as Deputy Surveyor of King's